North Carolina in the Connected Age

North Carolina in the Connected Age

Challenges and Opportunities in a Globalizing Economy

Michael L. Walden

The University of North Carolina Press
Chapel Hill

This book was published with the assistance
of the Anniversary Endowment Fund of the
University of North Carolina Press.

Set in Scala by Tseng Information Systems, Inc.
Manufactured in the United States of America

⊗ The paper in this book meets the guidelines
for permanence and durability of the Committee
on Production Guidelines for Book Longevity of
the Council on Library Resources.

The University of North Carolina Press has been
a member of the Green Press Initiative since 2003.

Library of Congress Cataloging-in-Publication Data
Walden, M. L. (Michael Leonard), 1951–
North Carolina in the connected age : challenges and
opportunities in a globalizing economy / Michael L. Walden.
p.   cm.
Includes bibliographical references and index.
ISBN 978-0-8078-3221-9 (cloth : alk. paper)
1. Industries — North Carolina. 2. Globalization — North Carolina.
I. Title.
HC107.N8W35 2008
330.9756 — dc22
2008008843

12 11 10 09 08   5 4 3 2 1

University of North Carolina Press books may be purchased at a
discount for educational, business, or sales promotional use. For
information, please visit www.uncpress.unc.edu or write to UNC
Press, attention: Sales Department, 116 South Boundary Street,
Chapel Hill, NC 27514-3808.

To the thousands of North Carolinians
who have touched my career—
thank you for the inspiration to write this book
about our great state.

Contents

Figures, Map, and Tables

Figures

Map

Tables

Preface

From Here to Where?

North Carolina's economy has gone through many transformations. Agriculture and an agrarian way of life dominated the state from its inception through most of the nineteenth century. Like most of America's residents, North Carolinians in the 1700s and 1800s lived on small subsistence farms. Turpentine, tobacco, and corn production were the state's leading industries, while the manufacturing industry consisted of a handful of textile mills that served only local markets.

Then, using cheap labor released from a mechanizing agricultural industry, the state developed three key manufacturing industries that would form its economic base for the majority of the twentieth century: furniture, textiles, and tobacco. North Carolina had long supplied lumber to northern furniture factories. In the early 1900s, the combination of available low-cost labor, proximity to plentiful forests, a favorable climate, and available rail transportation caused the furniture industry to shift its major base of operations from the North to North Carolina.

Similarly, the young nation's textile industry was centered in New England in the eighteenth and nineteenth centuries. Textile mills were usually fueled by waterpower and so had to be located on streams or rivers. By the twentieth century, however, the growing availability of electricity increased the number of possible mill locations. North Carolina offered easy access to southern-grown cotton and had always had a small textile industry: as with furniture, the lures of inexpensive labor, favorable climate, and natural input (cotton) caused North Carolina to attract industry from the North, and by the 1920s, the state had become the country's leading textile manufacturer. Apparel factories that turned fabric into finished clothing products quickly followed.

Unlike furniture and textiles, tobacco manufacturing was a homegrown North Carolina industry. Tobacco manufacturing did not exist until the late nineteenth century, when a machine for rolling tobacco into cigarettes was developed. North Carolina was already the leading producer of raw tobacco leaf, and cigarette-making entrepreneurs logically built their factories in the state.

By the 1920s, therefore, North Carolina's Big Three—tobacco, textiles, and furniture—were firmly established and on their way to dominating the state economy for the next four decades. In the 1960s, the Big Three directly accounted for two-thirds of the state's manufacturing employment and more than a quarter of its total employment.[1] In addition, facilities needed to support the Big Three created thousands of other jobs in the state.

At the end of the twentieth century, however, the availability of low-cost labor, which had helped to bring the Big Three to dominance, began to erode it. Technological developments that decreased the costs of worldwide transportation and communication and political decisions that dramatically lowered trade barriers among countries meant that manufacturers could access even lower-cost labor in foreign countries. To compete, American manufacturers needed to improve labor productivity—that is, find ways to produce the same output with less labor.

The resultant changes first and most dramatically appeared in the textile industry. Textile production increased only marginally in the 1980s and 1990s and then dropped 30 percent by 2005. Textile employment fell by more than two-thirds between 1970 and 2007. Similarly, 2007 employment at furniture factories totaled only two-thirds of peak levels, and production levels had slipped more than 10 percent between the late 1990s and the middle of the first decade of the twenty-first century.[2]

International competition plus changing consumer preferences led to contraction in North Carolina's tobacco industry. At the farm level, the federal tobacco program, begun in the 1930s, limited leaf production and kept leaf prices high. This situation benefited North Carolina tobacco farmers as long as no leaf substitutes were readily available. Such was the case until the 1990s, when Brazil, Zimbabwe, and other countries began to produce and market tobacco leaf of comparable quality. Tobacco leaf imports gradually rose, and North Carolina leaf production dropped. In 2005, the federal tobacco program ended.

In addition, prompted by mandated cigarette warnings begun in 1964, health concerns over tobacco led to major reductions in the U.S. per capita cigarette consumption. Cigarette production plunged 85 percent between 1977 and 2000.[3] Only cigarette companies' ability to increase prices prevented the industry from complete collapse.

Fortunately for the state, new industries emerged while the Big Three declined. This new growth was concentrated in five sectors—technology, pharmaceuticals, financial services, food processing, and vehicle parts—that became the new Big Five.

Drawn by national-caliber universities producing a steady stream of graduates, little labor union activity, and relatively low operating costs, research-oriented firms in the rapidly expanding technology and pharmaceutical fields began moving to North Carolina in the 1960s. The major beneficiary was the Research Triangle region bounded by Raleigh (North Carolina State University), Durham (Duke University), and Chapel Hill (the University of North Carolina).

Charlotte, the state's largest city, had long been the center of North Carolina's banking industry. Unlike most states, North Carolina permitted branch banking—that is, banks could operate offices across the entire state rather than in just a single locality. When first regional and then national banking became legal during the 1980s, North Carolina's financial institutions expanded aggressively, taking advantage of their experience in managing offices across wide geographical areas. By the end of the twentieth century, Charlotte was the nation's second-largest and the world's fourth-largest banking center by income.[4]

As the nation's appetite for alternatives to beef increased, North Carolina's poultry and swine industries also flourished, with each surpassing tobacco in gross farm receipts by the 1990s. Corresponding changes in household economics resulting from the increase in women working outside the home motivated increased purchases of processed meats. With the state's large herds of chickens and hogs, meat-processing plants constituted a logical addition. During the 1980s and 1990s, food-processing activity in the state increased by 150 percent.[5]

Foreign competition spurred the domestic auto industry to retool, and the South's low operating costs and population growth made the region a new home for auto manufacturing. International automakers, whose market share was growing, also found the South ideal for their expansion into the U.S. market. Although North Carolina did not attract any vehicle assembly plants, it developed a significant presence in the vehicle parts sector.

Beyond the new Big Five, the state's economy changed in other major ways during the late twentieth and early twenty-first centuries. North Carolina agriculture was remade from a crop industry to a livestock industry. The state's beaches and mountains had always been popular for tourists and retirement living, but the economic growth of the late twentieth century, fueled by the maturing baby boom generation, carried this economic activity to new levels. Tourism, second homes, and retirement communities became the primary industry in several coastal and mountain counties as well as in the golfing region (Pinehurst/Southern Pines) in central North Carolina.

This latest transformation of the North Carolina economy is part of a larger, worldwide era I dub the Connected Age. Built on technology, trade, competition, and the expanding service sector, the Connected Age has fully integrated all parts of the state into a national—indeed, international—network of interlinked commerce. Trade and communication between North Carolina and all parts of the rest of the world are easier today than was the case between any two cities in the state during the early twentieth century. Labor markets in North Carolina (and the country) are no longer insulated from those in the rest of the world. In the Connected Age, domestic workers are increasingly engaged in one-on-one competition with their foreign counterparts, and technology even makes possible the direct transfer of jobs out of the state to other countries.

On the surface, the transformation of the North Carolina economy during the Connected Age appeared to improve the state's aggregate indicators of well-being in the last thirty years of the twentieth century. Both aggregate and per capita income increased faster in North Carolina than in the nation as a whole, and the state's average income levels moved closer to the national average. The proportion of high school graduates attending college soared, and the percentage of workers with college degrees approached the national level. The fastest-growing occupational group between 1970 and 2005 was professional and scientific workers.[6]

Yet as North Carolina entered the twenty-first century, some observers raised questions and concerns about the new economy. For the textile and furniture components of the traditional Big Three, China's entry into the World Trade Organization accelerated employment losses. In addition, legal and health concerns and foreign competition still confronted the tobacco industry. The decline in tobacco's economic clout was symbolized by the sevenfold increase in the state cigarette tax approved by lawmakers in 2005.

The Big Five also faced problems at the dawn of the new century. In the late 1990s, the technology bubble burst, and significant reorganization and downsizing occurred in the industry. North Carolina lost 30 percent of its employment in these fields, and the jobs did not return over the next decade or so.[7] Many industry observers worry that international competition and outsourcing will jeopardize future expansion in these high-tech sectors. The financial services industry is also undergoing restructuring, with mergers and consolidations resulting in pared payrolls and more modest forecasts.

Although the pharmaceutical industry's outlook remains bright as an aging population increases the consumption of medical services, two unknowns cloud the future. Public concerns about rising drug prices raise the possibility of governmental price regulation. In addition, reports of unexpected negative side effects from drugs already on the market risk an investor backlash and a plunge in asset values.

For the food-processing industry, environmental and safety issues may impede future growth. A major problem with hog farming is the disposal of large amounts of waste, which can threaten critical groundwater supplies. Worker safety at processing plants also constitutes an ongoing issue. Finally, uncertainty about gas prices and the health of U.S. auto firms raises questions about the future of both the vehicle assembly and vehicle parts industries.

At the same time, questions have arisen about how the new North Carolina economy has affected North Carolinians of different skill and income levels. The good-paying jobs in technology, pharmaceuticals, and financial services require significant formal education beyond high school. Yet the tens of thousands of workers released from the Big Three rarely have more than high school diplomas. Without retraining, they most likely can find employment only in lower-paying service jobs.

North Carolina's low-skilled workers also face another challenge. Between 1990 and 2000, the state's Hispanic population increased by more than three hundred thousand; most of this 400 percent gain came from immigration.[8] These immigrants certainly have benefited the state's economy and social diversity, but most of these newcomers have little formal educational training and thus compete in the low-skilled labor market. As a result, some observers worry that the migration has swollen the pool of low-skill employees, depressed their wages, and widened the income gap between skilled and unskilled workers.

The transformation of the modern North Carolina economy has also left a geographic imprint. The highest levels of educational attainment occur in metropolitan counties, particularly in the Research Triangle Park and Charlotte regions. These counties have benefited most from expansion in the technology, pharmaceutical, and financial services industries and have lost the least from downsizing in the traditional Big Three industries. Conversely, nonmetropolitan counties, especially those far from tourist and retirement destinations, have suffered the greatest losses from the downsizing of the Big Three, and any employment gains have largely occurred in the lower-paying food-processing and service industries. In addition, with the fastest job growth in metropolitan counties, cross-county commuting for work has increased.

This progression of events in Connected Age North Carolina raises several critical questions. Will the state's traditional Big Three industries continue to decline and eventually completely disappear, or can their competitiveness be restored, albeit at a smaller stable level? What common strategies must the Big Three pursue to regain their economic footing? With an increasingly integrated world economy, will the technology sector in particular soon follow the path of the Big Three, or do its economic characteristics differ so fundamentally that the industry will survive in the new world? Or will the technology sector endure only in a dramatically different form?

And how will the impacts of the economic transformation change? Will the state's economic divides between skilled and unskilled households, growing and declining industries, and robust and struggling regions continue and widen, or will they close? Are workers lacking college degrees doomed to a declining standard of living, and do some college-educated workers face the same fate?

Some people say that new industries will ride to North Carolina's rescue—industries such as biotechnology, nanotechnology (the science of small scale), advanced telecommunications, and perhaps industries related to the development of space. How viable are these industries, and what role will they play in North Carolina's economic future?

Finally, what is the proper role of government in these issues? Does the state government have the proper mix of taxing and spending policies for the twenty-first-century economy? More fundamentally, to what extent can state and local governments guide economic development? Can the state pick industry winners and lure those companies to the state, or should government's role in economic development be more passive?

This book explores the progress, pitfalls, and prospects for the North Carolina economy in the Connected Age. Chapter 1 provides the national context by examining how the Connected Age evolved and what major impacts it had on the U.S. economy. Chapter 2 presents a macro, or aggregate, view of how the North Carolina economy has changed during the Connected Age, identifying shifts in industries and discussing the broad forces behind these shifts. Chapter 3 turns the focus to a microanalysis of the key industries in the North Carolina economy, including both the traditional Big Three as well as the industries of the new economy, and highlights and evaluates factors particular to each industry's performance.

Chapter 4 moves the discussion to the household and worker. How did the trends of the Connected Age affect households of different occupations and educational backgrounds as well as people of different races and genders?

How did the era affect the allocation of time between work and family, and how did the pattern of income distribution in the state change? Finally, how did the two migrations, one domestic and the other international, change the composition of the state's workforce and households?

Chapter 5 turns to the geographic effects of recent economic change, identifying location trends of growing and declining industries along with the effects on county population and income. The chapter shows that disparities among counties in educational and skill levels constitute a major determinant of the geographic differences.

Chapter 6 examines whether the state's public policies are appropriate for the new North Carolina economy. The chapter presents trends in North Carolina's public spending and taxes and identifies issues before evaluating the broad range of alternative public policies that affect economic development.

Finally, chapter 7 looks ahead to the future of the North Carolina economy. Will the current transformation continue, or will a new one begin? What industries will expand, and what industries will downsize in the future economy? Can North Carolina workers remain competitive in a globalized economy, or are the state's best economic days behind it? What kinds of policy changes are needed to deal with the future economy, and will they be easy to make? Is economic prosperity for all people and all regions an achievable goal? These and other questions conclude the book.

Since this is a book about economics—in this case, the economics of a state and its people—economic concepts and terms are used to some extent. These terms have logical and intuitive meanings but are nevertheless briefly explained at their first mention in the book. Longer explanations and discussion appear in "A Primer on Economic Concepts," following chapter 7.

The starting date for the modern North Carolina economy is set at 1970 for two reasons.[9] First, 1970 represents the beginning of the twilight for the state's traditional industries—in particular, for tobacco and textiles. The structure of the tobacco industry was fundamentally changed by the issuance of the surgeon general's 1964 report, and the downward trend in per capita cigarette consumption consequently began during the 1970s. Textile employment in the state peaked in 1973; improvements in manufacturing productivity and foreign imports subsequently began to whittle away at the industry's jobs.

Second, 1970 is a threshold year for the development of the new North Carolina economy. It began the first decade after passage of the national Civil Rights and Voting Rights Acts, which reduced the stigma of racial tension in the South and made business location in the region more acceptable. During the 1970s, energy costs became a bigger factor in business location, a development that benefited the South, with its shorter winters. Finally, North Carolina's technology industry blossomed after the opening of the Research Triangle Park in the 1960s.

Perhaps the single best word to describe the early twenty-first century is "anxiety"—anxiety regarding international terrorism, anxiety regarding the loss of jobs to foreign countries and its impact on the U.S. standard of living, and anxiety regarding an unknown future in a rapidly changing world. In North Carolina, the industries that sustained the state for more than fifty years are now crumbling, and the industries that have replaced them appear shaky in many ways. This book may not relieve this anxiety or accurately predict the future, but knowing what has happened and why and knowing the forces that are shaping the modern North Carolina economy may in some small way help to guide the future path.

This book grew out of thirty years of living in, working in, and studying North Carolina. Although I, like millions of my fellow residents, was not born in the state, I have regarded North Carolina as my home for a long time. I have traveled to most of the state's counties and to the majority of its major cities and towns, and I am continually amazed by my home's beauty and diversity as well as by the energy, openness, and vitality of the people. North Carolina truly is a special place.

While it would be appropriate to thank virtually everyone with whom I have been associated in North Carolina, space permits me to mention only a few people. My colleagues past and present at North Carolina State University, especially those in the Department of Agricultural and Resource Economics, have motivated many questions, provided many answers, and created a supportive work environment. Blake Brown and Kelly Zering particularly stand out in this regard. My two immediate bosses, department head Jon Brandt and Dean Johnny Wynne, relieved me from a semester of teaching duties so I could devote more time to this book. Other colleagues and coworkers—at the University of North Carolina School of Government, the North Carolina General Assembly's Fiscal Research Division, the N.C. Association of County Commissioners, and the N.C. League of Municipalities—provided information and statistics, as did two generous reviewers, Dan Gerlach and John Kasarda. I was inspired by the writings and analysis of academics in other states, such as Richard Vedder and Gavin Wright, who can craft a good story around seemingly dry numbers and statistical relationships. I am indebted to David Perry, editor in chief at the University of North Carolina Press, for his interest in and support of the project, and I thank the entire production team at the press, including assistant managing editor Paul Betz and copyeditor Ellen Goldlust-Gingrich, for guiding the manuscript through to its final form. I also wish to acknowledge the generosity of North Carolina State University for partial financial support of the project.

But, as with my other books, my greatest appreciation goes to my wife, Mary, who provides balance, cheer, and best of all meaning to my efforts. Thank you.

North Carolina in the Connected Age

1. The National Context

The Creation of the Connected Age

As in all states, the economy in North Carolina is influenced by events at the national level. Indeed, because the U.S. economy is so highly integrated in national markets, much of North Carolina's change and development are linked to national trends. For example, national economic expansions and recessions are echoed at the state level by similar booms and busts. In addition, national technological, demographic, and production changes are mirrored at the state level.

This chapter sets the national context for North Carolina's economy by tracing the nation's economic development since 1970. This analysis serves as the basis for evaluating North Carolina's economic progress in chapter 2.

The Connected Age: Shrinking Space and Time

Although three and a half decades constitutes but the blink of an eye in recorded history, life changed more dramatically between 1970 and 2005 than was the case in some earlier centuries. Like never before, people, countries, and economies became interrelated and interconnected. Technology overcame distance and culture. Communicating halfway around the world became just as easy as talking to a next-door neighbor. Products and labor increasingly flowed to markets without regard to international boundaries. The world became linked digitally, globally, and competitively. The Connected Age arrived.

Since most change occurs with a degree of gradualism over time, many living through the Connected Age did not comprehend the massive changes it brought. Yet the cumulative impacts on life, work, and spending are eye-catching when some key indicators are compared for 1970 and the early 2000s.[1]

In 1970:

- cell phones, the Internet, and personal computers did not exist
- GM, Ford, and Chrysler dominated U.S. auto sales
- only one in twelve women had a college degree, and jobs held by women paid less than half as much as jobs held by men
- fewer than half of married women worked for pay
- one of every four workers had a factory job
- the average household had 3.15 persons
- households spent almost twice as much on food eaten at home as on food at restaurants
- households spent more on food than on transportation
- the average size of a new home was fifteen hundred square feet, and the average household owned 1.7 vehicles
- 639 airline miles were flown for every person in the country
- African Americans were the largest minority

In the early 2000s:

- the majority of households have cell phones and personal computers, and one-third of households are connected to the Internet
- the Toyota Camry is the best-selling sedan
- one in four women has a college degree, and jobs held by females pay 68 percent as much as jobs held by men
- more than half of married women work for pay
- one of every ten workers has a factory job
- the average household has 2.57 persons
- households spend half again as much on food eaten at home as on food at restaurants
- households spend more on transportation than on food
- the average size of a new home is 2,330 square feet, and the average household owns 2.1 vehicles
- 2,254 airline miles are flown annually for every person in the country
- Hispanics are the largest minority

These numbers demonstrate some key trends in the Connected Age. We bought and used new technology, we spent more on travel and traveled more by air, we bought more foreign-made products, women became more educated and worked for better pay outside the home, households became smaller, factory work declined, we ate out more, we bought bigger homes and more vehicles and relied less on doing things ourselves, and our population became more diverse. The following sections provide details on how the nation's work, life, people, technology, and government changed during the Connected Age.

Production: Shifts and Shakes

Americans produced more during the Connected Age. The national output of goods and services increased 138 percent, rising from $5.2 trillion in 1970 to $12.4 trillion in 2005 (both values in real, or inflation-adjusted, 2005 dollars).[2] This was an annual average growth rate of 2.5 percent, only slightly lower than the post–World War II growth rate.

Of course, a share of the economic growth resulted from the fact that more people lived and worked in the country. The nation's population jumped from 205 million to 295 million over the thirty-five-year period.[3] Therefore, it is perhaps more revealing to examine changes in production per person. Here the news is also impressive. Goods and services production per person grew from $25,380 to $41,959 (constant dollars), a 1.5 percent average annual increase.[4]

Although the national economy indeed expanded during the Connected Age, it did not do so in a consistent, straight-line way. A business cycle was evident, signifying an irregular but recurring pattern of growth followed by recession. Recessionary periods occurred six times in the Connected Age: December 1969–November 1970, November 1973–March 1975, January 1980–July 1980, July 1981–November 1982, July 1990–March 1991, and March 2001–November 2001.[5] As measured by the percentage decline in production, the recessions of 1974–75 and 1981–82 were the most severe, while those of 1969–70 and 2001 were the mildest.[6]

Even though national production increased, substantial variation occurred in the growth rates in specific economic sectors (figure 1-1). Growth was strongest in wholesale and retail trade, transportation/communications/public utilities (TCPU), agriculture, services, and finances and was weakest in manufacturing, construction, and government. As a result, the composition of the national economic pie changed. The goods-producing sector (manufacturing, construction, and agriculture) decreased from one-third of spending in the economy in the 1970s to less than one-fifth in the 2000s, while the service-producing sector (wholesale and retail trade, finances, TCPU, and services) correspondingly increased. And while a decline occurred in manufacturing's relative economic importance, total manufacturing output still increased (the growth rate for manufacturing is positive in figure 1-1). A

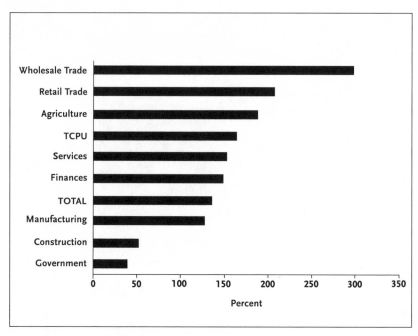

Figure 1-1. U.S. output growth rate by sector, 1977–2005.
DATA SOURCE: U.S. Department of Commerce, Bureau of Economic Analysis,
"Gross Domestic Product by State."
NOTE: Data not available before 1977.

marked shift also took place within manufacturing, with production moving to durable goods such as industrial machinery and electrical equipment and away from nondurable products such as apparel and printing.[7]

The nation's production became more integrated with world trade in the Connected Age. The share of national production sold to foreign buyers, termed "exports," more than doubled from 4.3 percent in 1970 to 10.5 percent in 2005. However, sales of foreign-made goods and services to U.S. buyers increased even more over the period, nearly tripling from 5.7 percent of national production to 16 percent.[8]

A key ingredient in any nation's economic progress is labor productivity, sometimes referred to as "working smarter." Labor productivity measures how much output a worker produces in a given period of time. Faster growth in labor productivity means that labor resources are being used more efficiently, so more can be produced with a given number of workers. Released workers can then be used in other enterprises. Earlier in the twentieth century, this process enabled workers to move to the growing manufacturing sector, just as more recent improvements in manufacturing productivity have provided labor for the emerging technology and service sectors. Higher levels of labor productivity allow U.S. firms to compete more effectively with foreign firms using lower-cost labor, and a more productive labor force can also help contain price inflation.

A major story of the national economy during the Connected Age was the acceleration in labor productivity. In the 1970s, labor productivity grew at an annual average rate of less than 1 percent; in the 1980s, the average growth rate was 1.6 percent; in the 1990s, the average rate rose to 2 percent; and during 2000–2005, the average growth rate hit 3.2 percent.[9] Several studies attribute this improvement to improved education and training of the workforce and the development and application of computer technology to the workplace.[10]

As the Connected Age progresses, these trends in production are expected to continue. Both the goods and services sectors will expand, but services will do so at a faster rate, enlarging the services piece of the total economic pie. Foreign trade's share of the national economy will increase from one-quarter to almost one-third of the economy, and exports—such as those to the growing Chinese market—will outpace imports.[11] Also, some forecasters are optimistic about labor productivity, believing that the historically high growth in worker efficiency enjoyed in the 1990s and early 2000s will be sustained.[12] Such an occurrence would have profound implications for the workforce, as I discuss later in this chapter.

Employment: Factory Flight

Employment in the national economy expanded along with production during the Connected Age, with the number of full- and part-time jobs increasing from 79 million to 142 million between 1970 and 2005.[13] However, the 1.6 percent average annual growth rate in jobs was considerably lower than the post–World War II average of 2.6 percent.[14]

Progress in the labor market is generally measured by the unemployment rate, or the percentage of people working or actively looking for work who are unemployed. The national unemployment rate demonstrated a decidedly downward trend in the Connected Age. The rate averaged 6.2 percent during the 1970s, 7.3 percent during the 1980s, 5.8 percent during the 1990s, and 5.2 percent between 2000 and 2006. The peak rate during recessions also showed a declining pattern.[15]

Yet the unemployment rate may give an incomplete picture of the labor market. The official statistics do not count as unemployed individuals who desire to work but who, out of frustration and lack of success, have stopped looking for work. Such individuals are termed "discouraged workers," and alternative measures suggest that they add between 0.3 percent and 4.0 percent to the official unemployment rate. However, no indicators point to an upward trend in the rate of discouraged workers during the Connected Age.[16]

The second issue with official unemployment is the concept of underemployment. Underemployment occurs when an individual is employed in a job that underutilizes his or her skills. Examples are a displaced computer engineer selling cars and a former stockbroker employed as the manager of a fast-food restaurant. No official measures of underemployment exist, but some observers have expressed concern that the large shifts in employment among economic sectors in the Connected Age have increased the prevalence of underemployment.[17]

Figure 1-2 shows these employment shifts. Employment gains were strongest in services, finance, construction, and retail trade. Employment increased but did so below the average rate for the government, wholesale trade, and TCPU sectors and decreased in agriculture and manufacturing.[18]

A comparison of figures 1-1 and 1-2 leads to several conclusions. First, total employment increased much less than total production (57 percent versus 126 percent), implying an improvement in labor productivity during the Connected Age. Second, employment in agriculture and manufacturing declined even as production in those sectors rose, again as a consequence of dramatic improvements in labor productivity in these sectors. Productivity of manufacturing workers rose at an average annual rate of 3.9 percent, while farm worker productivity improved at an annual average rate of 5.3 percent.[19] One study concluded that although total manufacturing employment fell, the number of highly skilled, highly productive manufacturing jobs increased between 1983 and 2002.[20]

The changes in industry output and industry employment caused corresponding changes in workers' occupations. A worker's occupation indicates what he or she does rather than the industry in which he or she works. During the Connected Age, a greater share of people worked in professional, sales, and service jobs, while fewer worked as clerks, craft workers, operatives, or farmers (figure 1-3). These moves are in line with the era's increased focus on skilled jobs requiring more education and on services.

Richard Florida focuses on an occupational group he terms the "creative class"—workers involved in developing new ideas, inventions, and technol-

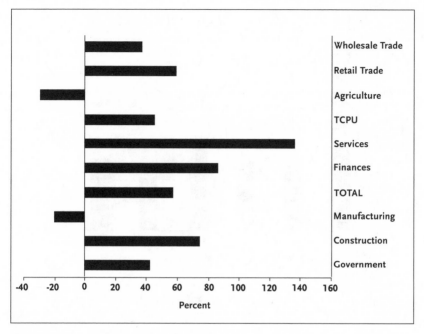

Figure 1-2. U.S. employment growth rate by sector, 1977–2005.
DATA SOURCE: Council of Economic Advisers, *Economic Report of the President*, tables
B-46, B-100.

ogies. In this group, he includes architects, engineers, scientists, artists,
writers, and high-end managers.[21] According to Florida, the generation of
ideas is critical to any country's modern economic development, since virtually any production job and many service positions now can easily move to
low-cost regions. Only countries with thriving creative classes, he argues, will
generate the new industries and businesses needed to prosper in the rapidly
changing world economy of the Connected Age. Florida estimates that in
recent decades, the creative class has comprised between 20 and 30 percent
of the workforce.[22]

Several trends influenced the labor market during the Connected Age,
including the increased labor force participation of women, the shift in compensation away from wages and salaries to benefits, the increased educational attainment of the workforce, and the growing importance of labor availability in foreign countries. I will now highlight key features of each of these
trends.

One of the most dramatic labor market changes in U.S. history occurred

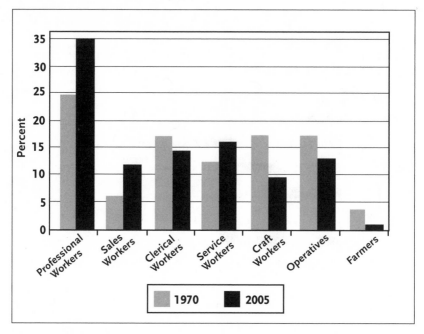

Figure 1-3. Distribution of employment by occupation, 1970 and 2005.
DATA SOURCE: U.S. Census Bureau, "Statistical Abstract of the United States," 2007, table 602, 1973, table 372.

in the latter part of the twentieth century with the increase in women's labor force participation. Between 1970 and 2003, the percentage of women ages twenty-two to sixty-five who were working or looking for work jumped from 46 percent to 70 percent.[23] Scholars have cited many factors as contributing to this rise in the number of working women, including their improved educational levels and thereby their prospects for better pay, the reduction in physically demanding jobs, the decline in large families, and improved household technology, which allows household tasks—still predominantly performed by women—to be accomplished in less time.[24] Research also suggests that some women enter the paid labor force to replace earnings reductions suffered by their husbands.[25]

A major byproduct of the increased proportion of working women has been increased household spending on services. As women have moved into the workforce, households have increased their use of paid services, such as child care and cleaning, lawn, and meal services. The proportion of total consumer spending going to services rose from 46 percent in 1970 to 58 percent in 2005.[26]

How workers are paid significantly changed during the Connected Age. Compensation paid from an employer to an employee can be separated into two parts, the wage or salary component and the benefits component. Wages and salaries are direct cash payments to the employee. Benefits are noncash payments for items such as retirement, vacation and sick leave, and health insurance. Benefits almost doubled their proportion of total worker compensation between 1970 and 2005, rising from 10.6 percent to 19.1 percent.[27]

Americans acquired more formal education during the Connected Age. In 1970, barely half of adult males and females had high school or college degrees, and only 13 percent of males and just 8 percent of females had college degrees. By 2005, these numbers had increased dramatically—almost 85 percent of adult males and females had finished high school or better, and 29 percent of males and 27 percent of females had obtained college degrees.[28] Although these numbers are impressive, observers have expressed some concern about the quality of the educational outcome. Trends in standardized test scores give mixed results, with some falling, some remaining relatively unchanged, and others modestly increasing.[29]

As the twenty-first century dawned, a new employment issue took center stage—U.S. companies moving jobs to foreign countries to take advantage of lower labor costs, a process alternatively referred to as offshoring or outsourcing. The globalization of the economy during the Connected Age accelerated the practice, which affected both blue-collar (factory) jobs and white-collar (service) jobs. In fact, by 2003, one estimate categorized half the offshored positions as service jobs; just under one in five were professional jobs.[30] One cost of offshoring is lost domestic jobs and the corresponding adjustments the former holders of these jobs must make. An estimated 9.9 million jobs were offshored in 2003, one-third more than in 1970.[31]

Some people view offshoring in a positive light. Some observers see it simply as an example of businesses using the economic principle of comparative advantage, where production moves to wherever input costs are lowest. Businesses using offshored labor can lower their costs and thus offer consumers lower prices. In this way, offshoring contributes to more affordable products and a higher standard of living.[32] Furthermore, while offshoring loses jobs for the country, inshoring—the placement of jobs in the United States by foreign companies such as auto and pharmaceutical manufacturers—gains jobs. In 2003, the United States had an estimated 5.7 million inshored jobs, and the gap between offshored and inshored jobs narrowed during the Connected Age.[33]

Again, no signs indicate that most of these employment trends will change in the near-term future. Between 2004 and 2014, official U.S. government forecasts show that eight hundred thousand manufacturing jobs will be cut, while employment in the broad-based service sector will jump by 18 million.[34] Jobs at both ends of the pay spectrum—professional occupations paying the most and lower-skilled service jobs in food preparation, health care support, personal care, and maintenance paying the least—will be the fastest growing.[35] More of the available jobs will also require more skills, and here the question is whether the U.S. labor market will be able to provide those skilled workers. If not, then more jobs—in particular, higher-paying positions— will move to foreign countries because of the traditional lower costs and the new availability of skilled labor. As the U.S. educational edge over developing countries such as China and India first narrows and then disappears, the off- shoring of jobs may extend to higher-paying occupations.[36] The role of the U.S. educational system, from K–12 to higher education, then becomes even more crucial in supplying the qualified workers needed to keep good-paying jobs in the country.[37]

One Connected Age trend that may have run its course is the movement of women into the paid labor force. During the first five years of the twenty-first century, the percentage of women in the paid labor force declined. Prelimi- nary analysis suggests that the labor market pull on women fell during this time.[38] If this finding is accurate and if the pull continues to lessen, a slow- down may occur in some segments of the service economy, such as prepared foods and home services.

Standard of Living: Has the Global Tide Lifted All Boats?

One of the most important issues associated with the Connected Age econ- omy is whether households improved their standards of living and, if so, whether some households improved more than others. With the numbers of factory jobs declining and of service jobs increasing, economists have ex- pressed concern that average worker pay fell. At the same time, the increase in the number of high-paying jobs has led to questions about widening in- come inequality. These questions are challenging because many alternative measures of economic well-being and different interpretations of these mea- sures exist.

Broad measures indicate that the average standard of living increased dur- ing the Connected Age. Between 1970 and 2005, after-tax personal income per person, in real dollars, rose 101 percent and personal spending per per- son, also in real dollars, jumped 121 percent.[39] Real dollar median household income per person rose a smaller but still healthy 58 percent.[40] The broadest measure of hourly compensation, which includes the value of both cash and noncash benefits, increased 54 percent in constant-purchasing-power dollars.[41] Yet a measure of hourly cash wages earned, which minimizes the effects of extremely high and extremely low wages and does not include the value of noncash benefits, showed only a 9 percent increase over the period.[42] Finally, wealth is another measure of well-being. Wealth is the accumulated value of a person's assets after subtracting what is owed (liabilities). In constant dollars, wealth per person rose 36 percent between 1970 and 2005.[43]

While all income numbers indicate an improved (to varying degrees) average standard of living over the time period, a further issue concerns whether all households shared in this prosperity. Unfortunately, total compensation and wealth data do not exist for persons or households of different income classes. However, wage rate, total income, and consumption have changed for households of various income levels. Both total income and consumption increased for all income categories, but the gains were greatest for the highest- and lowest-income categories and were more modest for the middle-income categories.[44] Wages earned per hour show a clear pattern in which workers earning higher wages receive the largest increases and workers earning lower wages receive the smallest increases.[45] Some measures show the real wages of both high school graduates and high school dropouts declining.[46]

Researchers studying standard-of-living patterns during the Connected Age have reached one major conclusion: the financial benefits of education and skills expanded during the period. The pay gap between college-educated workers and non-college-educated workers grew, as did the pay gap between professional workers and other workers. Analysts attribute the results to the changing nature of work and to the increasing importance of education in utilizing modern technology.[47]

Poverty is related to the standard of living. Between 1970 and 2005, the official poverty levels did not improve and in fact trended upward slightly.[48] However, this trend masked significant demographic changes affecting the poverty rate. Specifically, female-headed households, unrelated individuals, and lower-income immigrants increased their share of the total population during the Connected Age, and these groups typically have higher rates of poverty. Among two-parent households, poverty rates trended downward from 1970 to 2005.[49]

Some evidence indicates that one group, displaced factory workers, clearly faced economic challenges during the Connected Age. As I have already discussed, the number of factory workers declined as import competition and productivity improvements motivated manufacturing firms to rely more on technology and advanced machinery in their production processes. Former manufacturing workers tended to be older and less educated than workers who lost jobs in other sectors. Consequently, displaced factory workers comprised one of the groups least prepared to find good-paying alternatives in the Connected Age. Surveys show that when these workers found new employment, they suffered average earnings losses of 12 percent, with a quarter having losses of 30 percent or more.[50]

Finally, changes in the cost of living—also known as inflation—and in interest rates affected the standard of living. Rapid increases in inflation can reduce living standards if household incomes fail to keep up. High interest rates, which are directly tied to high inflation, inhibit households' ability to borrow money for big-ticket items such as homes and vehicles and make it more costly for businesses to update their machinery, buildings, and technology.

Declining trends in both inflation and interest rates have been a hallmark of the Connected Age. The average annual inflation rate dropped from 7.1 percent in the 1970s to 2.6 percent in the first decade of the twenty-first century.[51] The reduction was sharpest for manufactured products, where the spread of low-cost, worldwide production resulted in price reductions for apparel, technology, furniture, and appliance products.[52] Similarly, both short-term and long-term interest rates plunged by 3 percentage points between 1970 and 2005.[53] According to some observers, the reduction in interest rates resulted from the integration of world financial markets.[54]

More concerns and questions about future trends have perhaps arisen regarding the American standard of living than for any other element in the Connected Age. Long-run forecasts show the average standard of living, as measured by income available per person after taxes, continuing to rise.[55] Optimists see globalization as helping U.S. workers by moving them into more productive, higher-paying occupations and by keeping both the inflation rate and interest rates low as worldwide production takes place in low-cost regions.[56] Others are more pessimistic. They see U.S. workers' standards of living under increasing assault from cheaper foreign labor, the offshoring of even higher-paying jobs, domestic deregulation that forces businesses to cut costs even more, and the continuing decline of labor unions that protect the workers' interests.[57] Maybe nowhere are the expectations for the future of the Connected Age more divergent than for the standard of living.

Demographics: Who Will Do the Work?

The important demographic trends affecting the economy during the Connected Age include the aging of the population, the falling birthrate, and increased immigration.

Improvements in life expectancy and the aging of the baby boom generation combined dramatically to increase the percentage of the population qualifying as elderly. The number of people sixty-five years of age and older increased 83 percent between 1970 and 2005, much higher than the 45 percent increase in the total population. Consequently, the elderly population accounted for 12.4 percent of the total population in 2005, up from 9.8 percent in 1970.[58] The growing elderly population has profound implications for the workforce and government expenditures in the Connected Age, topics addressed later in this chapter.

At the same time, the relative size of the younger population declined. The population aged nineteen or under increased only 6 percent, dropping from 38 percent of the total in 1970 to 28 percent in 2005.[59] A major reason for this change was the decline in the birthrate. Between 1970 and 2004, the average number of births per woman dropped 23 percent, and average household size fell comparably.[60] These trends resulted from a delay in childbirth as a result of the increased time young women spent obtaining formal education and of their movement into the paid labor force.[61] In addition, economists have found a negative association between rising income and the birthrate. Children require parents to devote considerable time to child rearing and guidance. As average incomes rise, the value of parental time also rises. Hence, economists have long observed a correspondence between a declining birthrate and rising household income.[62]

A major demographic shift during the Connected Age was an increase in the rate of immigration. After declining each decade since the 1930s, immigration began to increase in the 1970s. By the twenty-first century, an estimated 1 million immigrants entered the country each year.[63] The composition of the new immigration also differed from that of earlier decades. Immigrants during the Connected Age have had lower educational levels and fewer formal skills than earlier arrivals and than the U.S. population as a whole.[64] Some research suggests that the increase in the supply of lower-skill immigrants in the U.S. economy contributed to the slow growth of wages for domestic low-skilled workers.[65]

A link exists between the three demographic trends of the Connected Age. The aging population has created a demand for low-skilled workers, especially in the construction and service industries. Immigrants have filled the gap in the supply of these workers created by the relatively slow increase in the domestic youth population and by the greater percentage of young people delaying entering the job market as they pursue college degrees. By the first decade of the twenty-first century, immigrants accounted for more than a third of the employment in the janitorial services industry and almost a quarter of the workers in the construction industry.[66]

In coming decades, the retirement of the baby boom generation, combined with the slower growth of subsequent generations, will cause the labor force to grow at its lowest pace in seven decades. Through 2050, labor force growth will amount to only one-third of 1970s rates and half the 1980s rates.[67] Without a tremendous surge in domestic fertility, the expected shortfall in workers will be made up by some combination of gains in labor productivity (each worker producing more) and foreign immigration. To achieve more productivity requires improved educational outcomes and investments in technology and equipment, but there are no assurances that these developments will occur. Past foreign immigration has already sparked political and social reactions that put its continuation in doubt. Therefore, the question of who will do the work in the future remains very much unanswered.

Technology: Digits over Distance?

If one characteristic defines the Connected Age, it is technology. Technology has digitally, globally, and competitively connected the country, workers, and businesses.

One of these technologies, air-conditioning, has existed for several decades, but only in the Connected Age did it become pervasive. While only one-third of all housing units had air-conditioning in 1970, almost two-thirds were equipped with it by 2005.[68] Although some people may consider the technology mundane, its importance should not be underestimated. Affordable, available air-conditioning made regions previously considered uninhabitable because of their hot, humid summers acceptable for year-round production and living. Air-conditioning particularly benefited the southern United States, which also had the advantage of relatively mild winters and thus low heating costs. Some economic historians have argued for a link between tropical environments and slower economic development.[69] Air-conditioning offers a way to break this link.

However, the technology most defining the Connected Age is the microchip. Initially developed in the 1950s, the chip underwent major improvements during the 1970s and 1980s that led to large-scale integrated circuits, programmable integrated circuits (microprocessors), and miniaturization. All of the signature tech applications of the Connected Age—personal computers, the Internet, and cell phones—constituted direct applications of the microchip technology. By 2005, 208 million people had cell phone service, and in 2003 62 percent of households owned a computer and 55 percent used the Internet.[70]

The most obvious way technology has affected the economy is in communications. One estimate suggests that the cost of communicating information fell by a factor of ten thousand between 1970 and 2000.[71] Increased communication not only has benefited the quality of life for families but also has promoted business efficiency by increasing the geographic range of contacts and reducing the time needed to detect and address business issues.

Technology has also impacted the economy in more subtle yet equally important ways. Businesses have long struggled with the issue of inventory management. If not enough product is kept in stock, customers will be turned away and business profitability will fall. Conversely, if overstocking occurs, future production is cut and workers are laid off. In fact, unwanted inventory accumulation is one of the main reasons for economy-wide recessions. Inventory-management programs using the technology of the Connected Age have significantly reduced the chances of both understocking and overstocking and bear partial responsibility for the shorter and milder recessions experienced in recent decades.[72] And although not technology in the strictest sense, significant improvements in ocean shipping containers helped to facilitate the great strides in world trade that occurred during this era.[73]

Thomas L. Friedman argues that these technological achievements have "flattened" the world economy, rendering distance increasingly obsolete and allowing companies around the world to compete with each other in the global marketplace.[74] He foresees this flatness increasing even more with further advances in technology that lower the cost of space. If he is right, then global competition will expand even more in the future and extend from manufacturing and simple services (catalog ordering, technical assistance) to professional and high-level services, possibly putting high-cost countries such as the United States at a disadvantage and slowing or reversing gains in living standards.

However, not all observers of the modern world agree. Edward E. Leamer argues that the world has been flattening for centuries as transportation and communications have advanced but that we perceive globalization as new because we are so caught up in today's gadgets.[75] But Leamer also presents evidence that the income disparities between countries such as the United States and Japan at the high-income extreme and China and India at the low-income extreme have not diminished but in fact have widened. According to Leamer, distance cannot be completely conquered by technology; rather, accessibility to customers and firsthand knowledge of customs and preferences will always have benefits. In addition, an assembly line will never duplicate talent, creativity, and innovation. This analysis suggests no requirement that incomes will flatten as world trade broadens.

Government: In the Way or Out in Front?

Government can play two major roles in the economy—directly, via the amount of tax revenue it takes and spending it generates, and indirectly, via the laws and regulations it enacts.

In terms of size, total government (federal, state, and local combined) grew modestly relative to other economic sectors during the Connected Age. Total government spending accounted for 28 percent of the economy in 1970 and 31 percent in 2005.[76] However, the composition of government spending shifted significantly during this time. Despite the additional defense spending allocated for the wars on terrorism and in Iraq and Afghanistan, federal defense spending as a percentage of the economy fell by more than 50 percent between 1970 and 2005. In contrast, federal health spending rose almost 300 percent and Social Security spending increased 45 percent over this period.[77] These spending increases were certainly driven by the aging population and the public's increased demand for health care. At the state and local levels, health, public safety, and public assistance spending took added shares of the economy, while relative spending on highways declined.[78]

Government spending falls into two categories: spending on government provision of services, such as building and maintaining roads, providing education in public schools, and paying police and firefighters to keep citizens safe, and spending on government transfers—that is, the government providing income to households or paying for a particular kind of spending, such as medical care. With transfers, only those who directly receive the income or have the cost paid obtain the benefits of the spending. During the Connected Age, government spending on services declined from 18 percent to 15 percent of the economy (gross domestic product), while government spending on transfers doubled from 6 percent to 12 percent of the economy, with the largest share of the increase going to health care expenditures.[79] These numbers imply that government did relatively less of those activities that all citizens collectively can see and appreciate (services) while doing more to support specific beneficiaries and functions (transfers).

Two important trends in governmental laws and regulations, particularly at the federal level, occurred during the Connected Age. Beginning in the late 1970s, the federal government deregulated several large industries—that is, removed or reduced rules and regulations about where and how companies operate and about the prices they charge. By the beginning of the twenty-first century, deregulation had been applied to the airline, telecommunications, trucking, energy, financial services, and agricultural industries. Advocates of deregulation claim that it has led to lower prices for consumers, greater choices, more responsive firms, and greater efficiency in resource alloca- tion.[80] Critics worry that deregulation has resulted in industry instability, lower quality, and a greater focus on short-run profits.[81] Nonetheless, deregu- lation clearly was aimed at increasing the degree of domestic competition in the economy, a key feature of the Connected Age.

The federal government also increased competition by agreeing to sev- eral international agreements that lowered trade barriers among countries. The most notable were the North American Free Trade Agreement (NAFTA), an agreement among the United States, Mexico, and Canada; the General Agreement on Tariffs and Trade (GATT), a worldwide trade deal; and the Cen- tral American Free Trade Agreement (CAFTA), a treaty involving the United States and various Central American countries. Estimates show that these agreements reduced tariffs on U.S. imports by as much as 60 percent be- tween 1970 and 2000.[82] At the same time, the fall of the Soviet Union and the removal of the iron curtain across Eastern Europe, combined with the inte- gration of China and India into the world economy, approximately doubled the world supply of labor and contributed to lower prices for many products and a moderating inflation rate.[83] Again, advocates and opponents of global- ization have sparred about whether trade agreements and closer international economic interaction have benefited or harmed the economy and workers.[84]

One of the biggest challenges for government at all levels will be managing the inevitable conflict between public spending and taxes. While this conflict has always existed—citizens want public services but prefer not to pay taxes for the provision of those services—the Connected Age arguably has intensi- fied and will continue to intensify this conflict. On the one side are economic and demographic pressures for higher rates of public spending—to educate workers so the country can compete in the global market, to repair and build public infrastructure to handle the increasing demands of trade, and to provide financial support both for the growing elderly population and for those households left behind in the era's competitive race. On the other side is the potential negative effect of higher tax rates on a locality's ability to attract and retain businesses and households in an increasingly mobile world. The tug-of-war between these two sides will only have a stronger effect on public decision makers in future decades.

Issues: What the Connected Age Hath Wrought

Improvements as well as challenges can be found in any era, and the Connected Age is no exception. Many prominent gains were made. The average household earned more, spent more, and became richer after 1970. More people acquired more education, and life expectancy grew. Economic ups and downs became milder, and the inflation rate and interest rates trended lower. Women's educational and employment opportunities increased, and more women took advantage of those opportunities. Technology created new worlds for consumers to explore and brought sophisticated production and management tools to business. Increased domestic and international competition expanded the ranges of choices and lowered many prices for buyers.

At the same time, the Connected Age created challenges. For decades, manufacturing had offered good-paying jobs to millions of workers with limited formal education. During the Connected Age, the manufacturing sector shed 3.5 million jobs.[85] Without retraining, many of these workers have had to accept lower-paying positions in the service sector. The bridge to the middle class that manufacturing for generations provided to individuals who did not pursue education beyond high school collapsed during the Connected Age.

In the Connected Age, education mattered as had never before been the case. Education replaced unions, experience, and personal connections as the major determinant of economic status. Workers with education got ahead in the Connected Age, and those without education increasingly struggled. The widening income disparity observed during the Connected Age was based on a gap between the highly educated and the less educated. Yet as the period progressed, even domestic workers with education faced competition from global competitors with the same training. While households' overall average income mobility apparently did not drop during the era, such mobility was reduced for young households and for households whose members did not possess college educations.[86]

The Connected Age produced a concern not seen in the country for several decades—whether a falling birthrate would fail to produce a sufficient supply of domestic workers. The baby boom generation (people born between 1946 and 1965) began to retire during the Connected Age and will be fully retired by 2020. Since the succeeding generation is smaller by 10 million persons, some observers forecast too few well-trained, well-educated workers to meet the country's future labor demands.[87] The shortage will have to be closed by some combination of increased worker productivity, increased immigration, and increased imports.

The greatest spending challenge confronting citizens in the Connected Age was health care. Both private and public budgets for health care exploded as the number of elderly persons grew and they lived longer and as medical technology and accomplishments improved. Attempts to rein in cost increases through limitations on care—the approach taken by health maintenance organizations—faced resistance. Meeting future health care demand within budgetary limits will constitute a major challenge in the future.

Many domestic businesses looked to foreign markets for opportunities during the Connected Age, just as foreign enterprises expanded sales in the United States. Technology had indeed shrunk the world and increased ties between continents and countries. Yet the memory of 9/11 and the dark cloud of international terrorism have raised questions about the safety and certainty of international linkages. Some observers worry that added measures to provide security for travelers in particular threaten the future vitality and productivity of the economy by restricting the movement of highly skilled and entrepreneurial individuals.[88]

Advances in communications and transportation and the enhanced competitiveness of the business world quickened the era's pace of change. Firms had to move fast and production had to change rapidly to keep up with altering consumer tastes and the constant repositioning of competing sellers. "Just in time" replaced "You'll have it soon." Long-term commitments became hazardous for businesses, and employees often paid the price. Pensions and health care increasingly shifted from being part of the employer-provided package to the employee's responsibility. In the competitive Connected Age, workers found themselves increasingly on their own.

Naturally, then, people frequently looked to government to provide shelter from the fallout from the Connected Age. Areas in which government has been asked to lead include education, worker retraining, health care, pension protection, and homeland and international security. In recent decades, government increasingly funded its spending through borrowing instead of taxes. This type of financing, combined with substantial spending promises to future citizens in the form of Social Security and Medicare, has led economists to predict significantly higher tax rates in the future.[89] Consequently, a looming public finance crisis may be one of the legacies of the Connected Age.

Finally, as the Connected Age moved into its fourth decade, an issue arose that affects virtually every household and individual—energy. Like its predecessor, the Industrial Age, the Connected Age was built on fossil-fuel energy. With the exception of a seven-year period between 1974 and 1981, oil and gasoline prices, in inflation-adjusted terms, trended downward, reaching historically low levels in the late 1990s. This cheap energy contributed to the era's economic growth and productivity improvements. However, as countries in Eastern Europe and Asia joined the economy of the Connected Age, world energy consumption rose dramatically after 2000, and energy prices followed. Some observers fear that worldwide oil and gas supplies will gradually become depleted, leading to a continual rise in energy prices and a consequent future curtailment of economic growth. Others see a combination of new supplies of oil, improvements in energy efficiency, and the introduction of alternatives to fossil fuels allowing the connected world economy to maintain its advance.[90] Whichever path proves correct, energy supplies and energy prices certainly will have a profound impact on the future of the Connected Age.

But what has the Connected Age brought to North Carolina, and where will it take the state? The next six chapters provide some answers and perspective.

2. The Macroeconomics of Change

Forces Transforming North Carolina's Economy

Few states have been impacted as much by the Connected Age as North Carolina. North Carolina's twentieth-century economy was built largely on the availability of plentiful low-cost labor. The dramatic opening of world markets and the ability to manage production over wide geographic areas with modern communications and transportation mean that low-cost labor no longer needs to be located in North Carolina or the United States but can be located in China, India, and Eastern Europe. Consequently, production has increasingly left North Carolina, and the state's dominant industries of the last century have diminished in size and importance.

But North Carolina has adapted. Capitalizing on Connected Age trends in education, deregulation, and consumer buying patterns, North Carolina fostered a new set of growing industries in sectors such as technology, health care products, food processing, banking, and vehicle parts. These industries compensated for the losses in traditional sectors and allowed the aggregate state economy to expand at rates exceeding national averages. Some might call this North Carolina's economic miracle.

But the miracle did not reach everyone everywhere in the state. People and firms that lacked the means or ability to adapt to the Connected Age's forces were left behind. Because those benefiting from the Connected Age and those losing were frequently separated geographically, the economic transformation has created pockets of prosperous regions on one side and groups of economically challenged regions on the other, with very little middle ground. By some measures, North Carolina's people and regions have grown farther apart during the era. Chapters 4 and 5 address this important topic in more depth.

This chapter tells a story of both endings and beginnings—an ending to North Carolina's traditional twentieth-century economy and a beginning to the new Connected Age economy. The chapter tracks broad changes in the state economy and compares them to those at the national level. It documents how North Carolina reacted to the key trends of the Connected Age and shows how these reactions contributed to contractions in traditional industries as well as expansion in new industries. The chapter concludes with a look to the future and how the North Carolina economy will further transform as the Connected Age matures.

North Carolina versus the Nation: Coming Together or Pulling Apart?

Overall, North Carolina's economy outperformed the national economy during the Connected Age. Table 2-1 shows real growth rates in key economic measures in both North Carolina and the United States from 1977 (the first year for which output data are available) to 2005. On both a total and per capita (per person) basis, North Carolina beat the nation on all measures.[1]

However, looking at annual changes reveals a possible change in the state's relative strength. Figure 2-1 tracks one of the broad measures, real per capita income, annually since 1977. The figure shows that real per capita income in the state has moved steadily higher during the Connected Age, with the exception of recession years, such as in the early 1980s, early 1990s, and early 2000s. The ratio of North Carolina per capita income to U.S. per capita income also trended higher until 1997, when it peaked at 93 percent. Since that year, while North Carolina's real per capita income has increased, it has risen slower than real U.S. per capita income; as a result, the ratio between the two numbers dropped to 89 percent in 2006. Other broad measures of North Carolina's economy relative to the national economy also peaked in the 1990s—per capita output in 1995 and per capita gross domestic product in 1999.[2]

North Carolina's economy has been approaching national measures over a much longer period as well. For example, from 1929 to 1962, North Carolina's per capita income rose from 48 percent of the national level to 73 percent.[3] Some economists argue that such results are to be expected because economically poorer regions will eventually catch up to (converge on) richer regions. Poorer regions will use their lower costs of production, especially labor, to attract firms and expand commerce, following the idea that resources flow to their highest use. This process most often occurs when fixed resources that cannot be duplicated or moved, such as rivers for power and harbors for freight, become less important as a result of technology and other factors.[4] As the regions grow, their wages and incomes will eventually become closer to national levels.

Table 2-1. Real Economic Growth Rates, North Carolina and the United States, 1977–2005

Measure	North Carolina	United States
Quantity of production	+194%	+182%
Quantity of production per capita	+85%	+74%
Real gross domestic product	+199%	+119%
Real gross domestic product per capita	+96%	+62%
Real per capita income	+81%	+64%
Employment growth	+80%	+66%

DATA SOURCE: U.S. Department of Commerce, Bureau of Economic Analysis, "Gross Domestic Product"; U.S. Department of Commerce, Bureau of Economic Analysis, "State Annual Personal Income."

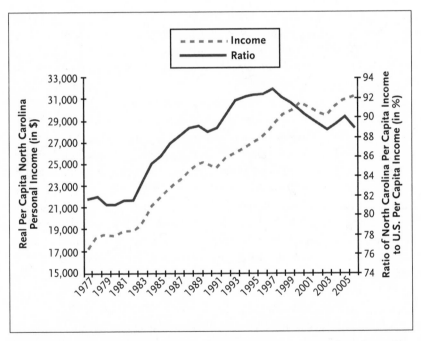

Figure 2-1. Real per capita North Carolina personal income and ratio of North Carolina per capita income to U.S. per capita income, 1977–2005.
DATA SOURCE: U.S. Department of Commerce, Bureau of Economic Analysis, "Gross Domestic Product."

Furthermore, when regions act to facilitate their attractiveness by enhancing positive features and correcting negative ones, this economic catch-up or convergence can accelerate. In the case of the South, economists have cited improvements in transportation and communication infrastructure, the development and installation of air-conditioning, and the removal of the negative stigma attached to southern race relations as important changes that made the South, including North Carolina, attractive to economic investment.[5]

Researchers have extensively examined the topic of economic convergence, and the results seem to favor similarity in economic measures over time among regions and states.[6] However, this finding makes North Carolina's post-1990s movement away from convergence all the more puzzling, as I explore later in the chapter.

While North Carolina's economy has moved faster than that of the nation as a whole throughout the Connected Age, the trip has also been bumpier. North Carolina's expansions have been stronger, but its recessions have been deeper. North Carolina's income and employment have grown one-third faster during Connected Age expansions, but the state's income losses have been two-thirds greater and job cuts have been almost twice as severe during recessions.[7]

A major reason for the greater volatility of North Carolina's business cycle is the larger importance of manufacturing to the state. Manufacturing traditionally has been more susceptible to the ups and downs of the business cycle because production needs lead time for scheduling and output can be stored. Therefore, if recessions cannot be predicted perfectly, manufacturers have unsold output; to minimize their losses, they contract production and reduce employment. During the Connected Age, manufacturing was half to two-thirds more important to North Carolina's economy than to that of the nation. Although manufacturing's importance fell in both North Carolina and the country as a whole during the period, the drop was greater in the nation.[8] Thus, relative to the United States, North Carolina became even more dependent on manufacturing.

Ominously, the size of North Carolina's expansionary upward bump declined over the last three expansions relative to the nation as a whole, while the severity of North Carolina's recessions has increased. In other words, the strength of North Carolina's expansions has become more similar to national expansions, but relative to the nation, North Carolina's twenty-first-century recession was more intense than the 1990s recession and was only slightly less severe than the very deep 1980s recession.[9] So, relative to the nation,

North Carolina's business cycle has recently featured more of the bad and less of the good.

The Transformation: The Economy Turned Upside Down

North Carolina's economy made impressive gains during the Connected Age. Yet these overall numbers hid a tremendous amount of churning—of adding and subtracting of both companies and jobs—beneath the surface.

Output growth in the major sectors of the economy is one arena in which this churning is apparent (figure 2-2). Like the nation (figure 1-1), three of the top four growing sectors by output during the Connected Age were wholesale and retail trade and transportation/communications/public utilities (TCPU). Services, manufacturing, construction, and government were the slowest-growing sectors. The biggest difference in the rankings between the nation and North Carolina is the financial sector, which was second-fastest-growing in North Carolina but only fifth in the United States.

Also following national trends, employment in North Carolina manufac-

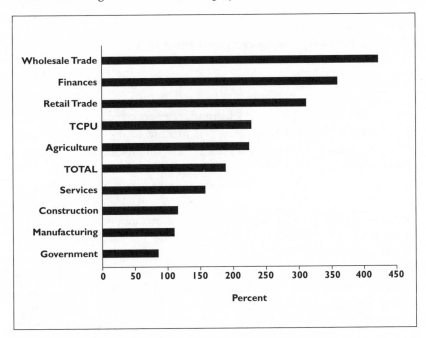

Figure 2-2. North Carolina output growth rate by sector, 1977–2005.
DATA SOURCE: U.S. Department of Commerce, Bureau of Economic Analysis, "Gross Domestic Product."

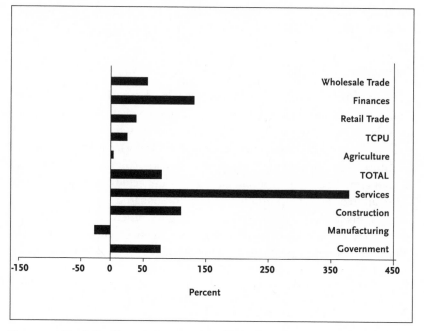

Figure 2-3. North Carolina employment growth rate by sector, 1977–2005.
DATA SOURCE: U.S. Department of Labor, Bureau of Labor Statistics, "Employment, Hours, and Earnings."

turing declined, while the largest job growth rates occurred in services, financial services, and construction (figure 2-3). Manufacturing output increased, while employment in the sector declined, the result of a significant increase in worker productivity.

Although tracking trends in broad economic sectors can be enlightening, any economy will be driven by a few key industries in which it has a competitive advantage. Such industries export a significant amount of production to buyers (both domestic and foreign) outside of the state and thus bring new income into the state. In the traditional North Carolina economy, these industries were tobacco, textiles and apparel, and furniture (the Big Three). In the North Carolina economy of the Connected Age, they are the new Big Five — chemical products (primarily pharmaceuticals), technology, food processing, banking, and vehicle parts.[10] Trends in the two categories demonstrate the state's dramatic economic transformation over the past quarter century.

In 1977, the traditional Big Three accounted for 22 percent of North Carolina's entire economy and 64 percent of the value of manufacturing produc-

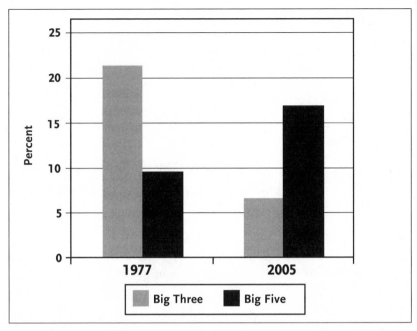

Figure 2-4. Big Three and Big Five shares of North Carolina economy, 1977 and 2005.
DATA SOURCES: U.S. Department of Commerce, Bureau of Economic Analysis, "Gross Domestic Product"; U.S. Census Bureau, "Annual Survey of Manufactures," North Carolina, table 1.
NOTE: Values are industry gross state product as a percentage of total gross state product.

tion. The new Big Five's share of the total state economy amounted to less than 10 percent, and its manufacturing component made up less than one quarter of all manufacturing production. By 2005, the shares were almost exactly reversed. The traditional Big Three held only 7 percent of the total economy and 32 percent of manufacturing, while the new Big Five had 17 percent of the total value of production and 43 percent of manufacturing (figure 2-4).[11]

Outside of financial services, the biggest changes in the service sector occurred in health care and professional and management services. Following national trends, each of these industries doubled its share of the state economy between 1977 and 2005.[12]

Learning to Swim with the Tide

The driving forces of the Connected Age have been education and technology, deregulation, and global trade. How has North Carolina adapted to these forces, and how have these forces affected the state economy and particular economic sectors?

Education

Virtually every study of recent economic growth has found a positive impact from education.[13] In the Connected Age, education matters for two reasons. First, educated workers are needed to operate the new technology developed for the workplace. Second, the nature of most jobs has changed, with analytical power substituting for muscle power. Machines do the heavy lifting, and computers increasingly perform the routine and unthinking tasks, leaving workers to deal with complex decisions requiring thought and analysis. Computerization has also accelerated the pace of job change and raised the value of verbal and quantitative literacy. Even the percentage of jobs that require only a high school education yet also necessitate complex communication and decision making has increased.[14] As a result, the wage premium paid for cognitive skills increased during the Connected Age.[15]

For most of North Carolina's economic history, educational attainment was a lagging characteristic. As recently as 1950, the average adult North Carolinian had less than an eighth-grade education, and in 1960 the average adult educational level remained under nine years.[16] Throughout much of the twentieth century, companies moved to North Carolina to take advantage of the low-cost, low-skilled labor supply.

In the Connected Age, the low-wage strategy no longer works because cheap labor is available and accessible outside the United States. To attract jobs — in particular, better-paying jobs — North Carolina had to respond to the educational challenge. And the state did. By 2000, North Carolina fell just 2 percentage points shy of the national average for adults with high school degrees (78 percent versus 80 percent) and had come within 1 percentage point of the national average for adults with bachelor's degrees (23 percent versus 24 percent).[17] Between 1970 and 2005, the percentage of adults in North Carolina with high school degrees increased twice as fast as the rate for the nation, and the percentage of adults with bachelor's degrees increased 10 percent faster.[18]

Perhaps even more impressive has been the improvement in educational quality as measured by standardized test scores. Between 1975 and 2005, the average Scholastic Aptitude Test (SAT) score for college-bound high school seniors increased more than four times as fast in North Carolina as in the nation.[19] The National Assessment of Educational Progress fourth-grade reading and math scores increased faster in North Carolina than in the nation between 1992 and 2005, and the same was true for eighth-grade math scores.[20]

How North Carolina achieved these gains is a matter of analysis and debate. North Carolina increased public educational spending per K–12 student faster than the nation did during the Connected Age, and class sizes also fell at a greater rate. Annual tuition and fees at public colleges are less costly in North Carolina than elsewhere, thereby making postsecondary training more attractive to more students. Chapter 6 explores the public policy issues related to K–12 and higher education in North Carolina during the Connected Age, while chapter 5 details geographical differences in educational attainment among North Carolina counties.

Worker Productivity

Characteristics of the labor supply have long been one of the most important factors — if not *the* most important factor — attracting business to a particular location. In the Industrial Age, observers argued that the South's labor advantage lay in its plentiful, cheap labor.[21] Even in the Connected Age's technological workplace, labor costs remain an important consideration, accounting for almost 60 percent of the total value of production.[22]

Several recent studies have highlighted the local labor market's role in economic development. Robert W. Crandall's analysis of the relocation of U.S. manufacturing from the North and Midwest to the South in the 1970s and 1980s found low wages and low levels of unionization to be attractive features for firm location among U.S. states, but only wages were important for North Carolina. Crandall found that wages and unionization were more important for high-tech firms in sectors such as chemicals, machinery, aerospace, and instruments than for other firms, a result he attributes to the greater mobility of tech-heavy companies.[23] Theodore M. Crone found similar results, as did John S. Hekman for computer manufacturers and Cletus C. Coughlin and Eran Segev for foreign-owned companies.[24] Geoffrey Tootell, Richard W. Kopcke, and Robert K. Triest found that regions with worker pay higher than the national average had slower employment and investment growth.[25]

Several researchers have focused on the South's low unionization rate as a key element in its post–World War II development.[26] Mancur Olsen in particular cites labor union and other interest group interference in market

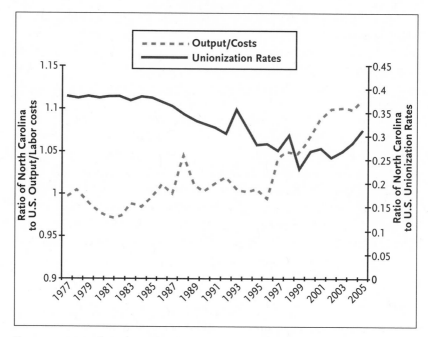

Figure 2-5. Ratio of North Carolina to U.S. output/labor costs and unionization rates, 1977–2005.

DATA SOURCES: U.S. Department of Commerce, Bureau of Economic Analysis, "Gross Domestic Product"; U.S. Department of Commerce, Bureau of Economic Analysis, "State Annual Personal Income."

NOTE: Output to labor costs data are the real value of output (gross domestic product) of the total economy per worker divided by real salaries and wages per worker in the same year, expressed as the ratio of the North Carolina measure to the U.S. measure. A value above 1 means that North Carolina workers are more productive than average U.S. workers.

forces as the origin of inefficiencies and higher costs that lead to economic decline. In contrast, Ronald L. Moomaw and Martin Williams found that states with higher unionization rates had higher levels of labor productivity and economic growth.[27]

Economic theory suggests that worker compensation relative to worker productivity, rather than worker compensation in isolation, is the key way businesses measure labor costs.[28] A worker paid twice as much as a counterpart who produces three times more in a given period of time is actually the lower-cost alternative. Therefore, worker pay relative to worker output is the more accurate way to measure labor costs.

Figure 2-5 shows the ratio of North Carolina output per labor cost relative to U.S. output per labor cost. The figure also gives the ratio of the North Carolina and U.S. unionization rates.[29] From the perspective of business location, North Carolina looks favorable, with higher output per labor cost and lower unionization rates over most of the Connected Age and particularly in the late 1990s and early 2000s.

Global Trade

The move to liberalize and open world trade began after World War II and represented a way to tie countries economically and reduce the likelihood of military conflict. Tariff rates (taxes levied on imports) were cut in half between the 1960s and 1990s among countries participating in world trade negotiations.[30] The reduction in tariffs was accomplished during several phases of negotiations in the General Agreement on Tariffs and Trade (GATT).

One exception to this reduction in trade barriers was for an industry very important to North Carolina—textiles and apparel. International trade in textile and apparel products after World War II was governed by a separate compact called the Multifiber Arrangement. This agreement allowed countries to impose quotas, or quantitative limits, on textile and apparel imports and helped protect the U.S. and European textile and apparel industries from lower-cost Asian producers.[31]

The institution of the North American Free Trade Agreement (NAFTA) in 1994 and the World Trade Organization (WTO) in 1995 opened global trade even further and, significantly for North Carolina, ended the special treatment for textiles and apparel. NAFTA eliminated or reduced tariffs and other trade barriers between the United States, Canada, and Mexico for products and services originating in those countries.[32] Trade barriers on textiles and apparel were reduced in steps over a ten-year period, with a total phaseout by 2003.[33]

More important was the WTO, which officially ended the Multifiber Arrangement and moved unrestricted trade to a worldwide stage. Trade barriers were removed in stages through 2005 for the organization's more than one hundred member countries.[34] The agreement allowed member countries facing a surge of textile and apparel imports to impose emergency quotas until 2008.[35] The WTO's impact expanded when China joined in 2001. Using low labor costs, China was expected to dominate much of the world's labor-intensive apparel production.[36]

These changes increased global trade but impacted the traditional and new

North Carolina economies in different ways. For the tobacco, textile, apparel, and furniture industries, more open world trade increased U.S. imports and moderated exports to other countries. In 2004, the value of U.S. tobacco exports reached only 26 percent of its 1994 level; U.S. furniture imports increased three times faster than exports between 1994 and 2004, a reversal of the situation during the preceding decade; the U.S. trade surplus in textiles declined after 1994; and the quantity of U.S. apparel imports increased faster in the decade after NAFTA and GATT than in the decade before. In contrast, U.S. exports increased faster than imports after 1994 for pharmaceuticals, financial services, and food processing.[37]

Consequently, the impacts of increased global trade during the Connected Age on traditional North Carolina industry production and employment cannot be overlooked. North Carolina's textile production peaked in 1994, apparel output topped out in 1995, and furniture production reached its highest levels in 1999.[38] Although employment in each of these traditional industries had been falling before the trade agreements, job losses accelerated thereafter.[39]

The post–World War II trend toward increased world trade reinforced another factor at work in manufacturing, the product cycle. Here the manufacturing of products moves through three stages. Development of the product takes place during the innovation stage, where highly skilled workers are needed to design and test the product, work out the kinks in the manufacturing process, and quickly interact with suppliers and customers. In the mature phase, production has been simplified and standardized and sales have been established. New production now can be sent to lower-cost regions and countries. In the third phase, complete standardization, all production moves to low-cost areas.[40] Ronald Ritter and Robert Sternfels argue that the product cycle most applies to goods for which demand is stable, inventory costs are low, and labor constitutes a high proportion of total costs.[41]

Textiles, apparel, and furniture have long been stable and standardized products whose production would logically involve low-cost labor. For much of the twentieth century, North Carolina supplied this labor, but in the Connected Age, such is not the case. Only trade restrictions prevented production from moving to low-cost countries, and when those restrictions were lifted, factory relocations increasingly occurred. Since the trade liberalization of the mid-1990s, imports have increased faster than exports for two Connected Age industries, technology and vehicle parts, suggesting that these products may be in the mature phase of the product cycle.[42]

Although North Carolina clearly has suffered job losses since the mid-

1990s as a consequence of enhanced global trade, particularly in textiles and apparel, some offsetting job gains may have occurred.[43] Some analysts estimate that increased international trade has reduced the average inflation rate and raised real economic growth.[44] If this finding is accurate, job gains in North Carolina resulting from these beneficial effects could have replaced a quarter to half of the direct job losses as a consequence of NAFTA and the WTO.[45]

Deregulation

Deregulation began in the 1970s with the airline industry and proceeded through the 1980s and 1990s with trucking, natural gas and oil, financial and legal services, agriculture, and telecommunications. Deregulation constituted a reaction to the low economic growth and high unemployment of the 1970s and was designed to boost production and reduce inflation. Analysts have generally concluded that deregulation has reduced prices paid by consumers and increased competition but has done so at the costs of market instability and worker dislocations.[46]

Deregulation of two industries, banking and tobacco, profoundly affected North Carolina's economy. Deregulation of banking was clearly positive for North Carolina and resulted from foresighted legislation passed almost a half century before the Connected Age. Tobacco industry deregulation was inevitable, and although the short-run impacts may be negative, the longer-run consequences may benefit the affected regions.

Banking experienced two types of deregulation in the Connected Age. Deregulation of services, authorized by the Gramm-Leach-Bliley Act of 1999, permitted banks to establish financial holding companies and to offer securities and financial products to complement their banking services. Banks could then advertise themselves as one-stop financial centers and potentially extend efficiencies in customer services.[47]

The second type of banking deregulation was geographic. Most states traditionally restricted banks to one site, and state and federal laws prohibited regional and nationwide banks. These restrictions stemmed from a historical concern about concentration of power in financial services. However, during the 1980s, individual states began passing laws that permitted branch banking and allowing banks from other states to purchase banks within the state's borders. By 1990, all but four states allowed at least some cross-state border purchases. In 1994, the federal Riegle-Neal Interstate Banking Act eliminated all interstate banking restrictions and allowed nationwide banking.[48]

North Carolina took greater advantage of banking deregulation than most other states because of the knowledge, experience, and competitive advantage North Carolina banks had gained in operating across large geographic areas for many decades. North Carolina had allowed branch banking within its borders since the 1920s, one of only twelve states that permitted branch banking prior to 1970. In the Southeast, only North Carolina and South Carolina allowed branch banking, and not coincidentally, North Carolina's banking center lay in Charlotte, on the South Carolina border. Studies have found that banks in states with branch banking were more efficient, with lower loss and cost ratios.[49] Hence, when first regional and then nationwide banking came, North Carolina banks used their experience and cost advantages to expand aggressively. Today, Charlotte is the country's second-largest banking center and the world's tenth-largest by assets and is home to two of the country's largest banks, Bank of America and Wachovia.[50]

The significance of banking deregulation in North Carolina goes beyond its benefits to the state's large banks. The efficiencies and advantages gained by the banking industry can be passed along to the general business community. For example, Timothy J. Bartik found that states having statewide branch banking had more small-business start-ups.[51]

Tobacco was one of the pillars of North Carolina's traditional twentieth-century economy. In part, the state's tobacco industry was maintained by a quota system, established in 1938, that restricted the quantity of tobacco produced and thereby kept tobacco prices high. With a relatively inelastic demand for tobacco products—meaning that consumption would fall, on a percentage basis, less than the percentage increase in product price—growers enjoyed high profits and a stable market.

The quota system worked well as long as there were few substitutes for North Carolina–grown tobacco, and for many decades, no such substitutes existed. Yet the high prices and profits provided big motivators for competition, and foreign-grown tobacco began to improve in quality and to compete using lower prices. U.S. cigarette manufacturers gradually increased their use of foreign tobacco, raising its share from 15 percent in the 1970s to 50 percent by 2000.[52] Also, although U.S. tariffs on imported tobacco leaf had always been low, NAFTA and the WTO further reduced these trade barriers. NAFTA's passage began a ten-year phaseout of all tariffs on tobacco and tobacco products from Mexico.[53] The WTO agreement mandated a 55 percent reduction in tariffs on cigarettes and, more importantly for North Carolina's tobacco industry, removed the requirement that cigarettes manufactured in the United States contain at least 75 percent domestically grown tobacco.[54]

As a result, the U.S. share of world tobacco trade fell from 20 percent in 1970 to 8 percent in 2002, and North Carolina's tobacco production (output) slid more than 80 percent between 1977 and 2003.[55] Faced with declining production and falling profits, the tobacco growers' industry agreed to a dismantling of the tobacco quota system in 2005. A buyout of quota holders compensated growers for their loss of profits between the new market-based system and quota system. The buyout will pay quota owners an estimated $4 billion over a multiyear period.[56]

Growth of the Service Economy

One of the major drivers behind the growth of the service economy during the Connected Age has been the movement of women into the paid workforce. This trend has led to an increased demand for convenience and time-saving devices and services. With working women still contributing the majority of time to child-rearing and household tasks, such women have had a strong motivation to ease their time burden by using products and services with low time inputs.[57] A major area where this shift took place is in food consumption. Spending on prepared foods (those requiring minimal cooking time) and restaurant eating increased dramatically during the Connected Age.

The shift to processed foods helped fuel the growth in North Carolina's meat industry, particularly in pork and poultry. At the farm level, between 1970 and 2003, hog production increased 485 percent by weight, and poultry output (broilers, chickens, and turkeys) jumped 295 percent by weight.[58] Output from the state's food-processing factories rose 234 percent from 1977 to 2003, more than three times the national increase.[59]

Two Economies, Two Directions

How did these Connected Age forces quantitatively impact the North Carolina economy as well as the individual sectors of the traditional and new economies? This section describes the results of an empirical investigation of this question that reveals a fundamental challenge to the state economy during the Connected Age. The Connected Age forces that have helped some sectors have hindered others.

Education, worker productivity, global trade, deregulation, growth of the service economy—a host of factors affected the North Carolina economy during the Connected Age. With the addition of two other forces—energy costs and government taxes—that can be movers of an economy during any age, disentangling the individual effects of any of these factors clearly becomes very difficult, especially when many of these forces are changing together.

Appendix A reports on the details of a methodology used to identify the impacts of the Connected Age forces on both the overall North Carolina economy and the performance of the traditional industries and the new economy industries. The analysis resulted in several important conclusions. Aggregate economic production in North Carolina rose with increases in the efficiency of labor (production per dollar spent on labor) and with improvements in educational performance. Also, rather than being adversely affected by globalization, total output from the state's factories, farms, and offices grew as tariffs were reduced and as China joined the world trading community. This finding is consistent with the argument that more open world trade promotes efficient resource use, lowers prices, and thereby improves economic activity.[60] The number of jobs in the state increased with a higher percentage of women in the labor force and with lower energy prices but decreased with improvements in worker efficiency.

However, the influences of the Connected Age forces differed dramatically for the traditional and new industries. With the exception of the paper industry, improvements in educational performance were not tied to changes in traditional industry production, and output in several of the traditional firms was not linked to labor efficiency. But output or employment in every traditional industry except agriculture has been adversely impacted by either reductions in tariffs or the opening of trade with China.

In contrast, increases in output in all of the new North Carolina industries have been linked to improvements in labor efficiency, and in the majority of the sectors, such increases are tied to improvements in student educational performance. Output in two of the new industries gained after China was included in the world economy, and declines in output only in the chemical industry were linked to tariff reductions, while another—the food industry— gained from those cuts. Increases in employment in two of the new economy industries are associated with educational improvements, and higher employment in computer equipment and in transportation equipment firms has occurred with lower tariffs. However, China's emergence was tied to fewer jobs in chemical product manufacturing. Furthermore, the analysis revealed a strong tie between expansion of the North Carolina banking industry and consolidation in the nationwide banking industry.

The statistical model used to derive these findings was also used to address the twenty-first-century puzzle in the North Carolina economy: Why has North Carolina's per capita income been falling relative to the nation's since 2000 after rising for much of the previous century? The answer appears not to be globalization or taxes, two commonly cited culprits. Instead, three other reasons predominate — the slowdown and recent slight reversal in gains of women working in the paid labor force, the rise in energy prices, and the improvement in worker efficiency. The rise of the working woman during the Connected Age not only helped propel North Carolina's food-processing sector but also contributed to consumer demand for products from the textile and apparel sectors and to employment gains in those companies. A turn-around in the labor force trends of women has added to the contractions of these still-important industries and reduced their ability to pay wages and hire workers, with the negative impact apparent in per capita income.

Similarly, North Carolina is more susceptible to rising energy prices than is the nation for two reasons. First, the energy-intensive manufacturing sector still comprises a much larger component of the North Carolina economy than it does of the national economy, meaning that increases in energy prices can have a more pervasive adverse impact on the state economy.[61] Second, energy prices have been consistently higher in North Carolina than in the nation, meaning that any increases add to an already relatively high cost base.[62]

Finally, the tremendous gain in worker efficiency (figure 2-5) has likely shifted employment away from lower-skilled workers to higher-skilled workers. While this outcome may be viewed as positive, it has also appar-ently resulted in a net job loss. That is, more lower-skilled jobs have been lost than higher-skilled jobs gained, and this trade-off, at least for now, has slowed North Carolina's income gains relative to those of the nation.

The Future: What Is the Next Big Thing?

The Connected Age therefore has reinforced if not created the division be-tween the traditional North Carolina economy of the early and mid–twenti-eth century and the new North Carolina economy of the late twentieth and twenty-first centuries. The era's forces have battered traditional industries while having either neutral or positive impacts on the new industries.

Trends associated with the Connected Age will likely continue. Further ad-vances in communications, transportation, and management and marketing techniques will effectively shrink the world even more and enhance interna-tional interdependencies. The net effect of these forces will vary widely by North Carolina industry.

For the state's traditional industries, the future is clear. More downsizing is expected. The U.S. Department of Labor projects that the value of production in the total North Carolina economy will grow 37 percent between 2005 and 2014; however, production value in tobacco manufacturing is expected to fall 46 percent, textile and apparel output will drop 13 percent, and value in furniture and its affiliated industries will grow at a subaverage rate of 19 percent.[63] As a result, North Carolina's traditional industry production will contribute half of its former amount—less than 4 percent—to the total state economy. Employment in the sectors will follow suit, shrinking by almost fifty thousand between 2005 and 2014.[64]

The forecasts are certainly better for the state's new industries. The largest growth in output will occur in electronic and computer products (up 113 percent), with good growth in financial services (37 percent) and transportation equipment (36 percent). Subaverage growth is expected for chemical products (17 percent) and food processing (16 percent). The Big Five's total contribution to the state's output will hold constant at near 17 percent. Employment in these sectors is expected to increase by only twenty thousand.[65]

A major driver of these projections for both the traditional and new industries is the position of both in the product cycle. Tariff reduction and other elements of globalization have shortened the time between the innovative stage, where initial production is located in high-wage countries, and the mature stage, where standardized production moves to low-wage countries. North Carolina's traditional industries are already in the mature phase. The future survival of parts of those industries will be based on their ability to develop innovative products. Perhaps the more important issue is how quickly North Carolina's new industries will move into the mature phase and to what degree they can counter that stage. Some segments of electronic and computer production and transportation parts production are likely already in the mature phase. Chapter 3 examines these issues in more detail.

Forecasts indicate that North Carolina will grow faster than the nation in coming years.[66] If North Carolina's traditional industries continue to shrink and if its new industries will collectively grow at only an average rate, what types of enterprises will take up the slack? The answer is support industries—information services, professional services, and wholesale and retail trade. All are forecasted to have above-average growth rates and together are expected to account for 85 percent of North Carolina's employment growth between 2005 and 2014.[67] In particular, the information services sector (broadcasting, publishing, software development, and telecommunications) is projected to expand more than 40 percent faster than the overall economy and could very well move from support status to basic industry status in the North Carolina economy.[68] It could become part of a new Big Six.

In the Connected Age, people are the major resource. Therefore, like most economies, North Carolina's economic future will be determined largely by the relative value of its workers. As has been demonstrated, two key characteristics of the North Carolina workforce, worker efficiency and educational performance, have accounted for the state's recent economic success. These characteristics will remain determining forces in the years ahead. To attract good-paying jobs in the world economy, the state's workers must remain competitive in knowledge and productivity. Continued improvements in educational attainment and rates of pay commensurate with output performance are needed to achieve these goals. In the Connected Age, productivity is paramount.

Some observers may ask, however, whether North Carolina workers—and indeed, U.S. workers—can ever effectively compete with foreign workers earning pay at a fraction of U.S. standards. The answer is no in some industries and yes in others. In industries with large labor inputs or where productivity gains are either not feasible or not valued, production will move to low-wage countries. Such is the case for common apparel, leather, and wood products. But in other industries where labor is a less important input and where substantial productivity gains can be achieved, domestic workers can compete effectively. In other words, U.S. workers can be a bargain compared to their foreign counterparts if higher rates of productivity more than compensate for greater costs.[69]

Furthermore, factors other than labor costs impact where firms locate. Such factors include access to customers; access to infrastructure such as roads, airports, and seaports; a predictable and reasonable tax code; protection of property rights; and a stable political system. In each of these areas, North Carolina and the United States have an advantage relative to many countries, especially developing countries.

Nonlabor factors could very well become more crucial determinants for business location as the Connected Age matures. The Connected Age places enhanced emphasis on speed and differentiation. Speed is important in several ways—to meet the demands of time-pressed buyers who are unwilling to wait, to service the product or product experience after the sale if problems or issues arise, and to ascertain changes in consumer demand and to follow up with appropriate changes in product design and content.

Differentiation of the customer base has also become an important marketing characteristic in the Connected Age. Tools are now available to identify and measure differences in customer desires and needs based on a variety of characteristics such as age, marital status, ethnicity, culture, religion, and residential location. In the Connected Age, one size fits all will no longer do—individualized sizes are necessary.

The net result is that the speed and differentiation required to meet modern customer demand are easier if the product provider has direct access to the customer base, a situation that argues for a location in close proximity to the customer. Although distant management and production are easier with the Connected Age's communication and transportation capabilities, at some levels these technologies cannot substitute for the flexibility and access gained by locating production close to buyers. Therefore, businesses serving the U.S. market—by far the largest in the world—still have reasons to locate in the country.

Still, foreign competition and the movement of domestic jobs to foreign countries will remain a fact of life for a substantial share of North Carolina workers. Studies show that an increasing number of service jobs, where direct personal contact with the customer is not required, will be susceptible to offshoring.[70] Conversely, offshoring can benefit the financial viability of some domestic firms and help them maintain domestic employment. By sending mundane, repetitive jobs to foreign contractors and reducing the costs associated with those tasks, companies can focus their domestic workforce on innovative tasks with high payoffs.[71]

While many people see the foreign competition associated with the Connected Age as a threat, others emphasize the benefits of globalization in terms of lower costs, lower prices, and expanded sales. Scott C. Bradford, Paul L. E. Grieco, and Gary Clyde Hufbauer estimate that the U.S. economy is richer by $1 trillion annually from increased world trade since World War II, and they see that number rising to $1.5 trillion if all remaining trade barriers were removed.[72] However, the benefits have not been evenly divided, with lower-wage workers who have lost their jobs or had hours reduced as a result of greater world trade likely suffering net losses.[73]

Just as a half century ago it was difficult to foresee the full effects of the coming economic forces on the North Carolina economy, it is impossible to accurately predict what the North Carolina economy will look like fifty years in the future. However, economic change certainly will not come in one large package but will come in many packages tied to individual industries and firms. Chapter 3 turns to these entities and these changes.

3. The Microeconomics of Change

The Remaking of North Carolina's Industries

As chapter 2 reveals, the economic forces of the Connected Age have profoundly affected individual North Carolina industries. Some industries have prospered during the age, while others have struggled. This chapter moves the focus to the individual industry level, tracing trends in each of the state's major industries in terms of output, employment, and productivity. I examine how each industry has been affected by and reacted to the Connected Age, with the goal of evaluating long-term prospects as the era proceeds.

Traditional Industries: Down but Not Out

North Carolina's traditional industries are furniture, lumber, and paper; textiles and apparel; tobacco products; and agriculture. These industries have become a smaller part of the North Carolina economy during the Connected Age (table 3-1). This section considers factors specific to each industry and to industry prospects in the next decades.

Furniture, Lumber, and Paper

Using ample supplies of oak, cherry, ash, maple, and walnut wood, a reliable railroad transportation system for moving lumber to factories, and plentiful low-cost labor, North Carolina established itself as the premier furniture manufacturing state by the 1920s. Furniture output doubled during that decade, slipped during the depression years of the 1930s, but rebounded after World War II and continued to grow through the 1970s.[1]

Furniture production traditionally has been procyclical, meaning that production rose when the economy expanded but retreated when the economy slipped into a recession and high interest rates curtailed home building.

Table 3-1. Relative Size of Traditional North Carolina Industries, 1977, at Peak, and 2005

	1977	At Peak (Year)	2005
Furniture			
% of GSP	2.2	2.3 (1978)	0.8
% of employment	3.5	3.6 (1978)	1.4
Output measure*	75.3	105.0 (1999)	80.0
Lumber			
% of GSP	1.1	1.3 (1979)	0.6
% of employment	1.5	1.6 (1978)	0.7
Output measure*	58.5	114.7 (1998)	112.1
Paper			
% of GSP	1.3	1.3 (1977)	0.5
% of employment	1.0	1.0 (1977)	0.4
Output measure*	93.2	123.2 (1988)	108.7
Textiles			
% of GSP	8.0	8.0 (1977)	1.0
% of employment	11.9	11.9 (1977)	1.7
Output measure*	84.3	129.4 (1994)	70.1
Apparel			
% of GSP	1.5	1.6 (1980)	0.5
% of employment	3.9	4.0 (1978)	0.6
Output measure*	87.7	115.0 (1994)	87.8
Tobacco Products			
% of GSP	5.9	6.2 (1978)	3.8
% of employment	1.2	1.2 (1977)	0.3
Output measure*	440.0	481.0 (1978)	65.0
Agriculture			
% of GSP	2.7	3.0 (1978)	1.1
% of employment	1.3	1.3 (1977)	0.7
Output measure*	25.5	100.0 (2000)	89.2

SOURCES: U.S. Department of Commerce, Bureau of Economic Analysis, "Gross Domestic Product"; U.S. Department of Labor, Bureau of Labor Statistics, "Employment, Hours, and Earnings"; Employment Security Commission of North Carolina, "Employment and Wages."
*Output measured as an index based on 100 for the value in 2000.

Figure 3-1 shows this pattern, with furniture output declining during the recessionary years of the early 1980s and 1990s.

The recession of 2001 was different. As a consequence of aggressive actions by the Federal Reserve to lower interest rates, home building increased rather than contracted in 2001 as well as in 2002–5.[2] Yet North Carolina's furniture production trended downward in that period, and in 2005 output

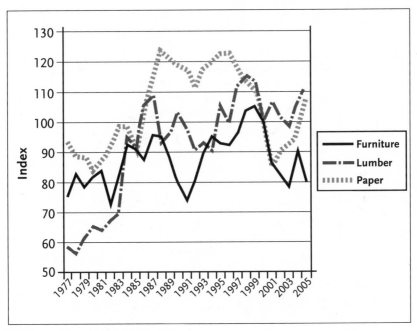

Figure 3-1. Output trends in North Carolina furniture, lumber, and paper industries, 1977–2005.
DATA SOURCE: U.S. Department of Commerce, Bureau of Economic Analysis, "Gross Domestic Product."

neared its lowest level in more than twenty-five years. Furniture was now seen as a declining industry in the state, similar to textiles, apparel, and tobacco.

What happened? In a phrase, foreign competition. With the expansion of world trade, imports of foreign-made furniture began to rise and increase their share of the domestic market in the 1990s. The domestic industry responded by improving labor productivity and offshoring production to lower-wage countries.[3] This strategy initially succeeded as production levels were maintained in the 1990s, albeit with fewer domestic workers (figure 3-2).

Then came China, whose 2001 entry into the world market dealt a blow from which the North Carolina furniture industry has never recovered. Chinese furniture exports expanded by almost 200 percent between the 1990s, when they occupied only a minor segment of the U.S. market, and 2005, when China accounted for almost half of all furniture exports to the United States.[4]

China's main advantage in furniture manufacturing is labor costs—the average wage in Chinese furniture factories is 40 percent of that in the United

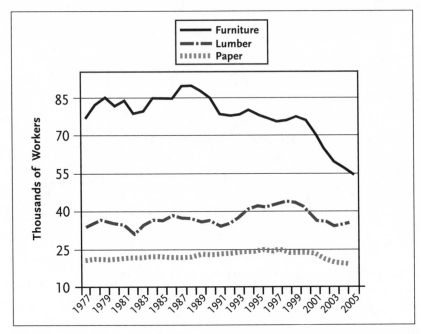

Figure 3-2. Employment trends in the North Carolina furniture, lumber, and paper industries, 1977–2005.
DATA SOURCE: U.S. Department of Labor, Bureau of Labor Statistics, "Employment, Hours, and Earnings."

States.[5] Although labor productivity in China is much lower and the freight costs of shipping from China are much higher, delivered Chinese furniture products remain 25 percent cheaper to the American consumer than U.S.-manufactured furniture. Improved shipping technology using modern containers has also greatly reduced the losses from breakage. Chinese furniture production now includes products of varying quality, and the country has improved its technology and finishing capabilities. These factors, combined with the country's large capacity for production, mean that China will remain a formidable furniture manufacturing competitor for the foreseeable future.[6]

Consequently, the furniture industry's impact on the North Carolina economy declined. Furniture manufacturing fell from 2.2 percent of the total state economy in 1977 to less than 1 percent in 2005.[7] More than thirty thousand jobs—one-third of the furniture manufacturing workforce—were lost over the same period, and furniture factory employment dropped from 3.5 percent to 1.4 percent of the state workforce.[8] Is it just a matter of time, therefore, before the last chair or dining room table is made in North Carolina? Is this once-great industry that was so important to the state economy dying a slow death?

Industry experts say that the answer to both questions is no. The furniture industry can survive in North Carolina, but it will be a smaller industry with a different focus. Specifically, North Carolina's furniture industry will have to restructure itself to emphasize four elements: productivity, customization, speed, and customer service.

Improved productivity is the only way higher-paid U.S. workers can compete against lower-cost foreign labor. Experts say that the furniture industry needs technology and equipment upgrades to improve its output/input ratios.[9] Labor productivity improved in the 1990s but slipped to some extent after the turn of the twenty-first century.

Even with improvements in productivity, analysts believe that the domestic furniture industry is unlikely to win in a direct competition against lower-cost foreign producers. Instead, furniture firms will have to capitalize on two of their innate advantages: knowledge of and closeness to the American consumer. A movement away from products for the mass market to innovative, customized products for smaller niche markets constitutes one way that domestic manufacturers can take advantage of their understanding of U.S. buyers' preferences and tastes.[10]

This strategy could be called a merging of the Starbucks model with the Dell model.[11] The Starbucks model taps into consumers' desire for products made specifically for them. In the case of furniture, this means products that fit customers' body types, functional desires, and design and finish needs. The Dell model then assembles standardized, individual parts into the customized final product desired by the customer. The just-in-time production process will keep inventory costs at a minimum.

In the Connected Age, waiting is out and speed is in, and despite modern communication and transportation techniques, foreign producers still have the disadvantage of distance from American furniture buyers. Successful furniture manufacturers will develop both distribution channels and supply chains that reduce the time of delivery to the customer. Similarly, Connected Age consumers value service after the sale, and the proximity of domestic producers to domestic customers should offer an advantage over foreign producers.

While the North Carolina furniture industry must pursue this strategy, the industry also has two advantages in facing the future. First, continued growth in the domestic population and in household wealth should keep the demand for furniture growing. The U.S. Department of Labor forecasts domestic furniture production to increase at an annual real rate of 2.5 percent through 2014.[12] Also, North Carolina and the eastern United States continue to provide quality wood for furniture production, so the major raw input for furniture manufacturing remains easily available.[13]

The North Carolina furniture industry will likely never resume the dominant status it held during the twentieth century. The internationalization of the furniture market is here to stay, and any changes may involve enhanced foreign competition from timber-rich countries such as Russia. North Carolina's furniture firms can survive with a different competitive model and different products, but even with these changes, employment is likely to continue its downward trend.[14]

The wood products or lumber industry has a longer history in the state than the furniture industry. The state's forests initially were valued for their by-products, such as tar and turpentine, rather than for their lumber. According to the oft-told story, North Carolina earned its nickname, the Tarheel State, when tar extracted from pine trees remained as a residue on residents' feet.

The lumber industry developed and prospered along with the state's furniture industry during the twentieth century. In the Connected Age, both output and employment rose except for downturns during recessions, when high interest rates curtailed home building (figures 3-1 and 3-2). In 2000, lumber output was 71 percent higher and employment was 22 percent greater than in 1977.[15]

Like the furniture industry, the outlook for the lumber sector changed in the twenty-first century. With records set in home construction in the early part of the decade, these years should have been strong ones for lumber production. Instead, North Carolina's lumber output and employment fell between 2000 and 2003, and output did not rebound until 2004 and 2005. With furniture manufacturing a major user of lumber, one reason for the decline certainly was the drop in furniture production. However, a second reason was international competition. The real value of wood product imports rose 50 percent between 2001 and 2005, with the largest increases coming from Canada and China.[16]

The North Carolina lumber industry faces a challenging future. Purchases from domestic furniture firms will increase modestly at best as that industry restructures to a permanently smaller size. Lumber demand from the domestic construction industry should be robust, but here the challenge will be from timber-rich countries such as Canada, Brazil, China, and Russia. Long-run forecasts show only modest increases in output and continued declines in employment.[17] North Carolina's lumber producers also face increased competition from alternative land uses, as state population growth fuels increased conversion of forestland to residential and commercial development. To increase output, the industry will have to improve productivity.

The paper industry has followed the Connected Age trends of its sister furniture and lumber industries. Output peaked in the late 1980s, and employment reached a high in the mid-1990s. Between 1995 and 2005, employment fell by five thousand jobs—22 percent of the total—and industry output had fallen 5 percent from its levels a decade earlier.[18]

Once again, a big reason is foreign competition. As chapter 2 reveals, output from North Carolina's paper mills has fallen with reductions in tariffs and with China's entry into the world's trading patterns. Between 2000 and 2005, paper imports grew twice as fast as exports, and Chinese sales of paper in the United States rose 180 percent.[19]

Factors outside of international trade also have resulted in the relative contraction of the domestic paper industry. One is the slow growth in the domestic market for paper products, where consumption has increased less than 2 percent annually in the late 1990s and early part of the following decade.[20] This relatively stagnant market has been caused in large part by the increasing use of digital records for the storage of information and the increased use of plastic for containers. Another factor is environmental. Pulp and paper mills have been linked not only to water pollution but also to some airborne illnesses.[21] The factories have faced mounting environmental regulations and their accompanying increasing costs.

The outlook for the state's paper industry thus remains uncertain. National forecasts suggest falling employment and annual output growth at less than 1 percent.[22] To compete effectively, domestic production will have to become more cost-efficient and environmentally cleaner, while some observers believe that converting paper mills to ethanol plants may be a viable alternative.[23] These are tall orders. But while the domestic market for paper products will grow slowly, the international market, especially in emerging countries, will offer opportunity. For example, paper consumption in China is growing at double-digit annual rates.[24] The question is whether North Carolina's paper firms can retool and reform to capture some of this growth.

Textiles and Apparel

Textiles and apparel are two separate but linked industries. The textile sector performs two functions, manufacturing yarn and fabric for use in the making of clothing and creating nonclothing products from fabric. The apparel industry focuses on making clothing from yarn and fabric.

As recently as 1973, North Carolina's textile and apparel industries employed 47 percent of manufacturing workers and 19 percent of all workers in the state. No other industry or economic sector came close to these numbers. By 2005, employment in textile and apparel firms had plunged 75 percent.[25] What happened, and can this longtime mainstay of the North Carolina economy ever recover?

Increased international competition is clearly one answer to the first question. Figure 3-3 shows that both textile and apparel output peaked in the mid-1990s and have subsequently trended downward. Of course, the two major agreements opening global trade, the North American Free Trade Agreement (NAFTA) and General Agreement on Tariffs and Trade (GATT), were passed and implemented beginning in the mid-1990s. Since that time, textile and apparel imports to the United States have almost doubled, exports from the United States to other countries have increased only marginally, and the trade deficit in textiles and apparel has doubled.[26]

Most of the swelling trade deficit has come from the apparel industry, where foreign-made finished clothing products have flooded the U.S. market. The trade balance for the domestic textile industry improved between 1994 and 2005, moving from a deficit to a surplus. One reason was the rules adopted as part of NAFTA that gave incentives for foreign manufacturers of apparel products to use U.S.-made yarn and fabric. However, because the majority of U.S. textile output is used as inputs for U.S. apparel production, the sharp decline in domestic apparel output pulled down domestic textile production.

John S. Hekman argues that the textile and apparel industries are excellent examples of the product cycle. The industry initially located in the Northeast to make use of the skilled workforce needed to develop and perfect production techniques. Automation and standardization of production in the late nineteenth century then allowed textile and apparel firms to migrate to the South to take advantage of lower-cost, unskilled labor.[27] With the domestic textile and apparel industries largely unprotected after the adoption of NAFTA and GATT, factories not surprisingly again moved to lower-cost locations. Textile and apparel production is particularly appropriate for developing countries because the needed labor skills are frequently taught and learned in the informal household economy.[28] Apparel in particular has traditionally been very labor-intensive because the industry has been unable to develop machines that can efficiently grasp and manipulate fabric with minimal losses.[29]

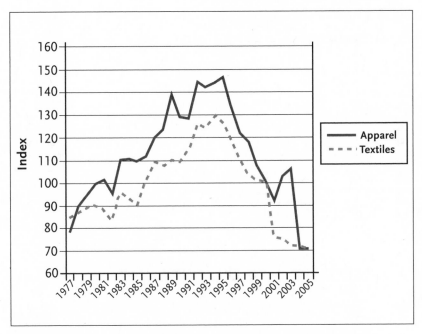

Figure 3-3. Output trends in the North Carolina apparel and textile industries, 1977–2005.
DATA SOURCE: U.S. Department of Commerce, Bureau of Economic Analysis, "Gross Domestic Product."

After the initial phase of trade liberalization in 1994, apparel imports increased from Western Hemisphere countries such as Mexico, Honduras, and El Salvador as well as Asian countries such as Bangladesh, India, Indonesia, Pakistan, and the Philippines. Since 2000, the origin of apparel imports has shifted to China. China doubled its share of U.S. apparel imports between 2000 and 2005 to 25 percent. Imports from the second-largest exporter, Mexico, actually dropped between 2000 and 2005.[30] China's advantages in apparel production lie in its high-quality products, its productive labor supply, and the availability of complementary components such as zippers and buttons.[31]

With the drop in textile and apparel output since the mid-1990s, employment in these industries has also fallen (figure 3-4). However, employment in both industries was falling before the mid-1990s, even while output was rising. Employment in North Carolina's textile and apparel firms fell 20 percent between 1977 and 1994, while output increased 50 percent in textiles and 80 percent in apparel.[32] The increased use of modern machinery and

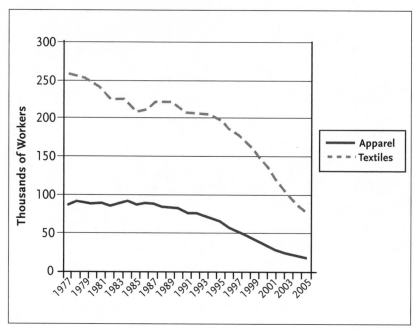

Figure 3-4. Employment trends in the North Carolina apparel and textile industries, 1977–2005.
DATA SOURCE: U.S. Department of Labor, Bureau of Labor Statistics, "Employment, Hours, and Earnings."

technology boosted productivity in the industries at a faster rate than in the overall economy.[33] But even though productivity gains continued and even accelerated after 1994, output losses and even larger job losses nevertheless occurred. In the decade after 1994, job cuts in the state's textile and apparel firms were three times greater than in the previous seventeen-year span.[34]

As with furniture, the outlook for domestic textile and apparel industries in the mass market is not good. The U.S. Department of Labor forecasts that both output and employment will decline in the two sectors through 2014. In both, output is projected to fall 3 percent annually, and employment is expected to drop 9 percent annually in apparel and 7 percent annually in textiles.[35]

Yet the industries are not expected to disappear. Evidence indicates that older, less efficient textile and apparel factories are being replaced by newer, more efficient plants. That is, at the same time that some workers exit the industries, other workers enter.[36] While the output and employment of the new factories have not offset the losses from the closed facilities, the fact that entrepreneurs and investors have been willing to enter the industries is a very positive sign, suggesting a belief that the industries will survive, albeit in a smaller form. And what form might it take? Experts think the industries will focus on two features: innovative products using technology, and small niche markets composed of fast-changing, time-sensitive buyers.

Innovative textile products, also called smart, brainy, or technical textiles, add features to fabrics that go beyond simply covering the user. Some of these fabrics use extremely small fillers and sensors to internally generate heat or cold, to monitor the user's vital signs, or even to change color. Other products include specially built fabrics for people with circulatory problems, antibacterial uniforms, and stronger airbags. These new fabrics are particularly useful for sports and public safety professions.[37] Other technical textiles have been developed for construction uses, such as sound insulation in hospitals and airports.[38] These products are valued for their technical performance and functional properties rather than just their aesthetics. Indeed, that part of the textile industry that manufactures fabric and fabric-made products for nonclothing uses has been growing. While much smaller than the clothing-oriented textile market, North Carolina's employment in this segment has increased since the 1990s.[39]

Successful firms in the apparel industry will direct their attention to two areas: markets where styles and fashions change rapidly and where buyers demand the latest trends and markets where speed of delivery and customization are valued. Like furniture manufacturers, domestic apparel producers possess the twin advantages of being nearer to and better understanding American customers than do foreign producers.

The North Carolina textile and apparel industries thus have come full circle in the product cycle. Originally the low-cost producer that used mass production of common products to gain a commanding market share, the domestic firms have now lost that production to new low-cost producers halfway around the world. To survive, the remaining firms will have to be innovative, productive, and fast. The workforce will increasingly come from the educated ranks rather than from low-skilled laborers. Output and sales will decline, but the remaining firms can still be profitable.

While trade liberalization has decidedly had a negative impact on North Carolina's textile and apparel firms and employees, the industries' products have had a positive effect on consumers. More open international trade in textiles and apparel has resulted in lower prices for American buyers. After consistently rising prior to the trade agreements in 1994, U.S. clothing prices have fallen an average of 1 percent annually since then.[40] One analysis estimates that U.S. consumers save $20 billion on clothing expenses each year as a result. North Carolina consumers' share of this amount would be $533 million.[41]

Tobacco Product Manufacturing

For decades, North Carolina was synonymous with tobacco. Profits from the industry were important in building the infrastructure and colleges and universities in the state during the twentieth century. The state's sports teams are still referred to as playing on Tobacco Road.

The big incomes from tobacco were derived from the manufacturing level, where farm-grown tobacco leaves were made into cigarettes, cigars, pipe tobacco, and snuff. Yet during the Connected Age, the output of manufactured tobacco products in North Carolina—mainly cigarettes—collapsed. Annual output fell 85 percent between 1977 and 2005.[42] Although peak employment in cigarette factories was less than one-tenth of the maximum number of jobs in textiles and apparel, tobacco jobs were cut by more than 60 percent during this period (figure 3-5).[43] The industry's production reductions would have been much worse if not for the fact that cigarette prices increased three times faster than the overall rate of inflation between 1977 and 2005.[44]

What brought about this decimation of the once-dominant industry in North Carolina? A perfect-storm combination of domestic and international factors, including a dramatic drop in domestic consumption, increases in domestic costs of production, and increases in the quality and competitiveness of foreign producers.

Per capita cigarette consumption in the United States topped out in 1963 and has fallen ever since. Per capita consumption in 2005 was 60 percent lower than the 1963 level.[45] Even with population growth, the total number of cigarettes sold in the country dropped 40 percent over that span.[46] One reason was price increases. From 1963 to 2005, cigarette prices rose 1,500 percent, triple the 500 percent increase for average prices.[47] A big factor was taxes, particularly since the late 1990s. As public acceptance of smoking declined, governments found it easier to increase cigarette taxes. In 2005, even legislators in the N.C. General Assembly voted to increase the state cigarette tax sevenfold.[48]

Increases in the cost of domestic production also drove up the cost of cigarettes. Major tobacco companies faced escalating costs in the wake of 1998's Master Settlement Agreement. In exchange for protection against liability

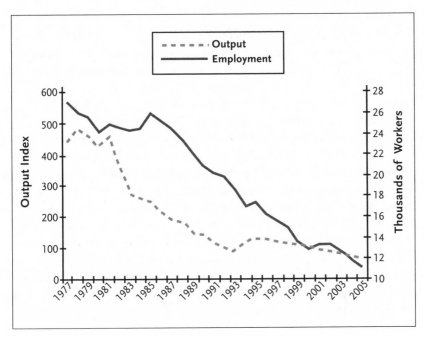

Figure 3-5. Output and employment in North Carolina tobacco manufacturing, 1977–2005.
DATA SOURCES: U.S. Department of Commerce, Bureau of Economic Analysis, "Gross Domestic Product"; U.S. Department of Labor, Bureau of Labor Statistics, "Employment, Hours, and Earnings."

lawsuits by smokers, the companies agreed to pay state governments more than $200 billion over twenty-five years and to fund research into reducing youth smoking.[49] The companies passed much if not all of these costs along to smokers in the form of higher cigarette prices.[50] And economic studies have found that large price increases reduce cigarette consumption.[51]

Noneconomic factors have also reduced domestic cigarette consumption. The 1964 U.S. Surgeon General's report officially linked cigarette smoking and lung cancer, and the Federal Trade Commission subsequently ordered that warning labels be placed on cigarette packs. Governments and businesses increasingly established smoking bans in buildings and restaurants and on public transportation.[52]

Domestic cigarette production has also been hurt by the increased international trade that has characterized the Connected Age. North Carolina traditionally produced the world's highest-quality tobacco. Cigarette manufacturers preferred North Carolina's tobacco, and its superior quality allowed the state's farmers to sell leaf at higher prices than world competitors received.

However, foreign producers in countries such as Brazil gradually closed the gap in quality.[53] Cigarette manufacturers then increased their use of cheaper imported tobacco: The foreign leaf content of U.S. manufactured cigarettes rose from 15 percent in 1970 to almost 50 percent in 2002.[54]

Cigarette manufacturers consequently have seen less and less reason to keep production in the United States. The market in this country is declining, the quality edge of domestically grown leaf has shrunk, and the cost of foreign-produced leaf is more attractive. Moreover, whatever future growth occurs in cigarette consumption will likely occur in foreign countries. The World Health Organization predicts no change in cigarette consumption in North and South America but annual growth rates between 6 percent and 16 percent in the rest of the world.[55] As a result, since the 1990s, several of North Carolina's cigarette factories have closed and their workers have been dismissed. Durham, once known as the City of Cigarettes, converted two large cigarette factories to retail and residential complexes and changed its nickname to the City of Medicine.[56] In just thirty years, the U.S. share of the world tobacco trade dropped by half.[57]

The outlook, therefore, is not bright for cigarette manufacturing in North Carolina. The U.S. Department of Labor forecasts that annual output and employment in tobacco manufacturing will decline 5 percent annually through 2014.[58] Furthermore, lawsuits against the industry, such as by nonsmokers alleging injury as a consequence of secondhand smoke, remain a concern.[59] One possible bright spot is the end of the price-support program for leaf production. Domestic leaf prices will now have to compete with world prices. If North Carolina farmers can produce at those prices, they may revive domestic purchases by manufacturers and provide more motivation for domestic production. Yet it is unlikely that this single factor will counteract all the others pointing to continued downsizing in North Carolina tobacco manufacturing.

Agriculture

North Carolina's final traditional economic sector is agriculture. Not surprisingly, agriculture's share of the state's economy shrank during the Connected Age. The sector's share of statewide income dropped from 2.7 percent in 1977 to near 1 percent in 2005, and its employment share declined from 1.3 percent to 0.7 percent over the same period (table 3-1). These trends mirrored

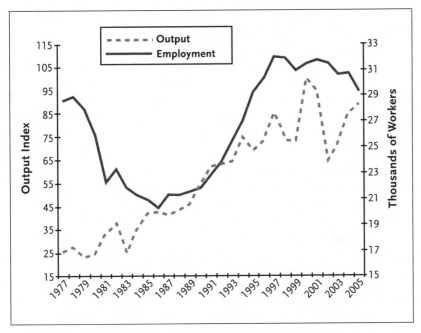

Figure 3-6. Output and employment in North Carolina agriculture, 1977–2005.
DATA SOURCES: U.S. Department of Commerce, Bureau of Economic Analysis,
"Gross Domestic Product"; U.S. Department of Labor, Bureau of Labor Statistics,
"Employment, Hours, and Earnings"; Employment Security Commission of North
Carolina, "Employment and Wages."

those at the national level.[60] However, despite agriculture's relatively small
size in the state, output more than tripled, and employment was higher in
2005 than in 1977 (figure 3-6). Also following national trends, the number
of North Carolina's farms dropped even as they grew in individual size, and
improvements in farm productivity allowed fewer farm workers to produce
more output.[61]

This story—of farming becoming a less visible part of the economy while
its productivity and output increased—is not new to the Connected Age but
has held true for agriculture for well over a century.[62] What is new in this
context is a dramatic change in farming's composition. An unprecedented
shift of resources and production from tobacco to livestock occurred.

In 1974, 39 percent of the total revenue from North Carolina's farms came
from tobacco, while 38 percent came from livestock and 23 percent came from
other crops. In 2002, the revenue share from other crops remained
virtually unchanged at 24 percent. However, tobacco's share had plunged to

only 5 percent, while livestock's share had mushroomed to 71 percent.[63] In less than thirty years, King Tobacco had been overthrown by the dual monarchs of King Hog and King Chicken.

The saga of tobacco farming parallels the story of cigarette manufacturing. Reduced domestic consumption of tobacco products, improved quality of foreign-produced leaf, and increased use of lower-cost foreign leaf caused North Carolina tobacco leaf production to drop by half between 1974 and 2003.[64] In addition, real prices paid to tobacco farmers fell by 55 percent during the same period.[65] Reduced production and plunging prices thus combined to shrivel tobacco's farm-level importance.

Just the opposite happened to livestock—specifically, to two segments of the livestock industry, poultry and swine. The annual number of North Carolina–raised birds sold for meat tripled from 225 million to 708 million between 1974 and 2002. Even more impressive was the expansion of swine production, which rose an incredible 1,500 percent, from 2.6 million to 42 million, over the same period.[66] By the start of the twenty-first century, North Carolina had risen to among the top states in both poultry and swine production.

Broad national as well as special local factors lay behind this transformation of North Carolina's agricultural sector. The increase in the U.S. working population, especially women, and the consequent higher demand for convenience foods fueled a national market for prepared meat products. Indeed, the statistical analysis reported in appendix A shows that the percentage of women in the paid labor force has had a positive effect on North Carolina's agricultural output. National chains such as fast-food restaurants and big-box retailers used their market power to require cost savings and efficiencies in meat production.[67]

The meat industry responded by developing integrated supply chains. Production of animals at the farm level, processing of the animals at slaughterhouses, and marketing of meat products to retailers and other final users were tightly coordinated to both reduce costs and produce a reliable and consistent result. Every aspect from genetics to groceries was organized into a seamless flow. The poultry industry pioneered the meat supply chain system in the 1950s, but the process was further refined and applied to swine production during the 1990s.[68]

This integrated meat supply chain, with its emphasis on lowering costs per unit, lent itself to large-scale operations because meat production costs have been shown to fall with increases in herd size.[69] As a result, the scale of operations at both the farm and processing levels increased for meat production during the Connected Age. The swine industry in particular became dominated by a handful of large firms that controlled the farm, processing, and marketing levels. Because transportation of live grown-out birds and hogs to processing plants risks significant losses, the industry sought to have farms and processing plants located in close geographic proximity.[70]

Within this national context, the expansion of North Carolina's meat industry differed for poultry and swine. Poultry production was attractive across the Southeast because of the region's rural nature, relatively low labor costs, and warm climate, which was well suited for raising birds. Health concerns regarding red meat and the expansion of convenience foods prompted growth in the industry across the area. Although the industry's growth in North Carolina was significant, it was not unique. Georgia's farm-level production of poultry increased faster than North Carolina's level from 1974 to 2002.[71]

The expansion of swine production in the state was unique because it occurred within a relatively stagnant national industry. Unlike the poultry industry, where per capita consumption doubled during the last three decades of the twentieth century, per capita pork consumption has remained virtually unchanged over this period.[72] Consequently, expansion of the North Carolina swine industry resulted from a relocation of the national industry to the state rather than growth based on a national expansion. In particular, pig production from the mid-Atlantic and southeastern states relocated to North Carolina.[73] Key to this relocation was the fact that the integrated supply chain techniques adopted for the swine industry were developed and tested by innovators in North Carolina, such as Murphy Farms, Prestage Farms, and Smithfield Foods.[74] Also important were the state's lower production costs, less stringent environmental standards, and special tax incentives for the industry.[75] When the world's largest hog-processing plant opened in North Carolina in 1992, therefore, all the pieces were in place for the explosive growth in the state's swine production.[76]

Any industry that experiences rapid growth is likely to raise issues, and for North Carolina's hog and pig farmers, the main issue is the perceived environmental impact of animal waste. The megafarms of the integrated supply chain system generate tremendous amounts of waste, which is channeled to large treatment lagoons, liquefied, and then sprayed on land as fertilizer. However, heavy rains and winds from significant storms, such as Hurricane Fran in 1996 and Hurricane Floyd in 1999, can break the lagoons and allow hog waste to contaminate lakes, streams, and groundwater. Odor from hog farms is also considered an environmental nuisance.

In 1997, North Carolina passed legislation imposing a moratorium on construction of new farms with more than 250 pigs. This moratorium has had an obvious impact on the industry. From 1970 to 1997, the state's swine industry grew at an annualized rate of 6 percent; from 1997 to 2005, however, North Carolina's hog inventory increased only 0.2 percent annually, two-thirds slower than the industry nationwide.[77] In 2007, the restrictions on hog farm expansion were made permanent, with the goal of motivating farmers to use environmentally sound systems for waste disposal.[78]

In 2000, the State of North Carolina entered into an agreement with two of the largest integrated hog firms to fund research for the purpose of identifying superior waste-management systems for hog farms.[79] The study reported its findings in 2006. While several alternative technologies were found, all would increase costs for the industry and result in long-run output reductions in the range of 12 percent to 24 percent.[80] Also in 2006, Smithfield Foods, the largest integrated pork producer, settled a lawsuit in which it agreed to take additional measures to stop hog manure from polluting waterways and groundwater. The agreement applies to all 275 Smithfield-owned farms in North Carolina and will mean installation of an early warning system to prevent spraying of liquid manure during wet weather. In 2007, the state banned the construction of new hog waste lagoons and the expansion of existing lagoons.[81]

Thus, several factors point toward expectations that North Carolina's swine industry will see its relative importance slide in both the agricultural and total economies. If environmental issues of waste disposal remain, they are likely to be addressed by continued restrictions on growth. If new technologies are used to address hog waste, these methods will probably increase costs of production and reduce the comparative advantage enjoyed by the industry in the state. Out-of-state producers, especially those in foreign countries such as Brazil, likely will copy the supply chain techniques of North Carolina's farms and become viable competitors.[82] Add the fact that national pork consumption is forecast to grow very slowly, and the prospect for further expansion in the North Carolina swine industry is highly questionable.[83]

The other major meat industry in the state, poultry, does not face the level of environmental issues that accompanies hog farming but does confront two challenges: worker conditions and disease. Worker conditions in the poultry industry came to the forefront with a 1991 poultry processing plant fire in Hamlet, North Carolina, that killed twenty-five people.[84] Workers' rights groups are also concerned about the low rate of pay and lack of collective bargaining for plant workers. Industry leaders worry that some suggested solutions will increase operating costs and reduce regional competitiveness.[85]

Then there is avian flu, a contagious animal disease that affects poultry and has caused some human deaths. Outbreaks have been reported in Asia and Europe, but as of 2007, none have occurred in North America. Nonetheless, the severe form of the disease is extremely contagious and deadly to poultry, with 100 percent death rates, potentially on the first day symptoms appear.[86] Hence, if an outbreak occurred in North Carolina, the economic loss would be enormous, for two reasons. First, the loss of the poultry flocks could impose economic costs of at least $2 billion.[87] Second, sales would be lost after the outbreak while the public hesitated to consume poultry products.

Economists expect U.S. poultry production to continue to expand as a result of continued growth in per capita consumption, domestic population growth, and added exports to markets in Asia, Europe, and Mexico. However, growth rates will be lower than during the 1990s as a consequence of stronger international competitors, such as Brazil, and an aging domestic demographic.[88]

Significant changes have also taken place in other agricultural commodities during the Connected Age. One good example is cotton. Of course, cotton was king in the South and in much of North Carolina in the nineteenth century, only to be decimated by the boll weevil and then replaced by synthetic fibers and other crops in the twentieth century. Increased interest in the environment and naturally grown products, development of controls for the boll weevil, and the discovery of technology for wrinkle-free cotton fabrics then combined to bring cotton back to the state. Although still far from its former levels, cotton production rose 1,000 percent in North Carolina between 1974 and 2005.[89]

North Carolina cotton production will increasingly be driven by international trade. With the decline of domestic textile manufacturing, two-thirds of the U.S. cotton output is now exported, and that portion should rise.[90] China has become a large net importer of cotton. The significant U.S. government subsidies for cotton, however, make it vulnerable to negotiated reductions in those subsidies from international trade talks. Any major reduction in those subsidies could reduce cotton's profitability.[91] The future of North Carolina's cotton thus will depend on its price, quality, and subsidies.

North Carolina nearly doubled its sales of fruits and nuts between 1997 and 2003.[92] The green industry, including nursery products such as shrubs, trees, planting, landscaping, and turf, has boomed as the state's population has increased and home building has expanded. Some estimates put the green industry's annual value at more than $8 billion in 2005.[93] Specialty or niche products have become a more important part of North Carolina agriculture. Such products include aquaculture, organically grown crops and free-range livestock, and hybrid products such as the sprite melon (a combination of a watermelon and a honeydew melon). Small farms located near expanding urban areas have found such niche products financially lucrative.

Finally, as energy prices in general and gasoline prices specifically took unprecedented leaps after 2000, interest in tapping into agricultural sources for alternative fuels grew. North Carolina jumped on the movement by outlining a strategic plan for biofuels and by financially supporting study and development of new fuels.[94] Several ethanol factories are planned for the state.[95] Analysts hope that alternative fuels will become a major additional component of the agricultural sector.

But before this development can occur, several questions will have to be addressed. Can U.S. drivers be weaned away from gasoline, or will alternative fuels simply be a passing fad for some and a hobby for others? Can North Carolina farmers expect to have a significant part of the market for the major alternative fuel, ethanol, or will Midwest producers always dominate the production? And how fast can the technology be developed to make cellulose-based fuels—those made from switch grasses, wood chips, and agricultural waste—practically viable and economically competitive? Some analysts think that these sources have the most potential as alternative fuels in North Carolina.[96] Observers have also expressed concern that since increased ethanol usage has dramatically increased corn prices and since corn is an input to the large North Carolina livestock industry, the net result may be negative for aggregate farm-level production in the state.[97]

Yet simply because of its size, North Carolina's agriculture will rise or fall with the state's major livestock industries, at least in the near future. The integrated hog farm system will continue, but expansion is unlikely as long as environmental issues remain. Likewise, the large increases in poultry production appear to have come to an end. North Carolina's farms will also continue to face pressure from continuing urbanization. Further productivity gains will be necessary to sustain output, which means still larger farms but fewer of them.

As has been the case several times in the past, North Carolina's agriculture will likely transform itself. From tobacco to cotton, cotton back to tobacco, and most recently tobacco to livestock, the leader of the state's farms has changed each century. What will the next change be?

New Industries: How Far to Go?

The new North Carolina industries that have developed and expanded during the Connected Age are technology, chemical products (primarily pharmaceuticals), vehicle parts, food processing, and banking. Table 3-2 highlights the key economic measures of these industries. This section explores factors behind the industries' development and issues in their future.

Technology

Before any discussion of the technology sector begins, the meaning and composition of the industry must be defined. Technology is a broad concept representing the current state of knowledge of how to develop, combine, and organize resources to produce economic outputs. Technology includes skills, processes, techniques, tools, and equipment. Technology therefore resides in workers' intellect and skills, in manuals and blueprints, and in machines and assembly lines.

Under this sweeping definition of technology, any economy includes a vast array of technologies. Certainly important in North Carolina are the knowledge and skills embodied in the state's people and workers and the educational institutions that facilitate this knowledge development and transfer. North Carolina has been home to the manufacturing of traditional technological equipment, including farm and textile machinery, commercial equipment such as vending machines and heating and air-conditioning apparatus, metalworking equipment, engine and power transmission equipment, and machinery for handling materials. Together, these activities had a market value of production of $3.5 billion in 2005, and they have consistently accounted for approximately 1 percent of the state economy in recent years.[98] Technology is also embedded in electrical equipment products, a category that added another $3 billion to the state economy in 2005.[99]

But the star of the technological world during the Connected Age clearly has been information technology—that is, the use of computers, transmission equipment, and related software to develop, process, and move information. The explosion of the information technology sector has been the most defining feature of the Connected Age. In 1977, no computers or software were sold in the United States, and ten years later, only $6.2 billion was spent nationwide on this technology. By 2005, the quantity of computer and software sales had grown 800 percent from 1987.[100]

North Carolina participated in this information technology explosion not only as a consumer but also as a producer. Production of information technology equipment, including computers and complementary machines and communications equipment, tripled between 1997 and 2005, and software output doubled (figure 3-7). Similar, but not identical, data from 1977 suggest

Table 3-2. Relative Size of New North Carolina Industries, 1977, at Peak, and 2005

Industry	1977	At Peak (Year)	2005
Information Technology			
% of GSP	1.9	3.4 (1999)	1.8
% of employment	1.7	2.2 (2000)	1.6
Output, hardware*	7	153.0 (2005)	153.0
Output, software*	0	101.0 (2005)	101.0
Chemical Products			
% of GSP	1.7	5.4 (2002)	4.3
% of employment	1.7	1.7 (1977)	1.1
Output measure*	18.6	150.3 (2002)	123.6
Food Processing			
% of GSP	1.6	1.9 (1983)	1.4
% of employment	1.9	1.9 (1977)	1.3
Output measure*	37.8	130.2 (2005)	130.2
Transportation Manufacturing			
% of GSP	0.4	1.2 (1994)	0.8
% of employment	0.5	1.0 (1999)	0.9
Output measure*	20.3	133.8 (2005)	133.8
Banking			
% of GSP	1.9	8.5 (2005)	8.5
% of employment	1.7	2.3 (2005)	2.3
Output measure*	15.6	154.6 (2005)	154.6

SOURCES: U.S. Department of Commerce, Bureau of Economic Analysis, "Gross Domestic Product"; U.S. Department of Labor, Bureau of Labor Statistics, "Employment, Hours, and Earnings."
*Output measured as an index based on 100 for the value in 2000.

a steady increase in production earlier in the Connected Age. Employment gains also occurred along with the increases in output. By 2000, North Carolina information technology firms employed more than eighty-five thousand workers.

The growth of the information technology sector in North Carolina was sparked by the establishment of the Research Triangle Park in the late 1950s and IBM's construction of a manufacturing facility there in 1965.[101] Over the next thirty years, encouraged by the proximity of three major universities (the University of North Carolina at Chapel Hill, Duke University, and North Carolina State University) that could supply a steady stream of well-trained workers as well as research collaboration and access to an international airport, several tech companies established their presence in the state, including

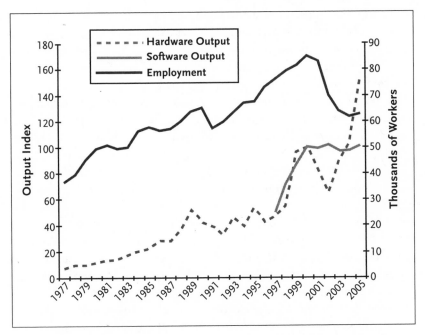

Figure 3-7. Output and employment in North Carolina information technology, 1977–2005.

DATA SOURCES: U.S. Department of Commerce, Bureau of Economic Analysis, "Gross Domestic Product"; U.S. Department of Labor, Bureau of Labor Statistics, "Employment, Hours, and Earnings."

NOTE: The Bureau of Economic Analysis has state output data for information technology hardware (computers) and software since 1997. Prior to 1997, the hardware component was included in the industrial machinery and equipment sector, and output for this sector is shown. No comparable software output data exist prior to 1997. Employment data for information technology hardware (computers) and software are available from the Bureau of Labor Statistics since 1990. The employment data shown for prior to 1990 are for the industrial machinery and equipment sector.

SAS, Nortel, Microsoft, EMC, Red Hat, and Lucent.[102] As a result of this growth, information technology became a more important part of the North Carolina economy. Information technology increased from less than 2 percent of total state income in 1977 to 3.4 percent in 1999.[103] The sector's employment share rose almost 30 percent over the same period (table 3-2).

Then came the crash—the bursting of the tech bubble in the late twentieth and early twenty-first centuries and the national recession that followed. Investors and others realized that the information technology sector had expanded too rapidly, leading to oversupply and overproduction, and a dramatic pullback in the industry and a downshifting of output and employment occurred. North Carolina's production of information technology hardware fell by one-third between 2000 and 2002, and nineteen thousand tech manufacturing jobs were axed from 2000 and 2004.[104] One of the state's leading tech companies, Nortel, saw its sales plunge by 50 percent in one year.[105] The software component of the industry fared much better, with output changing little and only three thousand jobs eliminated between 2000 and 2003.[106] But the episode constituted a major blow to the star status of this Connected Age industry.

As the national economy recovered from the recession, the fortunes of North Carolina's information technology sector turned around to some degree. Hardware production completely recovered by 2004 and reached a new record in 2005, while the software sector added a modest number of jobs. But jobs in tech hardware manufacturing never recovered. In 2005, tech hardware jobs remained one-third lower than their peak 2000 level. And plunging prices for computer hardware dropped the sector's contribution to the state economy almost 50 percent from 1999 to 2005.[107]

One viewpoint holds that a dichotomy exists for the economic future of tech hardware and tech software. The theory of the product cycle predicts that as production techniques become standardized in an innovative industry such as information technology, production will migrate to lower-cost locations, and this prediction appears to hold true in tech hardware production. In 2004, China for the first time surpassed the United States as the world's largest exporter of computers, mobile phones, and other digital products.[108] In addition, the United States has run a steadily increasing trade deficit in technology hardware since 1992. In 2005, the country imported one-third more tech hardware than it exported.[109]

Perhaps the most symbolic indication of this trend away from hardware production was the 2005 purchase of IBM's personal computer manufacturing unit by the Chinese computer giant Lenovo.[110] IBM at one time held 80 percent of the computer market, and the company's Research Triangle Park site was the largest in the world.[111] Today, IBM has retrofitted its manufacturing facilities into offices for its new focus on design, consulting, and financial management. One recent bright spot in tech hardware production in North Carolina was the construction of a Dell computer manufacturing plant in Winston-Salem in 2005. When fully functioning, it is expected to employ twelve hundred people.[112] However, just as the plant began production, Dell's sales slumped and its market share declined.[113] Analysts wondered if Dell needed a new retail model with a shift away from its direct-sales focus.[114]

Following the product cycle playbook, the future of information technology in both the United States and North Carolina appears to reside more in innovation and software and less in mass manufacturing. U.S. Department of Labor projections through 2014 show reductions in information technology manufacturing jobs but increases in software positions.[115] The United States possesses a strong advantage in software development, with an innovative labor force, available venture capital, and strong intellectual property protection laws.[116] North Carolina appears to be better positioned than other states to attract any forthcoming new technology jobs. Roger Riefler calculates that North Carolina pays relatively low money wages but relatively high real wages to information technology workers, a combination that is compatible with job expansion.[117] North Carolina's Employment Security Commission forecasts a modest rise (0.3 percent per year) in hardware manufacturing jobs but a robust 3 percent annual growth rate in computer software engineering positions.[118] Innovations in mobile commuting, wireless access over wide geographic areas, virtualization, and simulation are the leading areas in which new developments are expected to emerge.[119]

While the United States has led in information technology innovation and software development, no lead is safe in today's globalized economy. Software can be instantaneously sent electronically anywhere in the world, so few geographical barriers remain to the location of workers in this sector. In addition, both China and India are taking systematic approaches to training parts of their enormous labor supply in mathematics, science, and engineering. These countries will increasingly become competitors on the research and development side of information technology.[120] When the pressures to keep tech product prices low are factored in, it is easy to see that the traditional U.S. dominance in the technology of the Connected Age is far from being assured. The United States as a whole and North Carolina in particular will have to work hard to develop and promote the labor supply, risk taking, and business climate necessary to foster growth in this dynamic industry. Perhaps the country's (and state's) greatest asset is the freewheeling, "thinking outside the box" attitude that our open economy encourages.

Chemical Product Manufacturing and Pharmaceuticals

North Carolina has had a long history with the chemical product manufacturing industry. Much of the industry developed as a supplier of fertilizers, chemicals and dyes, synthetic fibers, and paints to the state's agricultural, textile, and furniture industries.[121] In the 1970s, the industry employed almost forty thousand workers and contributed just shy of 2 percent of the state's total income.[122]

During the Connected Age, the composition of the chemical manufacturing industry underwent a dramatic transformation and thereby helped to transform the North Carolina economy. In 1977, traditional chemically based products, primarily for industrial uses, comprised 75 percent of the state's industry. By 2005, these products accounted for less than one-third of chemical manufacturers' output.[123]

Pharmaceutical production made up the difference. Traditional pharmaceuticals are medical products derived from studying how chemical substances interact with living systems.[124] As the chemical industry found its markets stagnating in the 1970s, firms and entrepreneurs focused their attention on the growing health care sector.[125] With the elderly population growing in both numbers and purchasing power, the opportunities for drug development and sales expanded.

Figure 3-8 shows the output and employment trends in North Carolina's pharmaceutical industry during the Connected Age. Annual output expanded almost 500 percent between 1977 and 2005, while employment rose 165 percent between 1990 and 2005, far higher than the 10 percent rate for all of chemical manufacturing.

The growth in North Carolina's pharmaceutical industry eclipsed similar growth in the nation as a whole. Annual output increased four times faster in North Carolina between 1977 and 2005.[126] Similarly, as a percentage of total state income, pharmaceutical manufacturing's contribution jumped from 0.4 percent to 3 percent during the same time period.[127] By the twenty-first century, North Carolina ranked third behind only California and Massachusetts in the number of pharmaceutical companies located in the state.[128]

North Carolina's attractiveness to the pharmaceutical industry was based on the same fundamentals that brought the technology industry to the state. Much of the industry is centered in the Research Triangle region (Wake, Durham, and Orange counties) near Duke University, the University of North Carolina at Chapel Hill, and North Carolina State University.[129] Nationally recognized researchers and programs in chemistry, biological sciences, medicine, genetics, and agricultural sciences at these institutions helped lure the companies, offering intellectual firepower, possibilities for scientific collaboration, and a steady stream of highly trained graduates. Activist, business-oriented governors and a cheerleading industrial community also helped entice several firms to locate in North Carolina.[130]

As the Connected Age progressed, a new component of the pharmaceuti-

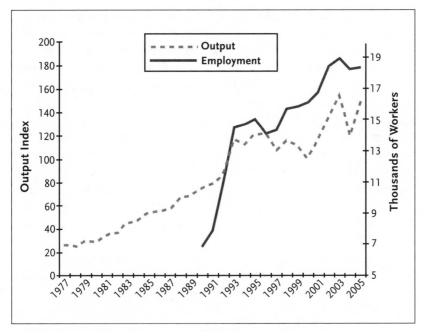

Figure 3-8. Output and employment in North Carolina pharmaceuticals manufacturing, 1977–2005.

DATA SOURCES: U.S. Census Bureau, *Economic Census, 1977*; U.S. Census Bureau, *Economic Census, 1992*; U.S. Census Bureau, *Economic Census, 2002*; U.S. Census Bureau, "Annual Survey of Manufactures," North Carolina, table 2; U.S. Department of Labor, Bureau of Labor Statistics, "Employment, Hours, and Earnings"; U.S. Department of Labor, Bureau of Labor Statistics, "Consumer Price Index."

NOTE: Employment in pharmaceutical manufacturing is available on an annual basis only since 1990. Data on output from the pharmaceutical manufacturing sector are not available. Estimates of the sector's output were constructed by dividing the value added in a given year by a price index for pharmaceutical products in that same year and then scaling the results based on a value of 100 for the year 2000.

cal industry emerged—the biotechnology sector. Whereas traditional pharmacology is based on chemical interactions with living systems and uses microbiology and enzymology as its scientific basis, biotechnology (biotech) is the direct manipulation of organisms and is a fusion of molecular biology and molecular genetics.[131] North Carolina led the nation in the growth of biotech companies from 1997 to 2001, and biotech employment in North Carolina doubled between 1992 and 2002.[132] In 2005, promoters announced the construction of a massive biotech campus on 350 acres at the site of a former textile factory near Charlotte. The $700 million project is expected to attract one hundred biotech firms and create five thousand tech jobs and thirty thousand other supporting jobs. Duke University and the University of North Carolina System are slated to participate in the venture.[133]

Therefore, the outlook for pharmaceutical manufacturing, including biotech, seems strong. A growing elderly population, rising pharmaceutical sales, and even more drug discoveries on the horizon should make for a profitable future. Nationally, while the entire chemical manufacturing industry is expected to grow slowly and employment is projected to drop, pharmaceutical production is forecast to increase rapidly, adding seventy-six thousand jobs between 2004 and 2014.[134] The trend of pharmaceutical manufacturing becoming a larger part of chemical manufacturing should thus continue. Growth prospects in North Carolina are also optimistic.[135]

Yet the industry may also take some backward steps, especially in the area of pharmaceuticals. One issue is price. Retail prices for prescription drugs and medical supplies surged 500 percent between 1977 and 2005, more than twice the rate for average prices.[136] Such increases have already created a consumer backlash, raising the possibility of government price regulation. Although the legality of price regulation of pharmaceuticals can be debated, the practical result would likely be reduced profitability and dampening of industry expansion.[137]

Another issue is the current regulatory environment for pharmaceutical products. Although the government does not directly control retail prices, the research and development process and the procedure by which drugs are brought to the market are highly regulated. The U.S. Food and Drug Administration has strict standards and processes that must be met and followed before drugs can be legally sold. As a result, pharmaceutical companies can spend hundreds of millions of dollars over more than a decade before a drug has positive earnings.[138] Studies have shown that stricter drug development regulations reduce the number of new drugs launched successfully.[139] More than half of pharmaceutical companies cite the regulatory approval process and associated costs as the top factor holding back advancement.[140] While companies recognize the need for government oversight, they would like the process to proceed more quickly and with less red tape. Observers have expressed concern that the drug approval rate has fallen while governmental approval times have increased.[141] These concerns and impacts will be heightened if the U.S. Congress approves legislation that would shorten the time before generic drugs can be marketed, especially if those drugs are not subject to the same requirements for clinical trials imposed on the drug's original developer.[142]

Finally, as with most industries in today's global economy, the issue of foreign competition arises. While U.S. companies account for almost 80 percent of worldwide pharmaceutical revenues, other countries are working hard to capture a larger share of this growing market.[143] The cost of developing drugs can be as much as 60–90 percent lower in India, Singapore, Taiwan, and China than in the United States.[144] China and India have also strengthened their intellectual property laws to attract pharmaceutical and biotech production.[145] Not only is competition from foreign-owned companies a threat, but so too is offshoring of U.S. company operations. On the other side of the ledger, legal restrictions that prevent U.S. citizens from purchasing foreign-retailed pharmaceuticals provide some protection for domestic sales.

The U.S. lead in scientific research and development, together with the dominance of American universities in worldwide scholarship, should nonetheless keep the pharmaceutical future upbeat, and North Carolina has the characteristics, interest, and commitment to maintain the industry's pulse there.[146] Applications of pharmaceuticals will continue to expand beyond medicine, in areas such as food, nutrition, and even crop and livestock production. Perhaps no other industry, including information technology, is developing and changing so rapidly yet has both exciting and still unknown impacts on human life and the economy.

Food Processing

The story of food processing in North Carolina parallels that of agriculture. Bakery and beverage manufacturing made up almost half of food processing output in 1977, while animal processing accounted for only 17 percent and fruit and vegetable processing comprised 7 percent of the total. By 2005, animal processing alone had reached 46 percent of all food processing, fruit and vegetable processing had increased to 13 percent, and bakery and beverage's share had dropped to 23 percent.[147] This shift resulted in increased prominence in the state for food processing. Both output and employment in the industry increased during the Connected Age, although gains in worker productivity reduced employment after the mid-1990s (figure 3-9). Furthermore, the increase in output was faster than both gains in total output in the state economy and output in the national food-processing sector.[148] However, because prices received by food processors rose only half as fast as average prices in the economy after the mid-1980s, the sector's share of state income fell from a peak of nearly 2 percent in 1983 to 1.4 percent in 2005 (table 3-2).[149]

The rise of the current dominant segment of the industry, animal pro-

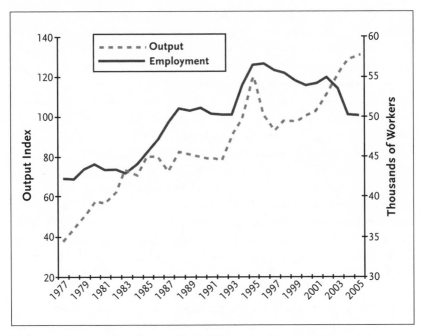

Figure 3-9. Output and employment in North Carolina food manufacturing, 1977–2005.
DATA SOURCE: U.S. Department of Commerce, Bureau of Economic Analysis, "Gross Domestic Product"; U.S. Department of Labor, Bureau of Labor Statistics, "Employment, Hours, and Earnings."

cessing, is recounted in the section of this chapter on agriculture. Lower operating costs, a favorable climate, and the proximity of a large supply of live animals—primarily hogs and poultry—combined to make North Carolina a national leader in food processing by the end of the 1990s. But environmental issues related to waste disposal caused the state to place a moratorium on hog farm expansion beginning in 1997.

Despite this constraint at the farm level, activity at North Carolina's meat-processing plants continued to make gains after 1997, in part as the result of a decrease in the exporting of live hogs out of the state for processing.[150] Nevertheless, future gains in the state's food-processing industry face challenges. One is based on the nature of food purchases. Economists consider food a necessity. Therefore, food consumption per person increases at a slower rate than income increases. As the nation's income and standard of living rise in the future, processed food consumption will likely rise more slowly, as forecasts from the U.S. Department of Labor confirm.[151]

In addition, the large gains in processed food that occurred during the Connected Age were in part pushed by increases in women working in the paid labor force. This trend has now slowed, and as chapter 1 notes, some information suggests that the process may have reversed. Although it is too early to tell whether such a switch will adversely affect the food-processing industry, future expansion of food firms will have to rely more on population growth than on socioeconomic shifts.

One of the major themes of the Connected Age is international competition. North Carolina's meat-processing sector benefited from international trade, moving from net importer to net exporter between 1955 and 2005.[152] International trade in processed food products is likely to increase in future decades, especially with improvements in transportation and food-preservation techniques. International agribusiness giants such as the Brazilian company Sadia will become significant competitors worldwide as well as in the United States.[153] If successful, they can take market share away from domestic companies, including those in North Carolina. Indeed, the U.S. trade deficit in processed foods increased 36 percent in real dollars between 2000 and 2005.[154]

Finally, demographic trends also play a role in shaping the food-processing industry. A growing elderly population should spark increased usage of processed foods specific for this age group. Similarly, the keen interest in nutrition and the fast-growing U.S. Hispanic population will motivate food manufacturers to shape and cater their products to these groups. North Carolina's location in the fast-growing Southeast should make the state attractive as a site for food manufacturing to serve a wide geographic area. In the first years of the twenty-first century, several food-processing companies announced plans for new facilities in North Carolina.[155]

Transportation Manufacturing

Who would have thought almost four decades ago that the South, including North Carolina, would become a center for U.S. transportation manufacturing? In 1970, Detroit was still the worldwide king of making vehicles. But the United States had yet to be hit by high gas prices, compact cars, and the invasion of foreign-built vehicles. North Carolina was just another state where auto enthusiasts eagerly looked forward to the unveiling of the next year's models. Few people in the state gave any thought to working in the auto industry.

Between the 1970s and the first decade of the twenty-first century, however, annual transportation manufacturing output in North Carolina increased more than 550 percent, employment tripled, and the industry's share of the state economy doubled (table 3-2 and figure 3-10). And all of these changes occurred while transportation manufacturing was declining nationwide.[156] Detroit lost its preeminent position in transportation manufacturing in both the nation and the world, but the South and North Carolina gained.

What turned the transportation world upside down during the Connected Age? Several factors converged to motivate the industry to move away from Detroit. First was intense cost competition brought on by foreign producers operating with nonunionized labor and modern factories. While the North's transportation industry workforce was highly unionized and its production facilities antiquated, the South offered union-free laborers and the ability to construct up-to-date factories. Lower energy costs also provided an advantage for the South.[157] This shift matched the paradigm of the product cycle.

A second important factor adding to the South's attractiveness was the development of innovative technologies for manufacturing transportation products. Fully completed, just-in-time modules completed off-site and produced just hours before delivery to the location where a vehicle was assembled replaced the traditional procedure of manufacturing many small parts and stockpiling them perhaps months before assembly. The new manufacturing method reduced inventory costs but required different factory floor arrangements and space allocations. Such modifications worked best in new factories, many of them located in the South.[158]

Another reason to locate transportation manufacturing facilities in the South was proximity to buyers. Vehicle manufacturing is more cost-effective if the plant is located close to ultimate buyers because moving completed vehicles across long distances is more expensive than moving vehicle parts and components to the final assembly location.[159] Hence, as the population of the South grew more quickly than the national population, locating new transportation equipment facilities in the region made economic sense.

Finally, international factors played an important role in the development of transportation manufacturing in North Carolina and the South. For several reasons—better-quality products, lower-cost production, and a product line more appealing to U.S. buyers—foreign producers, particularly those from Japan, have significantly increased their share of sales in the U.S. vehicle market. As their market share has increased, firms have had greater incentive to locate manufacturing facilities in the United States. As already mentioned, locating factories near buyers minimizes costs. In addition, moving factories to the United States blunted the call for restrictions on imports of foreign vehicles. Moreover, the persistent U.S. trade deficit gave foreign firms funds

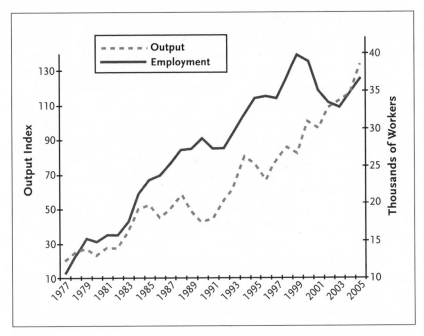

Figure 3-10. Output and employment in North Carolina transportation manufacturing, 1977–2005.
DATA SOURCES: U.S. Department of Commerce, Bureau of Economic Analysis, "Gross Domestic Product"; U.S. Department of Labor, Bureau of Labor Statistics, "Employment, Hours, and Earnings."

to invest in the United States. And when a foreign firm decided to locate a facility in the United States, the lower-cost yet growing South proved a logical site.

Several foreign-owned vehicle companies established factories in the region during the Connected Age, including Nissan in Tennessee, Mercedes and Honda in Alabama, and BMW in South Carolina. American companies Ford and General Motors have also put new factories in the South. North Carolina has repeatedly been short-listed for vehicle assembly plants, but the state has not yet made the cut. Instead, North Carolina's growing presence in transportation manufacturing has occurred in parts and components. More than two-thirds of manufactured transportation output in the state comes from vehicle parts, and production value from this sector grew more than 450 percent between 1977 and 2003.[160] As of 2005, more than one thousand North Carolina establishments manufactured parts, accessories, and components for automobiles, trucks, buses, and heavy equipment.[161] Studies show that parts factory locations within a day's drive (four hundred miles) from an assembly factory are acceptable sites, and on this basis North Carolina qualifies for many locations.[162] The state also has a growing presence in aerospace products and parts manufacturing, producing almost $600 million of output and employing more than eighteen hundred workers in these companies in 2005.[163]

Of course, any optimism about manufacturing in the Connected Age must be tempered by the prospect of foreign competition, and one country again stands out. Between 2000 and 2005, China went from being a net importer of vehicle parts to being a net exporter, and Chinese exports of vehicle parts soared from $1 billion to more than $15 billion annually.[164] As in other manufacturing sectors, North Carolina's transportation firms will have to meet international competition with gains in productivity and production efficiencies.

The U.S. Department of Labor predicts that output from transportation equipment manufacturing will grow at the national average for the entire economy through 2014 but that employment will increase at a much slower rate.[165] With the industry's preference for parts and assembly plants in close geographic proximity, North Carolina has a very good chance of eventually becoming the site of an assembly plant. Perhaps more open to question is whether the plant will fly the U.S. flag or the flag of an Asian or European country. The smart money would probably be put on the latter two.

Banking

Most new arrivals to North Carolina are surprised to learn that the state is one of the world's banking capitals. As chapter 2 discusses, a combination of foresighted state banking laws and federal laws deregulating the banking industry made Charlotte a banking center during the Connected Age. Modern technology also played a role by improving the efficiencies of large banks and easing long-distance management.[166] By the start of the twenty-first century, two of the nation's top five banks were headquartered in Charlotte; the city ranked second only to New York as a national banking center. Also, based on 1997 income, Charlotte was the world's fourth-largest banking center, trailing only New York, London, and Paris.[167]

A flurry of merger activity placed Charlotte and North Carolina in this position atop the national and world financial systems. Key was the 1998 merger of Nation's Bank of Charlotte with Bank America Corporation of San Francisco to form the Bank of America (also headquartered in Charlotte), the 2004 acquisition of Fleet Boston by Bank of America, and the merger of Wachovia and First Union in 2001 with headquarters in Charlotte. Bank of America and Wachovia are truly megabanks, with multi-hundred-billion-dollar assets and tens of thousands of employees nationwide. Also important is BB&T, the nation's tenth-largest bank holding company, which has its headquarters in Winston-Salem, and Raleigh-based RBC Bank, a subsidiary of the Royal Bank of Canada that had more than $300 billion in assets in 2003.[168]

Figure 3-11 clearly shows the explosive growth in North Carolina's banking sector. Output in particular leapt in the late 1990s after federal laws deregulated the industry both geographically and by offered services. Banking increased from a moderate 2 percent share of the state economy at the beginning of the Connected Age to a dominant 8 percent share by 2004 (table 3-2). However, because economies of scale frequently occur with mergers of companies, banking employment rose at a much smaller rate.

Because North Carolina's banking industry now operates in a national marketplace and has been driven by national factors, national trends will determine its future. Here, two aspects require consideration: trends affecting the banking industry as a whole and trends, particularly regarding mergers, that impact the megabanks.

The U.S. banking industry is considered to be healthy and to have a favorable outlook. The U.S. Department of Labor forecasts that through 2014, economic activity in banking will increase faster than the entire economy will grow. Employment, however, is projected to rise more slowly, reflecting economies of scale and increased efficiencies in the sector.[169] Banks will increasingly offer electronic services, but they will not necessarily diminish the role of brick-and-mortar outlets.[170] Although information technology allows customers to receive many of their financial services online, surveys show that households still value the physical proximity of a bank, and bank branch locations constitute the most important factor in people's choice of a bank. In fact, the number of branch locations has risen even as the number of bank companies has declined.[171]

Two demographic components will drive the future banking industry. One is the baby boom generation, whose main concern will be safety and accessibility for their investments in retirement. The second will be the immigrant population, whose relatively young age implies an initial focus on borrowing followed by a concentration on asset development. Both groups will provide banks with a steady supply of deposits while using the institutions' services and expertise.[172]

The giant growth spurt of the megabanks (those banks with assets greater

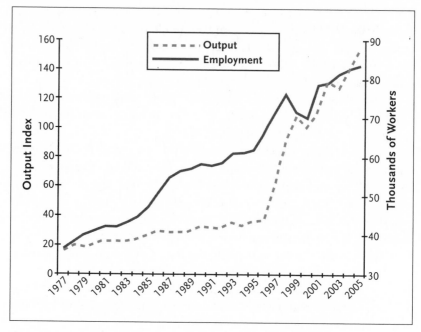

Figure 3-11. Output and employment in North Carolina banking, 1977–2005. DATA SOURCES: U.S. Department of Commerce, Bureau of Economic Analysis, "Gross Domestic Product"; U.S. Department of Labor, Bureau of Labor Statistics, "Employment, Hours, and Earnings."

than $10 billion) has likely ended, but experts believe that some consolidation in the banking industry will continue. For example, Kenneth D. Jones and Tim Critchfield see the number of banks dropping 15 percent between 2003 and 2013, a rate half that for the previous twenty years.[173] While most regional and midsize banks remain healthy and viable, they will remain targets for acquisition.[174] This outlook suggests that the dominant banks may see further growth not only from internal expansion but also from merger activity.

Perhaps the biggest question for the future of banking surrounds one of the last regulatory barriers faced by the industry—the wall between commerce and banking. In this case, the banking industry favors the regulation because it prohibits nonbank companies from providing banking services. Retail giant Wal-Mart would like to add banking to its portfolio of products and services. Company officials see a market for banking services because perhaps 20 percent of Wal-Mart's customers—twice the national rate—have no bank accounts.[175] Wal-Mart would also expect to use its successful retail model to be very competitive in pricing its banking services. If Wal-Mart entered the banking industry, other discount retailers such as BJ's, Costco, Kohl's, and Target would likely follow.

Although Wal-Mart and its companion discounters have significant economic and political clout, removing the legal barrier between banking and commerce remains a tall order. Thus, the outlook for North Carolina's banking industry is bullish. In fact, complementary financial service firms have found North Carolina an attractive location. For example, in 2004 Credit Suisse First Boston announced that it would locate one of its three world-wide global business centers in the Raleigh-Durham area, bringing four hundred jobs.[176] Even more significant, Fidelity Investments, the nation's largest mutual fund firm, announced in 2006 that it will construct facilities in the Raleigh-Durham area and create two thousand jobs over three years.[177] These moves will do even more to solidify banking and financial services as a key Connected Age economic sector of North Carolina's economy.

But there is always the possibility of a bombshell of a merger. North Carolina's banking sector could someday be shaken by an announcement that one of the state's major banks—especially one of the two megabanks—had been acquired in a merger. Because the necessary assets for such a merger would be enormous, a foreign-based bank would likely be the acquiring firm. Such a merger could jeopardize the North Carolina–based employment and operations of the merged bank. Although a merger of this proportion is unlikely, it would indeed threaten the state's banking sector.

Up-and-Comers

Other sectors emerged during the Connected Age and contributed importantly to North Carolina's economic growth but are not classified as basic industries. As the leisure industry grew in the nation in the late twentieth century, tourism gained increased importance in North Carolina, particularly on the coast and in the mountains. Similarly, the state's growth, its attractiveness to aging baby boomers as a second home and retirement site, and the favorable interest rate environment of the late 1990s and early twenty-first century sparked a construction boom that had its own economic impacts. Finally, with access a central feature of the Connected Age, the corridors of access, including highways, seaports, airports, and Internet access, become more important elements of economic development. Since these ventures are financed primarily by private funds, this chapter discusses seaports, airports, and Internet access.[178] Chapter 6 discusses publicly funded highways.

Tourism did not hit its stride in the modern North Carolina economy until the 1990s. Using hotel and lodging activity as a barometer, economic activity in tourism was flat from the late 1970s through 1990. However, from 1991 to 2005, the state's tourist activity jumped 85 percent, one-third faster than at the national level.[179] Calculations measuring tourism's comprehensive 2005 contribution to the state economy, including not only lodging but also tourist-associated spending on food, transportation, recreation, and retail products and services, found that tourism accounted for approximately 2.5 percent of the total state economy, about the same as at the national level, and employed more than 185,000 workers.[180] A noticeable drop-off in the numbers occurred after 9/11, but the industry rebounded four years later.[181]

Nationally, the tourist industry is expected to grow at rates comparable to or slightly above average growth in the economy for the foreseeable future.[182] Industry experts forecast that tourism will continue to shift its focus away from business stays to leisure stays by households. Retired baby boom households and emerging middle-aged Generation X households will be the main drivers of expenditures. The greatest upside in domestic tourist growth could come from Asian travelers, particularly those from China and India. As those two countries are rapidly modernizing and expanding their upper and middle classes, they have the potential to generate a surge in U.S. tourist activity. International travel is now growing at three times the domestic rate.[183]

With its central location, its varied topographies and activities, and prices competitive with those of other domestic tourist destinations, North Carolina should participate in the expanding tourist business. Once again, one challenge will involve developing tourist venues without downgrading the natural and related amenities (shoreline, lakes, mountain ridges) that initially made the destinations popular.

Logically, economic growth in North Carolina has brought with it construction activity. New jobs and new households to take those jobs require new housing units. But evidence suggests that the building boom proceeded beyond that needed to keep pace with expanding commerce. Between 1977 and 2005, construction's annual contribution to the state economy increased more than half of a percentage point, from 4.1 percent to 4.7 percent, while construction's national contribution remained steady over the same period.[184] In addition, the percentage of the state workforce devoted to construction rose from 4.9 to 5.9 during that time.[185] Finally, the increase in housing unit construction exceeded the increase in households in North Carolina: from 1980 to 2005, the number of households rose 64 percent, while the number of housing units increased 70 percent. Even more significant, after 2000, the difference became more dramatic, with households increasing 7 percent but housing units rising 12 percent.[186]

One big reason for the increased growth in housing units was the development of the second-home market in North Carolina. High-income working families as well as financially sound retired households fueled this market, especially after 1997, when the federal government liberalized tax laws regarding homeowner capital gains. According to one estimate, the second-home market accounted for 40 percent of total housing market activity between 2000 and 2005.[187] The state's less crowded conditions and lower susceptibility to hurricanes than Florida aided in the development of this market.[188]

The conditions that make North Carolina attractive for the second-home and retirement markets should persist. The state's year-round mild climate makes it especially suitable for such outdoor activities as golf and boating. Long and deep river basins and sounds have spurred development in the "Inner Banks" regions around Edenton, Bath, New Bern, and Sneeds Ferry, an alternative to the rapidly developing and higher-priced oceanside Outer Banks.[189] The development comes with a trade-off—the threat of increased water pollution, the curtailment of traditional coastal industries such as fishing, and even the potential that global warming will destroy coastal property.[190] National macroeconomic factors also affect the market. For example, the rise in interest rates in 2005 and 2006 was associated with a drop-off in both construction and sales in the state's second-home and retirement communities.[191]

With the boom in international trade during the Connected Age, activity at U.S. ports reached new levels. Between 1970 and 2002, total tonnage handled at U.S. ports doubled.[192] But cargo operations at the two major North Carolina ports, Wilmington and Morehead City, did not keep up. Wilmington tonnage increased 40 percent from 1970 to 2002, while tonnage at Morehead City declined in the late 1990s and early twenty-first century.[193] Part of the problem is North Carolina's proximity to competitive ports at Norfolk/Newport News, Virginia, and Charleston, South Carolina. In 2003, Norfolk/Newport News was the nation's eighteenth-busiest port, while Charleston was the thirtieth-busiest; Wilmington, by contrast, ranked sixty-sixth.[194] The ports directly contribute between $165 and $180 million annually to the North Carolina economy.[195]

Nevertheless, many observers see an opportunity for port development in North Carolina's future. In 2005, the N.C. State Ports Authority announced that it would begin planning a major new port facility near Wilmington. The plan calls for the port to be constructed to handle the world's largest cargo

ships. Supporters expect that such a modern port will spur economic development throughout the state and will increase the state's chances of attracting
large manufacturing facilities, such as an automotive assembly plant. However, any such port would have to contend with several challenges, including
the head start enjoyed by rival ports in Virginia and South Carolina and any
planned expansions at those operations, environmental impacts, and federal
government cooperation.[196]

As in the nation, air travel and airport facilities expanded during the Connected Age. Based on output, annual economic activity at North Carolina's
airports increased one hundredfold between 1977 and 2005, more than twice
as fast as for the nation.[197] A report commissioned by the N.C. Department
of Commerce found that air transportation in the state had a total economic
impact of almost $10 billion in 2006 and was directly or indirectly responsible
for more than sixty-nine thousand jobs.[198] Other analyses found the annual
impact to be more modest but still significant.[199] By the first decade of the
twenty-first century, North Carolina had seventy-four airport facilities, the
largest among them Charlotte's Douglas International Airport, the Raleigh-
Durham International Airport (RDU), and the Piedmont Triad International
Airport, which serves Greensboro and Winston-Salem. In 2004, Douglas
International Airport was the nation's eighteenth-busiest as measured by the
number of passengers boarded.[200]

North Carolina's major airports have grown in starts and stops. In the era
of the airport hubs during the 1980s, Douglas International served as a hub
for both Eastern and Piedmont, while RDU had an American Airlines hub. The
American Airlines hub was abandoned in the 1990s and was briefly replaced
by a Midway Airlines hub that closed when the airline declared bankruptcy
in 2001. Only the Piedmont (now U.S. Airways) hub remains at Douglas.
However, both Douglas and RDU have undergone expansion since the turn
of the century. Douglas is building a fourth runway and a parking deck, and
RDU is constructing a new terminal. Unlike many other U.S. airports, both
Douglas and RDU are in sites better suited for expansion and development.

In the Connected Age, airports are important not only for passenger travel
but also for the receipt and delivery of cargo. A total of 54 percent of U.S. exports move by air (up from 40 percent in 1990), and Connected Age firms
such as technology companies have a 50 percent higher demand for air transportation than traditional manufacturing companies. Air cargo is forecast
to triple over the next two decades.[201] Some futurists, such as John Kasarda,
see airports not only responding to economic development but actually driving economic growth. Air travel and accessibility to airports will become so

important that firms will be attracted to sites that are adjacent to major air terminals or that provide speedy travel to airports. Kasarda has coined the term "aerotropolis" to apply to the resulting complex, including manufacturing firms, high-tech facilities, and even retail centers to serve workers and travelers.[202] Empirical analysis has found that airport activity independently drives economic development.[203]

If one feature symbolizes the Connected Age, it is the connectivity provided by the Internet. Advances are being made so rapidly that in the very near future, every person will have the ability to connect to the Web via a relatively inexpensive, portable, handheld device. The private market will largely drive the development and spread of this technology, although governments and other collective organizations can be involved by providing public wireless Internet access.

North Carolina is becoming connected at a rate faster than the nation. In 1998, North Carolina ranked forty-seventh among the fifty states, with only 20 percent of households having Internet access. By 2003, North Carolina's ranking had improved to thirty-eighth, and 51 percent of the state's households had Internet access. This expansion of Internet access occurred almost 50 percent faster than the rate for the nation (157 percent versus 108 percent).[204]

Conclusions: The New North Carolina

The transformation of the North Carolina economy during the Connected Age completely altered the way in which the state contributes to national and world commerce. The dominant sectors throughout most of the twentieth century—tobacco, textiles and apparel, and furniture—are now mere shadows of their former selves. Their outlook is for further decline, although not total disappearance, with remnants focusing on smaller niche markets where speed of delivery and service and rapid adjustments to changing preferences are valued.

The other traditional industry, agriculture, was totally remade during the Connected Age and is now driven by livestock production: North Carolina has reached national prominence in swine and poultry output. However, further expansion in these sectors, especially swine, is hindered by environmental issues and public policy constraints. Thus, the open question is whether agriculture will be remade yet again or whether, like its sister traditional industries, it will slip into a long-term decline.

The new industries of North Carolina's Connected Age economy—information technology, pharmaceuticals, food processing, transportation parts, and banking—face a variety of challenges and futures. For information technology, the question is whether the domestic industry has matured and peaked, and if so, whether production will increasingly come from foreign firms. With an aging population and growing demand for medical solutions, the outlook for pharmaceuticals, including biotechnology, looks bright. Government regulation and the possibility of price controls pose the greatest threats to the sector's future.

Food processing will increasingly focus on nutrition and meeting the desires of more diverse consumers. However, the speed and shipping capacities associated with Connected Age transportation make international competition an increased threat. Vehicle parts and possibly even vehicle assembly look to be winners in North Carolina's future, but such success most likely will take place under foreign flags. Finally, banking is now firmly planted as a leading—if not *the* leading—industry in the new North Carolina, and it may soon be joined by other financial service companies.

Tourism, construction, and industries supplying today's connectivity (airports, seaports, and the Internet) expanded during the Connected Age and will continue to do so. Rather than following economic growth, these sectors and modes are now more likely to lead development.

North Carolina's economic transformation has meant big changes in what drives the state economy and in how commerce is linked to the rest of the nation and the world. The transformation has also meant big changes in terms of where the state's people work, how much they earn, and how they live. Chapter 4 turns to these and related topics.

4. Impacts on People

Many readers will find this the most important chapter in the examination of the modern North Carolina economy, because ultimately the effects that matter most are those on people. This chapter presents an in-depth look at how the changes that created and developed the North Carolina economy during the Connected Age affected the state's people, including the size and composition of the population, living standards, employment and occupations, and earnings. The analysis identifies winners and losers in the modern North Carolina economy. The final section assesses where the Connected Age will take North Carolina's residents and workers in the future.

A Larger, Older, and More Diverse Population

Between 1970 and 2005, North Carolina's population increased 70 percent (table 4-1), 60 percent faster than the national population grew over the same period. In each decade from 1970 to 2005, North Carolina's population growth exceeded the national rate.[1]

Three components make up population growth: internal growth, or the excess of births over deaths; in-migration, which is the movement of people from another state to North Carolina; and immigration, or the movement of people from outside the country to North Carolina. Between 1970 and 2003, North Carolina's birthrate (births per one thousand population) declined 27 percent, while the death rate fell 1.1 percent.[2] Internal growth accounted for about one-third of the state's population increase during the Connected Age.[3]

Domestic in-migration and international immigration accounted for the rest of North Carolina's population growth. The state has been a magnet for both types of migration during the Connected Age, trailing only Florida,

Table 4-1. Population and Quality-of-Life Indicators in North Carolina, 1970 and 2005

	1970 (alternate year)	2005 (alternate year)
Population Indicator		
Population	5,084,411	8,663,674
% under 25 years	47.9	34.7
% 25–59	40.0	48.9
% 60 +	12.1	16.4
Median age (years)	26.5	35.8
% white	75.9	69.6
% African American	22.2	21.0
% Hispanic	0.9	6.3
% other	1.0	3.1
Median family size (persons)	4.13	2.94
Birthrate (per 1,000 persons)	19.3	14.1 (2000)
Death rate (per 1,000 persons)	8.8	8.7 (2000)
Quality-of-Life Indicator		
Life expectancy (years)	69.2	75.8 (2000)
Infant mortality—whites (per 1,000 live births)	19.3	5.9 (2002)
Infant mortality—African Americans (per 1,000 live births)	36.1	15.6 (2002)
Adult smokers (%)	25.9 (1995)	22.6
Adults overweight or obese (%)	56.0 (1998)	62.6
Vehicles per capita	0.56	0.79
Median rooms per housing unit	5.0	5.3
Housing units with plumbing (%)	85.6	99.6
Homeownership rate (%)	65.4	69.8
Poverty rate (%)	20.3 (1969)	15.1
Urban %	45	60
Daily travel time to work (minutes)	9.2 (1980)	20.0
Per capita spending	(1972)	(2002)
On general merchandise	$1,163	$1,599
On building materials and garden supplies	$730	$1,108
At food stores	$1,961	$1,656
At restaurants	$516	$1,157
On apparel and accessories	$211	$500
On furniture	$243	$364
On pharmaceuticals	$510	$728
At auto dealers	$1,974	$3,299
At gas stations	$1,975	$2,052
On services	$1,508	$11,395

DATA SOURCES: U.S. Census Bureau, "Statistical Abstract of the United States"; N.C. State Data Center, "Log into North Carolina"; Centers for Disease Control, "Behavioral Risk Factor Surveillance System."

NOTE: All monetary values in 2005 dollars.

Nevada, and Arizona in population growth resulting from the arrival of persons from outside the state or country.[4] New York, Virginia, South Carolina, Pennsylvania, and Florida were the largest sources of in-migration to North Carolina, while Mexico was the biggest source of immigration.[5] This migration provided much of the fuel for the state's economic growth during the Connected Age.

In addition to growing in number, North Carolina's population also became older. The state's median age increased by almost ten years, from 26.5 in 1970 to nearly 36 in 2005. Between 1970 and 2005, the percentage of the state's population under age 25 fell from about half to nearly one-third, while the percentage in the prime working years (ages 25 to 60) rose from 40 percent to 49 percent and the percentage over the age of 60 jumped from 12 percent to 16 percent. Although the percentage of people under age 25 fell, their absolute numbers rose by a quarter, from 2.4 million in 1970 to 3 million in 2005.[6] This increase had implications for K–12 and postsecondary public education funding as well as for other governmental expenditures, topics that chapter 6 will discuss.

The third major feature of North Carolina's population change during the Connected Age was its increased racial and ethnic diversity. In 1970, non-Hispanic whites dominated the state, accounting for more than three-quarters of persons. African Americans comprised about 22 percent of the population, and other races made up only 1 percent. By 2005, non-Hispanic whites comprised just 71 percent of the population and the African American percentage had dropped slightly to 21 percent, but other groups totaled 8 percent. Growth in the state's Hispanic population (examined in the next section) bore responsibility for much of this increase.

While these changes in North Carolina's population and living standards moved the state closer to national levels, important differences still remain. Compared to the nation as a whole, North Carolina is younger and has a higher proportion of African Americans and, despite the recent rapid growth, a lower proportion of Hispanics. North Carolinians live in families with fewer members, and residents have shorter life expectancies. Infant mortality rates for both whites and African Americans are higher, as is the gap in the rates between the two races. A higher percentage of North Carolinians smoke, and a higher percentage are overweight or obese. North Carolina's poverty rate and percentage of persons living in rural areas are higher. Also, North Carolina households spend more on their homes (building materials, gardening, furniture) and on their vehicles (auto dealers, gas stations).

Demographers predict that North Carolina's population will continue to grow faster than the nation. The state's population is expected to increase by 16 percent in the first decade of the twenty-first century and 15 percent in the 2010s, topping 10.6 million by 2020.[7] With continued declines forecast in the state's birthrate, migration from both national and international sources will remain important. The state's age structure will also continue to change. The proportion of the population under age 25 will drop from 35 percent to 33 percent, while those aged 60 and above will grow from 16 percent to 21 percent. The future will differ from the 1970–2005 period in that the percentage aged between 25 and 60 will drop from 49 percent to 46 percent.[8] These changes will strain the workplace and will motivate three adaptations: (1) continued improvements in labor productivity, (2) pressure to keep more persons older than age 60 in the labor force, and (3) continued in-migration and immigration.

The Rise of the Hispanic Population

The overarching theme of the Connected Age is the interaction of economies throughout the world resulting in the freer flow of goods, services, money, and workers. Nowhere has the movement of workers been more dramatic in North Carolina than in the migration of Hispanic workers to the state.

North Carolina's Hispanic population grew from forty-three thousand in 1970 to more than five hundred thousand in 2005, a rise of more than 1,100 percent.[9] During the 1990s, the 400 percent increase in the state's Hispanic population led the nation.[10] Hispanics settled predominantly in the "urban crescent" region of the state, along the I-40 and I-85 interstate corridor from Raleigh to Charlotte, with a secondary concentration in the rural south-central counties. The Hispanic population is younger, has more males, and has less formal education than the rest of the state's population. As of 2004, the median age for Hispanics was thirteen years lower than the native population's median age: 35 percent were under age 18 (compared to 25 percent for natives), and 55 percent were aged between 18 and 44 (compared to 37 percent for natives). Fifty-six percent of Hispanics were male, compared to 48 percent of non-Hispanics, and Hispanics had 4.5 fewer median years of schooling than did native North Carolinians.[11]

As a result, the Hispanic migration has had a major impact on North Carolina's workforce. Between 1995 and 2005, Hispanic workers accounted for a third of the state's total increase in workers. Construction and wholesale and retail trade were the leading sectors employing Hispanics, with a significant number also in the food-manufacturing industry.[12]

Why have Hispanics come to North Carolina? The answer is simple—an imbalance between the demand for and supply of workers. On the demand side, Hispanics during the Connected Age have migrated to high-growth states, particularly in the South. The same is true within states, as the fastest Hispanic growth has been precisely in those counties with the fastest economic growth—in North Carolina's case, those metropolitan counties along I-40 and I-85.

But why were those jobs not filled by native workers? Because there were too few of them. The relative size of North Carolina's population cohort under age 25 shrank during the Connected Age. Even more important, the relative size of beginning workers—those aged 18 to 30—also contracted, from 20 percent of the population in 1970 to 17 percent in 2005.[13] In addition, a higher percentage of native young persons remained in school as the Connected Age progressed. So as the supply of native young workers fell, the supply of young immigrant Hispanic workers increased.

Hispanic immigration during the Connected Age has raised controversy about the impact on wages. Some researchers argue that the recent immigration of large numbers of relatively low-skilled Hispanic workers has reduced wages for all low-skilled workers. For example, Harvard economist George Borjas estimates that Hispanic immigration reduces real wage rates for high school dropouts, initially by 8 percent and ultimately by 5 percent.[14] Other researchers challenge this conclusion and point out that the Hispanic immigration has been concentrated in areas where job growth is strong and where any adverse effects on wages should therefore be minimal.[15]

One way to address this question for North Carolina is to compare real wage rate changes for industries where Hispanics have concentrated to real wage rate changes in other industries. For North Carolina, the industry with the greatest concentration of Hispanic workers is construction. In 2004, more than 40 percent of the state's Hispanic workers were employed in construction, compared to 10 percent for other populations. In that year, Hispanics accounted for one-third of all construction jobs.[16] Between 1990 and 2005, construction had the second-slowest growth in real wages of all industrial sectors.[17] Although this finding is consistent with the thesis that an influx of Hispanic workers to construction dampened real wage growth, it does not prove the relationship.

On the broader question of the Hispanic immigration's effect on the North Carolina economy, John Kasarda and James Johnson estimate that the private-sector impact has been significant—$9 billion of a total North Carolina annual economy of $323 billion.[18] This value may underestimate the impact of

Hispanic workers because it does not account for the improved productivity of native workers who moved into more skilled positions as a result of Hispanic immigration.[19]

Perhaps the most controversial aspect of the Hispanic immigration has been its impact on public-sector finances. Recent Hispanic immigrants have been poorer and thus have been more likely to use public services. They have also accounted for more than one-third of the increase in North Carolina public school enrollments between 1995 and 2000 and 57 percent of the increase between 2000 and 2004. Kasarda and Johnson estimate that while Hispanics contribute more than $700 million annually in North Carolina taxes, they use more than $800 million annually in public services. From the public-sector financial perspective, therefore, the Hispanic impact may be a net negative.[20]

Future Hispanic migration to North Carolina will depend on factors at the national, international, and state levels. Nationally, federal decisions about immigration limits, worker permits, and border control will influence how many Hispanic households consider migrating to North Carolina. Economic conditions in Mexico and other Hispanic countries will also affect the rate of immigration. Improving economic conditions would reduce the incentive to migrate, while deteriorating conditions would enhance the motivation. Finally, North Carolina's economic strength and age structure will continue to influence its attractiveness for immigrants. Economic growth above the national average and an aging workforce, together with a decline in the relative size of the younger worker cohort, will be a beacon for Hispanic immigrants.[21]

Quality of Life: Measuring What Counts

How did North Carolina's population live during the Connected Age, or in other words, how did the standard of living change in the state? This section considers quality-of-life measures apart from income and job characteristics, which the next section will address in detail.

Table 4-1 presents several quality-of-life indicators for North Carolina in 1970 and in 2005. Most of the indicators changed in a way that suggests an improved quality of life. Perhaps the key indicator, life expectancy, increased by more than 6.5 years. In addition, significant reductions occurred in the infant mortality rates for both whites and African Americans, although a gap remained.[22]

However, two behavioral factors affecting health showed mixed results.

While the incidence of adult smoking in the state has dropped, the percentage of adults classified as overweight or obese has risen from near half in 1998 to almost two-thirds in 2005. In 2005, North Carolina ranked seventeenth among states in the percentage of adults classified as obese.[23]

The consumption levels of North Carolinians increased during the Connected Age. Vehicles per capita increased by more than 40 percent, and the number of rooms per housing unit also grew. Since families and households decreased in size, individuals thus likely consumed more housing space per person in 2005 than in 1970. The quality of housing units also improved, as measured by the availability of plumbing facilities. The homeownership rate increased, and the poverty rate declined. Finally, real spending per capita on all categories of retail purchases except for food at stores (which dropped 16 percent) increased over the period.[24] Spending per capita both on apparel and in restaurants increased more than 100 percent, and service industry spending per capita rose by more than 650 percent. Moreover, the increase in spending per capita at restaurants fully countered the reduction in spending at food stores and resulted in total food spending per capita (both at food stores and in restaurants) rising 14 percent.

The changes to where North Carolinians lived receive a mixed evaluation. In 1970, the majority of the state's people lived in rural areas. By 2000, the reverse was true, with three out of five North Carolinians living in urban regions. While this shift may have brought greater access to shopping, educational, cultural, and medical facilities and activities, it also increased traffic congestion, as is evidenced by the doubling of the time spent in commuting to and from work each day.

Show Me the Money:
The Transformation of Work and Pay during the Connected Age

Behind all these changes—for better and for worse—is how North Carolinians earn their income. Where people work, what they do, and how much they earn lies at the core of any economy. Profound changes occurred in each of these facets during the Connected Age in North Carolina, and more changes are likely to come.

Where the Jobs Are and Will Be

The industries in which people worked and the occupations they held changed dramatically in North Carolina from the end of the twentieth century to the beginning of the twenty-first century. These industrial and occupational changes in turn affected the wage rates and incomes of North Carolina's workers and households.

Table 4-2 shows the distribution of North Carolina workers according to industry in 1970 and in 2005. Two broad trends, both consistent with the forces of the Connected Age, are obvious. First, employment in the traditional twentieth-century industries in North Carolina—agriculture, forestry, fishing, mining, and manufacturing—declined precipitously between 1970 and 2005. Employment in agriculture, forestry, fishing, and mining plunged 80 percent, while manufacturing's employment was cut in half. Second, the gaining industries have grown during the Connected Age. The financial sector's employment share jumped from 3.3 percent to 5 percent, a 50 percent gain. But most significantly, employment in service firms more than doubled, from just shy of 21 percent to just over 45 percent. North Carolinians put down their hoes, turned off the factory lights, and hung up their overalls and put on pressed shirts and ties and drove off to the office.

The changes brought on by the Connected Age were also reflected in what workers do—that is, their occupations. Table 4-2 also shows increases in white-collar occupations—professionals, managers, service providers, and sales and clerical workers. Collectively, these occupations expanded from 47 percent of all workers in 1970 to more than 72 percent of all workers in 2005. The largest gain was for professional workers and managers, a category that almost doubled its share. In contrast, the blue-collar occupations of farming, crafts workers, and operatives declined in relative importance from 47 percent of all workers to slightly less than 28 percent.[25] Occupations utilizing education, providing services, and managing and selling products replaced those making and maintaining products, tasks that increasingly became accomplished either by machinery and technology or by workers in foreign countries.

A general upgrading occurred in the skills and training of workers across most industries in the state. For example, in 1980 (the earliest year for such statistics), only 15 percent of North Carolina's manufacturing workers were in professional or managerial occupations; by 2005, more than 25 percent fell into that category.[26] Thus, although North Carolina manufacturing employment shrunk, it become more skilled. Similar increases took place in the professional and managerial worker share for all industries except agriculture.[27]

Forecasters expect that these employment trends will continue in the future and will result in a more bipolar job distribution—that is, the fastest

Table 4-2. North Carolina Employment by Industry
and by Occupation, 1970 and 2005

	1970	2005
Industry		
Agriculture, forestry, fishing, mining	5.1%	0.9%
Construction	6.2%	6.0%
Manufacturing	33.6%	14.8%
Transportation, communications, public utilities	5.2%	5.9%
Wholesale and retail trade	16.7%	16.1%
Finance	3.3%	5.0%
Services	20.9%	45.3%
Government	3.4%	5.7%
Unclassified	5.6%	0.3%
Occupation		
Professional and managers	17.7%	32.3%
Service	10.3%	15.8%
Sales and clerical	19.0%	24.2%
Farming	4.2%	0.8%
Crafts workers	18.3%	11.5%
Operatives	24.8%	15.4%
Unclassified	5.7%	0.0%

SOURCE: U.S. Census Bureau, *1970 Census of Population and Housing*; U.S. Census Bureau, "Public-Use Microdata Samples."
NOTE: All workers 14 and over; percentage of total.

employment growth will occur in both higher-skilled (and higher-paying) and lower-skilled (and lower-paying) jobs. For example, the N.C. Commission on Workforce Development projects that both the percentage of total jobs requiring education beyond high school and the percentage requiring no high school will increase between 2007 and 2017, while the percentage requiring only a high school degree will drop.[28] Similarly, the Employment Security Commission of North Carolina predicts that the fastest-growing jobs will be in the high-paying fields of business and finance, computer science and mathematics, and health care as well as in low-paying positions in food preparation, health care support, and cleaning and maintenance.[29]

Income: The Big Picture

For most workers and families, the key factor determining economic well-being and standard of living is income. Figure 4-1 shows trends in five alternative income measures for North Carolinians during the Connected Age. Mean per capita personal income is personal income from all sources less net government monetary transfers, divided by total population.[30] Median household income is the income level in the middle of the income distribution—that is, half of the household incomes are above this value and half are below.[31] The median wage rate is the earnings per hour of all persons working in the state, also measured in the middle of the distribution.[32] Mean worker pay is the simple average of wage and salary income per job, and mean compensation is the simple average of wages, salaries, and the value of benefits per job. The values of all measures are before taxes, are real values, and for ease of comparison have been converted to index values in which 1980 equals 100. The compensation measure was available only beginning in 1998.

Although all the measures show an increase during the period, the increase for per capita income is much greater. From 1970 to 2005, per capita income increased 106 percent, while household income rose 32 percent, the wage rate rose 26 percent, and worker pay rose 49 percent. One reason for the differences is the way "average" is measured in the alternative indicators. Per capita income and worker pay, with the largest increases, use a *mean* average and thus are influenced by extreme values—in particular, by large income increases for upper-income households that pull the average upward. In contrast, the household income and wage rate averages are *medians*, which are much less influenced by extreme values. The more rapid rise in per capita income therefore suggests some significant increases in the upper levels of the income distribution, a topic examined in detail later in the chapter. In addition, per capita income includes income from sources other than working, such as rents and investment earnings.

A less positive picture emerges from more recent income trends. From 1998 to 2005, both per capita income and the wage rate rose 2 percent and worker pay increased 7 percent, but household income fell 10 percent. The biggest gain was registered in compensation, which jumped 11 percent. These results suggest that employers have been shifting workers' pay away from salaries and wages and into benefits.[33] In addition, these results indicate that the aggregate averages likely are hiding fundamental changes that benefit some workers but hurt others, and these changes have become more pronounced in the twenty-first century.

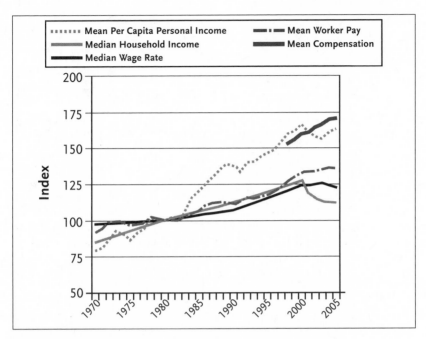

Figure 4-1. Alternative income measures for North Carolina, 1970–2005.
DATA SOURCES: U.S. Department of Commerce, Bureau of Economic Analysis, "State Annual Personal Income"; U.S. Census Bureau, "Public-Use Microdata Samples."
NOTE: 1980 = 100.

Behind the Numbers: Winners and Losers

The values in figure 4-1 are averages, so they hide many important changes. Table 4-3 shows how real household income and real wage rates as well as work hours changed for various categories of workers in North Carolina between the benchmark years of 1980, 2000, and 2005.[34] Only workers between ages 25 and 60 are analyzed to eliminate those who are in school or partially retired.

The patterns of wages and work diverged for full-time and part-time workers.[35] Full-time workers' median wage increased, even during the 2000–2005 period, as did their average annual work hours. The reverse was true for part-time workers—both their median wages and average annual work hours declined. Although the household incomes of both households headed by full-time workers and households headed by part-time workers declined between 2000 and 2005, the decline was much sharper for part-time worker households (10 percent) than for full-time worker households (3 percent).

Table 4-3. North Carolina Wage Rates, Work Hours, and Incomes during the Connected Age, Workers Aged 25–60, 1980, 2000, and 2005

	Median Wage Rate			Mean Work Hours			Median Household Income		
	1980	2000	2005	1980	2000	2005	1980	2000	2005
All workers	$11.87	$14.30	$14.30	1,887	2,002	1,947	$45,704	$56,183	$51,650
All full-time	$12.69	$15.19	$15.45	2,310	2,367	2,372	$50,933	$62,010	$59,935
All part-time	$10.39	$12.38	$11.72	1,308	1,305	1,265	$33,416	$39,195	$35,225
Full-time workers									
Gender									
Male	$14.37	$16.50	$16.53	2,370	2,439	2,439	$53,909	$67,860	$65,079
Female	$10.21	$13.60	$14.30	2,187	2,256	2,268	$30,397	$44,460	$50,173
Race and ethnicity									
White	$13.17	$16.16	$16.97	2,326	2,386	2,392	$52,962	$66,573	$66,319
African American	$10.37	$12.98	$12.91	2,224	2,287	2,321	$38,726	$47,970	$43,799
Hispanic	$11.98	$10.13	$9.93	2,333	2,323	2,296	$44,845	$45,747	$39,254
Other race/ethnicity	$10.54	$14.00	$14.90	2,300	2,388	2,361	$43,606	$58,500	$55,679
Income level									
Poverty	$3.60	$6.00	$5.31	2,408	2,428	2,304	$12,425	$14,625	$14,720
Education									
High school dropout	$10.66	$11.00	$9.93	2,288	2,301	2,318	$42,741	$45,302	$38,221
High school graduate	$11.98	$12.94	$12.91	2,290	2,322	2,338	$49,352	$52,954	$47,725
Some college	$13.77	$15.13	$14.90	2,308	2,360	2,358	$53,778	$60,840	$57,848
4-year college graduate	$18.93	$21.60	$22.35	2,394	2,447	2,434	$68,799	$86,580	$85,739

Occupation									
Professional workers	$15.97	$19.50	$19.87	2,398	2,424	2,431	$61,845	$77,220	$75,822
Service workers	$9.46	$10.69	$10.59	2,296	2,314	2,344	$41,446	$46,016	$40,287
Sales and clerical workers	$11.98	$14.06	$14.40	2,236	2,279	2,282	$52,302	$57,915	$58,468
Farmers	$7.19	$8.56	$8.34	2,486	2,456	2,385	$29,899	$39,078	$34,089
Crafts workers	$14.32	$14.91	$14.90	2,327	2,409	2,375	$49,825	$58,500	$54,542
Operatives	$10.78	$12.38	$11.92	2,255	2,319	2,333	$42,997	$50,310	$44,832
Industry									
Agriculture	$6.66	$9.56	$9.27	2,573	2,538	2,509	$38,688	$53,820	$49,894
Construction	$12.72	$13.78	$12.66	2,287	2,400	2,400	$48,580	$58,500	$50,720
Manufacturing	$12.77	$15.69	$15.89	2,242	2,307	2,318	$49,962	$61,437	$59,604
Trade	$11.83	$13.50	$13.71	2,419	2,425	2,422	$50,715	$60,255	$55,782
Transportation, communications, public utilities	$17.96	$17.60	$18.38	2,302	2,409	2,438	$58,166	$68,328	$65,079
Finance	$13.17	$17.18	$18.38	2,267	2,341	2,351	$59,548	$74,880	$77,062
Health and education	$12.97	$15.75	$15.89	2,262	2,306	2,299	$51,232	$59,085	$56,867
Professional and business services	$11.98	$16.88	$18.54	2,360	2,396	2,386	$54,805	$73,125	$73,364
Entertainment	$11.98	$14.56	$13.91	2,376	2,398	2,409	$50,198	$60,840	$51,650
Personal Services	$7.71	$11.25	$9.50	2,400	2,410	2,485	$42,342	$52,650	$50,617
Government	$14.37	$16.14	$17.48	2,326	2,404	2,395	$51,057	$60,840	$63,251

DATA SOURCE: U.S. Census Bureau, "Public-Use Microdata Samples."

NOTE: Median household income is for household head with stated characteristic. All amounts in 2005 dollars.

The percentage of workers aged 25–60 working part-time in North Carolina declined from 42 percent in 1980 to 34 percent in 2000 but then rose to 38 percent in 2005. Therefore, one reason for the wage stagnation in North Carolina in the first decade of the twenty-first century is the movement toward more part-time jobs.

The remaining entries in table 4-3 analyze the wage rate, work hours, and incomes of full-time workers with various characteristics. One of the major trends of the Connected Age has been the increased labor participation rates of females. Indeed, the percentage of North Carolina women aged 25–60 in married households who were employed for pay rose from 62 percent in 1980 to 68 percent in 2005. As the Connected Age progressed, the economic payoff to women dramatically improved. The median female wage rate jumped 21 percent between 1980 and 2000 and rose another 5 percent between 2000 and 2005. By comparison, the corresponding gains for men were 15 percent (1980–2000) and 0.2 percent (2000–2005). As a result, the female/male wage rate gap narrowed from 29 percent in 1980 to 13 percent in 2005. A big reason for this change was the improved educational levels for females relative to men. Between 1980 and 2005, the percentage of females aged 25 to 60 with college degrees increased twice as fast as the percentage for men. Full-time working females also increased their annual mean work hours more (3.7 percent) than did men (2.9 percent), and the income gains of households headed by full-time working females outpaced those of households headed by full-time working males. The Connected Age in North Carolina therefore had an overall beneficial effect for working females.

Significant differences also occurred in the economic progress of North Carolinians of different racial and ethnic backgrounds. The median wage rates of all racial/ethnic groups except Hispanics increased between 1980 and 2005, although African Americans saw a slight decrease in their wage rates from 2000 to 2005 and the African American/white wage gap rose slightly from 21 percent in 1980 to 24 percent in 2005. In 1980, Hispanic workers had the second-highest wage rate, trailing only whites; in 2005, Hispanics had the lowest wage rate among the racial/ethnic groups. This finding is explained by the change in the educational makeup of Hispanic workers in North Carolina. From 1980 to 2005, the percentage of Hispanic workers with no formal education tripled, while the percentage with only elementary school training rose more than 25 percent. At the higher end of the educational ladder, the percentage of Hispanic workers with some college or college degrees declined. Correspondingly, the median income of households headed by Hispanic persons fell between 1980 and 2005, while the median incomes of households of other racial/ethnic categories rose. Among those with gains, the increase was smallest for African American households and greatest for households of other races.[36]

Economic progress was mixed for North Carolina households defined as poor. The median wage rate rose between 1980 and 2000 but fell substantially from 2000 to 2005, when work hours also declined. Despite these changes, household income rose during both subperiods, likely because of the increased generosity of some public income support programs for the poor, particularly the Earned Income Tax Credit.[37]

The economic data relating education to income measures support education's status as one of the defining features of the Connected Age. Table 4-3 reveals several important associations. In all years, a higher wage rate was associated with increased levels of education, but the payoff to more education increased over the time period. For example, in 1980, the wage rate of college graduates was 58 percent higher than the wage rate for high school graduates, a number that rose to 67 percent in 2000 and to 73 percent in 2005. The changes in the wage rate over the entire time period were associated with the educational level—specifically, the more education, the greater the wage rate gain. Between 1980 and 2000, the wage rate gain was 3.2 percent for dropouts, 8 percent for high school graduates, 10 percent for those with some college, and 14 percent for college graduates. And from 2000 to 2005, the only workers enjoying an increase in their wage rate were college graduates. These patterns were repeated for household income, although households with college-educated heads experienced a slight drop in income between 2000 and 2005. Finally, more educated workers not only earn more but also work more. In all years, mean work hours increased along with educational level.

The effects of the Connected Age's dominating trends can also be seen in the earnings data for occupations. Professional occupations—those requiring the greatest amounts of education—led all occupations in wage rate gains between 1980 and 2005 (24 percent), followed by sales and clerical workers, farmers, service workers, crafts workers, and operatives. With the exception of farmers, whose earnings can be strongly influenced by government payments, wage gains for white-collar occupations (professional, sales and clerical, and service) dominated those for blue-collar occupations (crafts workers and operatives). Between 2000 and 2005, only professional sales and clerical workers achieved gains in their median wage rates. Professional workers also put in the most work hours in 2005 and were second only to farmers in 1980 and 2000, and households headed by professional workers experienced the greatest income gain from 1980 to 2005—a gain almost twice as large as that posted by the runner-up, farmers.

Table 4-3 also shows wage rates, work hours, and household income changes for workers classified by industry. Workers in all industries except construction registered wage rate gains over the entire 1980–2005 period, although the gains varied widely. The greatest gains took place in professional and business services (55 percent), finance (40 percent), and agriculture (39 percent), while the smallest gains were in transportation/communications/public utilities (TCPU), trade (wholesale and retail), and entertainment services. Changes in household income followed a similar pattern. Interestingly, the wages of manufacturing workers increased during the entire 1980–2005 period as well as between 2000 and 2005 as a consequence of the loss of thousands of lower-paying textile and apparel jobs (thereby raising the average wage rate of the remaining jobs) and the skill upgrades required for many holders of manufacturing jobs.

North Carolina's big income gainers during the Connected Age were women, college graduates, people in professional occupations, and people working in professional and business services and finance. That these groups were the winners makes sense because they benefited from the forces shaping the new era. Big losers have been Hispanics, primarily because the composition of the Hispanic population changed during the Connected Age—high school dropouts and workers with only a high school education, blue-collar workers (crafts workers and operatives), and workers in the construction, entertainment services, and TCPU industries. The rising tide of the Connected Age did not lift all boats. Some floundered.

Everything at Once

One problem with the preceding analysis is that it considers characteristics one at a time. It does not consider all factors simultaneously in a way that permits the isolation of the effects of individual factors. For example, since workers with professional occupations tend to be college graduates, looking at the change in the wage rate of professional workers does not allow the impact of the occupation to be separated from the impact of the education.

Statistical techniques, however, permit the isolation and measurement of the separate effects of individual characteristics such as gender, race/ethnicity, and educational, occupational, and industry factors. These techniques were used to analyze North Carolina workers' wage rates in 1980, 2000, and 2005. (For the methodology and details of the techniques, see appendix B.)

Table 4-4. Wage Rate Premium and Discount Percentages for Selected Characteristics, North Carolina Full-Time Workers, 1980, 2000, and 2005

	1980	2000	2005
High school graduate	17.7	11.6	5.8
Some college	29.2	23.9	19.6
4-year college graduate	64.0	80.3	88.5
Female	−39.1	−42.2	−40.5
African American	−15.6	−17.3	−29.3
Hispanic	−10.5	−15.1	−24.2
Other race/ethnicity	−9.8	−11.9	−17.4
Professional occupation	29.0	48.3	55.7
Service occupation	2.8	4.5	4.3
Sales and clerical occupation	16.6	21.2	26.9
Farmer occupation	57.8	35.0	29.4
Crafts occupation	7.8	8.1	13.6
Agricultural industry	−97.3	−73.3	−70.8
Construction industry	−26.6	−33.7	−45.1
Trade industry	−30.6	−28.5	−29.4
Transportation, communications, public utilities industry	9.4	−3.5	−3.7
Finance industry	−19.2	5.7	4.6
Health and education industry	−23.2	−26.4	−29.6
Professional services industry	−46.9	−24.5	−21.8
Entertainment industry	−33.5	−34.4	−38.5
Personal services industry	−56.9	−47.6	−63.8
Government industry	−14.8	−26.5	−26.7
Urban area	18.4	18.2	20.9

DATA SOURCE: Table B-1.

NOTE: These percentages are compared to the base case of the wage rate of a white, male high school dropout working as an operative in manufacturing and living in a rural area.

In short, the statistical method involves holding constant all characteristics except one, thereby deriving the specific impact of that characteristic.

Table 4-4 gives wage rate premiums and discounts for specific characteristics against the base case of a white, male, high school dropout working as an operative in the manufacturing industry and living in a rural area. In effect, the numbers in table 4-4 are the percentage increases or decreases in the base case worker's wage rate caused by changing a given characteristic. For example, the 17.7 value under 1980 for high school graduate means that if the base case worker was a high school graduate rather than a high school dropout but all other characteristics remained the same, his wage rate would be 17.7 percent higher. The −26.6 value for construction means that his wage rate would be 26.6 percent lower if he worked in the construction industry rather than in manufacturing.

The results for the education measures clearly show the increasing importance of education during the Connected Age. As expected, each of the three educational levels beyond high school dropout has an associated wage premium. But while the wage premiums for college graduates widened over time, from 64 percent greater than the wage rate for high school dropouts in 1980 to 88.5 percent greater in 2005, those for high school graduates and workers with some college narrowed. High school graduates earned a wage rate almost 18 percent higher than high school dropouts in 1980, but by 2005 the premium had shrunk to less than 6 percent. Likewise, the wage rate gain for workers with some college was 29 percent over high school dropouts in 1980 but only 20 percent in 2005. So while the Connected Age expanded the wage rate of college graduates, it compressed the wage rates of workers with less education.

Although North Carolina's female workers saw wage rate gains during the Connected Age, table 4-4 shows that these gains did not result from their gender. Indeed, comparing male and female workers with the same characteristics other than their gender (education, occupation, industry, and residence) shows that female workers consistently suffered a nearly 40 percent discount in their wage rate throughout the Connected Age. Other studies confirm that a gender pay gap persists even after accounting for worker characteristics such as education and experience. Researchers speculate that some of the gap may result from the potential loss in productivity of female workers when they take time from their careers for childbearing and child care. In addition, discrimination in the hiring and promotion of women may continue.[38]

Racial and ethnic groups other than whites also appear to be paid less in the modern North Carolina economy. The smallest discount is for workers of other races, the largest discount is for African American workers, and the discount for Hispanic workers falls in the middle. Further, these wage rate discounts for nonwhite workers increased during the Connected Age. These findings certainly are both controversial and troubling. One possible explanation is that the analysis is missing important information that would reduce or remove the discounts—information such as experience in current job, specific degree held, ratings of educational quality, job performance measures, and more detailed definitions of occupations and industries.[39] Some analysts argue that when such detailed information is included, racial/ethnic differences disappear. Other researchers disagree, contending that evidence continues to support the idea of racial/ethnic discrimination in wage rates.[40] Whether the racial/ethnic differences in pay result from unmeasured factors or discrimination will not be solved here, but such differences persist in North Carolina during the Connected Age.

All of the occupational categories command wage rate premiums over operatives, with professional occupations, farmers, and sales/clerical occupations having the largest premiums in 2005. Moreover, with the exception of farmers, the wage premiums of the occupations increased over time. The biggest increases occurred in professional occupations (a gain of 26.7 percentage points) and sales/clerical occupations (10.3 percentage points). Connected Age changes favored both of these occupations.

All of the industries paid a lower wage rate than manufacturing except for TCPU in 1980 and finance in 2000 and 2005. Over time, the wage rate discounts grew for construction, health/education, entertainment, personal services, and government; shrank for agriculture and professional services; and changed little for trade. The TCPU industry switched from paying a wage rate premium in 1980 to paying a discount in 2000 and 2005. The finance industry went in the opposite direction, paying a discount in 1980 and a premium in 2000 and 2005, likely because of the tremendous growth in the financial services sector. The fact that most North Carolina industries paid a wage rate discount relative to manufacturing indicates the adverse effect of the decline in the state's manufacturing job base on workers' economic welfare.

Finally, table 4-4 implies that workers in urban areas received a wage rate premium of approximately 20 percent over workers in rural areas. This premium probably does not represent a real gain for urban workers but rather reflects compensation for the higher costs of living in North Carolina's urban locations.[41]

This more sophisticated analysis reinforces some of the key trends of the Connected Age. Education was the most dominant worker characteristic, strengthening as the Connected Age progressed. The gap between college-educated workers and other workers went from a ravine to a canyon. White-collar occupations such as professionals and sales and clerical workers gained relative to other occupations, while the loss of jobs in the manufacturing industry hurt North Carolinians' overall wages.

Yet the analysis also confirms some lingering concerns that predate the Connected Age. Comparing workers with the same educational, occupational, and industry backgrounds revealed that females and nonwhites receive lower wage rates, and these wage discounts have increased over time. These results may reflect an inability to control for all relevant worker characteristics, including many that are difficult to measure, and these omitted characteristics could have become more relevant as the Connected Age matured. Conversely, the results may indicate gender and racial/ethnic discrimination that has not only continued but has become more rather than less acute.

Shifting Shares

Nationally, the Connected Age has featured a widening of the income distribution. The biggest income gains went to those at the top of the income distribution, resulting in a larger gap between higher-income households and both middle- and lower-income households. Analysts attribute the change to several factors: the greater gains received by those with advanced education and training, the increase in global competition for workers with less education and training, the increased supply of workers at the lower wage rate levels as a result of increased immigration and the movement of women into the paid labor force, and the reduced influence of unions.[42] Of course, the emphasis on education, more open global trade, increased immigration, and the greater participation by women in the paid workforce have constituted hallmarks of the Connected Age.

Figure 4-2 shows that a widening of the income distribution also occurred in North Carolina during the Connected Age. The change resulted primarily from a movement of households out of the lower- and middle-income ranges into the upper-income groups. The percentage of households in the lower three income categories (household incomes up to $15,000) declined from 17 percent in 1970 to 13 percent in 2005; the percentage in the middle four income groups ($15,000–$75,000) dropped from 71 percent to 60 percent; and the percentage of households in the upper two income categories ($75,000 and up) rose from 12 percent to 27 percent.[43] Furthermore, these changes did not result from the influx of women into the workforce and the resultant increase in two-earner households. Separate analysis of the trends in the income distribution for households with one working spouse and for households with two working spouses revealed the same pattern—reduced percentages of households in the lower- and middle-income ranges and an increased percentage of households in the upper-income ranges.

In one light, these results are positive. The fact that the percentage of households in the upper two income brackets more than doubled is truly remarkable and suggests that many North Carolina households benefited directly from the era's defining economic trends. Conversely, however, the

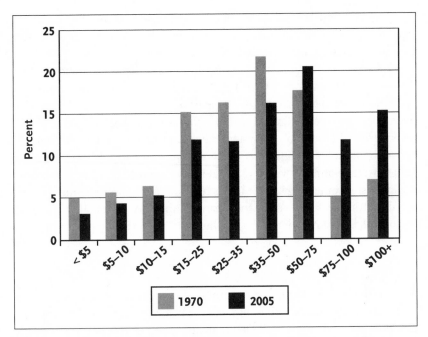

Figure 4-2. Distribution of North Carolina households by income, 1970 and 2005.
DATA SOURCE: U.S. Census Bureau, *1970 Census of Population and Housing*; U.S. Census Bureau, "Public-Use Microdata Samples."
NOTE: All income ranges expressed in thousands of 2005 dollars. For 2005, household income is used; for 1970, family income is used because household income was not available.

trends in the state's income distribution signal two dangers. One is a reduction in social cohesion. The middle class acts as a bridge between lower- and higher-income households. Lower-income households can set goals and benchmarks for economic progress by looking to households at the income rungs immediately above. As the proportion of households in the middle-income categories drops, however, lower-income households may see a removal of their role models for economic progress. The second concern involves control of monetary resources. As at the national level, a modest yet significant increase in the percentage of total income received by households at the top of the income distribution has occurred during the Connected Age in North Carolina. The percentage of total income received by the top 25 percent of income-earning households rose from 46 percent in 1970 to 49 percent in 2005.[44] Some observers view increasing income concentration as unhealthy for society. Others view the change with less alarm if it results from the changing structure of the economy, as occurred during the Connected Age, and if it provides individuals with incentives to improve their training to enhance their productivity and value.

However, considerable income mobility exists among households, even during the Connected Age. Although data specific for North Carolina are not available, national data show significant movement among income ranges for individual households. Over time, households move both up and down the income distribution. For example, Peter Gottschalk estimates that 58 percent of households in the lowest income range in the 1970s had moved into a higher range almost twenty years later, and almost half of households in the highest income range in the 1970s had fallen to a lower income category two decades later.[45] Preserving the means for this income mobility may be as important as the snapshot of the income distribution at any point in time.

Work and Family

Families and especially women in families faced difficult choices during the Connected Age. Forces both pulled and pushed women out of the home and into the paid labor force. Pull factors included women's increased access to education and training, which better qualified them for the jobs being created during the Connected Age, and the reduced physical requirements of many jobs as a result of modern machinery, equipment, and technology. The major push factor was the introduction of household equipment, appliances, and other technology that women could substitute for their time in performing household tasks.[46]

Consequently, the percentage of North Carolina's women of prime working age (between 25 and 60) in the paid workforce increased from 56 percent in 1970 to 73 percent in 2005. The jump was even more dramatic for married women with children at home: 51 percent of such women worked in 1970, compared to 71 percent in 2005.[47]

The increased proportion of working women has a host of social and economic ramifications, including the impact of working women on the social and intellectual development of their children and the growth of several industries, including child care, processed and fast foods, and restaurants.

The effect that working mothers have on the welfare of their children is an especially complicated and controversial subject that goes beyond cursory relationships. While some studies find that a mother's employment has an adverse effect on her child's cognitive and emotional development, other observers contend that the income derived from a mother's employment can improve her children's economic situation, which in turn can aid in successful child rearing.[48]

These conflicting views are reflected in various indicators of the welfare of children in North Carolina during the Connected Age. Table 4-1 shows improvement in several indicators of the material well-being of North Carolina households that bode well for children: the rise in homeownership, the increase in housing space per person, the increase in vehicles per capita, and the increase in spending per capita on most product and service categories. In addition, the prices of two key consumer commodities, food and clothing, fell between 1970 and 2005, meaning that households with children could afford more of these necessities.[49] Yet some key indicators of social and emotional success of the state's children declined. The rate of juvenile arrests rose by one-third between 1983 and 2004, while the rate of child abuse cases increased by one-quarter and the rate of child neglect cases jumped fivefold.[50]

The movement of North Carolina's women into the paid workforce during the Connected Age clearly caused an expansion in the state's child care industry. Between 1990 and 2004, the number of licensed child care facilities in the state more than tripled, while the capacity of these centers more than doubled.[51] An industry economic impact report showed North Carolina's child care firms generating $1.5 billion in gross receipts in 2004 and directly supporting forty-six thousand jobs. The industry has the capacity to serve almost one-quarter of the state's children aged 12 and under.[52]

Chapter 3 documents the growth of the state's food-processing industry, but the impact of the changing eating habits of North Carolinians—in part prompted by the increase in the proportion of working women—is also evident in the state's restaurant business. Food purchased and eaten away from home, in restaurants and other retail establishments, increased from 25 percent of all food spending in 1970 to 40 percent in 2005.[53] Restaurants in North Carolina doubled in number and quadrupled in sales between 1982 and 2002, stronger growth than that posted by all other businesses in the state.[54]

The increase in working women caused some tension in economic status between households with and without working spouses. Although real incomes increased for both household types over the 1970–2005 period, incomes increased faster for households with working spouses (155 percent) than for households without working spouses (143 percent).[55] Consequently, households with working spouses had 43 percent more income than households without working spouses in 2005; thirty-five years earlier, that number was 32 percent.[56]

Caught in Between

The transforming North Carolina economy during the Connected Age caught many workers between the old and the new economies. The extent of those caught in between can be seen in the data for announced business closings. From 1990 to 1993, an annual average of 103 businesses closed; from 1994 (the year of the North American Free Trade Agreement and General Agreement on Tariffs and Trade) to 2000, annual average closings jumped to 193; and from 2001 to 2005, closings soared to an annual average of 575.[57] The annual number of laid-off workers doubled between the 1990s and the first decade of the twenty-first century.[58]

First, who were these displaced workers? Perhaps not surprisingly, they tended to be older North Carolinians with less education who worked in manufacturing firms that restructured as a result of national and global changes in the economy.[59] In 2003, 85 percent of the displaced workers in rural areas had high school degrees or less, while 59 percent of such workers in urban counties lacked college training—precisely the types of workers least prepared for the Connected Age.[60]

And what happened to these displaced workers? First, many of them remained unemployed for a significant period. Studies show that between 20 and 40 percent of displaced workers were unemployed for at least six months.[61] Second, about half of displaced manufacturing workers who became reemployed took other manufacturing jobs, while the remainder found jobs in other industries—most commonly, administrative services, retail, and health care.[62] Third, and perhaps most important, displaced workers suffered losses in income. Studies of displaced workers both nationwide and in North Carolina show that their earnings fell between 15 and 50 percent.[63] Furthermore, the reduction in earnings persisted over time.[64]

Displaced workers are the major casualty of the Connected Age, and because North Carolina's traditional industries have been so adversely impacted by the economic trends of the period, the state's casualty count is high and likely will continue to grow. Balancing gains against the costs is a major issue for policymakers both nationally and in North Carolina.

Are We Better Off?

North Carolina in the first decade of the twenty-first century was much different than North Carolina in 1970. Led by migrants from other states and other countries, the state was a national leader in population growth. The state's population also became older and more ethnically diverse. A higher percentage of people worked as professionals, salespersons, and service providers, and a smaller percentage worked in the production crafts and trades. Jobs moved off the farm and out of the factory into offices, stores, hospitals, and schools.

But questions linger about whether such changes were all for the better. In the 1980 presidential debates, candidate Ronald Reagan asked Americans if they were better off then than they had been four years earlier. The same question can be asked of North Carolinians but with a longer time span: Are they better off after three-plus decades of the Connected Age?

On average and over the sweep of the entire period, the answer is a definite yes. North Carolinians became better housed, better clothed, and better fed during the Connected Age. They became more mobile and technologically connected, and they consumed more of just about every product and service available. Poverty, the infant mortality rate, and the death rate all declined, while life expectancy increased. Average wage rates and incomes rose and with a few exceptions did so for both males and females as well as for all races, education levels, occupations, and industries.

But the tide of the Connected Age lifted economic boats to varying degrees and allowed some to sink. The difference was most apparent for workers with different educational levels. High school dropouts regressed economically during the period, while other groups gained in proportion to their amounts of schooling. The Connected Age pitilessly awarded gains and losses. Workers and industries that benefited from the trends of the era (college graduates, professional occupations) reaped the benefits, while those whose characteristics were at odds with the trends suffered the losses (high school dropouts, workers in traditional manufacturing). The growth in the number of displaced workers and the widening of the income distribution were two manifestations of these outcomes. These patterns became even more pronounced after 2000, when globalization hit its full stride.

The Connected Age also failed to eliminate workplace differences resulting from characteristics other than education, occupation, and industry. No reduction occurred in the wage discounts paid to women and to nonwhite workers, and in some cases the discounts even grew.

The Connected Age thus favored some North Carolinians over others. Chapter 5 explores whether this result holds true for the different regions of the state.

5. Impacts on Places

Someone once said that all politics is local.[1] The same can be argued for economics. While international, national, and certainly statewide trends impact the financial fortunes of households and businesses, the greatest impacts come from the local economy. Local economies have elements that reflect characteristics of broader geographies but are not duplicates of their larger counterparts. Instead, local economies, just like people, tend to specialize in certain skills and industries. Thus, all states can have local economies moving in very different directions.

This chapter demonstrates that North Carolina has many varied local economies. Furthermore, the trends and forces of the Connected Age have affected these diverse economies in different ways. Some have benefited from and excelled as a result of the Connected Age's emphasis on education, deregulation, and international trade, while others have been battered and challenged to remain viable. Thus, at the ground level, in the multiple regions, counties, towns, and places that make up North Carolina, the story of the modern economy has been a dream for some and a virtual nightmare for others.

This chapter examines the impact of the Connected Age on North Carolina's places in two ways. I first present a comparative analysis of the state's local economies during the Connected Age, emphasizing how performance has varied during the era. Second, I analyze each of the state's local economies, showing how they have changed during the Connected Age and discussing their prospects for the future.

Comparative Performance of Local Economies

Any analysis of local economies initially confronts a practical question—how to define local economies. North Carolina is composed of 548 municipalities,

100 counties, 14 metropolitan statistical areas, and 7 economic development regions, plus several other administrative classifications.[2] Which of these properly defines a local economy?

While no correct or definitive answer to this question exists, this chapter uses commuting zones to define local economies. A commuting zone is a collection of counties between which a substantial movement of workers from their residences to their workplaces occurs, making the counties one cohesive economic unit, although economic diversity can still exist within each zone.[3] While commuting zones have no administrative structure, they are supported by an economic logic. North Carolina has twenty-one commuting zones (map 5-1).[4] These commuting zones will be the major basis for comparing North Carolina's local economies, with counties as a secondary source of comparison.

Walkers and Sprinters

A quick look at some key economic data for North Carolina's local economies shows that they performed quite differently during the Connected Age. Figure 5-1 displays the performance of the regions on two key measures — employment growth and average salary per job. Employment growth ranged between a high of 197 percent for the Triangle region and a low of 4 percent for the Roanoke region. Average salary topped out at $34,321 for Greater Winston-Salem and bottomed out at $21,010 for Roanoke.

The geographical income comparisons carry one caveat: prices, particularly for site-based products such as housing, vary between locations in North Carolina.[5] This price variation affects the purchasing power of income in different locations by increasing the spending power of earnings in low-priced regions and decreasing the spending power of earnings in high-priced regions. Research conducted in the 1990s showed the purchasing power difference to be as high as 25 percent between the highest-priced and lowest-priced locations. Furthermore, the high-priced locations tend to have the highest incomes, and the low-priced locations tend to have the lowest incomes. So North Carolina's high-income regions are not as well-off as they appear, and low-income counties are not as poor as they appear.

Yet the research also showed that the variation in prices within North Carolina is not as great as the variation in incomes. Indeed, the salary difference between the richest region (Greater Winston-Salem) and the poorest region (Roanoke) is 63 percent, considerably larger than the 25 percent measured difference in regional prices. The research on regional price differences also revealed that adjusting for those differences did not appreciably change the

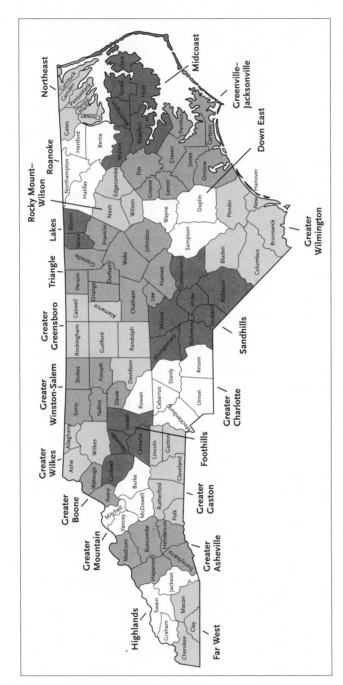

Map 5-1. North Carolina's local economies.

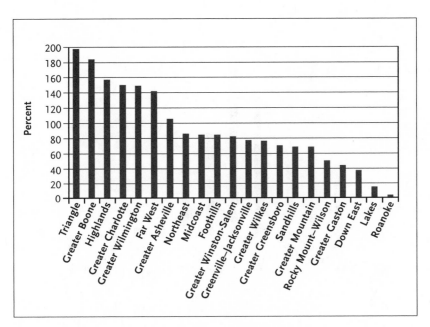

Figure 5-1a. North Carolina local economies, employment growth, 1970–2004.

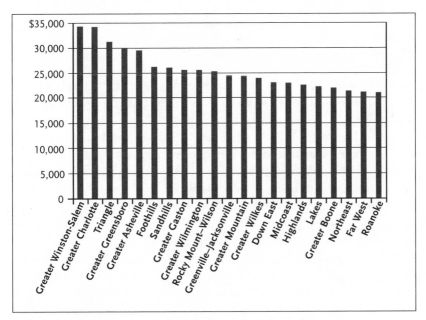

Figure 5-1b. North Carolina local economies, average real salaries per job.
DATA SOURCE: U.S. Department of Commerce, Bureau of Economic Analysis,
"Local Area Personal Income."
NOTE: The salary values are the average for 1970 and 2004, both in 2004 dollars.

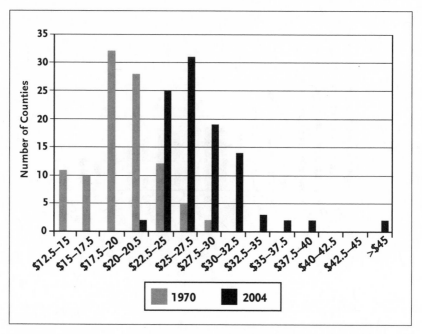

Figure 5-2. Distribution of North Carolina counties by real average salary per job, 1970 and 2004.

DATA SOURCE: U.S. Department of Commerce, Bureau of Economic Analysis, "Local Area Personal Income."

NOTE: All amounts in thousands of 2004 dollars.

income ranking of regions—that is, rich regions before the adjustment were also rich regions after the adjustment, with a similar conclusion for poor regions.

For further insight into the geographical differences, the distribution of average salaries in local economies in 1970 and 2004 can be compared. This resembles the comparison made in chapter 4 (figure 4-2) for workers' income distribution. To achieve a finer level of detail, the one hundred counties serve as the basis of comparison in this analysis. Figure 5-2 shows the results. Average real salaries per job rose over the period, and no North Carolina county suffered a decline in average real salary per job over the period.

Perhaps more revealing, in 1970, 60 percent of North Carolina counties fell in the middle ($17,500–$22,500) of that year's income distribution; in 2004, however, the income distribution was much wider, and the bulk of counties were bunched in the lower part of the distribution. Seventy-five counties fell into three of the four lowest income categories, and the upper tail of the distribution spread much longer. North Carolina's counties moved up the income ladder between 1970 and 2004, but several counties climbed many more rungs than did others.[6]

Common Threads

By comparing North Carolina's local economies on several measures, the regions can easily be grouped into a handful of categories defined by the differential impacts of the Connected Age. Seven characteristics are used to form the groupings: population density, population change, employment change, average salary, change in average salary, change in the number of traditional industries (agriculture; tobacco manufacturing; textile manufacturing; apparel manufacturing; and wood product, paper, and furniture manufacturing) firms, and change in the number of new industries (food manufacturing, pharmaceutical manufacturing, computer and electronic equipment manufacturing, transportation equipment manufacturing, and banking) firms.[7] Table 5-1 shows the groupings.

The first three groupings are local economies that have benefited from the trends of the Connected Age. Category 1—urban, new economy regions—includes the state's elite racehorses, propelled ahead at lightning speed by the evolving economy. These regions have enjoyed rapid population and employment growth, high average salaries, and robust income gains. They have been little affected by the downsizing of traditional industries, since the growth of new economy firms has greatly outpaced the losses in traditional, or old, economy firms. The Triangle and Greater Charlotte regions lead in this category, with Greater Wilmington and Greater Asheville posting somewhat slower growth as well as lower average salaries.

Category 2 includes small-city—or by some definitions small-town—regions that have also displayed substantial growth during the Connected Age.[8] They have gained new economy firms while losing few if any traditional companies. However, they differ from their urban counterparts in having slower growth and lower average salaries; in fact, average salaries in these regions are third-lowest among all regional categories. Similarly, category 3 includes two rural regions that have had strong growth—in fact, average employment growth in these regions has been as strong as that in the category 1 regions. Average salaries are near those in category 2, and the regions gained old economy firms over the period.

Categories 4, 5, and 6 are regions in transition, where the loss of old economy firms has been substantial and growth rates in both population and

Table 5-1. Categories of North Carolina's Local Economies, 1970–2004

Region	Density	Population Change	Employment Change	Average Salary	Salary Change	Old Firms	New Firms
United States	85	2.6%	4.4%	$33,969	2.0%	—	—
North Carolina	175	3.7%	5.0%	$28,678	2.8%	−653	3261
Category 1: Urban, New Economy Regions							
Triangle	525	6.1%	7.8%	$31,281	3.6%	−18	600
Greater Charlotte	888	5.0%	6.6%	$34,268	3.5%	−12	664
Greater Wilmington	393	4.8%	6.6%	$25,554	2.0%	−5	151
Greater Asheville	238	3.2%	5.2%	$29,495	1.7%	−3	148
Average	511	4.9%	6.6%	$30,150	2.7%	−10	391
Category 2: Small City, New Economy Regions							
Greater Boone	118	3.6%	7.6%	$21,996	1.7%	15	26
Northeast	91	3.2%	4.4%	$21,392	3.0%	−14	33
Midcoast	56	2.3%	4.4%	$22,935	1.9%	1	89
Average	88	3.1%	5.6%	$22,108	2.2%	0.7	49
Category 3: Rural, New Economy Regions							
Highlands	52	3.0%	6.8%	$22,579	2.1%	7	26
Far West	53	4.1%	6.4%	$21,086	2.7%	8	33
Average	52.5	3.6%	6.6%	$21,833	2.4%	7.5	30
Category 4: Urban, Transitional Regions							
Greater Winston-Salem	512	3.0%	4.3%	$34,321	2.0%	19	217
Greater Greensboro	413	2.9%	3.8%	$30,030	2.0%	−103	356
Sandhills	273	2.9%	3.7%	$26,045	2.6%	−62	173
Greater Gaston	332	2.4%	2.6%	$25,569	2.0%	−89	134
Average	383	2.8%	3.6%	$28,991	2.1%	−59	220

	Density	Population Change	Employment Change	Average Salary	Salary Change	Old Firms	New Firms
Category 5: Small-City, Transitional Regions							
Foothills	248[a]	3.7%	4.4%	$26,238	2.1%	-57	157
Greenville-Jacksonville	161	3.0%	4.1%	$24,473	2.6%	-70	156
Rocky Mount–Wilson	162	1.9%	2.9%	$25,317	3.3%	-46	85
Average	190	2.9%	3.8%	$25,343	2.7%	-58	133
Category 6: Rural, Transitional Regions							
Mountain	132	2.4%	3.7%	$24,413	1.6%	-9	47
Down East	134	2.1%	2.2%	$23,022	2.4%	-60	64
Greater Wilkes	75	2.0%	4.0%	$24,010	2.9%	-32	45
Lakes	131	2.0%	1.0%	$22,195	2.0%	-19	14
Average	118	2.1%	2.8%	$23,410	2.2%	-30	43
Category 7: Rural Stagnant Region							
Roanoke	61	-0.1%	0.3%	$21,010	2.9%	-104	43

DATA SOURCES: U.S. Department of Commerce, Bureau of Economic Analysis, "Local Area Personal Income"; U.S. Census Bureau, *County Business Patterns, 1970*; U.S. Census Bureau, *County Business Patterns, 2004*; N.C. State Data Center, "Log into North Carolina."

NOTE: Regional averages are unweighted means. Changes are annual rates.

[a] The Foothills region has a higher density than Greater Asheville, yet Greater Asheville is classified as urban and the Foothills is classified as small city because the central city of Greater Asheville (Asheville, population 73,189 in 2005) has a population almost twice as large as the central city of the Foothills region (Hickory, population 39,018 in 2005).

Density = persons per square mile in 2004

Population Change = average annual percentage change in population from 1970 to 2004

Employment Change = average annual percentage change in total employment from 1970 to 2004

Average Salary = salary per job averaged for 1970 and 2004 in 2004 dollars

Salary Change = average annual percentage change in average salary per job (in 2004 dollars) from 1970 to 2004

Old Firms = change in the number of firms in the industries of agriculture, tobacco manufacturing, textile manufacturing, apparel manufacturing, and wood product, paper, and furniture manufacturing from 1970 to 2004

New Firms = change in the number of firms in the industries of food manufacturing, pharmaceutical manufacturing, computer and electronic equipment manufacturing, transportation equipment manufacturing, and banking employment have been slower than for the regions in categories 1, 2, and 3. Category 4 includes urban, transitional regions where more than a quarter of the gains in new economy firms have been countered by losses in old economy firms. Although two of the four regions in top average salaries fall into this category, average salaries grew more slowly in this category than in all others.

Category 5 includes small-city, transitional regions. Here, more than 40 percent of the new firm gains were countered by losses in old firms. Category 6 is composed of the rural, transitional regions, where growth has been modest and where almost three old economy firms have been lost for every four new economy firms gained. Regions in this category also had the second-slowest average gains in population and employment.

Category 7 has only one region, Roanoke. It is the only region that lost population from 1970 to 2004, and the average annual gain in employment was an anemic 0.3 percent. The region has been devastated by the decline in North Carolina's traditional economy, with more than two old economy firms lost for every new economy firm gained. The region also has the lowest average salary.

Behind the Differences

What explains these differences in economic performance? Do better-performing regions have any features that poorer-performing regions lack? A look at past research on regional (substate) economic performance as well as some new analysis yields some answers.

One theme dominates the literature—differences in educational characteristics have constituted the driving force behind economic performance during the Connected Age. In an analysis of U.S. counties between 1970 and 1990, Jordan Rappaport found that higher shares of government spending on elementary and secondary education were positively related to real per capita income growth, net migration, and growth in median housing values.[9] Christopher H. Wheeler studied job growth in U.S. metropolitan areas between 1980 and 2000 and ascertained that higher fractions of workers with high school or less education were associated with slower job growth, while higher fractions of workers with some college training or a college degree were related to faster job growth. Wheeler also found these associations when jobs were divided between higher-paying and lower-paying occupations.[10] In their examination of economic growth, Mark Henry, David Barkley, and Haizhen Li found that between 1970 and 2000, southern counties with a higher share of college-educated workers among the adult population had faster growth in real per capita income.[11] Stephan J. Goetz and Anil Rupasingha derived the same result for all U.S. counties between 1990 and 2000 using the percentage of the population with high school degrees or more as the education measure.[12] Lorin D. Kusmin, John M. Redman, and David W. Sears examined determinants of real income growth in rural counties in the United States from 1979 to 1989 and found that rural counties with higher percentages of adults having high school degrees grew faster but that the percentage of adults with college degrees had no impact.[13]

Two recent studies have focused on analyzing economic growth among only North Carolina counties. Mitch Renkow found that the proportion of individuals aged twenty-five and older who held high school diplomas was positively related to the growth in real per capita earnings between 1970 and 1990.[14] Examining the 1981–95 period, Zulal Denaux found strong evidence that public spending on higher education was positively related to income growth but found no association between public elementary and secondary school spending and income growth.[15]

While these results clearly show that education matters for local economic growth in the Connected Age, several studies demonstrate that education matters more in some localities than in others. Specifically, the positive benefits of education matter more in urban counties than in rural counties, as Henry, Barkley, and Li; Goetz and Rupasingha; and Renkow found. Henry, Barkley, and Li showed that rural counties' growth premium from education amounted to only between half and two-thirds of the premium in urban counties. Goetz and Rupasingha found the rural growth premium from added education to be only one-third the size of its urban counterpart, while Renkow's analysis found the rural education premium to be half that of the urban education premium.

Two possible explanations for these results exist. First, urban areas offer more of a critical mass for maximizing the advantages of education. In more dense locations, educated workers have a greater ability to interact and benefit from each other's expertise, and this enhanced interaction creates a larger collective impact. Second, the benefits from education may be dampened in rural areas because those counties face the departure of their most talented workers to urban locations — a brain drain. Therefore, investors who might employ more highly educated workers in rural locations may be reluctant to do so for fear that the workers will migrate to other areas.

Studies have also found that factors in addition to education are related to growth — most notably, highway infrastructure. Both Goetz and Rupasingha and Kusmin, Redman, and Sears found that the presence of an interstate highway in a county was positively related to economic growth. Denaux measured highway infrastructure by the real dollar value of roads per square mile and found this measure to be positively related to economic growth.

Beyond highways, Kusmin, Redman, and Sears concluded that access to airport transportation is important to economic growth. In their study, rural counties within fifty miles of airports with scheduled passenger service had faster economic growth. Rappaport recognized that water as an amenity has increased in importance; his finding that counties with proximity to ocean coasts grew faster highlights an inherent advantage of local economies with beach access. Finally, studies have found conflicting evidence regarding the importance of local tax rates to economic growth. Denaux found that higher county property tax rates were associated with faster economic growth. Conversely, Kusmin, Redman, and Sears used the ratio of locally raised general revenues to local personal income to measure the local tax rate and found no relationship to economic growth.

Using these studies as a guide, a new analysis of North Carolina's local economic growth from 1970 to 2004 was performed with the county as the unit of analysis.[16] Appendix c reports the details of this analysis. Two measures of economic growth were studied: growth in average real salaries per job and employment growth. The analysis reconfirmed the importance of education. Growth in average real salaries has been lower in counties with initially higher percentages of workers with high school degrees in 1970 but higher in counties with larger increases in the percentage of workers with high school degrees over the entire period and much higher in counties with greater increases in the percentage of workers with college degrees. Some evidence also shows that the positive impact on real salaries from increases in the percentage of college graduates is strongest in urban counties. Noneducational variables had little effect on explaining differences in real salary growth among the counties.

The analysis generated somewhat different results for employment growth. For education, it was the change in attainment measures that mattered. Increases in the percentage of workers with high school degrees were related to slower employment growth, while increases in the percentage of workers with college degrees were tied to faster employment growth, and the impact of college degrees was much stronger. These effects did not differ between urban and rural counties. Highway mileage in the county, open space, and beach access were also linked to faster employment growth.

North Carolina's local economies clearly differ, and these differences have become more pronounced during the Connected Age. When differences in one of the crucial characteristics, education, are considered, North Carolina stands at both the very top and the very bottom of the nation. For example, in a ranking of U.S. counties by the percentage of workers with advanced college degrees, North Carolina's Orange County had the second-highest rate, while the state's Wilkes County ranked the lowest.[17]

What specifically drives or stalls North Carolina's local economies, and what are their prospects in the future? The next section addresses some of these questions.

Profiles and Prospects for North Carolina's Local Economies

This section profiles each of North Carolina's twenty-one (commuting zone) local economies, highlighting changes in their key industries, employment, and demographic characteristics. Because of data limitations, industry changes are examined between 1990 and 2004.[18] The industry measure used is gross local product (GLP), the counterpart to gross domestic product at the national level and gross state product at the state level. GLP measures the economic output of an industry produced within the local economy. It differs from the market value of output produced or sold in the local economy because it excludes the value of inputs imported from outside the local economy used to make the local output. For example, GLP for lumber produced at local sawmills would exclude the value of any cut trees brought to the mills from outside the local economy. In contrast, the market value of output of sawmills would include the value of the imported cut trees. Thus, GLP will be smaller in value than output, but GLP is preferable because it includes only the contribution of local economy inputs—in other words, the value added to the product in the local economy. GLP values for the major industries in each region in 1990 and 2004 appear in appendix D.

The profiles are presented in order of the categories of local economies from table 5-1 to permit easy comparisons between regions with similar characteristics. Table 5-2 gives key educational, demographic, and cost characteristics of the regions.

Urban New Economy Regions: The Racehorses

The Triangle, Greater Charlotte, Greater Wilmington, and Greater Asheville regions have been the racehorse economies of North Carolina during the Connected Age, adding people, workers, industries, and income. The regions

Table 5-2. Key Educational, Demographic, and Cost Characteristics of the Regions, Various Years (Regional Rank in Parentheses)

Region	Early in Connected Age			Later in Connected Age		
	College Attainment (1970) %	Median Age (1970) Years	Cost (1983) $	College Attainment (2000) %	Median Age (2000) Years	Cost (2006) $
United States	5.9	28.1	—	15.9	35.3	—
North Carolina	4.4	26.5	—	14.7	35.3	—
Triangle	6.8 (1)	26.3 (15)	359 (1)	22.5 (1)	33.3 (18)	757 (1)
Greater Charlotte	5.4 (2)	27.8 (10)	357 (2)	19.0 (2)	34.1 (17)	658 (2)
Greater Wilmington	3.4 (11)	27.0 (14)	306 (9)	14.3 (6)	38.0 (8)	626 (4)
Greater Asheville	5.0 (3)	31.4 (2)	288 (17, 18, 19)	16.4 (3)	40.6 (2)	580 (9)
Greater Boone	4.7 (6)	25.0 (19)	298 (12, 13)	16.2 (4)	32.2 (21)	617 (6)
Northeast	3.3 (13)	28.0 (8)	322 (5)	9.7 (14)	38.1 (7)	613 (7)
Midcoast	2.9 (17)	28.2 (6)	316 (7, 8)	11.9 (9)	39.8 (4)	561 (11)
Highlands	3.5 (9)	26.7 (11)	288 (17, 18, 19)	13.3 (8)	37.6 (9)	540 (14)
Far West	2.6 (20)	32.7 (1)	288 (17, 18, 19)	10.3 (12)	44.9 (1)	517 (17)
Greater Winston-Salem	4.9 (4)	28.5 (5)	325 (4)	15.0 (5)	36.7 (11)	599 (8)
Greater Greensboro	4.8 (5)	27.8 (9)	321 (6)	13.8 (7)	36.0 (15)	636 (3)
Sandhills	3.5 (8)	23.6 (21)	303 (10)	10.4 (11)	32.5 (19)	555 (13)
Greater Gaston	3.1 (14)	28.1 (7)	336 (3)	9.5 (15)	37.0 (10)	620 (5)
Foothills	3.4 (10)	27.6 (12)	297 (14)	10.2 (13)	36.6 (12)	556 (15)
Greenville-Jacksonville	3.5 (7)	23.9 (20)	294 (16)	11.2 (10)	32.4 (20)	539 (15)
Rocky Mount–Wilson	3.3 (12)	26.0 (18)	276 (20, 21)	9.3 (16)	36.3 (14)	577 (10)
Greater Mountains	2.8 (19)	29.5 (3)	295 (15)	8.1 (19)	38.2 (6)	538 (16)
Down East	2.9 (16)	26.2 (16)	316 (7, 8)	8.3 (17)	34.9 (16)	513 (18)
Greater Wilkes	2.0 (21)	29.3 (4)	298 (12, 13)	8.1 (18)	39.8 (3)	503 (20, 21)
Lakes	3.0 (15)	27.6 (13)	300 (11)	7.2 (20)	36.5 (13)	504 (19)
Roanoke	2.8 (18)	26.1 (17)	276 (20, 21)	7.1 (21)	38.3 (5)	503 (20, 21)

SOURCE: U.S. Census Bureau, "Statistical Abstract of the United States"; U.S. Department of Housing and Urban Development, "Fair Market Rents."
College Attainment = percentage of the population with four or more years of college education
Median Age = median age
Cost = average nominal monthly rent for a two-bedroom housing unit

benefited from the trends of the Connected Age, but a different force was prominent in each region. Moreover, the regions will face somewhat different future challenges and go in somewhat different directions.

Triangle: The Twenty-first-Century Economy

The Triangle region has been the state's premier growth area during the Connected Age, leading in both population and employment growth from 1970 to 2004 (table 5-1). Indeed, the Triangle is one of the premier regions of the country, regularly receiving "#1 best places" awards for jobs and quality of life.[19]

A glance at table D-1 shows why. New economy industries such as pharmaceuticals, software, research and development, computer terminals, and communications equipment led contributors to the region's GLP. The only traditional economy industry, cigarette manufacturing, ranked twelfth among the top fifteen sectors in 1990 and dropped from the list in 2004. The ten-county Triangle region expanded its GLP by a robust 97 percent between 1990 and 2004, when the region accounted for more than one-fifth of the total gross state product.

The main reason for the Triangle's success in the Connected Age is simple. The region leads the state in the percentage of its population with college degrees (22.5 percent in 2000), a rate well above the national level (15.9 percent). The Triangle's three Research 1 universities (Duke University in Durham, North Carolina State University in Raleigh, and the University of North Carolina at Chapel Hill) produce a continuous flow of highly educated workers, particularly in the scientific, technical, and financial fields so greatly valued by modern businesses.[20] In addition, this higher education complex attracts research dollars from both private and governmental sources that fuel the fires of innovation and make the Triangle attractive for creative workers and entrepreneurs. Annual research and development spending quadrupled in real dollars between 1990 and 2004, making this industry the seventh-leading sector in the region.

Many of the Triangle's new economy firms are located in the region's world-famous Research Triangle Park (RTP), positioned centrally between Chapel Hill, Durham, and Raleigh. RTP's tenants include IBM, GlaxoSmithKline, Cisco Systems, Nortel Networks, Sony Ericsson, and Bayer CropScience.[21] RTP pioneered the campus-style industrial park venue. The ties between the RTP firms as hirers of labor and the universities as suppliers of labor and as collaborators in research and development projects have been the most powerful force in the region's growth.

If a region were to be built from scratch for the Connected Age, a model better than the Triangle probably could not be found. The region has all the ingredients for success in today's global, competitive, and productivity-focused world. The regional economy has nevertheless endured some bumps. The most significant was the technology (dot-com) bust of the late 1990s. Overexpansion in the technology sector eventually led to contraction and retrenchment, and the Triangle did not escape the downside. Between 1999 and 2003, technology manufacturing employment in the region dropped by 30 percent, and as of 2007, these jobs had not been recovered.[22] Major employers such as Nortel and IBM permanently cut thousands of jobs. Indeed, table D-1 shows that the computer terminal manufacturing sector had a reduction both in output and in ranking in the region between 1990 and 2004.

The Triangle faces three vulnerabilities in its economic future. One is the risk that some of its key economic sectors will falter. As chapter 3 discusses, pharmaceuticals, telecommunications, and technology confront potential challenges in the decades ahead. The technology bust of the late 1990s provided a wake-up call, alerting the Triangle that continued expansion in the industries of the new economy is not inevitable. Triangle leaders have targeted fields such as biotechnology, biodefense, nanotechnology, informatics, and pervasive computing as sectors in which to expand.[23] In addition, the movement of RBC Bank's headquarters to Raleigh, the opening of a four-hundred-person office by Credit Suisse First Boston, and the announcement of the creation of a two-thousand-worker operation by the mutual fund firm Fidelity signals the region's increased attractiveness as a center for financial services.[24]

A second challenge comes from other domestic regions. At its establishment in the 1960s, the RTP represented a unique partnership between private-sector research and development firms and universities. Forty years later, many regions have copied this relationship, while many others, including Charlotte and Winston-Salem, seek to implement the same strategy. The RTP certainly enjoys unique advantages as a result of its size, synergies, and reputation, but the area may have to work harder in the future to maintain its position. In particular, the developing biotechnology center in the Greater Charlotte region will present competition for leadership in this field.

Third, the region's rapid growth presents challenges. Public schools, roads, and other infrastructure have become increasingly crowded and congested, and water rationing during dry summer months has become common. A citizens advisory committee in Wake County, the most populous in the Triangle, identified $12 billion in needed spending for school construction and another $12 billion for highway building through 2030.[25] The group recommended changes in the property tax, revisions in the state's funding formula for road construction, and the institution of new taxes to pay for the public costs related to growth.[26] Many of the region's outer counties, such as Johnston and Chatham, are experiencing even greater growing pains because they lack the large commercial and industrial tax bases to support the residential growth.

Even with these issues, the prospects for the Triangle remain bright. State government and the universities provide a relatively stable employment base.[27] Although rapid growth has pushed the region's cost of living to the highest in the state, it remains a relative bargain when compared to peer regions across the country.[28] The region has no natural boundaries to inhibit expansion. Fundamentally, however, the Triangle likely will remain among the nation's elite growth regions because of its almost one-of-a-kind education and research complex, which simply cannot be duplicated. The Triangle *is* the twenty-first-century economy.

Greater Charlotte: A Major League Economy

Located at the border of North and South Carolina, Charlotte, the dominant city of the Greater Charlotte region, has long been considered the economic capital of the Carolinas. Charlotte is the largest city in the two states, and the Greater Charlotte region ranked first in North Carolina in GLP and second only to the Triangle in employment in 2004. Although Greater Charlotte's growth in population and employment trailed the Triangle from 1970 to 2004, the six-county region posted the fastest growth in GLP in the state between 1990 and 2004 (table D-2).

In its role as the center of a two-state economy, Greater Charlotte performs functions as a wholesaling, retailing, and transportation hub. The share of GLP from these functions was by far the highest among all regions in 1990, and although its lead slipped by 2004, a large part of the Greater Charlotte economy still performs these central tasks.[29] Symbolic of this role is the presence of a U.S. Airways (initially Piedmont) hub at Charlotte's Douglas International Airport since the late 1980s.

Unlike its sister racehorse economy, the Triangle, the Greater Charlotte economy has had a major presence in North Carolina's traditional industries. In 1990, textiles, apparel, and tobacco were the region's fifth- and sixth-most important sectors, accounting collectively for almost 8 percent of GLP. The same year, new economy sectors such as banking, computer equipment, and food processing totaled only 5 percent of GLP.

Three major transformations occurred in the Greater Charlotte economy between 1990 and 2004. First, while the region continued to serve as a trade and transportation hub, the relative importance of this function fell. Second, a significant shift took place out of the old economy sectors of textiles and apparel and into new economy industries such as software processing, computer equipment, vehicle bodies and parts, and management services. Textiles and apparel did not even make the list of top fifteen industries in Greater Charlotte in 2004. Cigarette production maintained both its rank and percentage share of GLP between 1990 and 2004, but its importance will fall significantly with the announced closing of the large Philip Morris plant in the region's Cabarrus County.[30]

The most eye-catching change in the Greater Charlotte economy during the Connected Age undoubtedly was the meteoric rise in the banking sector. From 1990 to 2004, output from banking rose more than eightfold, banking's place among the region's top sectors jumped from ninth to second, and the industry's contribution to total GLP climbed from 2.2 percent to 9.1 percent. As chapter 3 discusses, this change reflected the aggressive and dynamic growth of North Carolina's banks during the period when the banking system was deregulated. Charlotte has become the nation's second-largest banking center, and the spin-offs and ripple effects in the region from the industry's growth are significant.

Whereas the Triangle's employment base is dominated by technology, health services, higher education, and state government, the Greater Charlotte job market is led by finance, trade, and management. The region's top entry in the technology sector, computer equipment manufacturing, contributed 2 percent to GLP in 1990. However, by 2004 the sector's share was cut in half, and employment dropped by 40 percent.[31]

Perhaps nothing symbolizes the Greater Charlotte region's ascension to elite status among U.S. metropolitan areas more than its acquisition of three professional major league sports franchises during the Connected Age. In 1988, the Charlotte Hornets began play as an expansion franchise in the National Basketball Association (NBA), while the National Football League's Carolina Panthers followed in 1995. After a dispute with the city over construction of a new arena, the Hornets left for New Orleans in 2002, but just two years later, the NBA took the unprecedented step of awarding Charlotte a second team, the Bobcats. Charlotte is also frequently mentioned as a possible site for a relocated Major League Baseball franchise, and auto racing at the 167,000 seat Lowe's (formerly Charlotte) Motor Speedway and other regional venues attracted an estimated $3.9 billion in spending in 2003.[32]

These professional sports teams and events provide the region with valuable national publicity.

While Greater Charlotte has a firm place in the new economy of the Connected Age, the downsizing of one old economy industry, textiles and apparel, has created adjustment issues. Most notably, when the giant Pillowtex plant in Cabarrus County closed in 2003, five thousand workers immediately lost their jobs.[33] Like a phoenix rising from the ashes, however, the $700 million biotechnology campus being constructed at the factory site (see chapter 3) represents the replacement of the old economy with the new, signifying Greater Charlotte's push to diversify into new economy industries beyond banking. With its geographical access to vehicle assembly plants in South Carolina, vehicle parts also are a natural industry for expansion in the region. In addition, Greater Charlotte's leaders have targeted machine manufacturing, plastics, medical equipment, and metalworking as viable sectors for the future.[34]

Thus, Greater Charlotte will forge ahead on two economic fronts. One front, like the Triangle, will pursue new economy industries that require advanced education and training—technology, pharmaceuticals, and of course banking. These efforts will take advantage of the expanding campus of the University of North Carolina at Charlotte, which is expected to grow from twenty-one thousand students in 2006 to thirty-one thousand students, including three thousand doctoral candidates, in 2016.[35] However, Greater Charlotte starts considerably behind the Triangle in both percentage of college-educated workers and annual number of college graduates. Competition with the Triangle for premier new economy firms therefore will be stiff, with Greater Charlotte having an advantage in lower costs but a disadvantage in available trained workers. Greater Charlotte's second front for economic development will focus on manufacturing and related industries, such as vehicle parts and machinery, that can tap into the area's blue-collar workforce.

As in the Triangle, public infrastructure will pose a challenge for continued growth in Greater Charlotte. Roads have become more congested, increasing the mean travel time to work in the region's most populous county, Mecklenburg, by 23 percent between 1980 and 2000.[36] Critics claim that even a planned light rail system in Charlotte—the first section of which opened in 2007—will not significantly decrease traffic congestion.[37] Public schools also have rising capital needs, and public support for school construction has ebbed and flowed over the years.[38]

Still, the Greater Charlotte region looks to have a positive future. Charlotte now enjoys comparisons to such major cities as Atlanta, San Diego, and even Washington, D.C., and in this light, the region enjoys an advantage in terms of cost of living and quality of life.[39] Greater Charlotte is in the major leagues to stay.

Greater Wilmington: Capital of the Coastal Boom

During much of the nineteenth century, Wilmington, the central city of the Greater Wilmington region, was North Carolina's largest city. As one of the biggest seaports on the East Coast, Wilmington's access to the outer world made it one of the most cosmopolitan and cultured cities in the entire South.

Then, as North Carolina's economy moved into the Industrial Age and as first rail and then road transportation replaced water transit, the cities of the state's Piedmont region (Charlotte, Winston-Salem, and Greensboro) over-took Wilmington in both size and status. As recently as 1990, the Greater Wilmington economy was led by traditional industries such as textiles, apparel, tobacco, and glass products as well as chemical and industrial oil plants (table D-3). However, real estate and construction was the leading sector, reflecting the economic transformation that was clearly under way in the region by 2004.

Real estate and construction's dominance subsequently increased. In fact, in only one other region, the adjacent Midcoast, did real estate and construction take such a large slice of the economy. Education moved up the list of important industries, reflecting the growth of the University of North Carolina campus at Wilmington, and consumer service industries—doctors, restaurants, and banking—had an enhanced role in the Greater Wilmington economy. New economy sectors such as food processing and transportation engines and parts (including those for boats) also emerged. The region retained an economic link to the past through such industries as industrial oils and paper products, but their shares of the overall economy either did not change or declined.

The real driving force behind the Greater Wilmington economy during the Connected Age is very simple—accessibility to the sun and sand of the Atlantic beaches. After World War II, the area became a vacation site, but growth in the number of aging and affluent baby boomers, combined with improved accessibility provided by the completion of I-40 to Wilmington in 1990, sparked interest in the area that far surpassed anything seen in the past. Wilmington served as a gateway to coastal development stretching from the South Carolina border to North Carolina's Outer Banks.

The region certainly continues to serve as a vacation magnet. In 2005, vacationer spending had an estimated $815 million economic impact, creating eleven thousand jobs.[40] But Greater Wilmington also has increasingly provided people, particularly retirees, with a permanent home. The median age in the region rose from twenty-seven to thirty-eight between 1970 and 2000, the fourth-fastest increase among the regions (table 5-2). Correspondingly, the percentage of the population under age eighteen fell below the state average.[41]

With the region's primary role as a service area meeting the demands of vacationers and retirees, construction, health and education, and personal and leisure services are the leading employment sectors, with percentages above the state average.[42] However, with these jobs comes a lower wage structure than is found in the Triangle and Greater Charlotte.

Two of the region's counties, Bladen and Columbus, do not touch the coast, and perhaps not surprisingly, these two counties have not developed in the same way as their coastal sisters. Employment in Bladen and Columbus counties remains oriented toward traditional industries, particularly agriculture, although food processing has also risen in importance. In fact, the largest pork-processing plant in the world is located in the Bladen County town of Tarheel.[43] A higher percentage of residents of the two counties commute out of their resident county for work than is the case in the rest of the region.[44]

With the retired population still growing and with the expected rapid growth in the number of households with incomes sufficient to afford vacation homes, national and state socioeconomic trends imply that more growth will occur in Greater Wilmington. However, as the limited number of sites at the coast escalate in price, the geographic path of development will likely move inland, following the courses of the region's rivers, creeks, and inlets. This pattern will help those interior counties that have lagged in economic development.

Four factors present challenges for the region. One is this escalation in prices, which will not only drive future growth inward but also push it along the coast away from Wilmington. The Greater Wilmington region now has the fourth-highest costs in the state, up from ninth in 1970 (table 5-2). Out-of-region counties such as Onslow, north of Wilmington, have already experienced rapid building as developers and households seek lower-cost locations. Higher prices can have another downside. During the nationwide real estate bust of 2006, house sales in Greater Wilmington fell by the largest amount of any of the state's metropolitan areas.[45]

The second and third potentially limiting factors are natural in origin—specifically, the threat of hurricanes and of damage to the environment caused by development. The North Carolina coast, including that around Wilmington, is susceptible to hurricanes, and the frequency and severity of these storms appear to have increased since the 1990s.[46] Hurricanes can create not only widespread damage but also long-lasting fears among potential vacationers and residents that can cost the region money.[47] One of the ironies of development around natural amenities is that it can damage the attractions (coastline, inlet, lake) that initially prompted the development. The natural tensions between developers and environmentalists and between short- versus long-run views will play significant roles in how quickly the region can or wants to grow.

The final challenge may take the Greater Wilmington region back full circle to its days as a major seaport. Promoters have proposed the development of the North Carolina International Port in Southport, to be completed between 2014 and 2016. The new port would be one of the largest on the East Coast and could create thousands of jobs. The project's supporters hope that limits on expansion at the competitive ports of Charleston, South Carolina; Savannah, Georgia; and Norfolk, Virginia, will soon bring those facilities to capacity and make them inadequate to handle the expected doubling of cargo traffic on the East Coast between 2005 and 2020. However, before the new port can become a reality, financing for the expected $1 billion cost must be found.[48]

Even if the North Carolina International Port becomes an enormous success, most North Carolinians will still see the Greater Wilmington region as a destination for fun, leisure, and retirement with the added amenities of a good-sized city and a university campus.

Greater Asheville: An Economy in the Clouds

Greater Asheville has been the slowest-running of North Carolina's economic racehorses during the Connected Age, but it has nevertheless posted an impressive performance. Jobs increased 105 percent between 1970 and 2004, seventh-fastest among the state's twenty-one regions, and GLP climbed 35 percent between 1990 and 2004.

Asheville, the central city of the region, has the largest population in the western third of North Carolina. Known as the Paris of the South because of its strong regional culture and art community, Asheville's temperate climate has drawn people seeking rest and relaxation since the nineteenth century.[49] The world-renowned Biltmore House, the largest private home in the United States, attracted some of the world's finest artisans and craftsmen to the region, and many stayed in the area to establish businesses that bolstered Asheville's reputation as a crafts capital.

During the twentieth century, traditional North Carolina industries such as textiles, apparel, and paper mills also became leading sectors. But personal service industries such as medicine, education, restaurants, and banking clearly dominated the regional economy, accounting for one-third of total employment in 1990.[50] The importance of these enterprises grew during the Connected Age. In 2004, eight of Greater Asheville's top ten economic sectors fell into the personal services or trade category (table D-4). Between 1990 and 2004, the relative importance of textiles and apparel to the region dropped by almost two-thirds, and the paper industry was reduced by more than half.

Like Greater Wilmington, its sister economy, Greater Asheville added a third function, serving as a permanent residence for retirees and as a location for second homes, to its roles as tourist destination and as regional trade center. In 2004, real estate and construction accounted for more than 9 percent of GLP, the seventh-highest share among all North Carolina regions and a rate higher than Greater Asheville's 1990 share. In 2000, the median age of Greater Asheville's residents was forty-one, five years higher than the state average and the second-highest among all regions. Greater Asheville's household in-migration rate for 2000 also came in well above the state average.[51]

Greater Asheville, therefore, is the mountain version of Greater Wilmington. Both regions have turned the demographic trends of the Connected Age into growth and prosperity. Yet the reliance on personal service jobs has a downside for workers. Real salaries in Greater Asheville rose at the second-slowest rate among all regions between 1970 and 2004. Only 7 percent of the region's 2004 jobs fell into the higher-paying finance and professional services sector, although this number had risen from 6 percent in 1990.[52]

While the region wants to retain its attractiveness to tourists, officials seek to diversify into other industries. The vehicle parts sector has a significant presence in the region, and local leaders would like to add firms and jobs in fields such as metalworking, optics, and forensic sciences.[53] Of course, these positions will require suitably trained workers. Asheville has a University of North Carolina campus, but it is primarily a four-year liberal arts school and has only thirty-three hundred students. The community college at Asheville graduates another six hundred students annually.[54] The region would need to bolster opportunities to train the labor force in specialties necessary to attract technology and durable manufacturing firms.

Leaders tout "MetaPop" (Major Port of Presence on the Internet) as having the potential to spur non-tourist-related development in the area. This federally funded project will bring fiber-optic cable high-speed Internet access to western North Carolina and link it directly to Washington, D.C.[55] This information superhighway will make Greater Asheville more attractive for technology firms and workers who value the region's climate and beauty.

Thus arises an inevitable conflict between growth and preservation. For regions such as Greater Asheville and Greater Wilmington that have developed largely as a result of their natural assets, growth implies some destruction or at least alteration of those assets. Defining the limits between growth that preserves the integrity of the natural assets and growth that ultimately is detrimental to the region's uniqueness and attractiveness perhaps constitutes Greater Asheville's greatest challenge.

The Racehorse Regions: Summary

The immediate future looks bright for each of the four racehorse regional economies, which in 2004 collectively accounted for 52 percent of the gross state product and 48 percent of the state's employment. The Triangle endured a setback with the tech bust of the late 1990s, but it has retrenched and is now diversifying into financial services. Still, its primary asset is its technology-oriented universities and the graduates they produce. The Triangle will remain a national center of research and development and health care. It has the physical room to grow, but it also faces the task of providing adequate public infrastructure to facilitate this growth.

The Greater Charlotte racehorse has been hitched to financial services, and as that sector soared, so did the regional economy. The region has felt some pains related to the downsizing of its textile and apparel component, but the positive spillover from financial services, combined with the area's continuing function as a warehousing and transportation hub, has put the region on the list of the country's top metropolitan areas. Greater Charlotte is trying to expand its relatively small technology sector, and like the Triangle, it must build schools and transportation facilities fast enough to prevent infrastructure shortcomings from limiting expansion.

Whereas the Triangle and Greater Charlotte's success is based on human assets (educated workers) and physical assets (universities, banks, airports), Greater Wilmington and Greater Asheville's assets are natural—sun, sand, and mountains. Consequently, their economies are tied to sectors that sell those assets to tourists, owners of vacation homes, and retirees. Two trends during the Connected Age—the increase in the retired population and the increase in both the number and income of upper-income households—have thus benefited these two economies. If these trends persist as expected, they will continue to stimulate growth in these two racehorse economies. The trick will be growing in a form and at a pace that preserves the natural beauty that originally attracted people. In addition, the regions' focus on tourism and personal services has resulted in salaries lower than those in the Triangle and Greater Charlotte. Greater Wilmington and Greater Asheville's goal of boosting salaries by adding professional and technology jobs will require support from educational institutions.

The racehorse regions thus promise continued growth during the Connected Age. But all residents do not view this promise in a positive light. Traffic congestion, crowded schools, and depletion of open space have spawned groups questioning growth in both the Triangle and Greater Charlotte. In Greater Wilmington and Greater Asheville, organizations concerned about preserving the natural environment have proposed stricter codes and requirements for development and in some cases outright limitations.[56] The outcome of these battles will greatly impact the future speeds of North Carolina's racehorse economies.

Small City, New Economy Regions: The Little Tigers

Greater Boone, the Northeast, and the Midcoast regions are the "little tigers" of the North Carolina economy, so called because although they are relatively small by the standards of the racehorse regions, their economies have benefited and grown significantly during the Connected Age.[57]

The three regions are tied by more than their size and growth. They have also been little affected by the downsizing in North Carolina's traditional economy because their links to that economy have been relatively small. But their greatest similarity lies in the common factor pushing their growth—tourism, second-home, and retirement development. In this way and in the issues they face, the three little tigers resemble their racehorse cousins, Greater Wilmington and Greater Asheville.

Greater Boone: Mountain Playground

The two-county Greater Boone region has an economy firmly planted in fun. When North Carolinians think of skiing in the winter or hiking in the summer, they think of Boone and the nearby communities of Blowing Rock and Banner Elk. In 2004, tourist-related industries such as restaurants, amusements and recreation, and hotels directly accounted for more than 10 percent of Greater Boone's GLP, the highest of any region in the state (table D-5).

The Greater Boone region had the second-fastest employment gain among all regions from 1970 to 2004. The biggest change between 1990 and 2004 in the region's economic composition was the elevation in the relative importance of education. Education's real output tripled between 1990 and 2004, and its share of the regional economy almost doubled from 8.5 percent to 15.4 percent as a consequence of the expansion of Appalachian State University, where enrollment rose 23 percent over the period.[58] Other major changes included the downsizing of textiles and apparel in the region and the growth of the banking and amusement and recreation industries. But the Greater Boone economy essentially has remained the same, based on the enjoyment of the natural beauty and wonders of the North Carolina mountains.

The building boom has not hit Greater Boone as it has other regions. While real estate and construction are important to the regional economy, the annual value of the sector changed modestly between 1990 and 2004, and its relative contribution actually declined, perhaps as a result of the harsher winter climate and more challenging terrain relative to Greater Asheville. As a result, Greater Boone has retained more of its small-town feel than has Asheville or Wilmington.

With its dependence on tourism, the regional economy has moved with the costs of and preferences for travel. For example, in the year after the 9/11 attacks, Greater Boone's regional personal income grew at a rate 96 percent slower than in the state as a whole. However, in the succeeding three years, travel and tourism rebounded, and the region's personal income grew at a rate comparable to that for the state.[59]

The tourism and vacation home industries have certainly been good to Greater Boone, but any region so closely tied to one industry seeks to diversify, if only to provide a cushion for the times when the key industry is down. Greater Boone has a small electronic components manufacturing sector, but its real output and relative share declined from 1990 to 2004. Nevertheless, the presence of Appalachian State University is a major asset for the region. The campus provides the training and intellectual stimulation that may be attractive to small, footloose technology firms that desire a location offering a wonderland in the winter and a cool, crisp respite during the summer.

Northeast: Fields and Frames

Tucked away in a corner of the state, the counties of the Northeast region are easy to overlook with so much attention focused on the powerhouses of the Triangle and Greater Charlotte. Indeed, the region's economy is relatively small, with a GLP of only $2 billion in 2004, less than 1 percent of the state total and fifth-smallest among the twenty-one regions. In 1990, the leading economic sector, after retail trade, was processed peanuts, and land-based enterprises such as farming and logging, together with federal military and nonmilitary spending and various kinds of personal services, composed almost the entire economy (table D-6).[60]

Yet within two decades, the Northeast economy came alive. Education and real estate and construction replaced retail trade and peanuts as the top two regional sectors, with output that tripled between 1990 and 2004 and shares of GLP that doubled. Federal government expenditures and personal services fell in the middle of the industry ranking, and land-based sectors brought up the rear.

Two changes transformed the Northeast economy. First, the University of North Carolina campus in the region, at Elizabeth City, expanded its student body by 44 percent, taking advantage of the Connected Age's heightened emphasis on higher education.[61] Second, tourists, retirees, and second-home owners discovered the region. Water sites abound in northeastern North Carolina, which includes the northern section of the Outer Banks and fronts the Atlantic Ocean on that side, has the wide and deep Albemarle Sound with its numerous inlets and river mouths on the south, and has the wide Chowan River to the west. Only the northern edge of the region is landlocked. With water sites so plentiful and varied, the area naturally became a destination for households seeking waterfront homes or vacation sites. The development of Currituck County, the region's easternmost county, which includes the Outer Banks, best illustrates this process. The county's population swelled 60 percent, twice as fast as the regional rate, between 1990 and 2004, and its stock of housing units jumped 45 percent between 1990 and 2000.[62]

One unique aspect of the Northeast region is its economic links to an out-of-state economy, the Norfolk/Chesapeake/Hampton Roads metropolitan area. Downtown Norfolk is only forty miles from Elizabeth City (the region's largest city), and one in six of the region's workers commute out of the region for work.[63] Hence, a major part of the region's economic fate is directly tied to the Norfolk/Chesapeake/Hampton Roads economy. Since the leading economic sector in the region is shipbuilding, particularly for the U.S. Navy, the prospects for immediate employment in the region will be strongly influenced by the federal defense budget. But salaries paid will not move up the ladder until educational attainment in the region, which in 2000 ranked fourteenth out of the twenty-one regions in college graduates and was 40 percent lower than the national average, improves.

If the market for alternative fuels takes off, the region's agricultural economy, which includes oilseed crops and grains, could benefit. Over the longer run, however, the region's economy will continue to develop around tourism and destinations for permanent retirees and second-home owners. As ocean and sound sites increase in cost, development will move westward along the area's sounds, rivers, and inlets, the so-called Inner Banks. The region's relatively modest cost of living and access to large population centers in Norfolk/Chesapeake/Hampton Roads; Washington, D.C.; and even Baltimore and Philadelphia will likely increase the rate at which housing frames replace open fields.[64]

Midcoast: From First Colony to First Flight to First Resort

North Carolina's Midcoast region has a history of being first and famous. The first colony was on the region's Roanoke Island. The Wright Brothers made the nation's first flight on the region's Outer Banks at Kitty Hawk. The country's tallest and perhaps most famous lighthouse also sits on the region's Outer Banks at Cape Hatteras.

What was said about the Northeast region can be also be said about the Midcoast except that the process has progressed at least a decade further. Bounded on three sides by water, the Midcoast region has more coastline than any other area in North Carolina. Most of the state's Outer Banks lie in the Midcoast region, and this stretch is the best known. Tourism, second homes, and retirement living move the economy, and the region has the state's fourth-highest median age of residents (table 5-2).

In 1990, the region's most important sectors were real estate and construction, trade, textiles and apparel, and a mix of wood-based and small manufacturing firms (table D-7). In 2004, the real estate and construction and trade industries pulled away from the rest, with the first sector alone accounting for almost 20 percent of regional GLP, the highest for any region. Also like the Northeast, the region's easternmost county, Dare, bordering the Atlantic Ocean, is the most prominent and has had the greatest development, while those inland to the west have more of a presence in agriculture, forestry, and small manufacturing.

In fact, the geographic divide between Dare and the region's five other counties is perhaps the widest of any region. Dare accounted for more than 40 percent of regional GLP in 2004, and the county's population grew 373 percent from 1970 to 2004. The next-fastest county population growth rate in the region was 28 percent, and three counties experienced virtually no change in population or lost population over the period.[65] For many tourists and part-time residents, the majority of the region is drive-through country on the way to the beach.

Yet circumstances may change in the future. Limited sites and high prices have already pushed the focus of new development off the region's coast and to its Inner Banks, a trend that will likely continue. Upscale residential communities have sprung up near the historic towns of Bath and Washington. Increased accessibility to I-95 and to the Triangle region via the interstate-quality state route 64 will continue to make the Midcoast region a beacon for households seeking rest and relaxation and possibly for telecommuters who desire water-based lifestyles. Of course, one continuing threat is that posed by hurricanes, as Hurricane Floyd demonstrated.[66]

The Little Tigers: Summary

The little tigers have grown as a result of their natural endowments—mountain air, scenery, and slopes in the case of Greater Boone and water and water-accessible home sites in the case of the Northeast and Midcoast. As long as increases continue in both the number of households and the income of those households whose residents like these natural endowments and want to visit or live in the regions, the little tigers should grow and expand their relative importance in the state economy.

But as the little tigers mature, they will face three important hurdles. One is relatively low incomes. Leisure service industry and supporting jobs tend to pay low salaries, and the average salaries of the little tigers are well below those of their racehorse cousins. Incomes may improve, however, in two ways. First, the regions may experience increases in the share of professional jobs as financial, medical, and other high-skill occupations are added to serve the increasingly important permanent retiree population. Second, the enhanced ability of many professionals to work remotely may open up the regions to more permanent residents with higher-paying occupations. The Greater Boone and Northeast regions, with their University of North Carolina campuses, may be particularly adaptable for this change.

The second issue concerns primarily the Northeast and Midcoast regions. Strong development and growth in these regions have been concentrated in coastal counties, and the economic pace has been slower inland. Time may even out this pattern, as the economies of resort and community development push future growth to less expensive sites. Nonetheless, a have/have-not separation will continue in the regions for many years.

Finally comes the potential clash between preservation and development, an issue explored in the section on Greater Wilmington. More beachfront homes increase the chances of erosion. More communities along sounds and inlets increase the chances of water pollution. More mountainside dwellings take away from the views of ridges and tree lines. The balance between preservation and development will be hard to find.

Rural, New Economy Regions: A Rebound for Real?

Few observers would guess that two of North Carolina's fastest-growing regions from 1970 to 2004 were the two regions in the far western corner of the state, the Highlands region and the Far West region. Yet these areas averaged population growth of 65 percent and employment growth of 150 percent during the period. Furthermore, the regions gained four new economy firms for every old economy firm lost.

The Highlands and Far West regions are tiny, with a combined 2004 GLP of only $2.6 billion, in part because national and state forests occupy almost half of their land mass.[67] The areas are mountainous and heavily forested, so large tracts are not available for industrial operations. In spite of these limitations, the regions posted impressive economic gains during the Connected Age. What did they do to cause such a revival, and is it for real?

Highlands: High Rollers and Higher Ed

In the nineteenth and early twentieth centuries, wealthy families from Charleston, South Carolina, traveled to the Highlands region to escape the summer heat and to enjoy resorts and hot springs.[68] Now, in the twenty-first century, visitors are returning for another form of recreation and relaxation — gambling. The region includes the largest Native American reservation in the state, that of the Cherokee tribe. In 1988, the U.S. Congress passed the Indian Gaming Act, which legalized gambling on reservations. Within a decade, the Cherokees established legal gambling operations on their land and hired Harrah's to operate a casino. In 2002, a multimillion-dollar conference center and hotel were constructed, and in 2005, a second resort hotel was added.[69] The casino industry alone accounted for 2.4 percent of the Highlands region's GLP in 2004, and its total impact through the lodging, restaurant, and retail trade sectors was even bigger.[70]

The Highlands region also includes Western Carolina University at Cullowhee, a campus of the University of North Carolina system, which grew from 5,125 students in 1970 to 8,396 students in 2004, a 64 percent increase.[71] In 2004, education accounted for more than 20 percent of the Highlands' GLP, more than double the share in 1990 and the highest rate for education among all the North Carolina regions (table D-8). The Highlands region also has the highest ratio of university students to population.[72] Western Carolina attracts students from across all of North Carolina as well as Tennessee and Georgia. Real estate and construction, retail trade, and personal service industries comprise the rest of the top sectors in the region. In addition to gambling and education, visitors are attracted to the region's public forests for hiking and camping and to the twenty-nine-mile-long, 11,700-acre Fontana Lake for water recreation.[73]

Without the growth of higher education and the emergence of the gambling industry, the Highlands region clearly would not have experienced such strong growth during the Connected Age. In the early part of the era, the region had a major presence in textiles and apparel, fertilizers, and paperboard mills, with these three industries collectively accounting for just under one-fifth of GLP in 1990. By 2004, only paperboard mills remained among the top fifteen regional industries, with less than a 1 percent share of GLP. Books and dice came to the rescue.

Far West: Atlanta Calling?

Residents of the Far West region can drive to Atlanta in half the time it takes to reach the North Carolina state capital, Raleigh. Atlanta Braves baseball is as frequently mentioned as the University of North Carolina Tarheels, North Carolina State Wolfpack, and Duke Blue Devils. People of the Far West often look south to Georgia rather than east to their fellow North Carolinians for directions to their economic future.

Like their partners in the Highlands region, the Far West economy was led as recently as 1990 by the traditional industries of textiles and apparel and furniture and by land-based sectors such as minerals and poultry, with a little light machinery production thrown in. These industries saw dramatic reductions in both their absolute and relative values by 2004. What was missing, however, was a significant replacement for these sectors. Although the region's growth numbers look good for 1970–2004, from 1990 to 2004 GLP stagnated and employment grew 40 percent slower than in the neighboring Highlands region (table D-9). The region's residents have also consistently been the oldest in the state, with the highest median age in both 1970 and 2004 (table 5-2).

A Rebound for Real?: Summary

Although the economic growth numbers look good for the Highlands and Far West regions during the entirety of the Connected Age, problems lurk beneath the surface. Education levels and salaries are low.[74] Moreover, the casino industry has become very competitive—direct employment from the casino and gambling industry grew 78 percent nationwide from 1990 to 2005—so continued growth in that arena is by no means assured.[75] In 2006, North Carolina instituted a state lottery, which will compete for gaming dollars. On the positive side, Western Carolina University is forecast to add eighteen hundred students between 2004 and 2012.[76] However, even the growth that has occurred in the region has sparked controversies over affordable housing, historic compatibility, and environmental impact.[77]

The regions may take advantage of their accessibility to Atlanta by comparing their pluses—low costs, a slower pace, natural beauty—to Atlanta's minuses of congestion, high density, and concrete. This contrast may attract selected firms and individuals who need to be close to but not in Atlanta. Indeed, the 1-575 corridor between Atlanta and western North Carolina has been one of the Atlanta market's fastest-growing areas.[78] But locked in by public forests and rugged terrain, the Highlands and Far West regions are unlikely to expand much beyond their niches of higher education and legalized gambling.

Urban, Transitional Regions: Twilight or Daybreak?

The four areas comprising the urban transitional regions have all had their day in the sun. Greater Winston-Salem was once the richest region in North Carolina as a center of banking and cigarette manufacturing. Greater Greensboro, adjacent to Greater Winston-Salem in the Piedmont Triad, specialized in textiles, apparel, and furniture and was for most of the twentieth century the second-largest region in the state. Likewise, the Sandhills, with its capital of Fayetteville, and Greater Gaston, just west of Charlotte, featured North Carolina's booming traditional industries.

With the downsizing of the traditional economy, the Connected Age has brought challenges and questions to these regions. If textiles, tobacco, furniture, and apparel are out, what is in? Can the regions attract sufficient jobs, with adequate pay, to continue growing and prospering? Are these urban regions in their twilight, or is a new economic era dawning?

Greater Winston-Salem: From Joe Camel to Michael Dell

During much of the twentieth century, the Greater Winston-Salem region was the cigarette capital of the world. The second-largest cigarette manufacturer in the world, R. J. Reynolds, was headquartered here, and a cigarette brand was named after each half of the region's name. Cigarette manufacturing alone accounted for 37 percent of the region's GLP in 1990, and textiles and apparel added another 5 percent (table D-10).

Not surprisingly, then, the region has been strained during the Connected Age. With cigarette, textile, and apparel production in decline, the region grew much more slowly than its urban cousins in the Triangle and Greater Charlotte (table 5-1). Real estate and construction, usually correlated with growth, also made subpar contributions to GLP. In 2004, cigarette production remained the leading sector, accounting for 27 percent of GLP, but this figure represented a 10 percentage point drop in tobacco's share, and the real value of cigarette production also fell. Both textile and apparel production and GLP share also dropped by one-third from 1990 to 2004.

The region was helped by the rise of banking in North Carolina. Despite the loss of the Wachovia Bank headquarters to Charlotte, the banking sector's share of GLP expanded from 2 percent in 1990 to almost 6 percent in 2004, giving Greater Winston-Salem the second-highest regional share in this sector, behind only Greater Charlotte.[79] The region is also a center for motor freight and warehousing and for air transportation, but these sectors showed little growth between 1990 and 2004.

With cigarette production as well as textile and apparel output expected to continue declining, the big question for Greater Winston-Salem is what will replace them. In 1994, perhaps the first step in answering this question came with the establishment of the Piedmont Triad Research Park. Conceived as a center for biomedical and information technology research and development, the park has progressed slowly and was taken over by Wake Forest University in 2002.[80] The second step came in 2004 when a leading computer manufacturer, Dell, announced that it would build an assembly plant in the region and would eventually employ up to fifteen hundred workers. Impact studies indicated that as many as six thousand additional jobs could be added at supplier and related firms. Although welcome news for Greater Winston-Salem, the Dell plant created considerable controversy because it involved public financial incentives potentially worth more than $200 million.[81]

The region is trying to attract new businesses in the technology, engineering, and medical fields and has many assets in pursuing this goal. First, the region is astride or near four interstate highways (I-40, I-77, I-74, and I-85), and it has easy accessibility to the Piedmont Triad International Airport— thus, transportation is a plus. Second, the region has an available labor supply, especially compared to a fast-growing region such as the Triangle. The unemployment rate in Greater Winston-Salem is typically 0.5 to 1.0 percentage points higher than the Triangle rate.[82] Third, the labor force is reasonably well trained, and excellent higher education facilities are available. The proportion of college graduates in Greater Winston-Salem is higher than the state average and ranks fifth among the regions, although the rate is slightly below the national average (table 5-2). The region is home to Wake Forest University, which offers graduate programs in all the science and technology fields, along with Winston-Salem State University and Central Carolina Community College. Fourth, costs are lower in Greater Winston-Salem. Building costs are among the lowest in the Southeast, and the cost of living is significantly less than those in the Triangle and Greater Charlotte.[83]

But are these positives strong enough for Winston-Salem to establish a core presence in technology that will mushroom into an authentic sector? Is Dell a dead-end street or the beginning of a superhighway?

Greater Greensboro: Attempting a Lift-Off

Greater Greensboro is the urbanized region in North Carolina that most represented the state's traditional manufacturing economy. Cigarette production, furniture manufacturing, and textile and apparel factories and mills were significant industries in the region in the twentieth century. The three sectors accounted for just short of 20 percent of the region's GLP in 1990 (table D-11). Anyone who wanted to see what kind of manufacturing typically drove North Carolina would go to Greater Greensboro.

Of course, as with its twin region, Greater Winston-Salem, Greater Greensboro's economy changed dramatically during the Connected Age. In 2004, cigarettes, furniture, and textiles and apparel collectively accounted for only 8 percent of GLP. Even the famous Furniture Market, held annually in the region's city of High Point, is in jeopardy of being spirited away to Las Vegas.[84]

Thus, Greensboro faces the same question as Winston-Salem: what now? The two cities have similar advantages—interstate highways, an international airport, available and skilled labor, institutions of higher education, and relatively low costs. Can Greensboro compete for technology and related companies with the racehorses of the Triangle and Greater Charlotte or even with Winston-Salem, or should it find another way?

Greensboro appears to be blazing its own path by emphasizing industrial manufacturing and air cargo. The vehicle parts sector, not even on the region's industrial list in 1990, was among its top fifteen sectors in 2004. In 2007, the Honda Aircraft Company announced that it would build a multimillion-dollar jet manufacturing factory in the region, with initial production due in 2010 as well as a complementary jet engine factory.[85]

But the biggest economic news for the region occurred in 1998, when FedEx selected Greater Greensboro for a $300 million air cargo and package sorting hub to serve the East Coast. With the opening expected in 2009, the fully operational hub could result in as many as sixteen thousand direct and spin-off jobs and could have a multi-billion-dollar impact on the regional economy.[86] Regional leaders hope that these developments will take Greater Greensboro out of its downward spin and move it to new heights. The question is whether enough new economy jobs can be created to offset the losses from the old standbys.

Sandhills: The Cavalry to the Rescue

One of the most important years in the economic history of the Sandhills regional economy was 1918, when the U.S. Army established Fort Bragg as an artillery training post for World War I soldiers. In the next year, Pope Field (later Pope Air Force Base), was created, and ever since, the economy of the Sandhills has been joined to the U.S. military. The combined Fort Bragg/Pope Air Force Base complex is one of the largest and busiest military installations in the world.[87]

The dominance of the military and military spending in the region can easily be seen in its economic profile (table D-12). In 1990, military spending directly accounted for 20 percent of GLP, a number that does not take into account spending at retail stores, restaurants, hospitals, and other consumer services linked to military personnel and their families.[88] In 2004, the direct impact of the military had increased to almost 24 percent.

The Sandhills, however, is in transition because of other sectors that have been important to its economy. As a region with ample supplies of relatively inexpensive labor, the Sandhills historically attracted textile and apparel firms, and mills and factories peppered the landscape. In 1970, at least one-fifth of regional employment was in textiles and apparel, and even in 1990 the two industries accounted for just under 10 percent of GLP.[89] Of course, as textiles and apparel have declined in relative importance during the Connected Age, both their output and employment in the Sandhills plunged. By 2004, only 2.5 percent of GLP and 11 percent of employment remained in these once-dominant industries.[90]

So does the future look bleak for the Sandhills? Not necessarily, again because of the military. Although the United States has reduced the number of military installations it operates, the resulting geographic reorganization of functions and training has helped the bases in the Sandhills. The recommendations of the 2005 Base Realignment and Closure (BRAC) Commission will result in an additional twenty thousand military personnel, civilian workers, and family members at Fort Bragg through 2015, although a small number of personnel will be lost when Fort Bragg absorbs Pope Air Force Base as Pope Army Air Field.[91]

The region's increased military presence, combined with the changing needs of modern armed forces, may help revive and reshape the local textile and apparel industry. The fabrics and clothing used by today's military have gone high tech, requiring uniforms resistant to both heat and cold as well as incorporating needs for communication, visibility, and stealth. North Carolina's textile and apparel firms are well suited to both develop and manufacture these products. In addition, a large local military will mean more opportunities for supplies of various products and services to the bases.

Discharged and retired military personnel can also be a resource for economic development in the Sandhills. These ex-military workers often possess valuable technical and sophisticated skills that have high value in the private sector. If they remain in the Sandhills area after their military service, they can attract a wide variety of companies from several economic sectors. The region also has a presence in transportation-related manufacturing, including tires and inner tubes and vehicle parts.

Of course, like every transitional region in North Carolina, education is an issue. The percentage of regional workers with college degrees is 35 percent below the state average and less than half the rate in the Triangle (table 5-2). The region has a campus of the University of North Carolina system, Fayetteville State University, but it has few technical and science graduates and virtually no graduate programs outside of education.[92] The region's best bet is to target small manufacturers of durable goods, especially those that value access to military buyers.

The Sandhills economy has one other positive feature. Most of North Carolina's regions that have been attractive to retirees are on the coast or in the mountains. The exception is the Sandhills. Large retirement communities exist near Fayetteville, Pinehurst, and Southern Pines. Many of the retirees — a large number of whom are former military — take advantage of the region's world-class golf courses and of its equine facilities, both of which are helped by the region's sandy soil. Keeping and attracting financially secure retirees is certainly an important economic development goal for the Sandhills.

At base, however, the near-term future of the Sandhills economy will rise or fall with the U.S. military. To date, the boost in the military presence has been an important offset to the decline in traditional industries, primarily in textiles and apparel. But with such a large part of the economy riding on one sector, especially a sector where decisions are made outside the region, the Sandhills economy will remain at risk for a major setback.

Greater Gaston: Ground Zero for Industrial Flux

Few regions in North Carolina have experienced the downside of the Connected Age like Greater Gaston. In 1970, an amazing two-thirds of the workforce was employed in manufacturing; in 2004, this number had fallen to less than one-quarter.[93] At one time, Gaston County, the most populous in the region, had more cotton mills than any other county in the country.[94] In 1990, textiles and apparel accounted for almost 16 percent of Greater Gaston's GLP, but only fourteen years later, their share had dropped to less than 6 percent (table D-13). In no other region of North Carolina was the loss of textile and apparel output between 1990 and 2004 as great as in Greater Gaston.[95]

On the upside, Greater Gaston borders South Carolina, where several vehicle assembly and related plants were established in the 1980s and 1990s. The number of firms manufacturing vehicle bodies and parts in the Greater Gaston region increased from four to twenty between 1970 and 2004.[96] As a share of GLP, this sector reached 5 percent during the Connected Age, the highest for any North Carolina region.

Still, transportation manufacturing has not replaced textiles and apparel. Both total GLP and total regional employment dropped between 1990 and 2004. The region was the only one with a reduction in GLP and one of only two with a drop in employment. With its tradition in textiles and apparel, the region suffers from low educational attainment and limited higher-educational facilities.[97]

So what can be done? Like other urban regions in transition, Greater Gaston has the benefits of an available labor force and relatively low costs. It can thus be attractive not only for transportation manufacturing but also for light manufacturing in plastics, small and household equipment, and metal fabrication.[98] Local economic developers will need to work with community colleges in neighboring Greater Asheville and Greater Charlotte to provide customized training for prospective employers.

Perhaps the most exciting opportunity for Greater Gaston will be in food processing. In 2005 a subsidiary of Dole announced plans to build and equip a vegetable-processing plant that will create nine hundred jobs by 2016.[99] The plant will partner with the biotechnology complex being developed in Cabarrus County (Greater Charlotte region). An industrial renaissance in the Greater Gaston region would be welcomed not only by its residents but also by the entire state.

Twilight or Daybreak?: Summary

The urban transitional regions in North Carolina share a common origin. They staked their claim to the traditional North Carolina economy in the twentieth century, and they have fallen on hard times in the Connected Age as the state's traditional industries moved to the rear of the economic stage. Each of the regions retains advantages in available labor, cost, and infrastructure, but the pace at which they can transform their economies is painstakingly slow and uneven. In addition, they must compete against regions that through luck or foresight have the characteristics to create momentum in the Connected Age.

Each of the four urban transitional regions has chosen a different path for its revival—technology in Greater Winston-Salem, air transport in Greater Greensboro, the military in the Sandhills, and food processing and vehicle parts in Greater Gaston. The regions may not catch up to the racehorses in the short term, but they are working to get out of the starting gate.

Small-City, Transitional Regions: The Little Engines That Try

Like the urban transitional regions, small-city, transitional regions had their economies tied to traditional industries prior to the Connected Age, but the downsizing of these sectors since 1970 has brought economic stress, and these regions are working to attract new industries to carry them through the twenty-first century. Their smallness, however, puts the transitional regions at a disadvantage relative to their urban counterparts because they lack the size and diversity to support a large array of economic specialties.

But each of the small-city, transitional regions has distinct advantages, and they are using those advantages in different ways to cope with economic change. The regions have used varied strategies and focused on different sectors in their approach to the Connected Age. Is this a case of different shoes for different feet, or will some regions find that their feet remain stuck in the economic mud?

Foothills: Another Miracle in the Making?

In 1944, the city of Hickory, the largest in the Foothills region, experienced what has come to be known as the Miracle of Hickory. A horrific outbreak of polio occurred, and afflicted patients overwhelmed hospitals in nearby cities. Hickory was too small for a hospital, but the enormity of the catastrophe prompted local residents to take matters in their own hands and construct a treatment facility in a mere fifty-four hours. The speed with which the building took place—the miracle—was credited with saving hundreds of lives.[100]

The Foothills region is trying to replicate the Miracle of Hickory in an economic way. In the twentieth century, the area was the center of furniture manufacturing in North Carolina—indeed, in the entire country. In 1970, one-third of the state's furniture factory jobs were in the region.[101] In 1990, furniture manufacturing accounted for almost 15 percent of GLP, more than four times furniture's share in Greater Greensboro, and furniture output was 50 percent higher than in Greater Greensboro (table D-14). Textiles and apparel production was the second-most important regional industry in 1990 (8.5 percent of GLP), and no other manufacturing sector was close. But from 1990 to 2004, the Foothills lost more than a third of its furniture and textile and apparel jobs, and the GLP shares held by furniture and by textiles and apparel were cut in half.[102]

The second miracle is that the region survived. Development came from an unlikely source—the tech sector. Using available labor from downsizing traditional industries, cooperative training programs from the local community college (Catawba Valley Community College), and abundant natural and energy resources, the region attracted investment from the burgeoning technology sector as early as the 1980s. In 1990, the sector accounted for 2.6 percent of GLP, and by 2000 the share had grown to 5 percent. In that year, 9 percent of the region's manufacturing workers were employed in the technology sector.[103]

Then came the technology bust, and what had been a positive for the Foothills economy turned into a big negative. Between 2000 and 2003, forty-six hundred technology jobs were cut (62 percent of the 2000 total), and the regional unemployment rate soared from 3 percent to 8 percent.[104] Some recovery occurred through the middle part of the decade, but in 2007 the regional unemployment rate remained above the state average.[105]

But the miracle may not be over. The Hickory Metro Higher Ed Center was established in the early twenty-first century to give greater focus to local skills development. Then in 2007, Google, the huge Internet search engine company, said that it would build a $600 million center in the Foothills town of Lenoir. The 215-acre facility will house thousands of computer servers and directly employ between 75 and 125 workers at almost twice the average regional salary. Google will remodel abandoned existing facilities and tap into local electricity and water resources developed for the furniture industry.[106] Regional leaders hope that this investment, combined with the high-speed

MetaPop from western North Carolina, will reconfirm the Foothills as a welcoming and logical place for technology companies.

The Foothills strategy is to turn human, physical, and energy resources, together with lower costs, into economic development. With both energy supplies and costs becoming more limiting industrial factors, the Foothills hold an advantage. Moreover, unlike some of its sister transitional regions, the Foothills can already point to success in implementing its strategy. Local leaders hope that success breeds success and that the miracle lives on.

Greenville-Jacksonville: Investing in Bullets and Bandages

Sometimes public decisions, made by political officials, can be more important to a local area's economic development than the choices made by private companies and individuals. Such is the case for the Greenville-Jacksonville region. In its history, three dates associated with important publicly made decisions stand out: 1792, 1941, and 1974. In 1792, legislators of the State of North Carolina, in the newly independent United States of America, moved the state capital from the regional city of New Bern to Raleigh. In 1941, the U.S. Navy Department established a marine base at the coastal regional town of Jacksonville. And in 1974, the North Carolina General Assembly appropriated funds to form a medical school on the campus of East Carolina University (ECU) in the region's largest city, Greenville.[107]

The movement of the state capital adversely affected the Greenville-Jacksonville region for obvious reasons. If the capital had remained at New Bern, the region would have been home to thousands of state employees, thousands of additional private-sector workers who benefit from being near the site of state government, and all the income and spending associated with both groups. The region would have become the center of the state's political power.

But the other two public decisions helped the region and established the core of the area's modern economy. During the Connected Age, military spending has consistently accounted for more than 20 percent of GLP (table D-15), a share second only to that in the Sandhills. Like Fort Bragg in the Sandhills, the Greenville-Jacksonville region's Camp Lejeune has escaped major reductions from the reorganization of military bases in the country, although the 2005 BRAC recommendations will result in a modest reduction in military and civilian personnel.[108] However, President George W. Bush's call for a 15 percent increase in the number of U.S. Army and Marine Corps soldiers between 2007 and 2012 should, if enacted, mean increased economic activity at Camp Lejeune.[109] The complementary Marine Corps Air Station at Cherry

Point is located near the town of Havelock.[110] Military spending from the two bases provides a steady stream of relatively reliable commercial activity for the region, although most of the associated private-sector jobs are in the lower-paid consumer and personal services sectors.

ECU's Brody Medical School, together with the university's other programs, has made education the second-most important economic sector in the Greenville-Jacksonville region. Education's share of GLP more than doubled between 1990 and 2004, when the sector's share stood at 10 percent. ECU has several professional and graduate degree programs, but the medical school stands out as the state's only medical school not located in the urbanized central Piedmont region.[111] ECU's medical school likely bears responsibility for the fact that the pharmaceutical industry has become the ninth-most important economic sector (by output) in the region. Most important, the expected growth in health care and medical research and development means that medicine and education will be major drivers of the Greenville-Jacksonville economy for decades to come.

Without the investments in the military and education, the Greenville-Jacksonville economy would be in trouble. Its coastal counties have and will continue to have investments in tourism, second homes, and retirement communities. Carteret County is home to the famed Crystal Coast, the coastal areas of Onslow County are benefiting from development moving north from Wilmington, and Pamlico and Craven Counties are part of the Inner Banks development. However, the economies of the region's landlocked counties have been based on traditional industries such as tobacco, textiles and apparel, paper products, and pulp mills.[112] The region's transition to the new economy of the Connected Age has been difficult enough with the presence of the strong military and education sectors. Without them, such a transition would have been virtually impossible.

For the foreseeable future, the education/military complex will be the mover in the Greenville-Jacksonville regional economy. Likely increases in medical treatment and research at the Brody School of Medicine will spin off private-sector jobs and collaborations in research and development and private treatment and care. A new dental school at ECU has also been approved.[113] Similarly, an increased military presence will require more private-sector support in everything from housing to food service to durable consumer goods. As in the Sandhills, opportunities may exist for niche developments in textiles and apparel. Also, as the region's coastal areas expand, retired military personnel may choose to remain. Specialty manufacturing, again related to military or medical needs, can also serve as a regional growth sector. Occupations requiring more training and education will command higher salaries, so the region should continue to focus on improving its k–12 facilities as well as increasing opportunities for advanced training at ecu and Pitt Community College.

Rocky Mount–Wilson: Too Far, Too Close, or Just Right?

A look at the map would suggest that the Rocky Mount–Wilson region has some big advantages. It sits midway between the racehorse Triangle region and the booming coast. The major north-south interstate, i-95, which carries millions of vehicles annually to and from the northeastern United States and Florida, passes through the center of the region. Another state route of interstate quality, nc-64, cuts through the region from west to east. The region is only 1 hour from Raleigh, 2.5 hours from Nags Head on the Outer Banks, 5 hours from Washington, D.C., and 3 hours from Myrtle Beach. Its location is a blessing.

Or is it a curse? The Rocky Mount–Wilson region may just be too close, a layover but not a destination. It is a place to eat and fill up the gas tank and then move on. It may always be overshadowed by its more prominent neighbors. If this assessment is accurate, local leaders will have to overcome this challenge.

Location has always been important to the region. The major city, Rocky Mount, developed around a train station serving as a shipping and shopping hub for the largely agricultural surrounding community in all directions. Tobacco (both raising and stemming and drying), textiles and apparel, and assorted other agricultural commodities formed the mainstay of the economy. In 1970, at least 20 percent of the workforce was directly involved in these industries, and as late as 1990, both tobacco and textiles and apparel numbered among the top fifteen industries ranked by shares of GLP (table d-16).[114]

The regional economy clearly suffered with the demise of North Carolina's traditional industries. Between 1970 and 2004, the area lost almost half of its tobacco, textile, and apparel firms.[115] Textile and apparel and tobacco's contribution to GLP fell by half between 1990 and 2004, with the real value of output falling by a third. Regional employment growth between 1970 and 2004 was the fifth-slowest of the state's twenty-one regions, and from 1990 to 2004 the region eked out only a 4 percent increase in jobs (table 5-1).

To their credit, the region's leaders have actively promoted the area's accessibility to the large Triangle market, proximity to the medical complex at ecu, transportation infrastructure, and lower costs.[116] These efforts appear to have paid off. Pharmaceutical production has become the region's largest industry, nearly tripling its output and doubling its share of the GLP between

1990 and 2004. Food processing is an up-and-coming local sector, with a national chain, the Cheesecake Factory, announcing in 2005 that it would build a bakery in Rocky Mount that would employ five hundred people by 2012.[117] Tire production, electronic components, glass products, and farm machinery all constitute relatively small yet important parts of the region's economy. A proposed entertainment complex in the Roanoke region to the north may have some positive spillover effects on jobs in the region. Leaders realize that continued progress will also require added investments in education and an upgrading of the skill composition of the labor force.[118]

The Little Engines That Try: Summary

In many ways, the changes associated with the Connected Age have been hardest on the small-city, transitional regions. These areas lack the status and name recognition of their urban counterparts and thus may lag behind in using their advantages in cost and eagerness to attract new interest. While the urban regions may have suffered equally in job losses and economic turmoil, at least those areas are in the major leagues—their names appear in company rolodexes. Many companies would be hard pressed to locate the small-city regions.

Yet considering that so many factors are stacked against them, the small-city regions have done remarkably well. The Foothills has a niche in the technology sector and could very well flourish in decades ahead. At least for now, the Greenville-Jacksonville region has growth from the military as well as public and private expansion related to the Brody School of Medicine at ECU and tourist and retirement investments in its coastal counties. The Rocky Mount–Wilson region is casting a wide net and hoping to become "Triangle lite"—the Triangle region without the high price tag and congestion. To pull off this transformation, however, the region will need a substantial upgrade in the upper ranks of its educational institutions.

These regions may ultimately make it, slowly but surely bringing their economies into the twenty-first century. They may combine a small-town feel, with low costs and without the hassles of life in a major urban area, with industries that will succeed in the globalized, connected world. They have already made perhaps the most important decision in this journey—they know they have to try.

Rural, Transitional Regions: Reviving the Real North Carolina

To many people, the regions in this category comprise the real North Carolina. They are not the North Carolina of big cities, with high-tech offices, modern factories, congested roads, and a fast pace that too often reminds people of the North. They are not even the North Carolina of medium-sized cities with links to tobacco, textiles, and furniture. But they are the North Carolina of unspoiled mountains, fertile fields, peaceful lakes and streams, and small towns where everyone knows everyone else's name. It is the North Carolina of postcards, dreams, and the past.

But is it the North Carolina of the future? All of the rural, transitional regions have strong ties to North Carolina's traditional twentieth-century industries. They have the added disadvantage of being off the beaten path, in more remote areas with low population densities and few of the amenities associated with urban regions. Beauty, yes; peacefulness, yes; economic growth—maybe.

Greater Mountain: Getting Away but Staying?

The counties comprising the Greater Mountain region have some of the best sites for natural beauty in the state—maybe in the entire country. From lush foothills to sparkling mountain streams to the highest peak in the eastern United States (Mount Mitchell), the Greater Mountain region inspires songs and uplifts spirits. Its majestic views are largely unspoiled by the development and commercialism affecting the Greater Asheville region to the south and the Greater Boone region to the north. Perhaps it should remain that way.

And it largely has remained that way since 1990. From 1990 to 2004, the region had virtually no employment growth and had the third-slowest rate of GLP growth among the state's regions. The reason was the same as in many other areas—a reliance on traditional sectors that have been in a state of decline. In 1970, three-quarters of regional employment was in manufacturing, and within manufacturing, at least three-quarters was in textiles and apparel and furniture.[119] Textiles, apparel, and furniture directly accounted for 27 percent of GLP in 1990 but only 12 percent in 2004. Some new economy sectors, like wiring devices, increased their share of GLP, but other new economy sectors (vehicle parts, food processing) saw their shares decline between 1990 and 2004 (table D-17).

One rather unusual industry in the Greater Mountain economy is pharmaceuticals. In 1970, a plant manufacturing intravenous solutions was built in the Greater Mountain region, and it is one of the largest such plants in the world.[120] The sector's share of GLP in 1990 was 6 percent, and by 2004 annual real output had increased by almost half and the GLP share had grown to 8 percent. The sector pays wages well above the regional average, and employment increased from twenty-three hundred to twenty-seven hundred between 1990 and 2004.[121]

The Connected Age saw a relatively new industry develop and flourish in the Greater Mountain region. This was the second-home and retirement-related construction and service industry. Much of the building has occurred around the region's sixty-five-hundred-acre Lake James, which sits at the base of the Blue Ridge Mountains and has direct access to the Pisgah National Forest and views of the surrounding mountain ridges. The region's GLP share from real estate and construction almost doubled between 1990 and 2004, and the region's median age was sixth-highest among all regions in 2000 (table 5-2). Only an hour from Asheville on I-40, the Greater Mountain region will likely draw increasing numbers of wealthy working households and active retirees who are interested in the rustic outdoors for a part-time or full-time residence.

The Greater Mountain region thus has the potential to grow around tourism, second-home and retirement development, and perhaps its niche in the pharmaceuticals industry. The question is whether it wants such growth.

Down East: Down on the Farm — and the Air Base

In 2003, the three counties that make up the Down East region had twenty-one hogs and pigs for every person.[122] On a drive along the roads and country lanes that lace the region, the large, efficiently run hog operations that supply pork to a big part of the country and world are easily seen (and often smelled). But the booms of supersonic F-15E Strike Eagles operating out of Seymour Johnson Air Force Base are also audible. Two industries that appear to lie at the opposite ends of the economic spectrum, traditional hog farming and the ultramodern military, define the modern Down East economy.

Geographically, the Down East region is a flat plain composed of sandy soil. The area receives good rainfall and has numerous lakes and small ponds and creeks. The region epitomizes the definition of "rural" — population density is low, and the area is one or two hours away from the urbanized Piedmont and the fast-growing coast. In the nineteenth and early twentieth centuries, railroads linked the region to the outside, but today accessibility is provided by a north-south interstate (I-95) and an east-west interstate (I-40).

Down East is not ideal for raising high-value crops, especially because of soil conditions. However, during the 1940s, agricultural entrepreneurs found that the region's openness and remoteness yet accessibility to transportation made it suitable for raising livestock, particularly hogs. Hog farms developed, and the region's first meatpacking plant soon opened.[123] As chapter 3 discusses, the development of an assembly line process of hog and pork production led to such rapid growth that by the 1990s, Down East had become the country's leading hog-producing region, surpassing the Midwest. The development of similar techniques for poultry production also caused this sector to grow. In the 1990s and first decade of the twenty-first century, farm-level hog and poultry production, together with the processing of the animals at packing plants, accounted for 10 percent of GLP, an amazingly high share for such sectors.[124] Farm-level vegetable production plus associated canning facilities added another 2 percent to GLP (table D-18).

Open space, combined with the political might of North Carolina's congressional delegation, brought the U.S. Air Force (initially the U.S. Army Air Corps) to the Down East region. Seymour Johnson Air Base was activated in 1942 as a training facility for World War II fliers. The base was deactivated in 1946 but reopened in 1956 during the Cold War and has subsequently remained active. It sits on thirty-three hundred acres and has six thousand active military and civilian personnel. At one time, the base was home to the B-52 bomber. Air combat groups from Seymour Johnson have participated in all active air operations, including those in the Middle East, during the past thirty years.[125] Military spending in the Down East region directly accounts for 8 percent of GLP, third only to the military's share in the Sandhills and Greenville-Jacksonville regions.

The growth of the agricultural sector and the continuing support from the military have been crucial for the Down East regional economy during the Connected Age, because one sector that was prominent is no more. In 1970, the region had thirty-five textile and apparel factories, and in 1990 the sector accounted for almost 5 percent of GLP. By 2004, only sixteen textile and apparel firms remained, and income generated from the industry accounted for less than 1 percent of GLP.[126] Few regions have seen such a dramatic decline in the once-powerful industry.

With the backbone of agriculture and the military, does the Down East region have to worry about its future economy? The answer is yes. Growth in the hog industry at the farm level has at least temporarily been restricted because of environmental concerns about animal waste. This issue will need to be resolved before the industry can resume its upward climb. Expansion remains possible, however, at the processing level, and growth also remains possible for farm-level poultry.

Although all signs point to continued growth in national military spending, Seymour Johnson Air Force Base still occupies a tenuous position. While the 2005 BRAC will result in more personnel at the base, earlier discussions considered substantially reducing or closing the facility.[127] North Carolina's political leaders have mobilized to remind both state and federal officials of the base's importance to the nation's defense as well as to the state and Down East economies, but no guarantees exist that these efforts will continue to meet with success.

Down East leaders therefore must contemplate the unpleasant possibility of life without Seymour Johnson and with a reduced hog industry. What options exist? What about alternative fuels, derived from grasses, grains, or animal waste? What about expansion of the vegetable industry, perhaps in concert with a focus on organically grown and nutritious crops? What about a bigger poultry industry, assuming waste issues can be circumvented? Given that educational attainment is exceedingly low in the Down East region, all is not necessarily well down on the farm and the air base.[128]

Greater Wilkes: Tomorrow's Resort?

The Greater Wilkes region can lay claim to a number of firsts and other points of notoriety. Sections of the region were part of the ill-fated late-eighteenth-century state of Franklin, which elected a governor and wrote a constitution but was never admitted to the new United States.[129] One of North Carolina's first toll roads ran through the region in the early nineteenth century.[130] The supermarket chain Lowes Foods began in the region in the early nineteenth century, as did Northwestern Bank, at one time North Carolina's fourth-largest financial institution.[131] The region was known as the moonshine capital of the world in the 1920s and 1930s, and the moonshiners' efforts to outrun the revenuers led to the legal motor racing industry; one of the earliest NASCAR speedways opened outside North Wilkesboro shortly after World War II.[132] In 1983, Greater Wilkes native Deneen Graham became the first African American woman crowned Miss North Carolina.[133]

While these firsts distinguish Greater Wilkes from many of the state's other regions, they share a common economic history. As in so much of North Carolina, the Greater Wilkes economy has been rooted in the state's traditional industries. In 1990, textiles and apparel and furniture combined for 12 percent of GLP and 14 percent of Greater Wilkes's employment. In 2004, the GLP share had dropped to 1 percent, and the employment share had fallen to 2 percent (table D-19). Slow employment growth in the Greater Wilkes region has put it in the bottom third of North Carolina regions during the Connected Age.

But continuing its history of uniqueness, Greater Wilkes has several economic elements compatible with the trends of the Connected Age. Food production and processing, primarily poultry, are significant sectors in the economy, although their GLP share fell from 13 percent in 1990 to 9 percent in 2004. Banking and vehicle parts are in the top fifteen of the region's economic sectors, and their relative importance grew in the 1990s and early twenty-first century. Most noteworthy, though, is the importance of management services, which at 16 percent stood as the top contributor to GLP in 2004, and exceeding its 2.5 percent share for the state. The region's specialization in this sector likely results from expertise and talent developed while Lowes Foods and Northwestern Bank were headquartered in the area.

Looking ahead, the Greater Wilkes region has several advantages for economic development. The availability of management services, a low cost of living, available labor, and a favorable geography and environment are pluses. The region is reasonably close to the urbanized North Carolina Piedmont, and the completion of the conversion of state Route 147 from two to four lanes gives the region interstate-quality access to I-40. These features may make the area favorable for the location of new economy manufacturing firms. A small electronic components manufacturing sector exists, but it has stagnated since 1990. Labor quality is an issue, with regional education attainment eighteenth among North Carolina's twenty-one regions (table 5-2).

The region could become the next hotbed for resort and retirement development for households preferring a cooler, foothills- and mountain-style climate. The region is located only an hour's drive from Winston-Salem, ninety minutes from Greensboro, two hours from Charlotte, and three hours from the Triangle. The region borders Greater Boone, and one index of housing costs shows prices in the Greater Wilkes region almost 20 percent lower than in Greater Boone (table 5-2). Real estate and construction activity should become a more prominent part of the future Greater Wilkes economy.

The Greater Wilkes region has long been known for its independent streak, from its days as part of the breakaway state of Franklin to the time that outrunning the revenuers was a favorite pastime. The region hopes to carve out an independent transition to the Connected Age and beyond.

Lakes: It's Already Here; They Will Come

The Lakes region is the smallest of the twenty-one regions in terms of GLP and employment. It also has the distinction of suffering the greatest reduction in jobs between 1990 and 2004.[134] Textiles and apparel and tobacco accounted for more than 20 percent of GLP in 1990, and no technology or new economy industries made the region's list of top sectors in that year (table

D-20). Based on this assessment, the economic outlook for the Lakes region might be assessed as gloomy.

However, the Lakes region has three major assets: Kerr Lake, Lake Gaston, and accessibility to the booming Triangle region. Kerr Lake and Lake Gaston are big—really big. Kerr Lake has 850 miles of shoreline with a capacity of 50,000 acres of water.[135] Lake Gaston has 350 miles of shoreline with a capacity of 20,300 acres of water.[136] Both are resources for power and drinking water, so they are important to the economic development of North Carolina and Virginia. But from the standpoint of the economy of the Lakes region, their value is also as an attraction and amenity for households seeking residences near water. Despite its job losses, the region has enjoyed a steady pace in new residential construction.[137]

Accessibility to the Triangle means that as that region's racehorse economy continues to grow, interest in residential development in the Lakes region should also increase. I-85 as well as the multilane state route 1 directly link the Lakes and Triangle regions, making the trip between most locations in the two areas only forty-five minutes to an hour—an easy drive for weekend visits by owners of second homes heading north or for shopping trips by permanent residents heading south. High-end residential development around the two lakes, therefore, should be on the upswing in coming decades.

The focus on residential development does not preclude commercial and industrial development in the Lakes region. The region can offer less expensive sites for companies that want to be relatively close to the action in the Triangle but do not need constant contact. Promoters established an industrial park, the Kerr-Tar Mini Hub, in 2005 to recruit just these kinds of firms.[138] However, the educational attainment of the local workforce is an issue, with the region ranking twentieth out of twenty-one regions in the proportion of college graduates.

The Lakes region will grow and develop, and its economic ties to the Triangle will strengthen. In fact, the Lakes likely will cease to be an economically identifiable region within twenty years. Some observers will be saddened by this development, while others will welcome increased economic opportunities and an enhanced standard of living.

Reviving the Real North Carolina: Summary

This category includes a diverse set of regions with unique characteristics and different outlooks. The Down East region has made an economic transition, but future growth is uncertain. The transition has been slow in coming to the Lakes region but likely will occur. The Mountain and Greater Wilkes regions fall in between. They have moved partway into the Connected Age, but how far can they go or do they want to go?

Like many other parts of North Carolina, a big part of the essence of re-viving the state's rural areas is their environmental beauty. Environmental quality has already become a major issue in the Down East region, and the moratorium on hog farm expansion has resulted directly from these con-cerns. If growth in the other three regions accelerates, environmental con-cerns could very well come to the forefront, pitting slow-growth or no-growth residents against pro-growth residents. Finding the middle ground will be tough work, requiring great persistence.

Rural Stagnant Region: Roanoke—Branson East?

It is ironic that the Roanoke region has been economically challenged for so long. In the eighteenth and nineteenth centuries, the region defined progress and prosperity. The Roanoke River, which begins in the Blue Ridge Mountains and flows to the Atlantic coast, moves through the region. A canal system developed in the nineteenth century served as a water highway for products and crops grown in the area's rich soil. The region brimmed with commerce until the railroad untied transportation from water and growth moved west-ward to the interior of the state.[139]

The Roanoke region is the only one of the state's twenty-one regions that lost population between 1970 and 2004. It had the slowest employment growth, lowest average salary, and the fifth-slowest growth in GLP between 1990 and 2004. It has been dead last in educational attainment. Textile and apparel production, agriculture, and other land-based enterprises, such as fertilizers and logging, dominated the regional economy in 1990 (table D-21). The demise of the textile and apparel industry removed a major piece from the regional economic puzzle.

The Roanoke region experienced one positive economic turn, the opening of a mini steel mill in 2000. The Nucor mill makes steel plates, directly em-ploys four hundred workers, and now constitutes the region's fourth-leading economic sector (4.1 percent of GLP in 2004).[140] However, the mill has not sparked an industrial revival. Its output and employment have remained un-changed since 2000, and employment in the host county, Hertford, has re-mained relatively unchanged since the mill opened.[141]

In 2005, regional leaders announced a new approach to economic devel-opment. The concept for Carolina Crossroads, a 700-acre entertainment park sitting along I-95, was unveiled. A public-private venture, Carolina Crossroads is billed as a venue for family entertainment, with music theaters, shopping hotels, restaurants, and recreational activities. An economic study estimated that the initial development of 116 acres will mean a $130 million investment and almost twenty-six hundred jobs, and completion of the entire project could generate more than twelve thousand jobs.[142] Still, the entertainment complex will compete with already established resorts near Richmond, Virginia, and Myrtle Beach, South Carolina. In addition, the majority of the affiliated leisure service industry jobs will pay at the lower end of the wage spectrum.

The Roanoke region faces fundamental challenges posed by its landlocked nature, its remoteness, and the very low educational quality of its workforce. The far eastern part of the region, along the Chowan River, has opportunities for second-home, vacation home, and retirement community development. The Nucor steel mill's track record shows that the region is not ready for durable goods manufacturing. Now the region is putting its chips on the entertainment card. Is it a good bet? Is Branson East in the cards?

Growing Apart or Coming Together?

The trends and forces associated with the Connected Age have affected regions in North Carolina in different ways. Several regions—most notably the racehorse Triangle, Greater Charlotte, Greater Asheville, and Greater Wilmington areas—have progressed and flourished. Other regions have grown much more slowly or have contracted. Three factors seem to determine which regions benefit from the Connected Age and which are challenged by it. Regions with greater concentrations of college-educated workers, regions with smaller concentrations (and therefore smaller reductions) of traditional industry firms, and regions bordering the coast tended to grow more quickly, while regions lacking these characteristics grew more slowly or declined.

Will this pattern persist in future decades? Although unpredictable twists and turns are always possible, the likely answer is yes. The trends and forces associated with the Connected Age will not disappear and may even strengthen. Continued advances in transportation and communication will shrink the economic world even further and put more of North Carolina's workers in direct competition with those in foreign countries. In this environment, education, ingenuity, innovation, and entrepreneurship become even more valuable, so regions that possess these features will grow while regions without them will not. Although trade liberalization will not advance in a straight line, the trend toward a more open worldwide trading system will continue. Finally, the retirement of increasing numbers of baby boomers and their attraction to resort-style communities with water as a main feature will certainly continue.

What role does public policy play in addressing the opportunities and challenges presented by the Connected Age in North Carolina, particularly as they relate to the differential impacts at the regional level? Can public policy even affect these issues? How has the era changed the fiscal priorities of both state and local governments, and how might these priorities change in the future? Finally, can the public sector reduce the divergence in regional economies that has occurred? The next chapter examines these and other questions.

6. Impacts on Policies

Reactions to economic change always occur both privately and publicly. Privately, individuals and households adjust in several ways. They change their time allocation to work and nonwork activities, alter their rates of borrowing and saving, change employers or even occupations, acquire more education, and perhaps even move their residences. Businesses may adjust their mix of inputs and products, hire different kinds of workers, expand or contract output levels, or—the ultimate change—cease operations altogether.

The public sector—that is, government—also reacts to economic change. Although observers constantly debate the relative size and role of government, no one would argue with the idea that government plays a major role in the economy, so governmental changes are unquestionably important. In the United States, government at all levels accounts for nearly 30 percent of all economic activity, with the state and local government share totaling close to 10 percent, a number that has remained relatively constant during the Connected Age.[1]

Government's impact on the economy is realized in two major ways. One is in how government collects public revenues, what mix of taxes and fees are used, and how both the total size of public revenues and the particular types of public charges affect private economic decision making. Second is how those revenues are spent, what programs are used, and the impacts of those programs on the functioning of the economy and the behavior and choices of households and businesses. Changes associated with the Connected Age have affected both of these public fiscal functions, while several fiscal changes have been enacted to attempt to alter the course of the Connected Age's trends.

This chapter examines how North Carolina has responded to the Connected Age in one area where citizens can have a collective voice—government policies. Have the changes been logical, appropriate, and productive, or are alternative policy prescriptions needed?

The Big Picture

Tables 6-1 (taxes) and 6-2 (spending) show trends in the relative size of North Carolina's government during the Connected Age. All revenue and spending amounts are expressed as percentages of gross state product (GSP) — that is, revenue and spending amounts are given as shares of the state's total yearly economic pie.[2] All revenue and spending amounts are for North Carolina's state and local governments combined to allow for easy comparisons over time, when the functions of the state and local governments might change. Combining state and local amounts also permits comparisons to other states, where the apportionment of functions between the state and local governments might differ from that in North Carolina.[3] Spending amounts also include federal money administered by North Carolina's state and local governments.[4]

The public revenue side indicates several trends. First, North Carolina's public revenues (total taxes and charges and fees) rose from 8.9 percent of GSP in 1972 to 11.5 percent in 2005.[5] Including revenues from the federal government (total public revenues), public revenue availability in the state increased from 11.1 percent to 15.3 percent during this span.

Second, the relative reliance on specific taxes and charges changed during the period. The take from the property tax, sales tax, and corporate income tax remained relatively constant, while the take from the individual income tax rose 85 percent (1.3 percent to 2.4 percent), and the share of GSP going to charges and fees — public levies for direct services received, such as college tuition and public hospital charges — jumped more than 80 percent. Revenues from federal sources rose by 73 percent. In contrast, the share of GSP going to vehicle taxes (gas tax and highway use tax) fell by 55 percent (1.1 percent to 0.5 percent).

So where did these public revenues go? Table 6-2, which shows the percentage of GSP allocated to the key categories of public spending in North Carolina, gives the answers. While little change occurred in the proportion of the state's economy allocated to K–12 public education, the share appropriated to public higher education jumped 50 percent, from 1.4 percent to 2.1 percent. Relatively more was also taken by public safety (police, fire, prisons) and by "other" spending.[6] But by far the largest increase took place in public spending categorized as "income transfers," which includes direct income-support programs such as cash welfare and Social Security as well as programs that subsidize certain household expenditures, such as food stamps, Medicare, and Medicaid. The share of GSP devoted to income transfers rose

Table 6-1. Public Revenues in North Carolina as a Percentage of Gross State Product, by Category, 1972–2005 (National Averages in Parentheses in 1972 and 2005)

	1972	1977	1982	1987	1992	1997	2002	2005
Property tax	1.8 (3.5)	1.7	1.7	1.6	1.8	1.7	1.8	1.9 (2.7)
Gas and highway use tax	1.1 (0.9)	0.9	0.7	0.7	0.7	0.6	0.6	0.5 (0.4)
Sales tax	2.1 (2.5)	2.2	2.2	2.3	2.5	2.3	2.2	2.3 (2.8)
Individual income tax	1.3 (1.3)	1.8	2.1	2.2	2.2	2.4	2.5	2.4 (1.9)
Corporate income tax	0.4 (0.4)	0.5	0.4	0.5	0.4	0.4	0.2	0.4 (0.3)
Total taxes	6.7 (8.6)	7.1	7.1	7.3	7.6	7.4	7.3	7.5 (8.1)
Charges and fees	2.2 (2.7)	2.4	3.1	3.1	3.6	4.0	4.1	4.0 (4.5)
Total taxes and charges and fees	8.9 (11.3)	9.5	10.2	10.4	11.2	11.4	11.4	11.5 (12.6)
Federal revenue	2.2 (2.6)	3.5	2.7	2.1	2.6	2.8	3.5	3.8 (3.5)
Total public revenue	11.1 (13.9)	13.0	12.9	12.5	13.8	14.2	14.9	15.3 (16.1)

DATA SOURCES: U.S. Census Bureau, "State and Local Government Finances"; and U.S. Department of Commerce, Bureau of Economic Analysis, "Gross Domestic Product."

Table 6-2. Public Spending and Public Debt in North Carolina as a Percentage of Gross State Product, by Category, 1972–2005 (National Averages in Parentheses in 1972 and 2005)

	1972	1977	1982	1987	1992	1997	2002	2005
Spending								
K–12 education	3.2 (3.9)	3.6	3.4	3.2	3.4	3.0	3.2	3.1 (3.8)
Higher education	1.4 (1.3)	1.6	1.8	1.7	1.7	1.6	1.7	2.1 (1.5)
Income transfers	2.0 (2.8)	2.4	2.7	2.3	3.7	4.1	4.7	4.9 (4.3)
Highways	1.5 (1.6)	1.1	0.9	0.9	1.0	0.9	1.0	1.0 (1.0)
Public safety	0.6 (0.7)	0.9	1.0	1.0	1.1	1.2	1.2	1.2 (1.4)
Other	2.3 (3.6)	2.9	2.8	2.6	2.8	2.8	3.2	2.9 (4.2)
Total	11.0 (13.9)	12.5	12.6	11.7	13.7	13.6	15.0	15.2 (16.2)
Debt	5.3 (8.0)	4.4	3.8	2.6	3.0	3.5	4.1	5.5 (7.0)

DATA SOURCES: U.S. Census Bureau, "State and Local Government Finances"; and U.S. Department of Commerce, Bureau of Economic Analysis, "Gross Domestic Product."
NOTE: State and local outstanding debt includes only bonds backed by the full faith and credit of the government; debt of public utilities is excluded.

almost 150 percent during the Connected Age, reaching 4.9 percent in 2005 and making it the leading category of government spending.

One class of public spending in North Carolina, highway expenditures, declined as a percentage of GSP. The rate fell from 1.5 percent in 1972 to 1.0 percent in 2005, with the entire 33 percent reduction taking place between 1972 and 1982. The implications of this change will be discussed in detail later in this chapter. Commensurate with the rise in total revenues, total public spending also trended upward.

These trends in taxing and public spending set up an interesting dichotomy. On the one side, North Carolina's tax take, particularly that netted by the income tax, increased during the Connected Age. On the other side, relative public spending devoted to perhaps the two most prominent and noticeable government functions, K–12 education and highways, either remained unchanged (K–12 education) or declined (highways). This dichotomy could provide a source of public frustration with government during the era.

Were these fiscal trends unique to North Carolina, or were they present in other states? Tables 6-1 and 6-2 present comparable average national values for the tax shares and spending shares in parentheses for 1972 and 2005. North Carolina's increasing reliance on the individual income tax parallels a national trend; however, the increase in North Carolina was much greater. While reliance on the property tax is much greater nationwide than in North Carolina, the property tax share declined nationally while remaining relatively stable in North Carolina. Similar trends occurred in both the nation and North Carolina in the corporate income tax, vehicle taxes, and sales tax, although the share of income taken by the sales tax was consistently lower in North Carolina. Charges and fees increased in North Carolina and the nation, but the nation's take remained higher. Federal revenues to North Carolina began lower than those nationally but surpassed the national average by 2005. The net result of these tax trends is that North Carolina's public revenues, whether measured by taxes alone, taxes plus charges and fees, or taxes plus fees and charges plus federal revenues, converged toward the national average between 1972 and 2005.

On the spending side of the ledger, just as in North Carolina, little change took place in the proportion of national income allocated to K–12 education. North Carolina's proportion, however, remained below the national average. An entirely different trend occurred for higher education. The percentage of income spent on higher education in North Carolina began slightly higher than the national average in 1972, and although the national average moved up modestly over the next three decades, North Carolina's rate rose much faster. Thus, while North Carolina spent 0.1 percentage points more of its income on higher education in 1972 than did the nation as a whole, the state spent 0.6 percentage points more in 2005. Income transfers also jumped more in North Carolina than in the nation. The state began the era below the nation in the percentage of state income allocated to income transfers, but thirty years later, the state surpassed the nation on this measure. North Carolina's trends in the other spending categories essentially paralleled those of the nation, especially in the decline in relative spending on highways. As with public revenues, total public spending in the state moved toward the national average between 1972 and 2005. The public spending difference between North Carolina and the nation dropped from 2.9 percentage points of GSP in 1972 to 1.0 percentage points in 2005. North Carolina's relative public debt (discussed in detail later in this chapter) also rose and moved closer to the national average.

As a result of North Carolina's faster growth in public revenues and spending, the state moved up in rankings of relative governmental size. North Carolina's ranking among states in state and local taxes as a percentage of the economy rose from thirty-seventh in 1970 to twenty-ninth in 2005.[7] Compared to other states in the southeast (Virginia, Tennessee, South Carolina, Georgia, and Florida), North Carolina's ranking also increased.[8]

This big-picture view thus reveals some key facts about North Carolina's public sector during the Connected Age. Foremost is the dependence on individual income taxes. The state relies more on the individual income tax than other states, and this reliance increased during the Connected Age. Conversely, North Carolina relies less on sales taxes and property taxes, although the gap for the property tax has narrowed in the past thirty years. Dependence on vehicle taxes dropped, while use of charges and fees rose, and other states matched these trends. In total, although North Carolina takes less of its income for public revenues than other states, it has moved closer to the national average. On expenditures, the state spends significantly more on higher education and income transfers, and the gap with other states has widened. But the state spends noticeably less on K–12 education and, like other states, allocated less to highways after 2000 than in the 1970s.

Is this mix of taxes and public spending right for North Carolina in the modern economic environment, or are changes needed to keep North Carolina competitive and improving? Since it is difficult to alter public policies without creating, at least in the short run, winners and losers, who would benefit from and who would be harmed by any policy overhaul? What kinds of tax changes might be necessary to adequately fund government in North

Carolina in light of expected demographic and economic changes? Are spending trends, particularly in higher education and income transfers, sustainable? The chapter now turns to these questions and issues, addressing them first from the tax side and then from the spending side.

Taxes

Connected Age trends have significantly affected government revenues in North Carolina, creating issues of many varieties. The size of the tax base (what is taxed) and its ability to grow with the economy have been affected by the expansion of the service economy, new technology that facilities out-of-state purchases, and the differences in economic growth among regions of the state. Heightened competition created by deregulation, globalization, and new technology has put added attention on tax rates and how their levels affect the location of increasingly mobile households and businesses. The added returns to education and the widening gap between those with and without advanced training have raised concerns about the incidence of the tax system (who pays) and especially any proposed changes. Finally, extending an issue that predates the Connected Age, the volatility of public revenues over the business cycle continues to focus concerns on the stability as well as adequacy of revenues.

The following subsections highlight the issues, debates, and potential remedies the Connected Age poses for North Carolina's major sources of public revenue.[9]

Individual Income Tax: Rates Too High?

As the preceding section demonstrated, North Carolina relies more on the individual income tax than do other states, and this reliance increased during the Connected Age. Further, income tax rates in North Carolina are high, ranking eleventh among all states, fifth among the fifteen largest states, and second among southeastern states.[10]

In the Connected Age, where household mobility is greater and workers, especially those with higher income, have more options for their residential locations, a state tax system that utilizes the individual income tax more and has relatively high rates may deter more affluent households and retard economic growth. Indeed, empirical evidence supports this concern.[11]

Many advocates of tax reform, both nationally and in North Carolina, have supported changing the individual income tax to one with a broader base and lower rates. A subcommittee of the 2007 N.C. State and Local Fiscal Modernization Study Commission recommended broadening the tax base by limiting exemptions and deductions while lowering tax rates to at least those prevailing in neighboring southeastern states. In 2007, the state lowered the top marginal individual income tax rate.[12] The changes sought to make the state individual income tax less of a factor in economic decision making, particularly for more tax-sensitive, higher-income households.

Corporate Income Tax: Double Taxation?

Issues regarding the state corporate income tax echo those for the individual income tax—corporations are increasingly mobile and sensitive to state taxes, and North Carolina's corporate income tax rate ranks high, most notably among southeastern states.[13] However, unlike the individual income tax, North Carolina's relative corporate income tax revenues failed to rise during the Connected Age, for three reasons: legislated exemptions, enhanced corporate ability to move taxable income to low-tax states, and a shift to smaller firms that pay taxes under the individual income tax.

Calls for reform of North Carolina's corporate income tax have come in two varieties. Some observers advocate outright abolition of the tax because individual income taxation of interest and dividends reaches the same base as corporate income tax and therefore represents double taxation.[14] And the fact that not all corporate dividends and interest will be paid to taxpayers residing in North Carolina is balanced by North Carolina's gains from taxing dividends and interest received by residents from out-of-state corporations.

More modestly, two state tax commissions as well as other reformers have called for changes in the corporate income tax that mirror those for the individual income tax—that is, broadening the base by limiting corporate deductions, exemptions, and credits and then reducing the corporate tax rate.[15] To prevent corporations from shifting income to low-tax states, analysts have also recommended that corporations submit a single, or combined, income report for all their operations and subsidiaries.[16]

Sales Tax: Broaden the Base?

No tax has been more affected by the trends of the Connected Age than the sales tax. The expansion in the proportion of higher-income households and the shift of females into the paid labor force have led to service sector growth that has outpaced overall economic growth. But the North Carolina sales tax is applied primarily to tangible goods and not to most services. Consequently, the state's sales tax base steadily declined from 60 percent of disposable income in 1970 to 40 percent in 2002.[17] To maintain revenues, the falling sales tax base has prompted public decision makers to increase the sales tax rate. For example, between 1988 and 2003, the North Carolina General Assembly increased the sales tax rate by 50 percent.

The North Carolina sales tax base of tangible goods was established in the 1930s when the service economy was virtually nonexistent. An obvious solution to the eroding base is to broaden it to include consumer spending on services. In fact, every comprehensive study of reforming the North Carolina tax code has recommended broadening the base to services.[18] Such a change would permit a reduction in the sales tax rate, perhaps by as much as half.[19] While the initial change would be revenue neutral (that is, the increased revenues from broadening the base would be countered by lower revenues from rate reductions), sales tax revenues would grow more quickly than under the current system as further shifts to service spending are realized.[20]

Technological innovations during the Connected Age in the form of Internet shopping (also known as e-commerce) have also hurt the sales tax base by taking taxable sales away from bricks-and-mortar locations in the state and moving them to nontaxable sales in cyberspace. Estimates indicate that North Carolina lost more than $350 million in sales tax revenues, or 2 percent of total state tax revenue, from e-commerce in 2001 and that the loss will rise to 5 percent of state tax revenue in 2011.[21] Although North Carolina law requires taxpayers to report Internet purchases and to pay the corresponding sales tax when they file their annual income tax returns, enforcement is virtually impossible. The issue ultimately lies beyond the state's control and will have to be solved by a national agreement among all states.

Property Tax: Up to Date?

The property tax is the major source of revenue for North Carolina's local governments, accounting for almost three-quarters of local government tax revenue in 2005.[22] As such, the property tax is crucial for the smooth operation of public functions that are primarily locally funded, like school construction and local police and fire protection. Whereas the traditional sales tax base has contracted during the Connected Age, the opposite has been true for the property tax base in regions that have benefited from the era's trends. In areas such as the Triangle, Charlotte, fast-growing coastal communities, and mountain resorts, the property tax base has expanded rapidly as economic growth has surged.

The problem is the way that the property tax base is taxed. North Carolina law requires real property (real estate) to be reassessed (have its value updated to market value) at least once every eight years. The majority of North Carolina counties use the eight-year interval, while most of the rest use a four-year interval.[23] As a result, in most years, the current or market value of property is not being taxed; instead, an out-of-date value is being used. Thus, the property tax base does not remain current with the economic base. Then, when property values are reassessed, the onetime change represents the accumulation of many years of annual changes. Property owners naturally rebel against this sticker shock, and local officials are often unable politically to sustain the increases. Property tax rates frequently are rolled back so that when they are applied to the new, higher property values, taxes remain the same or only modestly higher than before the reassessment.[24] In fast-growing regions, taxing out-of-date property values causes local governments difficulty in paying for the current costs of infrastructure, such as school buildings, when they are largely based on current land values.

A reasonable solution to this problem is more frequent property reassessments, as a subcommittee of the 2007 State and Local Fiscal Modernization Study Commission recommended.[25] More frequent reassessments would result in smaller annual changes in property values and smaller increases in property tax payments, which owners would find more acceptable, especially if the increases fall into line with inflation and economic growth. More frequent reassessments would also result in improved revenue flow to counties and municipalities from property values.[26] For low-income or fixed-income property owners who might have difficulty affording annual increases in property taxes, a deferral of some part of the payment until the property is voluntarily sold could be applied.

Vehicle Taxes: Too Little?

The two vehicle taxes, the motor fuels (gas) tax and the highway use tax, provide most of the funds for highway construction and maintenance in the state.[27] As table 6-1 shows, revenues from these taxes as a percentage of the state economy have trended downward during the Connected Age. The reason is quite simple—neither tax has kept pace with inflation. The gas tax rate per gallon of gasoline, after adjusting for inflation, declined by half between 1970 and 2006.[28] The decline is even larger if improved gas mileage is factored in.[29] For the highway use tax (a sales tax on vehicles) the problem is not the rate (a flat 3 percent) but the base to which the rate is applied. For commercial vehicles, the dollar limit for the tax payment is not automatically adjusted for inflation. More generally, vehicle prices have risen substantially more slowly than the overall rate of inflation during the Connected Age.[30]

Public resistance to very visible and frequently paid taxes, like the gas tax, is likely one major reason for these results. In addition, North Carolina's gas tax rate is among the nation's highest.[31] Drivers therefore resist increases in the state rate. Yet the rate is high only because of the almost unique way the state finances road projects. Most states split the financing of highway projects between the state and local governments. For the average state, 39 percent of road spending is financed at the county and city levels, and the funding comes mainly from property taxes. In North Carolina, virtually all highway spending is financed at the state level from the gas and vehicle license taxes.[32] North Carolina's gas taxes are high, therefore, primarily because property taxes are not used for road purposes, as is the case in most other states.

If political resistance can be overcome, a straightforward remedy to the problem of road financing is indexing both the gas tax rate and the vehicle license tax to inflation.[33] For the vehicle license tax, the payment cap would be indexed annually to inflation and the tax rate would be adjusted when vehicle price inflation fell short of general inflation.

Other observers say that the only long-run solution to public road financing is to abolish the gas tax and replace it with a mileage tax, since mileage driven is really the best measure of highway usage.[34] A mileage tax would also eliminate the problem of declining revenues per mile when fuel efficiency rises.

The state also is actively considering a change to the entire philosophy behind road financing, moving away from public financing to private financing, as the 2002 establishment of the N.C. Turnpike Authority indicated. The authority is charged with investigating and where practical securing authorization to establish and construct toll roads. Supporters of toll roads see two advantages. Road projects might be built more quickly, especially in rapidly growing regions, because funding would go directly to the designated roads and not through the state-level allocation process. In addition, toll roads appeal to backers of economic efficiency, because direct users of the roads pay for their construction and maintenance. As of 2007, several toll road projects had been investigated, and some had received approval, but none had yet received funding.

Incidence: Who Bears the Burden?

The Connected Age's emphasis on competitiveness, productivity, and economic efficiency has stimulated a rethinking of taxes in North Carolina. The era's three tax commissions recommended a restructuring of the state's taxes that would promote these goals and enhance the state's growth in the global economy. Key in this restructuring would be a movement away from income taxation, at both the individual and corporate levels, and to sales taxation.

While some observers argue that such a change would improve the state's investment climate, it could also shift the burden of taxation from higher-income to lower-income households.[35] Estimates for North Carolina indicate that lower-income taxpayers pay a much higher percentage of their income in sales taxes than do higher-income taxpayers, while the reverse is the case for the state's individual income tax. For example, the N.C. Budget and Tax Center calculates that the lowest 20 percent of taxpayers by income pay 6.9 percent of their income in sales taxes, while the top 1 percent of households by income pay only 1.2 percent of their income in sales taxes. The situation is almost exactly reversed for the individual income tax: the poorest 20 percent of taxpayers pay 1.3 percent of their income for the individual income tax, but the richest 1 percent of taxpayers pay 6.9 percent.[36]

Analysts have proposed two solutions to this problem. One is to exempt some key purchases that are relatively important to lower-income households from the sales tax. For example, groceries are already exempt from the state component of the sales tax.[37] This exemption could be expanded to include items such as clothing and services such as medical care. However, this approach would be complicated and costly to administer. One alternative is to implement a North Carolina form of a negative income tax, called the Earned Income Tax Credit (EITC) and modeled after the federal version. First developed by the late economist Milton Friedman, an EITC pays money to eligible low-income households rather than collecting taxes based on their income (hence the term "negative income tax").[38] Supporters say that such a tax is easy to administer, can be targeted to certain households, and can offset any increase in a lower-income households' relative tax payments that might result from an expansion of the state sales tax. North Carolina legislators passed a state EITC in 2007.[39]

Volatility: Easing the Cycle

Volatility refers to the degree to which tax revenue growth is erratic, increasing at faster rates in some years while increasing at substantially slower rates or even declining in other years. Volatility is tied to the general business cycle, wherein a pattern of economic growth and expansion is followed by retrenchment and recession. Volatility is not an issue new to the Connected Age, but as North Carolina's government has grown larger and is being looked at to address many of the issues associated with the Connected Age, the significance of volatility has increased.

The revenue statistics for the largest of North Carolina's public budgets, the state General Fund, clearly show this volatility. For example, in the recessionary fiscal years of 1991–92 and 2000–2001 and the almost recessionary fiscal year of 1995–96, General Fund revenue grew an average of only 1.1 percent. In contrast, during the economic growth fiscal years of 1989–90, 1993–94, and 1999–2000, General Fund revenue grew an average of 12.6 percent.[40]

Volatility generates problems regarding expectations and planning. The political process creates strong incentives for the spending of all public revenue. Therefore, when revenue growth is strong, spending plans implicitly are based on the continuation of this growth rate. However, when revenue growth ultimately slips, planned spending often exceeds revenue availability, creating the difficult political choice of cutting planned spending, increasing tax rates, or some combination of the two.

Volatility of public revenues likely cannot be eliminated because the business cycle cannot be prevented, but measures can moderate the volatility and better cope with its existence. Annual increases in spending can be limited. Three tactics have been discussed. The strictest would limit spending in one year to revenue availability in the previous fiscal year. The second would allow for spending increases from the previous year but would limit them to a factor related to population growth and inflation.[41] The third and most generous technique would specify that spending each year could be no more than some fixed percentage of the state economy (GSP or total personal income).[42] In the early years of the twenty-first century, North Carolina considered an annual spending cap for the state General Fund based on average personal income growth for the previous ten years, but the measure was not adopted into law.[43]

One measure for dealing with volatility that has been employed in the state is the rainy-day fund. The idea of this fund is simple. During good years, when the economy is strong and public revenue growth is high, all revenue will not be spent. Instead, some will be set aside. Then, when the economy sours and revenue growth is shaky, the fund will be used to augment revenues and support state spending. In this way, revenue availability can be provided more evenly across the ups and downs of the business cycle.

North Carolina established a rainy-day fund during the Connected Age, but its relative size has varied, ranging between 0 percent (the fund was depleted) and 5 percent of the state General Fund. The concept is difficult to implement because it requires public decision makers, many of whom have short time horizons related to their next election, to refrain from spending now. The temptation also arises to use the rainy-day money for non-business-cycle emergencies, as was the case with North Carolina's fund for Hurricane Floyd recovery in the early twenty-first century. Nonetheless, the concept is viable and practical as long as public decision makers can force themselves to take the longer-run view. However, fiscal experts recommend that the fund total at least 10 percent of the state budget.[44] In North Carolina's case, this would require a tripling of the fund as it stood around 2005.[45]

Debt: Delaying Payment?

Although borrowing is technically not a tax, debt is used to raise revenues for public purposes, so it is an alternative to taxation. Government borrowing and government debt have negative connotations among the general populace, but public borrowing has a legitimate purpose in the proper circumstances. Where projects are long-lasting, such as roads, bridges, and school buildings, they can logically be financed with debt rather than with current revenues. Paying for projects only with currently raised revenues (that is, tax revenues) imposes costs entirely on current taxpayers. Borrowing the funds and then repaying them over a period that approximately matches the life of the project allows the costs to be spread out over both current and future taxpayers, all of whom presumably benefit from the project.

Unlike the federal government, which can use debt financing to pay for both long-lasting projects and programs with short lives, most state and local governments use debt only for infrastructure projects. In North Carolina, public borrowing finances highways, bridges, school and college buildings, and other government buildings. Again, the rationale is that these projects span several decades and give benefits to multiple generations of taxpayers.

Although North Carolina uses debt financing logically, the issue of the relative size of the state's public debt arises and is best measured as outstanding state and local debt in a given year as a percentage of state income (GSP) in that same year.[46] The last line of table 6-2 shows how this measure changed during the Connected Age. From 1972 to 1987, the relative size of outstanding debt fell by 50 percent, but it subsequently rose and reached its high for the era in 2005. Such a pattern is not unusual. Infrastructure spending is "lumpy" — that is, when the required spending corresponding to a wave of growth is completed, more spending will not be required until a further wave of growth occurs. Infrastructure spending thus typically goes through patterns of intense activity followed by a lull, followed by more activity and another lull, and so forth.

Table 6-2 also demonstrates that North Carolina has been a more frugal user of debt financing than have other states. In both 1972 and 2005, the relative size of the state's debt was lower than that for the nation. However, North Carolina was closer to the national average in 2005 than in 1972, likely because of the state's above-average growth during the Connected Age and corresponding greater need for infrastructure projects. Moreover, in 2003, the North Carolina General Assembly authorized the use of certificates of participation to fund public facilities. Unlike traditional public debt, which is backed by the government's general taxing power, certificates of participation use the funded project as collateral for the loan and identify a specific revenue stream for the loan's repayment. As of 2006, $1.4 billion in certificates of payment had been approved for issue in North Carolina.[47] These certificates do not require voter approval but carry higher interest rates than standard public debt.

Some experts see North Carolina going through an intense period of infrastructure building and rebuilding in the coming decades. The American Society of Civil Engineers estimates that $46 billion will be required through 2030 to replace and expand airports, bridges, dams, water systems, rail lines, and roads.[48] The majority of the debt ($29 billion) is for roads. In the unlikely event that all of this debt were financed at once, it would quadruple the state's relative debt load. Public infrastructure requirements and the associated financing will remain key issues as the Connected Age matures.

In 2005, North Carolina joined the majority of other states in approving the use of tax-increment financing, a technique that allows local governments to sell bonds to pay for public improvements such as highways and water and sewer lines that will enhance the value of a location and make it more attractive for development. However, the bonds are financed not by general tax revenues but by the anticipated added property tax revenues forthcoming from the development.[49] Supporters say that tax increment financing can spur economic improvement in blighted areas, while detractors claim that it dangerously commingles private goals with public purposes and that worthy private projects should be able to acquire standard private financing.[50]

Spending

What government spends money on, in addition to how much it spends, is always controversial, and the Connected Age has been no exception. But the era has perhaps seen added scrutiny on government spending for two reasons. First, as discussed earlier, the relative size of government spending in North Carolina has risen since 1970. And second, the massive economic changes occurring during the Connected Age have caused many people to look to government for guidance, support, and solutions to these new challenges and issues.

This section examines changes and questions related to the major categories of government spending in North Carolina, including K–12 education, higher education, transfer spending, and highways, as well as strategies and tactics for economic development. The questions probed include past impacts of the spending, debates about the appropriate size and type of spending, and recommended directions for the future.

K–12 Spending: What Works?

North Carolina made significant progress in K–12 education during the Connected Age. From 1970 to 2005, the percentage of adults (persons twenty-five years old and over) with high school degrees rose 118 percent, from 39 percent to 84 percent, and the state almost reached the national average for this measure. In 1970, North Carolina stood 14 percentage points below the national average for adults with high school degrees; in 2005, the state trailed by only 1 percentage point.[51] In 1972, North Carolina high school students taking the Scholastic Aptitude Test (SAT) scored 8 percent below the national average, but in 2006, the state's deficit had dropped to less than 2 percent.[52] And maybe the most impressive of all statistics are the state's results for the respected National Assessment of Educational Progress, a nationally designed test given to fourth- and eighth-graders since the 1990s. North Carolina has either consistently scored above the national average or has moved from under the national averages to closer to or above the national averages.[53]

At the same time, an increase occurred in the major inputs to K–12 education. North Carolina boosted its spending per pupil, in inflation-adjusted terms, dramatically during the Connected Age. From 1972 to 2004, real spending per pupil increased 176 percent, faster than the 142 percent increase for the nation.[54] In 1972, North Carolina spent 25 percent less per pupil than the national average; in 2004, that gap had shrunk to 15 percent, moving North Carolina from forty-third to thirty-eighth among states in per pupil K–12 educational spending.[55]

Similar improvements took place in pupil/teacher ratios and teacher salaries. The average K–12 pupil/teacher ratio in North Carolina fell 37 percent between 1970 and 2003, moving the state from above the national average on this measure to below the national average.[56] Real teacher salaries in North Carolina improved 35 percent from 1972 to 2004, faster than the 24 percent national increase and halving the state's 16 percentage point deficit versus the national average.[57] However, the real salaries of North Carolina's teachers rose slightly more slowly than the real salaries of all the state's workers during the period.[58]

Since this all appears to be good news, what issues confront K–12 education in North Carolina? First and foremost, although progress has occurred, is it enough? Educational standards and performance are increasing in the rest of the world, and with the continuing march to greater globalization, North Carolina's students and workers will increasingly compete with those in foreign countries.[59] Therefore, a higher percentage of high school students will need to have the abilities and preparation for college, and the state cannot rest on its laurels.[60]

Second, while educational attainment and achievement have improved, a significant proportion of students still do not achieve in a timely manner. In 2004, North Carolina ranked eleventh out of forty-six states in the high school dropout rate, and the rate trended higher through the first years of the twenty-first century.[61] In addition, only 68 percent of the state's 2002 high school freshmen graduated four years later.[62] This proportion has not improved since 1973, and in 2000 North Carolina ranked sixth-worst on the measure among all states and the District of Columbia.[63]

Third, a racial achievement gap not only still exists but by some measures has worsened. In 1995, the average African American SAT score was 82 percent of the average white score; in 2005, that number had dropped to 80 percent. Similarly, in 1995 the average Hispanic SAT score was 93 percent of the average white score; ten years later, that figure had fallen to 90 percent.[64] In addition, African American students comprised 85 percent of the enrollment at the seventeen North Carolina high schools designated "low-performing" in 2004–5.[65]

Finally, demographic trends suggest that a larger percentage of future students will come from more challenged backgrounds. By 2050, half of North Carolina's population is expected to be African American and Hispanic, and the proportion of the school-age population drawn from these two groups will be even higher.[66] Because these two groups currently underperform other racial categories in academic achievement, policymakers will need to increase their focus on improving the performance and skills of members of these groups to increase college enrollment and continue to record educational advances. At the same time, some observers worry that the attention on underachieving students is drawing resources away from those who are more talented.[67]

The answers to these questions are both complex and uncertain. A starting point is to review the trends and issues affecting the two major inputs into educational outcomes — those who deliver the training (teachers) and the means by which the training is delivered.

Teachers

The front line for addressing virtually any issue in education is the teacher. And absolutely no doubt exists that trends associated with the Connected Age have made it much more difficult to attract and retain highly qualified and successful teachers. K–12 teaching was once one of the few fields that accepted professional women, and even today they dominate the field.[68] Yet educational and occupational opportunities for women clearly have expanded during the Connected Age. Other fields now compete for the college students — especially females — who traditionally went into teaching. As a result, the number of the most academically qualified individuals completing teaching degrees has declined.[69] A 2003 analysis of the SAT scores of students in twenty-one college majors nationwide showed that education majors had the third-lowest math scores and second-lowest verbal scores.[70]

One important issue for teachers, as for people in any occupation, is money. An examination of 2006 occupational data from the Employment Security Commission of North Carolina shows that the estimated beginning, average, and experienced wage rates for teachers are lower than those for all but one comparable occupation requiring a college degree.[71] A national study comparing teaching wage rates to the wage rates of other professional workers found similar results for North Carolina.[72]

An additional concern is how North Carolina teacher salaries change with experience. Typically, a worker's salary rises with experience because more experienced workers are deemed to be more productive and hence more profitable for the firm. In North Carolina, a teacher's salary changes over time in a pattern dictated by the state's salary schedule. So attracting and retaining teachers requires not only a competitive starting salary but also competitive salary changes with experience.

Figure 6-1 compares the salary experience profiles of North Carolina teach-

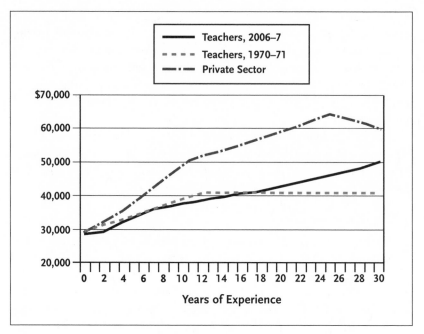

Figure 6-1. Actual and alternative earnings profiles of North Carolina teachers, 1970–1971 and 2006–2007.

DATA SOURCES: N.C. Association of Educators, *History*; N.C. Association of Educators, "Teacher Salary Percentage Increases"; Murphy and Welch, "Empirical Age-Earnings Profiles," 207–9.

NOTE: All salary data are real 2006 dollars. Teacher salaries are for holders of bachelor's degrees.

ers in 1970 and 2006 as specified by the salary schedules in those years against a fictitious 2006 teacher salary schedule if teacher salaries followed the average earnings profile in the private sector. North Carolina changed the teacher salary schedule between 1970 and 2006 to give greater salary boosts for experience, especially after twelve years. Indeed, in 1970, no salary premium existed after twelve years of experience. Also in 2006, the rate of salary gain for teachers fairly closely matched the rate of gain for private-sector workers after ten years of experience and was actually better for teachers late in their careers (after twenty-four years of experience). But North Carolina's teacher salary schedule still comes up short in the salary bumps during the first twelve years of experience.

To attract qualified individuals to teaching, the New Commission on the Skills of the American Workforce recommends a significant increase in both the beginning salary and salary earnings profile of teachers, but with a big caveat.[73] Teacher pay should be linked to student performance. North Carolina has instituted such a linkage, but the program has three limitations: the amount (two thousand dollars) is modest, is not indexed to inflation (and in fact has never been changed), and is tied to the academic performance of the entire school rather than of the particular teacher's students. Ironically, one of the most detailed studies on the benefits of financial incentives for teachers analyzed a North Carolina pilot program that ran from 2001 to 2004 and paid teachers a bonus if they agreed to work in high-poverty or academically failing schools.[74] The researchers found that the bonus increased the retention rate for teachers. A recent national study also found a statistical linkage between teacher merit pay plans and student academic performance.[75]

Experts argue that if North Carolina were to move to paying teachers based on performance, their pay should be based on their students' relative rather than absolute performance.[76] Absolute performance looks at some grade or standard achieved by students, whereas relative performance looks at the change in the grade or standard. Using absolute performance would reward those teachers with the highest-achieving students, irrespective of how much improvement the students made. In contrast, relative performance rewards those teachers whose students improved the most, no matter their ending level. North Carolina has in place a system for tracking the relative performance of students and linking that performance to individual teachers, but as of 2007, no plans existed to use that information for differential pay raises for teachers.[77] Research also suggests that for merit pay plans to create the intended incentives, the rules must be structured so that much fewer than half of teachers receive the bonus.[78]

Although appealing in concept, pay for performance can be divisive and potentially counterproductive if teachers do not embrace the methodology for evaluation.[79] Rather than following this path, North Carolina has focused on improving teacher training. The state has had one of the most aggressive programs to increase the proportion of teachers with advanced training certification, and some analysts credit this approach with generating the impressive gains in student achievement.[80] However, the academic community is far from unanimous in this view. Several studies question the alleged tie between teacher certification and student performance, instead recommending that schools focus on retaining teachers who have already demonstrated an ability to improve student achievement.[81]

Teachers are a—perhaps *the*—key part of the K–12 education equation. Highly qualified and highly motivated individuals are unquestionably the ideal for teachers, especially with education's increased importance in the Connected Age and beyond. But how can this goal best be attained? The added competitive pressures associated with this era suggest that more attention should go to the roles of teacher incentives in both motivating and directing their behavior. By implication, some movement to matching pay and performance will likely need to be made.

Means of Delivery

This section discusses all the other inputs in the K–12 education process, chiefly those involving technology, curriculum, and the hotly contested issue of school choice. In each of these areas, significant change and debate took place during the Connected Age.

As one of the defining features of the late twentieth and early twenty-first centuries, technology appropriately entered the classroom. Real spending per pupil on classroom technology, including funds for computer centers, media, and associated staff development and training, increased 38 percent nationwide between 1992 and 2005. Yet in North Carolina, that increase amounted to only 5 percent.[82] Other data show that North Carolina spent $16 per pupil on technology in 2001, compared to $104 for the nation as a whole.[83] The relative timidity with which North Carolina has adopted technology for use in K–12 education may be appropriate given a national study questioning its effectiveness. The research found that student test scores were not significantly higher in classrooms that employed reading and mathematical software products.[84] Similar research in North Carolina reached inconclusive results on the role of technological equipment in student outcomes.[85]

But just a few studies do not constitute the last word on technology's role in education. Technology's uses as a teaching aid, ability to provide individualized student instruction, and coordination with traditional classroom teaching methods are in their infancy. As the cost of technology falls and as technological devices become more widely used, especially among youths, North Carolina schools will find more effective ways to employ these products and techniques in learning.

Analysts have long debated whether public education should emphasize broadly educating students as citizens or providing specific training for specific occupations. Should public schools, especially high schools, primarily instruct students in core academic subjects that will serve them throughout their lifetimes, regardless of their occupations? Or should high schools provide options for vocational training, which necessarily means less time for the basics? This debate may have gained vigor during the Connected Age given the upheaval occurring in the state's job market.

North Carolina consequently edged the pendulum toward the vocational side. While the state does not have technical or vocational high schools, it does have an impressive post-high-school community college system that provides mostly technical two-year-degree programs. In 2004, the state instituted the Learn and Earn program, a five-year high school curriculum that allows students to acquire high school degrees and community college associate degrees. Begun modestly, the program is slated by 2008 to be in seventy-five high schools and to offer forty thousand online community college and university courses to high school students.[86]

Three factors have motivated the move to make high school more job-focused. First is North Carolina's high dropout rate and low high school completion rate, which observers assume are at least partly related to the fact that some students do not see a practical purpose for high school. Second, forecasts hold that the state will create more technical positions for auto mechanics, computer technicians, laboratory assistants, and the like than it is currently on track to fill.[87] To eliminate this gap, more high school students need to graduate and receive some postsecondary education. Third, research shows that programs linking school to work increase the likelihood that less motivated students—especially males—will complete school and become gainfully employed.[88] Still, debate continues about how far such programs should expand and at what cost to broader objectives regarding an informed citizenry.[89]

The most intensely contested aspect of delivering K–12 education during the Connected Age concerned school choice. A vocal group of academics, educators, and parents has argued that a stiff dose of competition will go a long way toward curing the perceived ills of public schools and improving elementary and secondary education overall. Just as competition in the private marketplace brings greater effectiveness, greater efficiency, lower prices, and increased attention to customers' desires, advocates believe that competition in education could result in lower costs, higher student attainment, and greater recognition of individual student needs.[90]

In North Carolina, the policy initiative addressing school choice is charter schools. Authorized in 1996, these schools receive public operating funds but are privately run and have greater flexibility in their curriculum and functioning than traditional public schools. Parents apply for admission for their children, and the state monitors the schools' progress and makes periodic evaluations for continuation of the charter. In 2001, eighteen thousand North Carolina students, or 1.3 percent of total K–12 enrollment, attended charter schools, and 93 percent of the state's limit of one hundred charter schools had been allocated.[91]

The major public policy question for charter schools is whether they work—that is, do they result in improved student outcomes? The evidence to date from North Carolina's charter schools is no. Two major studies of charter schools in North Carolina, by Robert Bifulco and Helen F. Ladd and by Caroline M. Hoxby, either found no difference between the performance of charter school students and that of other students or found that charter school students performed more poorly.[92] Reexamining Hoxby's results, Craig M. Newmark found no difference overall between the two groups of students but also found that more established charter schools and students with longer attendance at charter schools had better results than students at traditional schools.[93] Although it is both too early and too difficult to accurately access the full effects of charter schools, these findings strongly indicate that the state is unlikely quickly or significantly to raise the current numerical limit on charter schools.

During the Connected Age, North Carolina experienced controversy over educational financing. Since the 1930s, the state government has funded the majority of K–12 education. In 2003–4, for example, the state paid 63 percent of the costs of education, while the federal government paid 10 percent and local governments paid 27 percent. In the average state, the state and local split is almost even.[94] Nonetheless, a group of North Carolina's low-wealth counties sued, claiming that their relatively poor economic status hindered their ability adequately to fund the local share. The North Carolina Supreme Court agreed, ruling in 1997 that the state constitution guarantees every child an opportunity to receive a basic education and directing the state to fulfill that guarantee. Since the ruling, additional state funds have been allocated for K–12 education in designated low-wealth counties, and by 2005, spending per pupil from all sources in the state's lowest-wealth counties exceeded comparable spending amounts in the highest-wealth counties.[95]

This discussion of K–12 education leads to three key conclusions. First, attracting and retaining academically elite individuals as teachers has become more difficult during the Connected Age. Therefore, both salary levels and earnings profiles will need to be brought more in line with private-sector jobs, particularly those that are close substitutes for individuals with an aptitude for teaching. The New Commission on the Skills of the American Workforce recommends that compensation be shifted out of funding teacher pensions, where levels are typically more generous than the private sector, to augmenting salaries. In other words, teachers should be paid more while they are working and less when they are retired.[96]

"Performance," "productivity," and "achievement" are terms associated with the more competitive and results-oriented environment of the Connected Age, and these standards eventually will reach κ–12 education. To some extent, the federal No Child Left Behind legislation and North Carolina's evaluation of individual schools' progress have already implemented these measures at the κ–12 level. But the next step will be to take these assessments to the level of the individual teacher and to link salary gains to student performance. To succeed, however, the process will have to be transparent, considered fair by teachers, and implemented in a way that maintains good collegial relations. Basing student performance on a relative standard is a necessity. The value of teachers' postdegree training and certification will remain subject to debate.

The process of delivering κ–12 education will also likely evolve. Complementary technological techniques that provide more customized instruction to the individual student, allow for more parental involvement, and give students more real-world applications for their knowledge will be refined and implemented. Technology may eventually permit the transfer to the classroom of noninstructional resources in administration and transportation.

However, behind all these conclusions lies the sobering matter of how much schools can really do. An analysis of the academic performance of North Carolina students from 1989 to 1992 found that all the inputs provided by schools, including the quality of teachers, time allocated to each student, technology, and other equipment, collectively could account for at most 20 percent of the variation in student achievement. The most consistent school factor linked to improved outcomes was lower student/teacher ratios, and even more important were the influences of parents and the neighborhoods where students lived.[97] Other analyses have confirmed this conclusion.[98]

North Carolina's economic success during the Connected Age is tied to improvement in κ–12 education. Moreover, κ–12 education is a multifaceted process that involves schools, students, parents, and the wider environment. Coordinating all these factors to produce a student ready for the challenges of the Connected Age in many ways poses the most daunting challenge of all.

Higher Education: Who Pays?

North Carolina has long been a leading state in higher education. The University of North Carolina at Chapel Hill was the nation's first public university.[99] In the 1950s, the state's community college system pioneered customized training for businesses.[100] At its inception, the state recognized the value of education by stipulating in its constitution that higher education "as far as practicable, be extended to the people of the state free of expense."[101]

North Carolinians responded to the increasing value of higher education during the Connected Age by enrolling in colleges and universities at rates never before seen. Enrollment in four-year public universities, two-year public community colleges, and four-year private colleges and universities rose from 190,594 in 1972 to 467,987 in 2005, a 147 percent increase.[102] More telling, the state's percentage of college-aged persons (eighteen- to twenty-four-year-olds) enrolled in higher education jumped from 27 percent in 1972 to 52 percent in 2005; the percentage of the total population enrolled in higher education increased from 3.6 percent to 5.4 percent over the same period.[103] As a result, the percentage of adults with bachelor's degrees rose threefold, from 8.5 percent in 1970 to 25.4 percent in 2005.[104]

As table 6-2 shows, state policymakers acted on the perceived need to expand opportunities for higher education by increasing the relative share of the state's total resources devoted to public funding of higher education institutions by 50 percent (from 1.4 percent of GSP in 1972 to 2.1 percent in 2005). This increase fell roughly in line with the expansion in enrollment (that is, the increase in the percentage of all persons enrolled in college also represents a 50 percent gain).

Yet many people, especially those who strictly interpreted the state constitution's mandate on the cost of higher education, were disturbed by the commensurate rise in student costs. In-state tuition and required fees, in inflation-adjusted terms, rose steadily at both the public university and community college levels (figures 6-2 and 6-3). From 1972 to 2004, real public university tuition and required fees for in-state undergraduates increased almost 90 percent, and real community college tuition and required fees rose 120 percent. All of the increases occurred after 1980.

Even with these increases, public higher education in North Carolina remained a bargain compared to other states. In 2005, average tuition and required fees at the state's public universities were twelfth-lowest in the nation; tuition and fees for two-year public community colleges were sixth-lowest.[105] In addition, estimates show that in 2006, student tuition and fees accounted for only 18 percent of the academic budget of the University of North Carolina campuses and 13 percent of the cost of the North Carolina Community College System.[106]

Still, the rise in real tuition costs to students is worrisome, given the goal of raising the state's academic achievement levels. But another important policy element, the amount of student financial aid, must be considered in the student cost of higher education. Figures 6-2 and 6-3 show two adjustments to tuitions, termed "net tuition," which give the cost to in-state undergraduate students after accounting for public financial assistance.[107]

The measures display some interesting patterns. For in-state University of North Carolina System undergraduates (figure 6-2), the net tuition after subtracting scholarships and grants follows the overall pattern of total tuition except at a much lower level. Although this measure has risen since the 1980s, its 2004 level was only marginally higher than its 1972 level. The net tuition measure subtracting scholarships, grants, and loans also follows the pattern of the other two measures, although at a still lower level, until the late 1980s, when total tuition began its aggressive rise. The second measure of net tuition began to drop dramatically, suggesting that policymakers used loans to counteract the rise in paid tuition. In the 1990s and early part of the following century, the second measure of net tuition turned negative, meaning that the average student received enough financial aid to completely cover tuition and fees and had funds remaining for other expenses.

The pattern for community college tuitions (figure 6-3) differs. Here, scholarships and grants totally countered the rise in paid tuition since the late 1980s, making net tuition after subtracting these forms of financial aid negative by the turn of the century. Adding loans increased this trend only slightly.

Thus, public policy responded to the rising cost of higher education in the Connected Age by significantly increasing student financial aid. State-funded financial aid for higher education in North Carolina rose an incredible 2,400 percent in real terms between 1989 and 2003, and North Carolina ranked sixth among all states in its percentage increase in aid from 1993 to 2003.[108] The percentage of students enrolled in the University of North Carolina System receiving scholarships and grant awards rose from 22 percent to 85 percent from 1989 to 2003.[109] National research shows that the availability of college financial aid is linked to increases in college enrollment.[110]

But if the additional financial aid to higher education counteracted higher tuition and fees, couldn't the rise in tuition and fees have been moderated, thereby eliminating the need for more financial aid? Richard Vedder argues that higher education has practiced a form of market segmentation during the Connected Age.[111] Market segmentation is a widely used business technique of separating customers into different groups based on their sensitivity to the price of the product or service. Those less sensitive to price changes pay higher prices, and those more sensitive pay lower prices. Businesses have found that using market segmentation, where practical, can lead to higher profits than when all customers are charged the same price.

Public universities and colleges do not, of course, earn profits, but their objective of increasing enrollment can also be met through market segmentation. In this case, customers (students) who are less sensitive to price (tuition)

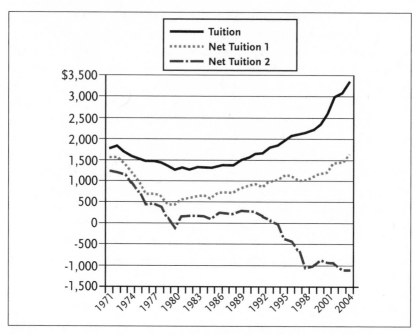

Figure 6-2. Average in-state undergraduate annual tuition at University of North Carolina System campuses before and after financial aid, 1971–2001.

DATA SOURCES: University of North Carolina Board of Governors; U.S. Department of Labor, Bureau of Labor Statistics, "Consumer Price Index."

NOTE: All amounts in 2004 dollars.

Net tuition 1 = net student tuition and fees after accounting for scholarships and grants

Net tuition 2 = net student cost after accounting for scholarships, grants, and loans

changes are charged higher prices, while more tuition-sensitive students are charged lower prices. The means of segmenting students is income (usually of the parents), and the method of altering the price is financial aid. Students who have higher-income parents and whose attendance decisions presumably are not as impacted by increases in tuition are charged the full tuition price, while students whose parents have lower incomes and who are more affected by increases in tuition receive financial aid and thus pay a lower net tuition. Analysis of University of North Carolina System data show that net tuitions for students from lower-income households have been rising at much slower rates than net tuitions for students from higher-income households.[112]

With the increasing emphasis on higher education as the way for North Carolina to compete in the globalized economy and to raise standards of

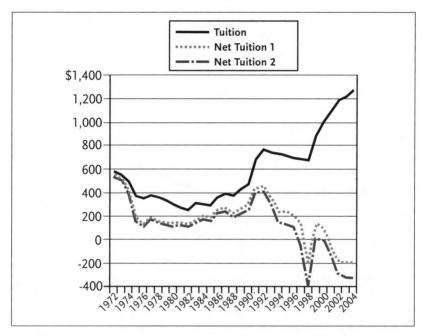

Figure 6-3. Average annual tuition at North Carolina Community College System campuses before and after financial aid, 1972–2004.
DATA SOURCES: University of North Carolina Board of Governors; U.S. Department of Education; U.S. Department of Labor, Bureau of Labor Statistics, "Consumer Price Index."
NOTE: All amounts in 2004 dollars.
Net tuition 1 = net student tuition and fees after accounting for scholarships and grants
Net tuition 2 = net student cost after accounting for scholarships, grants, and loans

living, enrollments are expected to increase at rates more than double the rate of general population growth.[113] This situation presents the state with an enormous funding challenge, implying that a larger share of GSP must be devoted to publicly funded higher education. With increases in other demands on public budgets, particularly from income transfers for medical support for the elderly and indigent as well as infrastructure needs, a greater share for higher education cannot be assumed to be forthcoming.

Without greater public funding support, the expansion of public higher education in North Carolina can be financed in two ways. One is through improved productivity—increasing the ratio of output (student degrees) to inputs (faculty, buildings, equipment). Student output is typically measured by the five-year completion rate—the percentage of undergraduate students who finish their degrees within five years. For example, for the University of North Carolina System, 54 percent of entering freshmen in 2001 finished within five years.[114] More intense counseling and advising of students, earlier identification of the most appropriate major and plan of work, and even substantially higher tuitions for students taking longer than four years are potential methods for improving the speed with which students complete their degrees. In particular, some evidence indicates that the time taken to complete a degree is linked to tuition rates. A 2004 study found that lower tuition rates were associated with increasing amounts of time to graduation.[115]

Improving input productivity means more efficiently utilizing both human inputs (faculty) and physical inputs (buildings, equipment) in the higher education process. For example, faculty productivity rates could be improved by increasing class sizes, by increasing the number of classes each faculty member teaches, or by some combination of the two.[116] Of course, any of these measures would have the potential downside of less faculty time per student and hence could adversely affect the quality of instruction.[117]

Distance learning has expanded during the Connected Age and is likely to continue to expand. The number of students served by distance, or online, courses at University of North Carolina System campuses jumped 189 percent from 1999 to 2003, and the rate of growth is expected to climb further in the future.[118] While current studies show that distance courses provide no faculty or physical input savings to the university, this finding may result from the relatively small size of distance learning courses to date.[119] The technology has the potential to transform the delivery of education, however. Direct student-instructor interaction, classroom discussions, and even simulated laboratory experiments are already possible. Of course, students lose the benefits of the campus experience.

Higher education institutions can also garner resources outside of state appropriations through higher tuitions. Tuition increases to keep pace with inflation (leaving real tuitions stable) certainly are to be expected, so the question is whether tuition hikes beyond this level will occur. The answer is likely yes, as such increases enable universities and colleges to continue their successful market segmentation plan. To garner public acceptance, such increases must meet two conditions. First, the real tuition increases must be accompanied by corresponding real financial aid increases, thereby allowing students who lack financial resources to have opportunities for higher education. Second, even with the higher real tuitions, the student rate of return, measured by the gain in future income compared to the tuition cost, must remain substantial and superior to most investments.[120]

Finally, the impending retirement of almost two-thirds of the faculty by 2025 will dramatically affect the future costs of North Carolina's public universities and colleges and potentially impede their ability to elevate the educational level of future residents of the state.[121] Two trends will adversely affect not only replacement of this faculty but also the hiring of additional faculty to meet increased student numbers: the smaller size of the replacement generation and expanded opportunities for employment of highly educated individuals outside of education. Attracting replacements and new hires will likely require significantly higher real salary offers, which will further exacerbate the fiscal pinch in higher education. From 1970 to 2005, the average salaries of University of North Carolina System faculty rose at a rate no higher than that for all workers in the state, while salary increases for North Carolina Community College System faculty trailed those of other jobs.[122] These trends cannot be sustained in the future.

One alternative, sure to be very controversial, involves using technology to hire remote faculty in foreign countries to teach North Carolina–based and –credited online courses. The faculty could be full time or adjunct, would be evaluated based on their credentials and performance, but presumably could be paid at discounted rates if they were from developing countries such as India, China, or those in Eastern Europe. Increasing the faculty pool to include foreign competitors could also put downward pressure on salaries for domestic hires. Although this practice has not yet been considered, it may become a viable option as pressures on higher education mount and communication technology brings the world even closer together.

North Carolina's public higher education sector will almost certainly grow in relative size in the coming decades as a consequence of the payoff in terms of expanded income, added jobs, and an improved standard of living. The big questions are how this expansion will happen and who will pay for it. To what extent will higher education's delivery model of bricks and mortar and in-person lectures be replaced by the cyberspace technique of online courses? Will this shift be enough to boost higher education's productivity and avoid massive and costly new construction efforts? With the growth of the Hispanic population, particularly among the college-age population, will undocumented individuals receive lower in-state tuition rates? How much more will educational institutions have to pay for increasingly scarce new faculty, and could foreign faculty play an increased role? At what cost? Finally, what combination of added state appropriations and higher real tuitions will pay the bill for expansion that is not funded through productivity improvements? And does it even matter? Examining most states between 1977 and

2002, Vedder found a positive association between state appropriations for higher education and higher education enrollment, yet this connection was relatively weak. According to his model, increasing state appropriations by 20 percent reduces the proportion of those not attending higher education institutions by only 1 percent.[123] The benefit of a higher education degree in today's economy may be so strong as to surmount any impediments created by cost.

Early and Late Education: Effective, Enough?

Although K–12 and higher education form the core of North Carolina's public commitment to academic achievement, two other educational components received added attention during the Connected Age: early childhood or preschool education and adult education, better known as worker retraining.

The goal of improving elementary education outcomes, in particular, sparked a new focus on early childhood education. Studies have documented that crucial learning takes place before children enter school, and if this learning is impeded or incomplete, academic achievement in elementary school and beyond can be reduced.[124] Thus, with education perhaps the top policy priority of the Connected Age, policymakers have put new emphasis on preparing children before they reached school.

The focus began at the federal level with Head Start. Created in 1965, Head Start provides child care assistance and learning programs for children aged three, four, and five from income-disadvantaged families. In 2002, Head Start served approximately nine hundred thousand children annually, including twenty thousand in North Carolina.[125] Detailed research has found that Head Start children show gains in vocabulary and that these gains persist over time unless counteracted by other circumstances.[126]

North Carolina added to the federal efforts in early childhood education with two programs instituted during the Connected Age. In 1993, Smart Start began as a collaboration of public and private resources to assist locally based programs that helped disadvantaged children become ready for school. The program operates through county child care facilities and helps pay for equipment and child care subsidies. By 2004, Smart Start was assisting children in every North Carolina county at an annual cost of approximately $200 million.[127]

A state-funded early childhood program more directly focused on education was added in 2001. The program, More at Four, operates in more of a classroom-based setting than does Smart Start, although the teaching can take place at schools as well as at child care and Head Start centers. By the sixth year of the program, More at Four was serving more than twenty thousand children at an annual cost of $85 million, with a planned expansion to near thirty thousand children in the next year.[128]

As with Head Start, a major question concerns the effectiveness of the two North Carolina programs. Both Smart Start and More at Four have been subject to ongoing evaluations. The latest research suggests that participation in Smart Start helps in the development of some learning capabilities but not others. For example, Smart Start children were found to have improved abilities in applied math, language recognition, counting, print awareness, and book knowledge, but they also showed no significant gains in social skills, positive behaviors, letters named, and story comprehension.[129] The results were more consistent for More at Four, where participating children demonstrated improvement in all learning categories.[130] It is too early to determine if these benefits persist over time.

Early childhood learning programs, especially for at-risk children, have probably become a permanent part of the educational system. The relative success of the programs must be monitored, both while children participate and later, when they move into k–12 classrooms and beyond.

At the other end of the age spectrum, worker retraining attained a new level of importance during the Connected Age, given the massive reshuffling of jobs in the state. As earlier chapters document, the downsizing of traditional manufacturing industries in North Carolina left hundreds of thousands of workers without employment in the only kinds of occupations many of them had ever held. Without upgrading their skills, most would be left to eke out a living in service-related jobs at the lower rungs of the pay ladder. Studies show that retraining older workers can succeed: one analysis demonstrated that for every year of training for older displaced workers, their long-run earnings increased between 8 and 10 percent.[131]

However, worker retraining is not easy. It requires not only funds for schooling but also time—time away from earning a living and from other responsibilities. It also requires a psychological adjustment as the trainee, who is usually older, returns to the classroom. North Carolina, like most states, has relied primarily on federal money for worker retraining programs. Yet these federal funds have been decreasing rather than increasing during the Connected Age. Between 1985 and 2003, federal worker retraining funds dropped 29 percent in real terms.[132]

The solution for adequately funded worker retraining programs may not lie in North Carolina or for that matter in federal monies from general tax-

payer sources. Instead, funding may need to come from those who have benefited from the conditions that created much of the job churning. A large proportion of the job losses in traditional manufacturing in North Carolina have
resulted from international trade agreements that allowed a good share of
this production to move to foreign countries. These agreements had domestic
beneficiaries—specifically, consumers who purchased lower-priced foreign-
made products.

For example, since the North American Free Trade Agreement and General Agreement on Tariffs and Trade were approved in the mid-1990s, clothing prices have fallen almost 1 percent annually, resulting in savings in 2003
of $20 billion to U.S. clothing purchasers. A special 5 percent sales tax applied
to clothing purchases in the United States, with the proceeds targeted to the
retraining of former textile and apparel workers, would still leave clothing
consumers with annual savings of $10 billion but would allow $12,000 to be
provided annually to every textile and apparel worker displaced since 1994.[133]
These funds could be used for education, financial support during retraining,
and relocation. Similar programs could be established for former workers in
other trade-affected industries.

In the absence of such substantial funding, the best way North Carolina
can assist displaced workers is with a robust community college and university system that is receptive to the needs of older, career-changing workers
and that offers affordable tuition rates and supportive financial aid. To its
credit, North Carolina appears to be providing such a system, although doing
so will likely become more difficult in the future.

Highways: Stuck in Potholes; Any Way Out?

As table 6-2 reveals, spending on highways is one of the few government
functions whose share of GSP declined during the Connected Age. This drop
in spending is directly linked to the relative decline in taxes devoted to highway spending and in particular to the inability of those taxes to keep pace
with inflation.[134] As a result, real highway spending per vehicle in the state
was lower in 2004 than in 1972.

Three adverse consequences have arisen from this situation. First, evidence indicates that the quality of North Carolina's roads has suffered. The
state's roads, bridges, and even interstates have consistently been rated poor
and have ranked in the bottom ten among the fifty states in condition during
the 1990s and early twenty-first century.[135] The state has also been well above
average on fatality rates per mile traveled.[136] Second, traffic congestion has

increased, particularly in such large urban regions as Charlotte and the Triangle, where it is forecast to double by 2030.[137] Third is an estimated backlog in required maintenance spending that the American Society of Engineers put at $29 billion between 2005 and 2030.[138]

In addition to these problems, North Carolina faces the continuing issue of the distribution of highway funds. As already noted, the vast majority of the state's highway funds are dispensed at the state level. An analysis of data from 1990 to 2004 showed considerable variation in highway spending per vehicle mile traveled among regions in the state, with rural counties tending to win out over urban counties. For example, the large urban counties of Mecklenburg (Charlotte), Wake (Raleigh), Forsyth (Winston-Salem), and Guilford (Greensboro) ranked seventy-third, seventy-fifth, ninety-fifth, and fifty-first, respectively, among the state's one hundred counties in highway expenditures per daily vehicle mile traveled.[139] These counties also came up short when the amount of highway spending was measured as a percentage of state gas taxes paid.[140]

Addressing highway issues will first and foremost require more money. Problems with North Carolina's gas and vehicle taxes have already been noted, and solutions have been proposed. North Carolina also loses out on the federal gas tax, receiving only 86 cents in federal highway funds for every dollar of the tax sent to Washington in 2003. This imbalance has led to calls for abolishing the federal gas tax and allowing states to add that rate to their state tax.[141]

The distribution issue in North Carolina could be addressed by splitting the state gas tax into two parts—a state component that would still be allocated by state-level decision makers and a local component where revenues would be spent only in the region where the funds were collected. Another way of accomplishing the same objective would be to keep the current form and level of the state gas tax but give local governments the authority to add local versions. In 2007, North Carolina moved toward more local involvement in road construction by removing the seventy-year-old ban on road construction by county governments.[142]

The most difficult transportation issue to address may be congestion, especially in the fast-growing urbanized communities. Both Charlotte and the Triangle have attempted to add light rail to their transportation options. Charlotte's system is further along, with the initial ten-mile, $427 million line of a multi-billion-dollar project having opened in late 2007. The Triangle project currently is on hold as a result of the denial of federal funding. Analysts say that Charlotte, with its one-center focus, is better suited to rail transit than the multicentered Triangle.[143] Still, skeptics argue that neither region is dense enough to attract significant ridership, and the large up-front construction costs and heavy operating subsidies would be better spent on using traditional highway projects to reduce congestion.[144]

Alternatively, many economists think that creative pricing is the efficient way to motivate drivers to account for congestion in their commuting behavior. Ideas such as congestion fees required for entering a highly urbanized and crowded area, high-occupancy vehicle lanes that reward vehicles carrying multiple riders, and altering the charges on North Carolina's future toll roads to reflect varying levels of congestion are behavioral approaches that use incentives to control traffic levels.[145]

Income Transfers: Can the Growth Be Contained?

Numerous images can be used to describe the growing size of income transfer spending—the program with the insatiable appetite, the eight-hundred-pound boulder at the budget table, and the budget line with no limits. Income transfer spending undoubtedly is the fastest-growing part of public spending in North Carolina, more than doubling its share of the state economy in less than twenty-five years and with no end to the growth in sight. Like the old saying about a star athlete, "Don't expect to control him, just hope to contain him," North Carolina is struggling to even get close to containing income transfers.

Broadly defined, income transfers are government payments to help support people with their expenses. Specifically, these transfers include programs such as Social Security, Medicare and Medicaid, income maintenance (welfare), unemployment insurance, and veterans' benefits. Some of the programs pay cash, while others pay providers for services delivered to people.

With the growth of income transfers during the Connected Age, they not surprisingly became a more important part of individual financial support. Income transfers to individuals increased from 7 percent of total personal income in 1970 to 16 percent in 2005.[146] Perhaps more significant, income transfers became even more dominant in low-wealth counties. In the state's ten lowest-wealth counties, income transfers rose from 9 percent of personal income in 1970 to 25 percent in 2005. In contrast, in the state's two wealthiest counties, Mecklenburg and Wake, income transfers increased only from 5 percent to 8 percent of personal income.[147]

Many of the income transfer programs, including Social Security, Medicare, and veterans' benefits, receive all of their funding from the federal government, which directly pays individuals or those who provide services to individuals. The state has no financial involvement in these programs. Other income transfer programs are federally funded but administered by the state—for example, the Food Stamp program. Still other programs—most prominently, Temporary Assistance for Needy Families—are funded jointly by the federal and state governments. Finally, Medicaid, which assists income-qualified households with their medical expenses, was funded by the federal, state, and local (county) governments in North Carolina. By the twenty-first century, this program had grown into one of the dominant factors—if not *the* most dominant factor—in both state and county budgets.

All states are required to share in the cost of Medicaid, and as in most states, North Carolina's state-level costs increased rapidly during the Connected Age. Medicaid participants jumped from 8 percent of the state's population in 1979 to more than 18 percent in 2005.[148] In 1979, state costs in 2005 dollars were estimated at $129 million, or 0.2 percent of GSP. By 2005, state costs had risen to $2.8 billion, 0.8 percent of GSP.[149] In 2006, Medicaid took a larger share of the state's General Fund than all but K–12 public education. Just between 1996 and 2006, Medicaid's share of the General Fund doubled.[150] These increases resulted from the rising number of participants, the increased real costs of medical care, and expanded coverage.[151]

But North Carolina was one of only six states requiring counties to pay part of Medicaid's costs.[152] As a consequence, North Carolina's counties bore some of the rising burden of Medicaid expenses, with real expenditures in 2005 dollars growing from $23 million in 1979 (0.02 percent of GSP) to $494 million in 2005 (0.14 percent of GSP).[153] The local funding requirement especially stressed the budgets of low-wealth counties, which had the fastest relative growth in Medicaid participants to go along with the slowest-growing economies. In 2005, eighteen counties spent more than one-fifth of their property tax revenues on Medicaid expenditures, and all but two of these counties had average property wealth below the state average.[154] In 2009, the state will assume the county share of Medicaid spending; in return, the counties will transfer part of the local sales tax to state coffers.[155]

The growth in Medicaid is not expected to slow. The Congressional Budget Office predicts that between 2006 and 2017, federal expenditures on Medicaid as a percentage of the national economy (gross domestic product) will increase by 50 percent, from 1.4 percent to 2 percent. Such growth would imply a comparable increase in state Medicaid spending in North Carolina from 0.9 percent of GSP to 1.4 percent.[156]

Such increases may well be both expected and necessary as the population ages and the usage of health care per person expands. However, some observers believe that the growth in Medicaid threatens other public programs or might lead to higher relative tax payments. Proponents of this view have made two proposals to contain Medicaid costs in North Carolina. First, the apparent generosity of Medicaid payments could be reduced by tightening eligibility requirements and limiting financial assistance. By some measures, the state's Medicaid spending is the highest among southeastern states.[157]

The other proposal involves shifting Medicaid from a supply-side program that directly covers medical expenses to a demand-side program that enables participants to purchase private-market medical insurance. Under this plan, the allotted Medicaid budget would be converted to medical insurance vouchers, which clients would use to purchase private insurance. Because users would face limitations on and incentives for their behavior imposed by the insurance policies, supporters believe that the plan would lead to more efficient use of medical facilities and slower growth in total spending. Florida, South Carolina, and Oklahoma have experimented with Medicaid vouchers.[158]

North Carolina has already made changes to another income-transfer program, cash welfare, that have resulted in declining usage. As part of a national overhaul of welfare in which its open-ended, or entitlement, status was revoked and replaced with limited annual budgetary amounts, North Carolina instituted the Work First program in 1997. Work First sought to use a combination of positive and negative incentives to move welfare recipients off the rolls and into self-sufficient work. The positive incentives included providing child care, transportation, and other assistance for recipients enrolled in educational and training programs, while the negative incentives included a time limit of two years for the receipt of cash welfare.[159] However, Work First did not affect recipients' ability to continue receiving benefits from other income transfer programs such as Food Stamps and Medicaid.

Strong evidence indicates that Work First has reduced reliance on cash welfare. The number of individuals receiving cash assistance dropped by two-thirds in the decade beginning in the mid-1990s, and the percentage of the population on the cash welfare lists fell from 4 percent to 1 percent over the same period.[160] Labor market participation and labor earnings for former users of cash welfare have both risen, while their rate of unemployment and incidence of poverty have fallen. But these changes have had inconsistent results with regard to child well-being.[161]

Economic Development: In Search of a Policy Direction

Economic development policy can be interpreted broadly or narrowly. Broadly, it includes all of the state's public policies that impact economic development—education, highways, worker training, and income transfers, plus tax policy and any specialized policies for recruiting businesses. Narrowly, it is limited only to policies related to business recruitment. Since the chapter has already discussed all the topics except business recruitment, this section focuses on that area.

North Carolina has had a long history of active business recruitment. The state, along with most of its southern sisters, began pursuing outside businesses after tremendous productivity gains in agriculture released hundreds of thousands of workers from the formerly labor-intensive industry. Recruiters naturally stressed the region's advantages—low wages, available labor supply, low taxes, and ready land. Financial incentives in the form of property tax exemptions and direct subsidies through industrial bonds were also used. North Carolina was one of the least aggressive players in financial incentives, preferring to emphasize not only its labor costs but also its superior educational system.[162]

However, prompted by the South's success in business recruitment and by job losses in traditional southern industries, states in both the North and South began a bidding war during the 1980s over trophy firms, upping the financial enticements to such companies.[163] Auto manufacturers provided a particularly appealing target in these bidding wars, and the South won many of the battles, with Saturn going to Tennessee, Toyota to Kentucky, BMW to South Carolina, and Mercedes-Benz to Alabama.[164]

But North Carolina registered none of these wins, and with neighboring South Carolina's success in developing an auto assembly and parts sector to cushion the loss of traditional manufacturing jobs, North Carolina's leaders faced pressure to become more active and aggressive in business recruitment. Since the 1990s, therefore, North Carolina has implemented three programs to provide direct financial incentives to new or expanding firms. The Lee Act offered tax credits to offset up to 50 percent of a company's state corporate income or franchise tax liability. The Job Development Investment Grant program allowed companies to receive grants ranging from 10 percent to 50 percent of the personal income tax withholdings from newly created jobs. The One North Carolina Fund set up a pool of money to be used at the governor's discretion in business recruitment. The programs have been widely used. The liability associated with the Lee Act is expected to approach $1 billion by the early twenty-first century. The Job Development Investment Grant program used $100 million in 2002–4 and is forecast to have used a cumulative $500 million by 2010. The One North Carolina Fund is stocked at the rate of $10 million annually, with a provision for an emergency supplement of $20 million.[165] In 2007, the state added a program to provide incentives to existing companies that upgrade their physical capital and meet other standards.[166]

Although the programs' goals—bringing or keeping good-paying jobs for North Carolinians—may be widely accepted, the means and outcomes of the programs have faced criticism. The Lee Act uses a multitiered system that provides more benefits to companies locating in lower-income counties. However, the majority of grants have gone to firms moving to richer counties.[167] The Lee Act has also received criticism for its ineffectiveness. One study estimated that only 4 percent of the new jobs associated with the program would not otherwise have been created.[168] The Job Development Investment Grant program and One North Carolina Fund have also been cited as disproportionately assisting businesses in less economically distressed counties.[169]

Supporters of these programs have countered by arguing for the importance of creating new employment in the state, no matter where the jobs are located. Unemployed or underemployed workers may be better off with new jobs, even if they involve cross-county commuting or residential relocation, as long as earnings, net of the commute or residential move, improve.

The biggest controversy over North Carolina's active business recruitment efforts has been for efforts outside of these three programs. In several instances, the state has approved large—sometimes more than $100 million— financial incentives packages for individual firms.[170] Criticism of the packages has focused on two areas. Opponents have launched a legal challenge on the basis that many of the financial incentives involve tax reductions and that this practice violates the state constitution because it benefits specific firms rather than the general public.[171] In 2006, a North Carolina Superior Court judge dismissed the suit on the grounds that the plaintiffs had not shown that they suffered direct injury.[172] Second, critics have questioned technical points in the state's economic model used to estimate the relative benefits and costs of offering financial incentives to attract firms.[173]

More broadly, public financial incentives as a business recruitment tool raise two issues: What is the economic logic behind the tool, and is it effective? An economic explanation for the use of financial incentives is again based on the notion of market segmentation. If a state seeks to maximize some measure of economic activity, such as production, jobs, or income, then it may find that the best way to do so is to charge different tax rates to different categories of firms. Firms already located in the state and for whom relocation would require major expenses would likely be less sensitive to changes in state tax rates. Conversely, firms not currently committed to either expanding or locating in a state would be more sensitive to state tax rate changes. In this situation, the state rationally should charge existing firms the full state tax rate and newly locating or expanding firms a lower tax rate via financial incentives.[174]

Most academic studies find financial incentives for business recruitment ineffective, reaching this conclusion either by asking firms to rate the relative importance of incentives in their business location decisions or by using statistical analysis to measure the importance of incentives to a state's economic growth or to the economic growth of individual firms.[175] Yet such studies face challenges on two levels. First, survey results may be suspicious if business owners hesitate to claim the benefits of incentives.[176] Second, scholars have difficulty controlling for all relevant factors before isolating the impact of incentives in statistical analyses.

An innovative study addressed both of these potential shortcomings by comparing the economic outcomes in locations that used incentives to attract companies to the economic outcomes in runner-up locations—that is, counties that also bid for companies but did not get them. The authors assumed that companies examine all possible locations and winnow the list to two or three that are virtually identical in all important characteristics. At this point, financial incentives become important because they can break the tie. The authors found that winning locations indeed had stronger economic growth than runner-up locations.[177]

In addition to the financial incentive programs for recruiting businesses, the state has implemented two organizational structures with an economic development mission. The Microelectronics Center of North Carolina was established in 1980 as a nonprofit organization to lead and coordinate development in the technology sector. The Microelectronics Center works on research and technology transfer issues predominantly through the public university and community college systems. In 1986, the North Carolina Rural Economic Development Center was formed to focus and coordinate stimulus efforts for the state's rural counties. It conducts research, serves as a clearinghouse for information about rural areas, and manages some grant programs assigned by the General Assembly.

The state went beyond its role of recruiter, catalyst, information coordinator, and financer of standard infrastructure (water, sewer) with one—some would say ill-fated—project, the Global Transpark, begun in the early 1990s. The concept involved having the state construct a modern air cargo jetport capable of handling the world's largest planes. The plan was that just-in-time manufacturing firms would locate adjacent to the jetport and fill orders from clients around the world. The Transpark was placed in an economically distressed region in eastern North Carolina and was expected to do for that area what the Research Triangle Park had done for the central part of the state. Supporters projected a total of one hundred thousand jobs and a multi-billion-dollar impact by 2010.[178]

But the project fell far short of those goals. After spending $112 million in public money, the complex has generated little in the way of jobs or commerce.[179] Some observers cite environmental issues as hindering the project from the start, while others believe that the state's existing major airports are adequately handling the cargo function and still others see the project as just ahead of its time.[180] For whatever reasons, the Global Transpark never got off the ground and has been a major disappointment for the state's economic development strategy.[181]

The failure of the Global Transpark brings the discussion of North Carolina's economic development policy full circle to the debate between passive and active policies. The Global Transpark was the epitome of an active policy. The state clearly selected a specific development project and funded it, but it failed. Opponents of the active strategy cite this example to argue against such activism. Public decision makers have no particular ability to select winning economic development projects or winning firms. And when failure occurs, the public money spent is lost. These thinkers believe that a better approach involves following the passive economic development strategy of spending public money on what is known to work—education, highways, and a general tax structure that is conducive to private-sector investment, risk taking, and entrepreneurship.

But the passive approach also has its major downside—time. Passive strategies, by their nature, focus on long-term policies that can take years to bear fruit. A decade or more may pass before the educational standards of a generation of workers can be raised permanently. Likewise, road building and other infrastructure investments are time-consuming and tedious, and tax impacts, while they can be quick, usually gain significantly in strength after a year or more.[182] Many people and regions lack the time to wait for results.

The dimensions of people and regions have given rise to a second, complementary debate in economic development policy. Simply stated, should development efforts focus on people by training them to succeed in the modern economy and then letting either the jobs come to them or the trained people go to the jobs? Or should public policy stress improving particular places and bringing development to the regions as part of a balanced growth strategy for the entire state? For example, such a policy would attempt to stem the brain drain that has occurred when rural areas lose their best and brightest students and workers to the greater economic opportunities of metropolitan counties.[183]

North Carolina may implicitly be following a middle strategy that merges elements of the active and passive and people versus places approaches. First, the majority of public resources are devoted to education. North Carolina spends more on higher education per state income than does the nation as a whole and has significantly increased access to its public universities and community colleges. The state has also achieved impressive improvements in K–12 educational attainment. This approach has been complemented with targeted business recruitment efforts, but with the amount of business incentives received by a firm tied to the firm's performance. If job targets are not met, the incentives are scaled back with tax credits linked to the company's production levels.[184]

Second, the major effort must be devoted to improving the training and educational credentials of people, wherever they reside, and policymakers must accept that people, especially young people, are mobile and will have a tendency to migrate to the fastest-growing job centers. When actions are undertaken to attract jobs to a particular location, especially an economically lagging area, utilize the local community college to upgrade the training capabilities of the local workforce, thereby combining the person and place economic development objectives.

Third, use government to improve the information about local economies that is available to potential investors. Web sites detailing local areas' strengths and assets, such as available land, building space, labor supply and costs, tax structure, and laws and regulations, must be updated and be available to companies and investors throughout the world. The Web sites can reduce the costs outside entrepreneurs incur in learning about North Carolina and its regions and can attract more detailed inquiries.

Policy Choices for a Connected Economy

As the Connected Age economy moves ahead at ever faster speeds, public decision makers struggle to keep up. A century ago, when times were slower, the arduous process of reaching political decisions about public issues could be tolerated. Not so today. The failure to act swiftly and decisively can mean missed opportunities that may never reappear.

Perhaps nowhere is this more clearly seen than with taxes. North Carolina's current tax system was developed in the 1930s, before the service economy, before globalization, before the Internet, and before both households and businesses enjoyed tremendous mobility. A consensus appears to be growing that the tax system needs to be changed and updated, most likely by expanding the tax base while lowering rates and reducing deductions and exemptions, but the trouble lies in getting from here to there. Tax codes are notoriously resistant to change for the simple reason that each component has a supporting constituency.

Tax change can proceed in one of two ways. It can occur in tiny steps, where small pieces are altered either as a result of the opposing constituency being overwhelmed and outvoted or the constituency being bought out by other public benefits. Or a "grand design"—a massive overhaul—can impose short-term pain on all constituencies but garner support through recognition that the resulting improved economic tide will eventually lift all boats. Because the current system is untenable over the long run, tax change will inevitably come. The questions are how soon and in what form?

Spending may even be a tougher issue than taxes because of the growing clash between education and transportation on the one hand and income transfers on the other.[185] A greater share of public resources will be needed for highways in the future, both to address future growth as well as to handle backlogs from subpar spending in the past. At the same time, higher education in particular will require more relative funding to keep pace with the rising share of the population attending college. Yet these growing demands will continue to bump up against the increasing portion of the budget consumed by income transfers. These three functions account for almost three-quarters of all public spending in North Carolina. So with pressures on each segment to grow, the inevitable result is an overall expansion in the relative size of the state's government. However, this growth can create a competitive problem if the increased spending continues to push North Carolina up in the state rankings of relative government size.

One way to address the public spending dilemma is to fund education, highways, and income transfers at their projected higher levels by increasing tax rates. If taxpayers believe that the economic returns from the additional spending more than compensate for the greater relative tax bill, this approach will both benefit citizens and improve North Carolina's economic standing among states.

A second approach is to privatize part of the payment for the additional public services, following the notion that where possible, direct beneficiaries of a public service logically should pay part of the costs. For higher education, this approach would mean increasing the share of total academic costs covered by tuition; for highways, it would imply greater use of toll roads. Converting the Medicaid program to a voucher system would force recipients to follow the financing rules established by private insurance vendors. In addition to shifting the financing burden from general taxes to a form of user fees, privatization may have the further benefit of motivating more efficient use of the public services.[186] On the downside, privatization could tilt more of the payment share for public services to lower-income households and thereby impede their access to these services.

Improving the productivity of the education, highway, and income transfer programs as well as of the programs comprising the other 25 percent of public spending in North Carolina is the third method of addressing the increasing pressures on public budgets. Raising productivity implies achieving more output with the same inputs or having output grow more quickly than inputs. One problem with this approach is that it assumes that output and inputs can be measured for each program. While inputs (program dollars spent, public employees hired) usually can be calibrated, outputs are sometimes more challenging. In education, reasonable outputs might be average test scores, graduation rates, and time to receive degrees, but what are the comparable outputs for medical care programs? And how can the influence of nongovernmental factors be removed so that only the relationship between government inputs and outputs is observed?

These are tough questions, but they are worth asking as ever-tighter public budgets make performance standards more valuable. One rather dramatic way of enforcing such standards is through use of a sunset provision in government budget deliberations—that is, the requirement that after a certain number of years, a government program is abolished unless legislators reauthorize it. Sunset provisions force public decision makers to reconsider and rejustify public programs in their entirety on a regular basis rather than merely to debate and vote on marginal changes. This process brings to the forefront such questions as whether the program requires public funding, what its objectives are, whether its goals could be accomplished as well in the private sector, and how the program has performed in the past.

Many public policy issues with which North Carolina has grappled during the Connected Age can be put in the context of the long-standing economics clash between efficiency and equity. In many ways, this clash became heightened during the era. As the Connected Age embraced international competition, deregulation, and productivity, the pressure to use all resources, both human and physical, to their utmost efficiency was raised. Getting the most from each dollar or person increasingly became the mantra. The move to reform welfare, the efforts to improve the educational levels of new workers, and the calls to measure the performance of teachers and government programs all exemplify this focus.

Yet the era clearly has left losers—high school dropouts and traditional manufacturing workers, among others—in its wake, and so equity plays an enhanced role in the Connected Age. Equity is the goal of providing more balance in the availability of resources to households of different earnings levels. A compassionate society will not let those at the bottom of the economic ladder be disproportionately and permanently disadvantaged. And as society's general standard of living has increased, what is considered acceptable for disadvantaged households has changed. Thus, programs such as Medicaid and Food Stamps and the national Earned Income Tax Credit have expanded their scope.

State and local budgets will continue the tug-of-war between efficiency and equity in coming decades. Efficiency will move public decision makers toward programs promoting self-sufficiency, establishing user fees, linking benefits and costs, and offering modest taxes and modest spending. Equity will attract leaders to adequacy, fairness, the fulfillment of basic standards, redistributive taxes, and larger budgets. How this tussle will be resolved, if at all, will partially determine the course of the Connected Age and its impacts on North Carolina's households and incomes.

7. North Carolina's Future

in the Connected Age

North Carolina has taken a long journey through the Connected Age, and the trip is not over. Most of the major trends associated with the era—globalization, deregulation, advances in communication and transportation technologies, stronger educational requirements, and increases in service spending—will not be reversed and likely will accelerate. North Carolina is now part of the international economy, where money, ideas, products, and even labor—through immigration and offshoring—move more easily across geographic and political boundaries. Economic opportunities have multiplied, the potential gains from success have never been higher, but those who are not prepared or who have been unlucky have quickly fallen behind.

Any shift in the underlying fundamentals of an economy will create pluses and minuses—winners and losers. That is the very essence of change. Those who persist in doing things the old way lose out, while those who adopt the new methods win. The Connected Age clearly has created classes of winners and losers in North Carolina at many levels. Industrially, the Big Three of tobacco, textiles, and furniture is out, replaced by the new Big Five of technology, pharmaceuticals, banking, food processing, and vehicle parts. College-educated workers have gained income, while non-college-educated workers have experienced real income declines. Urban regions with steady streams of college graduates as well as resort and retirement communities have thrived at the same time that small towns and rural regions still dominated by the old economy have struggled.

However, North Carolina has not reacted passively to the Connected Age's trends. The Big Three are adapting to a future of smaller and more specialized markets. Agriculture has totally remade itself. North Carolina is a national leader in student improvement at the K–12 level, and college enrollments have reached record highs. Lagging regions are taking stock of their assets and moving into new directions of technology, light manufacturing, tourism, and retirement living.

Yet as is jokingly said about economics, it is easy to predict the past; predicting the future is the problem. Many questions remain about where North Carolina is headed. Some of the questions have clear answers; others have answers that are less certain. Still, asking the right questions is half the battle.

❡ *If North Carolina's era of cheap labor has ended, how can the state compete with countries where workers earn a fraction as much as their U.S. counterparts?* North Carolina can remain competitive by recognizing that what counts in labor costs is not just the wage paid to the worker but also the productivity of the worker compared to the wage. North Carolina's workers can compete as long as their productivity—what they produce in a given period of time—per dollar paid to them is higher than the same measure for other domestic or foreign workers. The good news is that North Carolina workers have rated very high on this measure. For the future, this lead must continue and even grow. Well-trained workers must be matched with the latest technology and production techniques.

To remain in the game, North Carolina also needs to realize that location still matters, even in the era of a flat world. Elements outside the factory, office, or farm, such as highways and other infrastructure, public safety, access to educational facilities, taxes, and access to customers both for determining preferences as well as for postsale service all retain some degree of importance, though it may be slight for some elements and higher for others. Nevertheless, these factors can tip the balance in favor of a North Carolina location.

❡ *With the Big Five replacing the Big Three, can North Carolina relax in knowing that the new industries will anchor the state economy for decades to come?* No. The globalized economy has shortened the product cycle—the pattern that carries products from their initial high-cost, innovative site to a low-cost, standardized manufacturing location. For many segments of the new Big Five, such as biotechnology and nanotechnology, the industries are in the innovative stage, where access to research scientists and highly skilled labor is essential. Such conditions favor the industries' continued presence in North Carolina. But after the products are standardized and amenable to straightforward manufacturing, use of the lowest-cost labor and facilities will become more important. At that point, North Carolina will have to compete for this production on the basis of labor productivity relative to labor costs and other nonlabor elements.

In the long run, therefore, the state must make itself a center of innovation, where the next big idea can flourish and take root, if only for a while. The state must also build as much flexibility as possible into educational and training programs. In the Connected Age, what is here today could very well be gone, or at least downsized, in just a decade or two.

¶ *Will education continue to grow in importance?* A clear connection has existed between economic growth and education in the Connected Age and is likely to continue and perhaps even strengthen. The spread of technology in the workplace will require workers not only to use those tools but also to analyze and interpret the results. This requires both how-to skills and reasoning skills. In addition, as the level of education has been elevated throughout the national and international economies, even more education and training will be needed to stand out. Said another way, college has become the new high school—many Connected Age employers expect workers to hold college degrees, whereas a generation ago high school degrees sufficed.

Does this imply that high school graduates or dropouts will have no jobs in the future economy? Not at all. According to the N.C. Commission on Workforce Development, jobs in the state will grow fastest over the coming decade for college graduates and for high school dropouts.[1] That is, jobs requiring both the top skills and the least skills will become bigger parts of the state's workforce. High school graduates who cannot find jobs will be forced to take lower-skilled positions.

What about the wage premium for a college education? This premium, which measures the additional hourly earnings college graduates receive over high school graduates, widened considerably in North Carolina during the Connected Age (see chapter 4). With an increase in the percentage of college graduates in the labor force in coming years, this premium may well level off or decline slightly. A college education will remain worthwhile in financial terms, but perhaps less so than has been the case in the past.

¶ *Will balanced economic growth come to North Carolina? That is, will economic disparities within the state narrow and economic growth among regions become more similar?* Probably not. More likely, the geographic range of the fast-growing regions—like the Triangle, Greater Charlotte, and Greater Wilmington—will incorporate more counties. These regions still have plenty of growing room internally as well as nearby. The regions' economic advantages will not disappear or be replicated anytime soon. They will continue to attract workers from other parts of the state as well as from elsewhere in the nation.

However, this forecast does not preclude certain slower-growing regions from accelerating their performance. The best candidates for such a turn-around will be smaller regions that enjoy proximity to fast-growing areas but can offer significantly lower land costs and less congestion. Examples are Rocky Mount–Wilson and the Lakes near the Triangle and the Foothills and Greater Gaston adjacent to Greater Charlotte.

¶ *Can any public policy issues be easily solved?* Yes, transportation—or, more specifically, highways—is one. As chapter 6 shows, public revenues raised for and spending on highways decreased as a portion of the state economy during the Connected Age. Highway taxes fell just as the demands on transportation infrastructure rose. Consequently, the condition of the state's highways has deteriorated and a multi-billion-dollar backlog of highway maintenance and construction projects has been created.

The simple solution is for drivers to put more of their money into funding highways. Highway taxes are an excellent example of user fees. Users of the public project—in this case, roads—pay to build and maintain them. North Carolina legislators should consider indexing the two main state highway taxes, the motor fuel (gas) tax and the highway use (car sales) tax, to inflation or, better yet, to inflation in highway construction costs. Or North Carolina should institute a mileage tax based on how many miles a person drives, again indexed to inflation. Privately constructed toll roads offer another option.

¶ *Is it just a matter of time before most of North Carolina's manufacturing jobs will be offshored to foreign countries, and will offshoring eventually take a sub-stantial share of the state's good-paying professional and technical jobs? Will the globalized economy of the Connected Age ultimately reduce the North Carolina (and U.S.) economy to predominantly low-paying service jobs?* Many Carolini-ans think the answer to all these questions is yes. Some of the scenario will almost certainly come true. For example, total manufacturing employment in North Carolina will likely continue to drop as textiles, apparel, and other traditional manufacturing sectors shed jobs. But some parts of manufactur-ing employment will grow, and overall manufacturing output will increase. Indeed, in 2006, North Carolina's manufacturing output reached an all-time high.[2] The nature and type of manufacturing will change, but the sector will retain an important presence in North Carolina for the foreseeable future. Tomorrow's manufacturing will be more of a high-output, low-employment industry, much like agriculture.

Economists have reached no consensus regarding the degree and extent of job losses due to offshoring, particularly in higher-paying positions. This area represents one of the biggest wild cards of the future. Technological advances logically will increase the number of professional and technical tasks that can be performed off site, including in foreign countries, and more work will flow in this direction if it can be performed at lower cost. Such tasks presently are limited to routine and mundane work, where little personal interaction is necessary, but technology will probably facilitate greater interaction and may even overcome language and cultural barriers. Today's Indian call service and technical assistance centers could be expanded to additional professional services. The potential certainly exists for offshoring to have a large adverse effect, either directly (through job losses) or indirectly (through lower domestic wages), on higher-paying domestic occupations.

This pessimistic view assumes a static world (that is, where there are no reactions), and two reactions could easily limit the scope of offshoring for professional and technical jobs. One is the addition of domestic workers providing services that cannot be duplicated by foreign competitors. For example, a domestic tax preparer can promise in-person defense of any returns audited by the Internal Revenue Service. Or a North Carolina architect can guarantee on-site supervision during construction. The second reaction is in the competitive foreign country. As development occurs and incomes improve, demand for professional and technical services will increase, and upward pressure will begin to be asserted on the foreign workers' salaries. Both trends will limit the foreign country's ability to compete for U.S. (and North Carolina) work.

Finally, trade is a two-way street. Yes, the media has focused on the large U.S. trade deficits and the loss of manufacturing jobs to China and office jobs to India. But despite their growth, these two countries, like other developing nations, have many limitations — massive poverty, inadequate infrastructure, environmental issues, more rigid and controlling governments, and a much shorter tradition with a flexible, market-oriented economy than the United States possesses.[3] U.S. exports to China and India have grown impressively and should increase even more as those two countries' middle classes expand.[4]

¶ *Education is the crucial competitive factor of the Connected Age. Although North Carolina has made significant and important advances in this area, other states and countries have also done so, raising the education bar. Can any magic bullets improve educational outcomes and expand educational opportunities?* K–12 education certainly has many candidates — smaller class sizes, improved teacher training and certification, higher teacher pay, more technology in the classroom, expanded school-to-work programs, linking teacher pay to student performance, and more competition in the provision of education (see chapter 6). Some studies support the role of each of these factors in improving education, while other studies debunk that role. Although economists may lean toward those techniques that emphasize incentives (tying teacher pay to student performance and competition in the provision of education), this view does not hold universal sway and is not overwhelmingly supported by the evidence. Many programs will likely continue to be debated and tried, and perhaps this approach is wise. However, the success of these methods must consistently and objectively be evaluated after a sufficient period of time.

The situation differs at the higher education level. Competition for students already exists because students choose rather than are assigned to schools, as at the K–12 level. In addition, greater flexibility often exists in awarding instructors differential pay based on an evaluation of performance, especially at four-year schools. Instead, the issue in higher education is twofold: how to expand the opportunities for higher education to more individuals, and how to allocate the costs of public higher education between the student and the general taxpayer.

On the one hand, higher education should remain within the financial reach of as many individuals as possible, because the Connected Age requires more college-educated workers. Therefore, direct student costs should remain low. On the other hand, North Carolina already heavily subsidizes higher education, and the subsidy will grow (as a percentage of gross state product) as the rate of college attendance expands. Moreover, individual students benefit most from obtaining degrees. These points support the idea of a larger student contribution to higher education costs. Wrestling with these competing realities and apportioning the benefits and costs of higher education between its public (taxpayer) and private (student) components will be a constant source of tension during the Connected Age.

❡ *The public sector—government—is an important part of the economy, and it has taken on an additional degree of importance during the Connected Age. But government can both impede progress through taxes and fees and promote progress through its important spending functions, particularly in education and infrastructure. Can these conflicting views be resolved to find consensus regarding the proper size and scope of government?* Because government is everyone's business, conflicts always have arisen and always will arise over its proper role, size, and policies. But as government has become relatively larger in North Carolina and as the political turf has become more competitive, these conflicts have become sharper and more intense.

North Carolina faces some serious public-sector challenges. The tax system is clearly antiquated and in need of updating. Many people can easily agree on the goals of a tax system—public revenue should grow as the economy expands, rates should be relatively low to avoid impinging on private decision making, revenue availability should be more stable than the business cycle, and low-income households should pay lower effective tax rates than higher-income households. But reaching those goals is another matter. One problem is that virtually every detail in the current tax code has a backer or group that benefits from its existence. Change, therefore, is tortuous and involves an enormous expenditure of time and political capital. A major crisis in government finance may have to erupt before this pattern changes.

Such a crisis may be coming. The two major parts of government spending—on services (specifically education and highways) and on income transfers (mainly Medicaid)—are moving closer to conflict. Pressures continue to mount to increase spending in all three areas, but because these categories are so large, increases cannot occur unless the total relative size of North Carolina's government expands. However, an expanding government slice of the economic pie creates the worry that North Carolina has priced itself out of the market—that is, that the size and scope of government have become so large that they deter investors and impede economic growth.

This conflict may be avoided by seriously scrutinizing government for ineffective spending and spending for which costs far exceed benefits. However, just as with taxes, every government program and line item of spending has its supporters, so the political process is unlikely easily to find such savings. One option is to have elected leaders agree to an independent commission similar to the one that recommended military base closures and to stipulate beforehand that the commission's recommendations on spending reductions will be adopted. Another approach involves privatizing parts of the public budget. Doing so would mean increasing tuition costs to college students, building more toll roads, and converting Medicaid to a voucher program.

Disagreements about government will continue during the Connected Age, simply because some people see government as a burden while others see it as a savior. It is to be hoped that the increased access to information and analysis that marks the era will allow the debate to move beyond rhetoric to real evaluations and conclusions.

❡ *What will North Carolina look like after twenty more years of the Connected Age?* As the 1950s saying goes, this is the $64 million question (although with inflation, today the amount would need to be closer to $470 million).[5] Everyone wants to know what the future will hold, and varying scenarios are easy to imagine and cannot be dismissed as incorrect—no one will know if the vision is right or wrong until the future is here.

The private choices of millions of people and firms, many not yet in the state or born, will ultimately determine the future course of the state and its economy. Furthermore, the big economic forces and trends discussed in chapters 1 and 2 will motivate these private decisions. Government can have a role—a very important one—but will always take a backseat to the winds of change sweeping across the economic landscape.

Some safe predictions can be made about the economic future. North Carolina will have more people and workers, as the state, like others in the South, will grow faster than the nation as a whole. The South still has room to expand; is newer than the rest of the country, with more modern infrastructure and construction; and has an attractive climate with more sun and milder winters than in the North. Adverse change in the regional climate might derail this growth, however. Hotter and drier weather in the South combined with milder and more temperate seasons in the North could reverse the migration flow.

North Carolina, like the nation, almost certainly will be older and more ethnically and racially diverse in the future. Almost surely, more residents will have college degrees and work in professional and technical jobs. The payoff for a college degree is just too high and the job availability just too great for individuals not to extend their time in school.

The bleeding of jobs in traditional manufacturing will slow to a trickle for the simple reason that so much has already been lost. Manufacturing employment overall will still decline, but much less so than in the 1990s and early twenty-first century. The move to get the most out of each worker and each job will become even more pervasive. The tools of reducing waste, managing costs, and motivating workers with performance bonuses will keep companies profitable in the competitive, connected world.

More North Carolinians will live in urbanized areas, so congestion and commuting costs will grow and pressures on the transportation system will intensify. As a result, remote working, staggered hours, and flexible schedules will become attractive to more firms and workers, although they will remain in the minority. The bulging numbers of older baby boomers and retirees will continue to spark development in coastal and mountain regions, which in turn will intensify the disagreements between developers and conservationists.

The North Carolina of 2025 will be more linked to the world economy and international trade than it is now. In particular, the state's agriculture, technology, and finance sectors will tap into growing foreign markets, most notably in Asia. Formal education in foreign languages and cultures will increase in the state's universities, colleges, and even high schools and grade schools. On the flip side, foreign investment in the state—including that from China and India—will rise, providing jobs for thousands of members of the state's workforce. The international linkages will put a premium on access to airports and will intensify development around these key centers.

Perhaps the biggest unknown of the future involves further advances in technology. What new technology will develop, and how will it affect the workplace, commerce, and the home? Will retail outlets become obsolete as online shopping becomes more sophisticated? Will shopping malls become ghost towns, and if so, could this change improve traffic congestion but decimate local governments' property tax revenues? Will further breakthroughs in communications and virtualization turn the home into the workplace, thereby dramatically reducing commuting costs for millions of workers? Could improvements in online education replace lecture halls as the way millions of college students learn and thereby save the state government billions of dollars in spending to construct and maintain college buildings? Or have the big leaps in technology already taken place, reducing further improvements to just the edges?

These questions are both exciting and scary. But they are representative of the Connected Age, which has brought developments that few people could have projected a mere half century ago. The Connected Age turned North Carolina's economic world upside down and inside out, and the transformation is not complete. The genie is out of the bottle—the forces of the Connected Age will not be stopped. Awareness of the era's trends, flexibility in adapting to them, and the pursuit of opportunities created by the age represent the best strategies for prospering in its path. For North Carolinians, this approach should be second nature; it is what the people of the Old North State have been practicing for more than three centuries.

A Primer on Economic Concepts

This is a book about the economy of North Carolina; as a result, economic concepts are used throughout. Like any discipline, economics has its own jargon. Jargon is really simply a shortcut for ideas that may take several sentences to explain. I believe—maybe because I am an economist—that economics jargon is not mind-numbing but is really based on common sense. Using jargon is a way to get to the point—and the good stuff—more quickly. This section includes an alphabetical list of some key economic terms and ideas used in the book, along with their explanations. There aren't many of them, and I hope you'll agree they're fairly commonsensical, but if you come across one in the book and are confused about what it means, this primer serves as an easy reference for getting you back on track.

Business cycle: Over time, most economies, including the national economy and the economy in North Carolina, expand over time. Employment increases, commerce grows, and the incomes of most workers increase. But these positive changes do not happen in a straight line. Instead, employment, commerce, and incomes improve for a while before a pullback occurs when many of the aggregate economic measures regress. After this pause, however, growth again returns, followed by another pullback, and so on.

The periods of growth are called *expansions*, and the periods of pullback are called *recessions*. One complete combination of an expansion and its complementary recession is called a *business cycle*. In the United States, ten business cycles have occurred since World War II, with the last one ending in 2001.[1] As of 2007, the economy was in the expansion phase of the eleventh business cycle.

The business cycle is important for several reasons. It is an economy-wide phenomenon that affects the nation, all states, and all industries and companies. But it does not equally impact states, regions, and industries. The business cycle is more volatile in North Carolina (expansions are stronger but recessions are deeper) than in the nation as a whole. In addition, the strength of the business cycle varies among industries. Some industries are barely impacted, while others are severely affected. A few countercyclical industries go against the grain, doing well during recessions but contracting during expansions. And because government derives its revenues from the private economy, recessions adversely affect government resources. However, recessions are often the time when government is asked to do more to help those hurt by the economic downturn. So the recessionary part of the business cycle presents very difficult challenges to public decision makers.

The causes of business cycles and policies designed to eliminate them or to at least smooth their ups and downs have been subjects of intense study and debate among economists.[2] These discussions lie beyond the scope of this book, but the business cycle is an economic concept with which North Carolina will likely continue to live during the Connected Age and beyond.

Employment: Unless otherwise noted, employment numbers cited in the text include full-time and part-time employment. When categories of employment are examined, they are usually broken down into groups based on the type of *industry* (construction, manufacturing, services, trade, government, and so forth) that employs workers or based on *occupation* (that is, what the worker does, such as sales, clerical tasks, operating machinery, and so on). Many economists think that a closer link exists between a worker's occupation and his or her pay than between the industry of the worker and pay.

Employment in an industry often serves as an indicator (sometimes, *the* indicator) for the relative importance of that industry. One problem with this approach is the implicit assumption that workers in different years make the same contribution to production. This assumption is wrong because a worker's *productivity* frequently changes over time. Worker productivity measures how much a worker accomplishes in a given period of time—for example, how many bushels of corn a farmer can harvest per acre in a year or how many monitors a worker in a computer factory can assemble in an eight-hour shift. Worker productivity tends to rise each year, especially in industries such as manufacturing and agriculture, so a decrease in the number of factory workers or farmers does not necessarily mean less factory and farm production.

Gross domestic/state/local product: Gross domestic product (GDP) is a measure designed to capture the total amount of economic activity in a geographic area. GDP is the total value of production, including both goods (tangible products) and services, in dollar terms during a period of time (usually a year) in a country, state, or substate region. At the country level it is called GDP; at the state level, the measure is often labeled gross state product (GSP); for substate areas, it is termed gross local product (GLP). GDP, GSP, and GLP can also be calculated for individual industries.

GDP is not simply a totaling of all sales in the economy, which would count more than once products that go through many processing transformations and a sale at each stage. For such products, GDP includes only the additional value, or *value added*, at each stage. GDP also does not include the value of inputs made in another geographic area. So, for example, if a computer is manufactured in North Carolina using parts made outside the state, only the value of the assembled computer greater than the sum of the parts' value would be considered for North Carolina's GSP.

In addition to tracking the size of an economy, GDP is also commonly used as the standard by which to judge relative economic size. In this context, GDP (or GSP or GLP) is the total economic pie, while relative size is a slice of that pie. To judge the size of manufacturing in North Carolina, for example, one approach would be to calculate manufacturing's percentage of North Carolina's GSP. Similarly, to evaluate the size of the state's government, government spending as a percentage of North Carolina GSP could be compared over many years.

Income: Everyone knows what income is—money coming into a household, business, or government. But especially for households, several alternative definitions of income exist. The broadest measure is income from all sources, including work, investments, and public assistance from government. But even income from work has different components. *Wage and salary income* is what workers see in their paychecks; implicit income comes from *employer-paid benefits*, such as vacation, sick leave, and company health insurance. When wage and salary income are added to the value of employer-paid benefits, the result is *compensation*. A difference also exists between a worker's total wage and salary income and what that worker earns per hour—the *hourly wage*. Finally, each of these measures can be expressed *before taxes* are paid or *after taxes* are paid.

Output: In economics, we measure most concepts in dollars for two reasons. Dollar values are a universal concept understood by almost everyone, and dollar values from different corners of the economy can easily be added. For example, GDP is a dollar-value concept that allows the combination of economic activity from disparate industries such as computer manufacturing and hog farming.

But the value of computer production in North Carolina is obtained by multiplying the number of computers manufactured by the sales price of each computer. Likewise, the value of hog farming results from multiplying the number of hogs sold by the price per hog. As a result, no one-to-one correspondence necessarily exists between the output—the physical number of units produced—and the value of that production. A high price per unit can make a production value look high even though the physical output is low.

Measures of the physical quantity of output—called *output* or sometimes *production*—are available for the entire economy as well as for individual industries. These measures provide an indicator of how much physical production is occurring from a factory, farm, or office. The measures are not calibrated in terms of the specific physical units, like number of computers, pounds of tobacco, or number of haircuts, but are provided as *index numbers* around some base year. For example, an index number of 150 for computer production in 2006, using a base of 100 for 2000, would mean that 50 percent more computers came off the assembly line in 2006 than in 2000.

Real dollars: Who would want unreal, or counterfeit, dollars? Are real dollars simply legal dollars printed by the government?

This definition is close, except that "real" refers to *purchasing power*. Real dollars are those that are the same in terms of the quantity of products and services they can purchase. Over time, the average of prices of products and services we buy tends to rise. This is called *inflation*. The rate of increase (the *inflation rate*) is not the same each year, but the direction is definitely up. This means a dollar will not be able to buy as many products and services this year as in past years—in other words, the purchasing power of dollars falls over time. Most people know this, but the confusing aspect is that no adjustments are made to dollars to reflect this reality. For example, we know that fifty thousand dollars today will not buy what fifty thousand dollars bought twenty years ago, but salaries and prices in different years are usually quoted in their actual dollar amounts (economists call them *nominal dollars*) without any consideration for the difference in their purchasing power.

Real dollars correct this. For example, Joe Smith earned thirty thousand dollars in 1985, when he started working, and earned forty thousand dollars in 2006. Since these are nominal dollars, they have not been adjusted for the differences in purchasing power of the dollar between 1985 and 2006. An adjustment would show that earning thirty thousand dollars in 1985 is like earning almost fifty-four thousand dollars in 2006. In other words, having a salary of fifty-four thousand dollar in 2006 is the same as having a salary of thirty thousand dollars in 1985. Expressing Joe's salary in 1985 as fifty-four thousand dollars, *in real 2006 dollars*, allows a direct comparison to what he actually earned in 2006, which was forty thousand dollars. So when *real dollars* are used, Joe's salary went down, not up, from 1985 to 2006. The real dollar amounts have to be expressed in terms of prices in a certain year (2006 in this example); a recent year is usually used, since people will have knowledge of contemporary prices. But any year can be used—what is important is that the adjustment is made and real dollars are used. Real dollars are sometimes termed *constant dollars*, to imply that the dollars are constant in purchasing power.

Appendix A

Determinants of North Carolina's Economic Growth during the Connected Age

This appendix reports on an analysis of North Carolina's economic growth during the Connected Age. A regression analysis is used to measure the relationships between two measures of the North Carolina economy (an index of output and total employment) and several factors important in the Connected Age (the efficiency of workers [WORKEFF], average Scholastic Aptitude Test scores of North Carolina students [SAT], the average tariff rate on products imported to the United States [TARIFF], the years in which China became an active part of the world economy [CHINA], the percentage of women working in the labor force [WOMENWORK], and the proportion of national bank assets held by the top ten banks [BANKASSET]). Also included are the comparable measures of the U.S. economy (USOUTPUT in table A-1, USJOBS in table A-2) to control for trends at the national level.

The analysis was repeated for the individual industries of the traditional economy (apparel, textiles, tobacco products, furniture, lumber and wood, paper, and agriculture) as well as for the individual industries of the new Connected Age economy (food processing, chemical products, computer products, transportation equipment, and banking). Tobacco products captures economic activity at the manufacturing level (mainly cigarette manufacturing), while agriculture includes the farm-level value of tobacco leaf production as well as other farm products. BANKASSET was included only in the banking equations. In these regressions, the national measures of output and jobs were those of the comparable national industry.[1]

In addition to the factors related to the Connected Age, the literature suggests other factors important to economic growth. One is energy prices. By increasing the costs of production, higher real (inflation-adjusted) energy prices may cause reductions in production.[2] However, the impacts on employment can be more complicated. Employment may fall as a result of production falling. Or, with higher real energy prices making equipment and other capital inputs more expensive, companies may substitute labor for capital and increase employment. Alternatively, the two effects may cancel out each other, leaving no impact on employment. To control for these possible impacts, the analysis includes real energy prices (ENERGYPR).

A second factor is taxes. All else equal, higher taxes would be expected to deter economic growth by removing resources from households and businesses. However, the government can spend tax revenues on public services valued by households and businesses. If households and businesses place a higher value on these services than on the tax cost, taxes have a positive impact on growth. If households and businesses value the services at less than the tax cost, taxes have a negative impact on growth. And if the service value and tax cost are the same, taxes have no impact on growth.

Comprehensive studies include measures of the tax burden and public services together in the analysis, and a large majority of such studies show that spending on education or measures of the results of educational spending have a positive impact on growth, a smaller majority show that public infrastructure spending has a positive impact on growth, and a little more than half show that the tax burden is associated with a negative impact on growth.[3] In this analysis, SAT captures the effects of educational spending in North Carolina. The major type of infrastructure spending in the state, highway spending, is measured by the proportion of gross state product devoted to this public good (HIGHWAY). The analysis accounts for the North Carolina tax burden through state and local taxes and fees as a proportion of gross state product (TAXES).

Table A-1 shows the results of the analysis for output, while table A-2 shows the results for employment. The statistically significant values for USOUTPUT, WORKEFF, and SAT in table A-1 indicate that North Carolina's aggregate output increased with increases in national output, the efficiency of the state's workers, and the educational performance of the state's students. North Carolina's output also increased in years after trade with China increased. The statistically significant negative value of TARIFF means that state output rose as tariff rates dropped, and the statistically significant negative sign on energy prices means that state output fell as energy prices rose. The percentage of working women, bank assets, and highway spending had no impact on state output. Also, the relative size of taxes had no effect with the educational and highway measures included.

The table also shows a clear dichotomy between the traditional industries and new economy industries. WORKEFF has the most consistent effect, being

Table A-1. Determinants of North Carolina Economic Output, Total and by Sector, 1977–2003.

	North Carolina	Traditional Industry							New Economy Industry				
		Apparel	Textiles	Tobacco	Furniture	Lumber and Wood	Paper	Agriculture	Food Processing	Chemical Products	Computer Products	Transportation Equipment	Banking
USOUTPUT	0.8	1.4	1.3	1.0	1.2	0.6	0.8	-0.1	1.1	0.9	0.6	0.6	0.8
WORKEFF	10.7	35.2	4.9	-.4	23.5	34.8	35.4	17.5	36.6	18.3	26	18.4	6.8
SAT	0.08	0.0	-.3	-1.2	-0.2	0.4	0.2	0.3	-0.4	0.8	0.2	0.4	0.2
TARIFF	-2.7	9.6	3.4	22.2	1.9	-3.3	6.3	-12	-8.5	6.8	-.2	3.3	-0.2
CHINA	2.4	-18	-3	43.1	-3.7	-14	-5.2	1.9	26.4	-5.9	5.7	2.9	3.9
WOMENWORK	0.4	2.9	5.1	1.6	-0.1	1.4	0.6	1.9	1.1	-1.4	2.0	4.4	-1.3
BANKASSET	0.0	—	—	—	—	—	—	—	—	—	—	—	1.1
ENERGYPR	-0.5	2.1	-.4	-10	0.2	2.2	1.2	-2.8	-1.3	1.7	-.9	3.6	-0.7
HIGHWAY	0.7	-5.8	-.9	21.7	-1.5	-5.4	-4.3	15.2	4.4	-0.4	2.1	-1.6	-0.1
TAXES	-0.1	0.5	0.0	-2.0	0.1	0.6	0.3	-1.4	-0.4	0.2	-.2	0.1	0
R²	0.99	0.93	0.99	0.99	0.90	0.92	0.98	0.95	0.98	0.99	0.96	0.98	0.99

DATA SOURCES: U.S. Department of Commerce, Bureau of Economic Analysis, "Gross Domestic Product"; U.S. Census Bureau, "Annual Survey of Manufactures"; U.S. Department of Commerce, Bureau of Economic Analysis, "Gross Domestic Product; N.C. Public Schools, "North Carolina 2005 SAT Report"; Council of Economic Advisers, *Economic Report*, tables B81, B104; U.S. Census Bureau, "Statistical Abstract," 2007, table 571; Federal Reserve Board, "Bank Structure Data"; U.S. Department of Energy, "State Energy Consumption"; U.S. Census Bureau, "State and Local Government Finances."

NOTE: Statistically significant parameter estimates are in boldface, with a two-tail significance level of 10 percent or better.

USOUTPUT = U.S. gross domestic product

WORKEFF = real gross product per worker divided by real wages and salaries per worker

SAT = combined verbal and math Scholastic Aptitude Test score for North Carolina students

TARIFF = import duties as a percentage of value of imported goods and services

CHINA = a categorical variable taking the value of 1 for years after 1999, when the United States and China signed a bilateral trade agreement paving the way for China's entry into the World Trade Organization

WOMENWORK = percentage of women in the labor force

BANKASST = percentage of bank assets held by the ten largest domestic commercial banks

ENERGYPR = real dollars per Btu, specific for North Carolina

HIGHWAY = proportion of gross state product devoted to highway spending

TAXES = state and local taxes and fees as a proportion of gross state product positive and statistically significant in four of the seven traditional industries and all five of the new economy industries. SAT is positive and statistically significant in three of the new economy industries and is negative and statistically significant in one of the new economy industries (food processing). The findings for SAT are reversed for the traditional industries — negative and statistically significant in two industries and positive and statistically significant in one industry.

The differences continue with the trade variables, TARIFF and CHINA. Except for tobacco and agriculture, output is either positively related to higher tariffs or negatively related to years of increased trade with China for all of the traditional industries — in the cases of apparel and paper, both. Tobacco output is positively related to CHINA, and higher agricultural output is associated with lower tariffs. In contrast, output in two of the new economy industries is positively related to CHINA, and in none of the new economy industries is output negatively related to CHINA. Likewise, output is positively related to higher tariffs in only one new economy industry (chemical products), and output is negatively related to higher tariffs in the food-processing industry.

The increased presence of women in the paid labor force (WOMENWORK) has helped traditional North Carolina industries more than the new industries. Output in apparel, textiles, and agriculture rose with increases in WOMENWORK. Among the new economy industries, the same result was obtained only for transportation equipment, while banking services fell as WOMENWORK increased. ENERGYPR is negatively related to output in tobacco, agriculture, food, and banking but positively related to output in paper and transportation parts. Highway spending and taxes are not statistically significant in any of the output equations, but banking services rose with BANKASSET.

In the analysis of employment for the North Carolina economy as a whole (table A-2), employment fell as worker efficiency rose, rose as the rate of working women increased, and fell as energy prices climbed. No statistically significant relationships were found between total North Carolina employment and the two trade measures, TARIFF and CHINA.

Employment in the majority of individual industries followed employment trends of the same industry at the national level. Indeed, this finding held true for each of the traditional industries and for all of the new economy industries except computer products and banking. Changes in WORKEFF affected employment in only two industries, agriculture and transportation equipment and did so in a positive way. The negative effect of WORKEFF on aggregate employment therefore must result from changes in individual industries not analyzed here.

Table A-2. Determinants of North Carolina Employment, Total and by Sector, 1977–2003

	North Carolina	Traditional Industry									New Economy Industry		
		Apparel	Textiles	Tobacco	Furniture	Lumber and Wood	Paper	Agriculture	Food Processing	Chemical Products	Computer Products	Transportation Equipment	Banking
USJOBS	0.0	.05	1.28	0.3	0.2	.05	0.05	0.01	0.02	.07	.06	.01	.03
WORKEFF	-.01	-5.4	4.9	-0.03	-6.7	-5	-0.7	1.17	2.4	-1.5	-3.4	4.5	-0.2
SAT	0.0	-0.3	-0.3	-.06	0.0	.08	0.01	0.2	-0.1	0.3	-0.6	-.04	0.3
TARIFF	-.01	10.2	3.4	2.1	6.3	0.2	0.4	-3.6	-1.6	0.9	-14	-3.3	0.8
CHINA	0.0	0.51	-2.9	2.2	-6.1	-7.2	-0.5	-0.1	-1.1	-3.6	-1.5	0.3	2.2
WOMENWORK	.002	2.14	1.2	0.4	0.1	0.2	0.08	-0.2	1.2	0.6	2.8	1.9	0.5
BANKASSET	0.0	—	—	—	—	—	—	—	—	—	—	—	0.6
ENERGYPR	-.01	0.72	-0.4	-0.5	2.1	0.5	0.23	-0.9	-0.7	-0.4	-1.7	-0.4	-1.4
HIGHWAY	-.3	-2.7	-0.9	1.3	-2	-1.2	-0.5	1.8	1.1	-2.2	3.2	0.3	-1.1
TAXES	0	0.24	0.0	-0.11	0.1	0.1	0.05	-0.2	-0.1	0.2	-0.2	-.01	.08
R^2	0.98	0.99	0.99	0.97	0.96	0.87	0.81	0.95	0.96	0.94	0.87	.099	0.97

DATA SOURCES: U.S. Department of Labor, Bureau of Labor Statistics, "Employment, Hours, and Earnings"; U.S. Department of Commerce, Bureau of Economic Analysis, "Gross Domestic Product; N.C. Public Schools, "North Carolina 2005 SAT Report"; Council of Economic Advisers, *Economic Report*, tables B81, B104; U.S. Census Bureau, "Statistical Abstract," 2007, table 571; Federal Reserve Board, "Bank Structure Data"; U.S. Department of Energy, "State Energy Consumption"; U.S. Census Bureau, "State and Local Government Finances."

NOTE: Statistically significant parameter estimates are in boldface, with a two-tail significance level of 10 percent or better.

USJOBS = U.S. employment

WORKEFF = real gross product per worker divided by real wages and salaries per worker

SAT = combined verbal and math Scholastic Aptitude Test score for North Carolina students

TARIFF = import duties as a percentage of value of imported goods and services

CHINA = a categorical variable taking the value of 1 for years after 1999, when the United States and China signed a bilateral trade agreement paving the way for China's entry into the World Trade Organization

WOMENWORK = percentage of women in the labor force

BANKASST = percentage of bank assets held by the ten largest domestic commercial banks

ENERGYPR = real dollars per Btu, specific for North Carolina

HIGHWAY = proportion of gross state product devoted to highway spending

TAXES = state and local taxes and fees as a proportion of gross state product

Table A-3. Determinants of North Carolina Real Per Capita Income, 1977–2003

U.S. real per capita income	0.70	BANKASST	12
WORKEFF	−1976	ENERGYPR	−253
SAT	14.3	HIGHWAY	−128
TARIFF	−73	TAXES	15
CHINA	83	R^2	0.99
WOMENWORK	295		

DATA SOURCES: U.S. Department of Labor, Bureau of Labor Statistics, "Employment, Hours, and Earnings"; U.S. Department of Commerce, Bureau of Economic Analysis, "Gross Domestic Product; N.C. Public Schools, "North Carolina 2005 SAT Report"; Council of Economic Advisers, *Economic Report*, tables B81, B104; U.S. Census Bureau, "Statistical Abstract," 2007, table 571; Federal Reserve Board, "Bank Structure Data"; U.S. Department of Energy, "State Energy Consumption"; U.S. Census Bureau, "State and Local Government Finances."
NOTE: Statistically significant parameter estimates are in boldface, with a two-tail significance level of 10 percent or better.
WORKEFF = real gross product per worker divided by real wages and salaries per worker
SAT = combined verbal and math Scholastic Aptitude Test score for North Carolina students
TARIFF = import duties as a percentage of value of imported goods and services
CHINA = a categorical variable taking the value of 1 for years after 1999, when the United States and China signed a bilateral trade agreement paving the way for China's entry into the World Trade Organization
WOMENWORK = percentage of women in the labor force
BANKASST = percentage of bank assets held by the ten largest domestic commercial banks
ENERGYPR = real dollars per Btu, specific for North Carolina
HIGHWAY = proportion of gross state product devoted to highway spending
TAXES = state and local taxes and fees as a proportion of gross state product

A contrast appears in the findings for SAT and TARIFF between the traditional and new economy industries. SAT is negatively related to employment in textiles, positively related to agricultural employment, and has no impact on employment in the other traditional industries. But SAT is positively related to employment in two of the five new economy industries and is negatively related to employment in only the computer products sector. Among the traditional industries, higher values for TARIFF are related to higher employment in apparel, textiles, tobacco, and furniture and lower employment only in agriculture, while lower values for TARIFF are positively related to higher employment in two of the new economy industries.

The results for CHINA are more mixed. Increased trade with China lowered employment in the traditional industries of furniture and lumber and wood and increased jobs in tobacco. However, Chinese trade also lowered employment in the new economy industry of chemical products.

The other factors generated similar results in the traditional and new economy industries. Increases in WOMENWORK were related to increases in employment in two traditional industries (apparel and textiles) and four new economy industries. Higher energy prices lowered employment in tobacco, agriculture, food processing, computer products, and banking but increased employment in furniture. Highway spending and taxes had no employment impacts in any of the industries, and changes in BANKASSET had no statistically significant relationship to employment in the banking industry.

The same factors (plus U.S. real per capita income) were used to analyze determinants of changes in North Carolina real per capita income. Table A-3 shows the results. Four factors were found to be statistically significant. North Carolina per capita income rose with increases in U.S. per capita income, fell with increases in worker efficiency, rose with the rate of women in the labor force, and fell with increases in energy prices. These results imply that the ratio of North Carolina to U.S. per capita income falls as worker efficiency increases, rises as the percentage of women in the labor force rises, and falls as energy prices increase.

Appendix B

Determinants of Real Wage Rates for
North Carolina Workers during the Connected Age

This appendix presents an analysis of real (inflation-adjusted) wage rates for North Carolina workers during the Connected Age. The analysis is confined to full-time workers between the ages of twenty-five and sixty to eliminate issues related to schooling, retirement, and choices between part-time and full-time work. The data are from the 1980, 2000, and 2005 public-use samples of the U.S. Census Bureau for North Carolina. Although including data from 1970 would have been beneficial, data regarding hours of work—other than over intervals—were not available for that year. This omission precluded calculation of precise wage rate information.

Real wage rates in each year are analyzed separately. The real wage rate is determined by the worker's education, age, gender, racial and ethnic characteristics, occupation, industry, and urban or rural location. Education is a key factor in the Connected Age, and it is measured by four categorical variables: high school dropout, high school graduate, some college, and four-year college graduate. Age can be directly related to work experience, so a positive effect of age on the real wage rate might be expected. However, this positive effect likely is nonlinear—that is, the positive impact of an additional year of age declines as the worker is older. Therefore, the analysis includes both age and age squared, and the impact of age squared is expected to be negative.

Gender is measured by a categorical variable indicating whether the worker is male or female. Four categorical variables describe the worker's racial/ethnic characteristics: white race but not Hispanic, African American race, Hispanic ethnicity, and other race. Six categorical variables describe the worker's occupation: professional, service, sales/clerical, farmer, craftsperson, or operative. Because different supply and demand conditions are likely to be associated with different occupations, a worker's occupation is expected to have an impact on the real wage rate. Likewise, supply and demand condi-

Table B-1. Determinants of the Real Wage Rate for North Carolina Full-Time Workers Aged 25–60, 1980, 2000, and 2005

	1980	2000	2005
Intercept	−3.44	−7.35	−14.27
High school graduate	2.19	1.56	0.74
Some college	3.62	3.21	2.51
College graduate	7.94	10.81	11.35
Age	0.73	0.92	1.30
Age squared	−0.01	−0.01	−0.01
Female	−4.85	−5.67	−5.19
African American	−1.93	−2.33	−3.76
Hispanic	−1.30	−2.03	−3.11
Other race/ethnicity	−1.21	−1.59	−2.23
Professional occupation	3.60	6.49	7.14
Service occupation	0.35	0.60	0.55
Sales and clerical occupation	2.06	2.85	3.45
Farmer occupation	7.17	4.71	3.77
Craftsperson occupation	0.97	1.09	1.75
Agriculture industry	−12.06	−9.86	−9.09
Construction industry	−3.31	−4.53	−5.79
Trade industry	−3.81	−3.83	−3.77
TCPU	1.16	−0.47	−0.47
Finance industry	−2.38	0.76	0.59
Health and education industry	−2.88	−3.55	−3.80
Professional services industry	−5.82	−3.30	−2.80
Entertainment industry	−4.16	−4.63	−4.94
Personal services industry	−7.05	−6.40	−8.19
Government industry	−1.84	−3.57	−3.42
Urban	2.28	2.46	2.68
R^2	0.26	0.19	0.28
Number of observations	51,998	106,732	21,356

DATA SOURCE: U.S. Census Bureau, "Public-Use Microdata Samples."
NOTE: All amounts in 2005 dollars.

tions are likely to be present for different industries, which in turn will affect the real wage rate of workers in those industries. Industries are divided into eleven categorical variables: agriculture, construction, manufacturing, trade, transportation/communications/public utilities (TCPU), finance, health/education, professional services, entertainment, personal services, and government. Finally, because cost-of-living factors, especially those related to housing, are typically higher in urban areas, employers in those areas will be compelled to pay higher wage rates to compensate workers. Therefore, workers in urban locations would be expected to receive higher real wage rates than workers in rural locations.

The effects of categorical variables must be compared to the effects of some other category—usually called the left-out category—whose impact is captured in the intercept of a regression equation. Here, the left-out category is a high school dropout white male whose occupation is an operative, who works in the manufacturing industry, and who lives in a rural location.

A multiple regression analysis is used to determine the impact of the education, age, race and ethnic, occupation, industry, and location factors on real wage rates of North Carolina workers in 1980, 2000, and 2005. Table B-1 presents the results. All the parameter estimates are statistically significant at the 1 percent level. The parameter estimates for the three education categories show that relative to high school dropouts, workers with higher levels of education receive higher real wage rates. The positive parameter estimate on age and the negative parameter estimate on age squared indicates a nonlinear relationship with real wage rates, where the real wage rate increases with age but at a decreasing rate. Females receive less than males, and nonwhite racial and ethnic groups receive less than whites. Occupational and industry categories exhibit independent effects on real wage rates, and workers in urban locations receive a wage rate premium relative to workers in rural locations.

Near the bottom of the table, the line labeled R^2 provides some cautionary evidence from the analysis. The line indicates the percentage of the variation in real wage rates that is statistically explained collectively by the factors. Since the highest number is just under 30 percent, the results suggest that a large part of the variation in real wage rates is determined by factors not accounted for in the analysis.

To obtain the values in table 4-4, a two-step procedure was followed. First, the average real wage rate in each year was found for the base or left-out category of a high school dropout, white male, working as an operative in the manufacturing industry, and living in a rural location. For 1980, the amount was $12.40; for 2000, $13.45; and for 2005, $12.83. The parameter value in table B-1 for a specific factor was then calculated as a percentage of the base real wage rate, with this number reported in table 4-4.

Appendix C

Determinants of Economic Growth in North Carolina Counties during the Connected Age

This appendix develops and analyzes a model of economic growth in North Carolina counties between 1970 and 2004. Factors related to two measures of economic growth are studied: the percentage change in average real salary (in 2004 dollars) per job in the county (SALARYPC), and the percentage change in employment in the county (EMPLOYPC).

Two versions of the model are presented. Version 1 includes only educational variables. They are the beginning status of educational attainment in the county in 1970, measured by the percentage of workers with high school degrees (HSPC70) and the percentage of workers with college degrees (COLPC70). In addition, the changes in these two percentages are included— HSCHANGE for high school degrees and COLCHANGE for college degrees.

Version 2 adds other factors to the educational variables: paved highway miles per acre in the county averaged for 1980 and 2004 (HIGHWAYS); the percentage of housing units in the county with natural gas power averaged for 1970 and 2000 (GASPOWER); the county property tax rate (in cents per hundred dollars of real property value) averaged for 1980 and 2004 (TAXRATE); the real property value (in 2004 dollars) in the county averaged for 1980 and 2004 (PROPVALUE); the total amount of national, state, and local park and recreational acreage as a percentage of total acreage in the county in 2002 (OPENSPACE); air pollutant particles emitted from point sources in the county, in tons, averaged for 1985 and 1999 (POLLUTION); and a categorical variable indicating whether the county bordered the Atlantic Ocean (BEACH).[1]

The rationale for using the educational variables to explain differences in economic growth between counties is obvious. Perhaps the salient feature of the Connected Age is the positive relationship between economic growth and education. Furthermore, as chapter 5 reports, some researchers have found that educational effects are strongest in urban counties. To measure

Table c-1. Determinants of County Economic Growth, 1970–2004, Version 1

	Dependent Variable: SALARYPC		Dependent Variable: EMPLOYPC	
	(1)	(2)	(3)	(4)
Intercept	**31.89**	**32.69**	34.46	44.58
HSPC70	**−0.66**	**−0.63**	1.69	1.54
COLPC70	**1.64**	**1.20**	−2.71	−2.24
HSCHANGE	**0.26**	**0.34**	−1.84	−1.96
COLCHANGE	**0.70**	**0.42**	8.98	9.42
URBAN × HSCHANGE	—	**−0.44**	—	−0.32
URBAN × COLCHANGE	—	**1.62**	—	−0.64
R²	0.19	0.22	0.28	0.27
Number of observations	100	100	100	100

DATA SOURCE: U.S. Department of Commerce, Bureau of Economic Analysis, "Local Area Personal Income"; N.C. State Data Center, "Log into North Carolina."
NOTE: Boldface refers to a statistically significant result at the 10 percent level or better (two-tail test).

this possible impact, interaction terms between counties classified as urban (population density of two hundred persons per square mile or greater) and the change in the high school degree percentage (URBAN × HSCHANGE) and between counties classified as urban and the change in the college degree percentage (URBAN × COLCHANGE) are included.[2]

There are also logical reasons for including the noneducational explanatory variables in Version 2. Highways are one of the most frequently cited infrastructure factors related to local economic growth.[3] The presence of natural gas as an alternative fuel has been found to be related to economic growth.[4] The major source of local public revenues in counties is the property tax. Therefore, to capture the possible effects of local taxation on economic growth, an average property tax rate in the county is included in the analysis. However, because counties with higher property tax values can raise the same revenue with lower tax rates as can counties with lower property tax values with higher rates, an average of real property values in the county is included as a control factor. The impacts of both positive and negative environmental effects on county economic growth are measured by the open space and pollution variables. Finally, because counties with direct ocean beach access have been very popular for both residential and commercial activity during the Connected Age, the categorical variable BEACH is included to capture this impact.

Table c-1 presents the results of Version 1 of the analysis. Equation 1 finds each of the education variables to be statistically significant in the regression for real salaries. Counties with higher percentages of high school graduates in 1970 had slower growth in real salaries, while counties with higher percentages of college graduates in 1970 had faster growth in real salaries. Increases both in the percentage of high school graduates and in the percentage of college graduates were positively related to growth in real salaries, although the impact of increases in the percentage of college graduates was more than 2.5 times stronger.

Equation 2 adds the two urban interaction terms to the variables in Equation 1. The results resemble those in Equation 1 except in two important ways. First, the positive impact on growth in real salaries from increases in the percentage of college graduates is now statistically significant only in urban counties. This finding is indicated by the statistically significant coefficient on URBAN × COLCHANGE and the statistically insignificant coefficient on COLCHANGE. Second, while increases in the percentage of high school graduates in rural counties are associated with increases in real salaries — as shown by the positive coefficient on HSCHANGE — increases in the percentage of high school graduates in urban counties are now associated with decreases in real salaries.

Equation 3 shows the impact of the educational measures (without the urban interactions) on the growth in employment. Only the change in the percentage of high school graduates and the change in the percentage of college graduates are statistically significant, with more high school graduates leading to slower employment growth and more college graduates associated with faster employment growth. The impact of changes in college graduates is almost five times greater than the impact of changes in high school graduates. The addition of the two urban interaction terms in Equation 4 does not materially change the results.

Table C-2 presents the findings from Version 2, the extended model. In Equation 5, increases in real salaries are negatively related to the initial percentage of high school graduates and positively related to increases in the percentages of both high school graduates and college graduates. Among the noneducational variables, only HIGHWAYS is statistically significant, and the impact is negative. Equation 6 adds the two urban interaction terms, and they are not statistically significant. Among the educational measures, only the two high school variables are statistically significant. Among the noneducational variables, only OPENSPACE is statistically significant, with a negative effect.

Equations 7 and 8 repeat the extended model for the percentage change in

Table c-2. Determinants of County Economic Growth, 1970–2004, Version 2

	Dependent Variable: SALARYPC		Dependent Variable: EMPLOYPC	
	(5)	(6)	(7)	(8)
Intercept	**34.10**	**38.35**	**−48.83**	**−70.18**
HSPC70	**−0.42**	**−0.43**	−0.02	0.08
COLPC70	0.94	0.68	0.35	0.72
HSCHANGE	**0.19**	**0.23**	**−1.53**	**−1.57**
COLCHANGE	**0.77**	**0.65**	**8.27**	**8.47**
URBAN × HSCHANGE	—	−0.34	—	0.24
URBAN × COLCHANGE	—	1.34	—	−2.05
HIGHWAYS	**−10.44**	**−9.66**	**50.17**	**56.60**
GASPOWER	0.32	0.36	**−2.66**	**−2.59**
TAXRATE	16.11	11.37	55.51	63.54
PROPVALUE ($ millions)	21.04	−24.42	3.07	3.69
OPENSPACE	**−0.05**	**−0.05**	**0.40**	**0.41**
POLLUTION	0.00	0.00	0.00	0.00
BEACH	**−2.91**	**−2.23**	**90.36**	**91.61**
R²	**0.24**	**0.24**	**0.43**	**0.42**
Number of observations	100	100	100	100

DATA SOURCE: U.S. Department of Commerce, Bureau of Economic Analysis, "Local Area Personal Income"; N.C. State Data Center, "Log into North Carolina."
NOTE: Boldface refers to a statistically significant result at the 10 percent level or better (two-tail test).

county employment. For the educational variables, the results in Equation 7 are the same as those in Equation 3: the effect of the change in the high school percentage is negative, and the effect of change in the college percentage is positive and more than five times larger. Several of the noneducational variables have a statistically significant impact on employment growth, including HIGHWAYS (positive), GASPOWER (negative), OPENSPACE (positive), and BEACH (positive).[5] The results in Equation 8, which adds the two urban interaction terms, are virtually identical. The urban interaction terms are not statistically significant.

In conclusion, the analysis provides strong evidence that educational differences have significantly influenced differences in economic growth among North Carolina's counties. In summary, the findings show that growth in average real salaries per job has been lower in counties with initially higher percentages of workers with high school degrees but higher in counties with larger increases in the percentage of workers with high school degrees and much higher in counties with greater increases in the percentage of workers with college degrees. Some evidence indicates, though not conclusively, that the positive impact on real salaries from increases in the percentage of college graduates is strongest in urban counties. Noneducational variables do little to explain differences in real salary growth among the counties.

The conclusions differ somewhat for employment. Among the educational variables, the changes in the educational attainment measures are important. Increases in the percentage of workers with high school degrees are associated with slower employment growth, whereas increases in the percentage of workers with college degrees are related to faster employment growth, and the college effect is much stronger. These impacts do not differ in urban and rural counties. Highway mileage, open space, and beach access are also related to faster employment growth, while natural gas availability is associated with slower employment growth.

Appendix D

Gross Local Product by Major Industry in North Carolina's Regions, 1990 and 2004

The source for all the data in the tables is "IMPLAN" for North Carolina. All amounts are in millions of 2004 dollars.

Table D-1. Key Triangle Economic Sectors, 1990 and 2004

	1990	2004	% Change	Annualized % Change
Gross local product (GLP)	$32,194	$63,300	96.6	4.8
Employment	652,395	994,090	52.4	3.0

Sector	1990 value	% of GLP	Sector	2004 value	% of GLP
Real estate and construction	$2,776	8.6	Real estate and construction	$5,586	8.8
Education	$2,478	7.7	Education	$4,879	7.7
Retail trade	$2,064	6.4	Wholesale trade	$4,467	7.1
Wholesale trade	$1,831	5.7	Retail trade	$3,739	5.9
Communications equipment	$1,093	3.4	Pharmaceuticals	$2,753	4.3
Electric generation	$1,077	3.3	Software services	$2,712	4.3
Computer terminals	$930	2.9	Research and development	$2,476	3.9
Pharmaceuticals	$914	2.8	Telecommunications	$1,629	2.6
Physicians	$816	2.5	Medical practices	$1,541	2.4
Restaurants	$715	2.2	Hospitals	$1,463	2.3
State government	$661	2.1	Management services	$1,244	2.0
Cigarette manufacturing	$641	2.0	Banking	$1,203	1.9
Research and development	$623	1.9	Electric generation	$930	1.5
Software services	$539	1.7	Computer terminals	$709	1.1
Banking	$477	1.5	Communications equipment	$693	1.1

Table D-2. Key Greater Charlotte Economic Sectors, 1990 and 2004

	1990	2004	% Change	Annualized % Change
Gross local product (GLP)	$35,581	$72,525	103.8	5.1
Employment	623,323	937,483	50.4	2.9

Sector	1990 value	% of GLP	Sector	2004 value	% of GLP
Real estate and construction	$3,406	9.6	Real estate and construction	$7,084	9.8
Wholesale trade	$2,478	9.2	Banking	$6,586	9.1
Retail trade	$2,619	7.4	Wholesale trade	$5,692	7.8
Electric generation	$1,931	5.4	Management services	$4,455	6.1
Textiles and apparel	$1,662	4.7	Retail trade	$3,389	4.7
Cigarettes	$1,116	3.1	Education	$2,875	4.0
Motor freight & warehousing	$1,033	2.9	Cigarettes	$2,458	3.4
Medical practices	$808	2.3	Medical practices	$1,629	2.6
Banking	$798	2.2	Software processing	$1,326	1.8
Air transportation	$797	2.2	Restaurants	$1,294	1.8
Education	$727	2.0	Motor freight & warehousing	$1,113	1.5
Computer equipment	$703	2.0	Electric generation	$1,007	1.4
Restaurants	$609	1.7	Computer equipment	$711	1.0
Food processing	$477	1.3	Air transportation	$626	0.9
Hospitals	$375	1.1	Vehicle bodies and parts	$505	0.7

Table D-3. Key Greater Wilmington Economic Sectors, 1990 and 2004

	1990	2004	% Change	Annualized % Change
Gross local product (GLP)	$6,335	$11,426	80.4	4.2
Employment	137,620	214,591	55.9	3.2

Sector	1990 value	% of GLP	Sector	2004 value	% of GLP
Real estate and construction	$651	10.3	Real estate and construction	$1,529	13.4
Retail trade	$529	8.4	Education	$851	7.4
Chemical manufacturing	$454	7.2	Retail trade	$826	7.2
Electric generation	$368	5.8	Electric generation	$600	5.3
Wholesale trade	$265	4.2	Medical practices	$464	4.1
Education	$258	4.1	Wholesale trade	$434	3.8
Industrial oils	$206	3.3	Restaurants	$319	2.8
Textiles and apparel	$181	2.9	Paper mills and products	$292	2.6
Restaurants	$176	2.8	Banking	$273	2.4
Medical practices	$175	2.8	Industrial oils	$179	1.6
Paper mills and products	$164	2.6	Hog processing	$165	1.5
Banking	$139	2.2	Motor freight & warehousing	$120	1.1
Motor freight & warehousing	$88	1.4	Aircraft engines and parts	$106	0.9
Tobacco	$59	0.9	Glass products	$105	0.9
Glass products	$59	0.9	Hotels	$56	0.5

Table D-4. Key Greater Asheville Economic Sectors, 1990 and 2004

	1990	2004	% Change	Annualized % Change
Gross local product (GLP)	$8,373	$11,288	34.8	2.1
Employment	182,348	223,410	22.5	1.4

Sector	1990 value	% of GLP	Sector	2004 value	% of GLP
Retail trade	$685	8.2	Real estate and construction	$1,062	9.4
Real estate and construction	$664	7.9	Retail trade	$934	8.3
Paper mills	$533	6.4	Education	$749	6.6
Textiles and apparel	$375	4.5	Medical practices	$583	5.2
Medical practices	$349	4.2	Wholesale trade	$445	3.9
Wholesale trade	$308	3.7	Restaurants	$352	3.1
Education	$270	3.2	Hospitals	$320	2.8
Hospitals	$267	3.2	Paper mills	$302	2.7
Plastic products	$237	2.8	Banking	$275	2.4
Restaurants	$210	2.5	Federal nonmilitary	$201	1.8
Motor freight & warehousing	$185	2.2	Vehicle parts	$154	1.4
Photographic equipment	$183	2.2	Textiles and apparel	$149	1.3
Electric generation	$160	1.9	Motor freight & warehousing	$143	1.3
Banking	$153	1.8	Hotels	$142	1.3
Vehicle parts	$143	1.7	Plastic products	$127	1.1

Table D-5. Key Greater Boone Economic Sectors, 1990 and 2004

	1990	2004	% Change	Annualized % Change
Gross local product (GLP)	$984	$1,599	62.5	3.5
Employment	29,803	37,883	27.1	1.7

Sector	1990 value	% of GLP	Sector	2004 value	% of GLP
Real estate and construction	$146	14.8	Education	$247	15.4
Retail trade	$104	10.6	Real estate and construction	$155	9.7
Education	$84	8.5	Retail trade	$153	9.6
Restaurants	$45	4.6	Restaurants	$73	4.6
Medical practices	$38	3.9	Medical practices	$72	4.5
Wholesale trade	$34	3.5	Wholesale trade	$58	3.6
Hospitals	$34	3.5	Hospitals	$53	3.3
Textiles and apparel	$29	2.9	Amusements & recreation	$53	3.3
Greenhouse & nursery products	$25	2.5	Banking	$41	2.6
Hotels	$24	2.4	Hotels	$37	2.3
Electronic components	$22	2.2	Greenhouse & nursery products	$21	1.3
Motor freight & warehousing	$18	1.8	Electric generation	$20	1.3
Amusement and recreation	$15	1.5	Electronic components	$17	1.1
Banking	$15	1.5	Minerals manufacturing	$13	0.8
Electric generation	$13	1.3	Textiles and apparel	$12	0.8

Table D-6. Key Northeast Economic Sectors, 1990 and 2004

	1990	2004	% Change	Annualized % Change
Gross local product (GLP)	$1,372	$2,187	59.4	3.3
Employment	35,244	45,930	30.3	1.9

Sector	1990 value	% of GLP	Sector	2004 value	% of GLP
Retail trade	$139	10.1	Education	$238	10.9
Processed peanuts	$133	9.7	Real estate and construction	$200	9.1
Real estate and construction	$80	5.8	Retail trade	$190	8.7
Wholesale trade	$74	5.4	Wholesale trade	$101	4.6
Education	$74	5.4	Federal nonmilitary	$99	4.5
Military	$63	4.6	Military	$71	3.2
Federal nonmilitary	$62	4.5	Medical practices	$62	2.8
Medical practices	$41	3.0	Restaurants	$54	2.5
Textiles and apparel	$39	2.8	Banking	$51	2.3
Restaurants	$27	2.0	Logging and sawmills	$46	2.1
Banking	$24	1.7	Oil seed crops	$33	1.5
Oil seed crops	$22	1.6	Greenhouses & nursery products	$25	1.1
Motor freight & warehousing	$22	1.6	Grains	$23	1.1
Logging and sawmills	$22	1.6	Vegetables	$23	1.1
Electric generation	$18	1.3	Poultry and eggs	$21	1.0

Table D-7. Key Midcoast Economic Sectors, 1990 and 2004

	1990	2004	% Change	Annualized % Change
Gross local product (GLP)	$2,176	$3,501	60.9	3.4
Employment	59,672	73,563	23.3	1.4

Sector	1990 value	% of GLP	Sector	2004 value	% of GLP
Real estate and construction	$262	12.0	Real estate and construction	$661	18.9
Retail trade	$225	10.3	Retail trade	$295	8.4
Wholesale trade	$130	6.0	Education	$247	7.1
Textiles and apparel	$109	5.0	Restaurants	$152	4.3
Education	$98	4.5	Wholesale trade	$101	2.9
Restaurants	$81	3.7	Fertilizers	$97	2.8
Electric housewares	$55	2.5	Banking	$83	2.4
Electric generation	$52	2.4	Textiles and apparel	$71	2.0
Wood partitions	$43	2.0	Medical practices	$64	1.8
Banking	$43	2.0	Logging and sawmills	$54	1.5
Logging and sawmills	$41	1.9	Hospitals	$51	1.5
Wood furniture	$35	1.6	Wood partitions	$48	1.4
Boat building	$31	1.4	Boat building	$44	1.3
Oil bearing crops	$28	1.3	Electric generation	$41	1.2
Motor freight & warehousing	$28	1.3	Motor freight & warehousing	$41	1.2

Table D-8. Key Highlands Economic Sectors, 1990 and 2004

	1990	2004	% Change	Annualized % Change
Gross local product (GLP)	$743	$1,286	73.1	3.9
Employment	22,210	30,145	35.7	2.2

Sector	1990 value	% of GLP	Sector	2004 value	% of GLP
Real estate and construction	$95	12.8	Education	$261	20.3
Education	$70	9.4	Real estate and construction	$148	11.5
Retail trade	$57	9.3	Retail trade	$89	6.9
Fertilizers	$62	7.7	Restaurants	$48	3.7
Textiles and apparel	$52	7.0	Medical practices	$38	3.0
Hotels	$29	3.9	Casinos	$31	2.4
Paperboard mills	$27	3.6	Hospitals	$30	2.3
Restaurants	$21	2.8	Hotels	$26	2.0
Hospitals	$20	2.7	Plastic products	$25	1.9
Furniture	$15	2.0	Furniture	$23	1.8
Medical practices	$14	1.9	Banking	$22	1.7
Greenhouse & nursery products	$8	1.1	Greenhouse & nursery products	$20	1.6
Plastic products	$8	1.1	Wholesale trade	$16	1.2
Electric generation	$8	1.1	Electric generation	$15	1.2
Amusement and recreation	$7	0.9	Paperboard mills	$10	0.8

Table D-9. Key Far West Economic Sectors, 1990 and 2004

	1990	2004	% Change	Annualized % Change
Gross local product (GLP)	$1,295	$1,318	1.8	0.1
Employment	24,545	29,524	20.3	1.3

Sector	1990 value	% of GLP	Sector	2004 value	% of GLP
Fertilizers	$339	26.2	Real estate & construction	$163	12.4
Real estate & construction	$99	7.6	Retail trade	$153	11.6
Retail trade	$90	6.9	Education	$86	6.5
Textiles and apparel	$62	4.8	Hospitals	$48	3.6
Electric generation	$57	4.4	Restaurants	$42	3.2
Minerals	$50	3.9	Banking	$39	3.0
Motors and generators	$46	3.6	Medical practices	$37	1.8
Education	$31	2.4	Electric generation	$24	1.7
Restaurants	$22	1.7	Amusement and recreation	$22	1.8
Medical practices	$21	1.6	Gaskets & related products	$20	1.5
Hospitals	$21	1.6	Wholesale trade	$20	1.5
Poultry and eggs	$18	1.4	Motors and generators	$12	0.9
Gaskets & related products	$15	1.2	Greenhouse & nursery products	$12	0.9
Instruments	$15	1.2	Hotels	$9	0.7
Furniture	$13	1.0	Textiles and apparel	$8	0.6

Table D-10. Key Greater Winston-Salem Economic Sectors, 1990 and 2004

	1990	2004	% Change	Annualized % Change
Gross local product (GLP)	$18,680	$23,147	23.9	1.5
Employment	259,515	305,268	17.6	1.1

Sector	1990 value	% of GLP	Sector	2004 value	% of GLP
Cigarettes	$6,958	37.2	Cigarettes	$6,236	26.9
Retail trade	$973	5.2	Banking	$1,359	5.9
Textiles and apparel	$946	5.1	Retail trade	$1,248	5.4
Real estate and construction	$832	4.5	Real estate & construction	$1,248	5.4
Wholesale trade	$648	3.5	Education	$1,219	5.3
Education	$573	3.1	Wholesale trade	$919	4.0
Hospitals	$461	2.5	Textiles and apparel	$712	3.1
Medical practices	$396	2.1	Hospitals	$671	2.9
Banking	$379	2.0	Medical practices	$601	2.6
Motor freight & warehousing	$319	1.7	Restaurants	$405	1.7
Air transportation	$267	1.4	Motor freight & warehousing	$395	1.7
Restaurants	$258	1.4	Industrial instruments	$363	1.6
Breweries	$218	1.2	Air transportation	$238	1.0
Electric generation	$165	0.9	Air and gas compressors	$88	0.3
Furniture	$150	0.8	Electric generation	$77	0.3

Table D-11. Key Greater Greensboro Economic Sectors, 1990 and 2004

	1990	2004	% Change	Annualized % Change
Gross local product (GLP)	$25,057	$34,325	37.0	2.2
Employment	508,840	585,553	15.1	1.0

Sector	1990 value	% of GLP	Sector	2004 value	% of GLP
Textiles and apparel	$1,999	8.0	Wholesale trade	$2,644	7.7
Wholesale trade	$1,765	7.0	Real estate and construction	$2,460	7.2
Retail trade	$1,742	7.0	Retail trade	$2,449	7.1
Cigarettes	$1,721	6.9	Education	$1,866	5.4
Real estate and construction	$1,690	6.7	Cigarettes	$1,158	3.4
Furniture	$857	3.4	Textiles and apparel	$1,093	3.2
Motor freight & warehousing	$595	2.4	Medical practices	$1,093	3.2
Education	$589	2.4	Pesticides	$911	2.7
Medical practices	$577	2.3	Banking	$804	2.3
Hospitals	$500	2.0	Restaurants	$760	2.2
Restaurants	$494	2.0	Motor freight & warehousing	$710	2.1
Breweries	$367	1.5	Hospitals	$601	1.8
Banking	$364	1.5	Furniture	$484	1.4
Pesticides	$283	1.1	Vehicle parts	$377	1.1
Electric generation	$224	0.9	Wiring devices	$354	1.0

Table D-12. Key Sandhills Economic Sectors, 1990 and 2004

	1990	2004	% Change	Annualized % Change
Gross local product (GLP)	$12,142	$18,326	50.9	2.9
Employment	273,974	333,227	21.6	1.4

Sector	1990 value	% of GLP	Sector	2004 value	% of GLP
Military	$2,474	20.4	Military	$4,356	23.8
Textiles and apparel	$991	8.2	Education	$1,428	7.8
Retail trade	$886	7.3	Retail trade	$1,139	6.2
Real estate & construction	$687	5.7	Real estate & construction	$979	5.3
Education	$444	3.7	Medical practices	$581	3.2
Medical practices	$368	3.0	Textiles and apparel	$452	2.5
Tires and inner tubes	$340	2.8	Wholesale trade	$418	2.3
Wholesale trade	$325	2.7	Restaurants	$362	2.0
Hospitals	$255	2.1	Banking	$284	1.5
Restaurants	$242	2.0	Tires and inner tubes	$260	1.4
Mineral mining	$188	1.5	Motor freight & warehousing	$252	1.4
Banking	$176	1.4	Hospitals	$244	1.3
Motor freight & warehousing	$148	1.2	Vehicle parts	$111	0.6
Processed food	$105	0.9	Pesticides	$108	0.6
Poultry processing	$98	0.8	Poultry processing	$108	0.6

Table D-13. Key Greater Gaston Economic Sectors, 1990 and 2004

	1990	2004	% Change	Annualized % Change
Gross local product (GLP)	$10,219	$9,872	−3.4	−0.2
Employment	198,869	190,296	−4.3	−0.3

Sector	1990 value	% of GLP	Sector	2004 value	% of GLP
Textiles and apparel	$1,583	15.5	Retail trade	$774	7.8
Fertilizers	$1,228	12.0	Real estate & construction	$690	7.0
Retail trade	$651	6.4	Education	$652	6.6
Vehicle bodies and parts	$543	5.3	Textiles and apparel	$577	5.8
Real estate and construction	$483	4.7	Vehicle bodies and parts	$482	4.9
Wholesale trade	$407	4.0	Wholesale trade	$426	4.3
Motor freight & warehousing	$300	2.9	Medical practices	$373	3.8
Education	$263	2.6	Electric generation	$236	2.4
Medical practices	$225	2.2	Restaurants	$227	2.3
Electric generation	$209	2.0	Hospitals	$211	2.1
Hospitals	$196	1.9	Banking	$185	1.9
Rubber and plastic products	$165	1.6	Motor freight & warehousing	$175	1.8
Restaurants	$160	1.6	Rubber and plastic products	$123	1.2
Glass products	$139	1.4	Glass products	$118	1.2
Banking	$112	1.1	Ball and roller bearing	$117	1.2

Table D-14. Key Foothills Economic Sectors, 1990 and 2004

	1990	2004	% Change	Annualized % Change
Gross local product (GLP)	$8,602	$12,053	40.1	2.4
Employment	199,369	229,463	15.1	1.0

Sector	1990 value	% of GLP	Sector	2004 value	% of GLP
Furniture	$1,243	14.5	Wholesale trade	$934	7.7
Textiles and apparel	$727	8.5	Retail trade	$881	7.3
Retail trade	$647	7.5	Furniture	$869	7.2
Wholesale trade	$504	5.9	Real estate & construction	$717	5.9
Real estate and construction	$416	4.8	Education	$690	5.7
Medical practices	$253	2.9	Fiber optic cable	$535	4.4
Motor freight & warehousing	$246	2.9	Textiles and apparel	$465	3.9
Wiring and instruments	$224	2.6	Medical practices	$407	3.4
Education	$209	2.4	Restaurants	$273	2.3
Restaurants	$206	2.4	Banking	$181	1.5
Plastic products	$196	2.3	Hospitals	$174	1.4
Hospitals	$196	2.3	Vehicle parts	$146	1.2
Electric generation	$133	1.5	Electric generation	$138	1.1
Banking	$125	1.5	Plastic products	$134	1.1
Paperboard products	$98	1.1	Foam products	$112	0.9

Table D-15. Key Greenville-Jacksonville Economic Sectors, 1990 and 2004

	1990	2004	% Change	Annualized % Change
Gross local product (GLP)	$10,471	$15,717	50.1	2.9
Employment	247,705	316,426	27.7	1.7

Sector	1990 value	% of GLP	Sector	2004 value	% of GLP
Military	$2,457	23.5	Military	$3,411	21.7
Retail trade	$778	7.4	Education	$1,596	10.2
Real estate and construction	$682	6.5	Retail trade	$1,025	6.5
Education	$487	4.7	Real estate and construction	$952	6.1
Textiles and apparel	$430	4.1	Medical practices	$562	3.6
Wholesale trade	$356	3.4	Wholesale trade	$466	3.0
Medical practices	$351	3.4	Restaurants	$403	2.6
Restaurants	$260	2.5	Banking	$284	1.8
Pharmaceuticals	$221	2.1	Pharmaceuticals	$158	1.0
Paper products	$165	1.6	Textiles and apparel	$138	0.9
Banking	$164	1.6	Motor freight & warehousing	$117	0.7
Tobacco	$143	1.4	Boats	$110	0.7
Boats	$130	1.2	Household appliances	$98	0.6
Motor freight & warehousing	$102	1.0	Metal valves	$89	0.6
Pulp mills	$84	0.8	Computer terminals	$87	0.6

Table D-16. Key Rocky Mount–Wilson Economic Sectors, 1990 and 2004

	1990	2004	% Change	Annualized % Change
Gross local product (GLP)	$5,274	$7,304	38.5	2.3
Employment	119,058	124,216	4.3	0.3

Sector	1990 value	% of GLP	Sector	2004 value	% of GLP
Retail trade	$416	7.9	Pharmaceuticals	$626	8.6
Real estate & construction	$336	6.4	Wholesale trade	$623	8.5
Wholesale trade	$295	5.6	Banking	$531	7.3
Textiles and apparel	$235	4.5	Education	$498	6.8
Pharmaceuticals	$217	4.1	Real estate & construction	$426	5.8
Education	$193	3.7	Retail trade	$406	5.6
Restaurants	$190	3.6	Medical practices	$200	2.7
Banking	$175	3.3	Tires	$177	2.4
Tires	$167	3.2	Restaurants	$138	1.9
Tobacco	$154	2.9	Textiles and apparel	$133	1.8
Medical practices	$143	2.7	Tobacco	$133	1.8
Motor freight & warehousing	$98	1.9	Food processing	$102	1.4
Vehicle bodies and parts	$70	1.3	Electronic components	$68	0.9
Hand tools	$64	1.2	Glass products	$63	0.9
Instruments	$82	1.2	Farm machinery	$49	0.7

Table D-17. Key Greater Mountain Economic Sectors, 1990 and 2004

	1990	2004	% Change	Annualized % Change
Gross local product (GLP)	$3,165	$3,706	17.1	1.1
Employment	77,749	78,049	0.4	0.0

Sector	1990 value	% of GLP	Sector	2004 value	% of GLP
Textiles and apparel	$497	15.7	Education	$350	9.4
Furniture	$344	10.9	Pharmaceuticals	$288	7.8
Pharmaceuticals	$196	6.2	Textiles and apparel	$241	6.5
Vehicle parts	$188	5.9	Retail trade	$240	6.5
Retail trade	$178	5.6	Real estate and construction	$227	6.1
Education	$160	5.1	Furniture	$163	4.4
Real estate and construction	$111	3.5	Wiring devices	$116	3.1
Minerals mining	$97	3.1	Medical practices	$105	2.8
Hospitals	$88	2.8	Wholesale trade	$102	2.8
Medical practices	$77	2.4	Hospitals	$86	2.3
Food products	$69	2.2	Restaurants	$77	2.1
Wiring devices	$53	1.7	Vehicle parts	$74	2.0
Restaurants	$53	1.7	Motor freight & warehousing	$70	1.9
Motor freight & warehousing	$50	1.6	Greenhouse & nursery products	$58	1.6
Wholesale trade	$46	1.5	Banking	$55	1.5

Table D-18. Key Down East Economic Sectors, 1990 and 2004

	1990	2004	% Change	Annualized % Change
Gross local product (GLP)	$3,679	$5,212	41.7	2.5
Employment	94,333	111,238	17.9	1.2

Sector	1990 value	% of GLP	Sector	2004 value	% of GLP
Military	$321	8.7	Education	$466	8.9
Retail trade	$288	7.8	Military	$427	8.2
Wholesale trade	$217	5.9	Retail trade	$346	6.6
Real estate and construction	$200	5.4	Wholesale trade	$246	4.7
Education	$189	5.1	Meat processing	$231	4.4
Textiles and apparel	$171	4.6	Real estate and construction	$218	4.2
Meat processing	$168	4.6	Poultry and eggs	$207	4.0
Poultry and eggs	$132	3.6	Medical practices	$133	2.6
Medical practices	$84	2.3	Pigs and hogs	$105	2.0
Fruit and vegetable canning	$71	1.9	Motor freight & warehousing	$92	1.8
Banking	$64	1.7	Fruit and vegetable canning	$88	1.7
Restaurants	$64	1.7	Banking	$77	1.5
Fertilizer	$53	1.4	Agricultural services	$65	1.2
Motor freight & warehousing	$53	1.4	Transformers	$60	1.2
Vehicle parts	$46	1.3	Rubber and plastic products	$58	1.1

Table D-19. Key Greater Wilkes Economic Sectors, 1990 and 2004

	1990	2004	% Change	Annualized % Change
Gross local product (GLP)	$1,721	$2,588	50.4	2.9
Employment	40,059	49,039	2.0	0.1

Sector	1990 value	% of GLP	Sector	2004 value	% of GLP
Retail trade	$218	12.7	Management	$415	16.0
Textiles and apparel	$147	8.5	Retail trade	$161	6.2
Poultry processing	$146	8.5	Real estate and construction	$149	5.8
Real estate and construction	$104	6.0	Wholesale trade	$139	5.4
Poultry and eggs	$69	4.0	Poultry and eggs	$120	4.6
Education	$64	3.7	Banking	$110	4.3
Furniture	$57	3.3	Poultry processing	$101	3.9
Wholesale trade	$56	3.3	Vehicle parts	$72	2.8
Electronic components	$52	3.0	Motor freight & warehousing	$54	2.1
Banking	$49	2.8	Medical practices	$48	1.9
Motor freight & warehousing	$43	2.5	Electronic components	$47	1.8
Glass products	$41	2.4	Restaurants	$44	1.7
Hotels	$41	2.4	Furniture	$29	1.1
Restaurants	$38	2.2	Hospitals	$25	1.0
Medical practices	$35	2.0	Wood products	$23	0.9

Table D-20. Key Lakes Economic Sectors, 1990 and 2004

	1990	2004	% Change	Annualized % Change
Gross local product (GLP)	$872	$1,149	31.8	2.0
Employment	26,724	24,781	−6.3	−0.4

Sector	1990 value	% of GLP	Sector	2004 value	% of GLP
Retail trade	$195	22.4	Education	$122	10.6
Textiles and apparel	$147	16.9	Retail trade	$100	8.7
Real estate and construction	$56	6.4	Wholesale trade	$58	5.0
Education	$45	5.2	Textiles and apparel	$56	4.9
Tobacco	$41	4.7	Real estate and construction	$56	4.9
Medical practices	$28	3.2	Glass containers	$48	4.2
Wholesale trade	$25	2.9	Medical practices	$40	3.5
Glass containers	$20	2.3	Motor freight & warehousing	$35	3.0
Hospitals	$18	2.1	Hospitals	$30	2.6
Restaurants	$17	1.9	Restaurants	$29	2.5
Electric generation	$14	1.6	Food processing	$24	2.1
Motor freight & warehousing	$13	1.5	Logging and sawmills	$21	1.8
Paperboard mills	$7	0.8	Pesticides	$17	1.5
Blowers and fans	$7	0.8	Tobacco	$14	1.2
Hotels	$6	0.7	Air purification equipment	$12	1.0

Table D-21. Key Roanoke Economic Sectors, 1990 and 2004

	1990	2004	% Change	Annualized % Change
Gross local product (GLP)	$1,905	$2,424	27.2	1.7
Employment	51,226	51,827	1.2	0.1

Sector	1990 value	% of GLP	Sector	2004 value	% of GLP
Paperboard mills	$189	9.9	Education	$248	10.2
Retail trade	$162	8.5	Retail trade	$203	8.4
Education	$126	6.6	Paperboard mills	$106	4.4
Wholesale trade	$123	6.5	Steel	$99	4.1
Textiles and apparel	$115	6.0	Wholesale trade	$81	3.3
Poultry processing	$92	4.8	Real estate and construction	$80	3.3
Electric generation	$87	4.6	Logging and sawmills	$74	3.1
Real estate and construction	$77	4.0	Poultry and eggs	$60	2.5
Logging and sawmills	$53	2.8	Medical practices	$54	2.2
Poultry and eggs	$50	2.6	Poultry processing	$50	2.1
Medical practices	$45	2.4	Electric generation	$50	2.1
Restaurants	$35	1.8	Restaurants	$48	2.0
Banking	$27	1.4	Plastic products	$42	1.7
Fertilizer	$25	1.3	Banking	$41	1.7
Plastic products	$24	1.3	Hospitals	$39	1.6

Notes

Abbreviations

BEA   U.S. Department of Commerce, Bureau of Economic Analysis

BLS   U.S. Department of Labor, Bureau of Labor Statistics

DES   U.S. Department of Education, "Digest of Education Statistics"

ERP   Council of Economic Advisers. *Economic Report of the President, 2007.* Washington, D.C.: U.S. Government Printing Office, 2007.

ESC   Employment Security Commission of North Carolina

LogNC   N.C. State Data Center. "Log into North Carolina." N.d. <http://linc.state .nc.us/>. Accessed 9 June 2007.

StatAbt   U.S. Census Bureau. "Statistical Abstract of the United States." N.d. <http://www.census.gov/prod/www/statistical-abstract-1995_2000.html>. Accessed 19 December 2007.

Preface

1. BLS, "Employment, Hours, and Earnings." Apparel employment is included with textiles. Tobacco includes farm-level production of the leaf plus processing value at the cigarette factories. Product value at the cigarette factories totals more than six times the value of the farm-level leaf.

2. Production is an index of output and is from the BEA, "Gross Domestic Product"; ESC, "Employment and Wages."

3. BEA, "Gross Domestic Product."

4. Dicken, *Global Shift*, 400.

5. As measured by an index of output. BEA, "Gross Domestic Product."

6. U.S. Census Bureau, *1970 Census of Population and Housing*; U.S. Census Bureau, "American Community Survey," 2005.

7. ESC, "Employment and Wages."

8. James H. Johnson Jr., "Changing Face," 17.

9. Data availability sometimes requires the analysis of the Connected Age to begin later than 1970.

Chapter 1

1. *ERP*; StatAbt, 1972, 2005; Riches, "Top 10 Best Selling Vehicles." Data for the 2000s are from various years, depending on availability.

2. *ERP*. The measure is gross domestic product.

3. Ibid.

4. Ibid.

5. National Bureau of Economic Research, "Business Cycle Expansions and Contractions."

6. BEA, "Real Gross Domestic Product."

7. Ibid.

8. Ibid.

9. *ERP*, table B-49.

10. Jorgensen, Ho, and Stiroh, "Projecting Productivity Growth"; Jorgensen and Stiroh, "Raising the Speed Limit"; Oliner and Sichel, "Resurgence of Growth."

11. Forecasts are from Su, "U.S. Economy to 2014," 14.

12. Oliner and Sichel, "Resurgence of Growth," 21.

13. *ERP*, table B-36.

14. Ibid.

15. Ibid., table B-42.

16. BLS, "Alternative Measures."

17. One survey found that 18 percent of recent college graduates were underemployed ("Underemployment Affects 18 Percent"). However, another study found no upward trend in job layoff rates in the 1990s and no evidence that low-wage jobs were disproportionately negatively affected by shifts in the economy (Clair Brown, Haltiwanger, and Lane, *Economic Turbulence*, 123).

18. Some of the decline in manufacturing employment occurred as a result of the increase in temporary hiring in the sector. In recent years, manufacturers have increasingly contracted with outside firms for support functions such as accounting, janitorial, and food services. These jobs are counted as nonmanufacturing employment in the contracted firms. However, when the jobs were part of the permanent manufacturing company base, they were counted as manufacturing employment. Between 25 percent and 30 percent of manufacturing job losses could have resulted from this change in classification (Congressional Budget Office, "What Accounts for the Decline?" 4).

19. *ERP*, tables B-46, B-51, B-99.

20. Dietz and Orr, "Leaner, More Skilled U.S. Manufacturing Workforce."

21. Florida, *Rise*.

22. Florida, *Flight*, 136.

23. Eckstein and Nagypal, "Evolution," 25. At the same time that women's labor force participation has increased, a much smaller reduction has occurred in men's labor force participation. This development suggests some substitutability in men's and women's paid work time and time spent in household activities.

24. For more discussion of the factors behind the increased participation of women in the labor force, see Blau, Ferber, and Winkler, *Economics of Women, Men, and Work*; Larry E. Jones, Manuelli, and McGrattan, *Why Are Married Women Working So Much?*

25. Alenezi and Walden, "New Look," 102.

26. BEA, "Real Gross Domestic Product."

27. Ibid.

28. StatAbt 2007, table 216; StatAbt 1973, table 175.

29. StatAbt 2006, tables 248, 252, 253, 254, 255.

30. BEA, "Trade in Goods and Services." Technically, "outsourcing" means the company transfers the work to an outside supplier, who may still be in the United States. "Offshoring" means the work is transferred to operations outside the United States.

31. Ibid.

32. Baily and Farrell, "Exploding the Myths," 1–2.

33. BEA, "Trade in Goods and Services."

34. Berman, "Industry Output," 46.

35. Heckler, "Occupational Employment Projections," 77.

36. For example, forecasts show the number of people holding science and engineering doctorates in China to go from 50 percent fewer than in the United States in 2003 to 26 percent more in 2010 (Bhide, "Venturesome Consumption," table 1a). A 2006 Duke University study found the lack of available skilled labor in the United States to be an important reason for firms to offshore employment (Cox, "Offshoring Blamed on Talent Gap"). Blinder ("Offshoring") sees a large increase in foreign competition for higher-paying U.S. jobs.

37. The National Center for Public Policy and Higher Education, "Income of U.S. Workforce," warns that supplying qualified workers may become even more difficult as retirees are increasingly replaced by younger employees from more challenged educational backgrounds.

38. Hotchkiss, *What's Up*. For example, the percentage of married women in the paid labor force fell from 62 percent in 2000 to 60.9 percent in 2004, and the percentage of married women with children in the paid labor force declined from 70.6 percent in 2000 to 68.2 percent in 2004 (StatAbt 2007, table 586).

39. *ERP*, table B-31.

40. Median household income per person was calculated by dividing median household income (U.S. Census Bureau, "Historical Income Tables") by persons per household (U.S. Census Bureau, "Families and Living Arrangements"). Median values are sometimes preferred because they moderate the effects of very high and very low incomes. Incomes could increase simply because people are working more. However, the data show that total hours worked increased less than both the number of households and the number of working-age people (Engemann and Owyang, "Working Hard or Hardly Working?").

41. Federal Reserve Bank of St. Louis, "Economic Data—FRED."

42. BLS, "Employment, Hours, and Earnings." However, Reynolds ("Unreal Wages") has criticized this measure as not being representative of the workforce.

43. Federal Reserve Board, "Flow of Funds Accounts," table B100.

44. Households in the top quintile of the income distribution had an average real (inflation-adjusted) income gain of 69 percent from 1970 to 2005, followed by gains of 37 percent, 22 percent, 16 percent, and 23 percent for households in the second, third, fourth, and fifth income quintiles, respectively (DeNavas-Walt, Proctor, and Lee, "Income, Poverty, and Health Insurance Coverage," table A-3). A similar pattern appears for consumer spending (BLS, "Consumer Expenditure Survey"). One factor contributing to the large gains in the top income quintile is the increased prevalence of two-worker households at that level (Reynolds, "For the Record").

45. Eckstein and Nagypal, "Evolution."

46. Levy and Murnane, *New Division*, 45.

47. Ibid.; Wheeler, "Evidence." For a contrary view suggesting that the link between technology and wage inequality is weak, see Card and DiNardo, "Technology and U.S. Wage Inequality."

48. DeNavas-Walt, Proctor, and Lee, "Income, Poverty, and Health Insurance Coverage," table B-1.

49. Ibid., tables B-1, B-2.

50. Kletzer, *Job Loss*, 43–53.

51. BLS, "Consumer Price Index."

52. Ibid.

53. Federal Reserve Board, "Selected Interest Rates."

54. Warnock and Warnock, "International Capital Flows."

55. Su, "U.S. Economy to 2014," 16.

56. Grossman and Rossi-Hansberg, "Trading Tasks."

57. Hacker, *Great Risk Shift*, chapter 1.

58. *ERP*, table B-34.

59. Ibid.

60. StatAbt 2007, table 77; StatAbt 1973, table 66; U.S. Census Bureau, "Families and Living Arrangements."

61. The median mother's age for a first birth increased from 21.7 in 1970–74 to 25.2 in 2003 (StatAbt 1982, table 94; Joyce A. Martin et al., "Births").

62. Willis, "Economic Theory," 63.

63. StatAbt 2007, table 5.

64. Borjas, *Heaven's Door*, 21.

65. Borjas, "Labor Demand Curve"; James P. Smith and Edmonston, *Immigration Debate*. A contrary view suggests that immigration has no adverse effect on wages of domestic low-skilled workers because the two groups are not perfect substitutes for each other (Ottaviano and Peri, *Rethinking the Gains*).

66. Camarota, "Jobless Recovery?," 6.

67. Toossi, "New Look," 20.

68. StatAbt 1973, table 1163; StatAbt 2007, table 952.

69. Landes, *Wealth and Poverty*, 6–7.

70. StatAbt 2007, table 1132; StatAbt 2006, table 1117.

71. Huber and Mills, *Bottomless Well*, 120.

72. Summers, "What Caused the Great Moderation?," 13–14.

73. Levinson, *Box*, chapter 14.

74. Thomas L. Friedman, *World Is Flat*.

75. Leamer, "Flat World."

76. *ERP*, tables B-1, B-82.

77. Ibid., tables B-1, B-80.

78. Ibid., tables B-1, B-86.

79. Ibid., tables B-1, B-83. Neither category includes government spending on public debt service.

80. Winston, "U.S Industry Adjustment," 101.

81. "Deregulation Was Supposed to Cut Prices."

82. Suranovic, "U.S. Tariff Policy," 1.

83. Greenspan, "Economic Outlook."

84. NAFTA has been the most analyzed of the trade agreements; for a positive view, see Hufbauer and Schott, *NAFTA Revisited*; for a negative view, see Robert E. Scott, "NAFTA's Hidden Costs." Hufbauer and Schott's numbers show that North Carolina had the highest percentage among all U.S. states of the labor force adversely affected by NAFTA.

85. *ERP*, table B-46.

86. Fields and Ok, "Measuring Movements," 465–67; Gittleman and Joyce, "Have Family Income Mobility Patterns Changed?," 308–11.

87. Gordon, *2010 Meltdown*.

88. Florida, *Flight*, 262–69.

89. Kotlikoff and Burns, *Coming Generational Storm*, chapter 7.

90. For a provocative discussion of the energy future, see Huber and Mills, *Bottomless Well*. Although the U.S. use of energy increased 47 percent between 1970 and 2005, energy used per dollar of economic production fell by 50 percent (*ERP*, table B-2; U.S. Department of Energy, "Energy Consumption by Sector").

Chapter 2

1. On the broadest measure of economic activity, quantity of production, North Carolina's growth rates exceeded national growth rates in every decade of the Connected Age. The state's growth rates in quantity of production per capita were also higher than national rates in every decade except the first years of the twenty-first century.

2. BEA, "Gross Domestic Product."

3. Hanna, "Income in the South," 252–53.

4. Garrett, "Growth in Manufacturing."

5. Cunningham, "Structural Booms."

6. Carlino and Mills, "Are U.S. Regional Incomes Converging?"; Choi, "Reexami-

nation"; Sherwood-Call, "1980s Divergence"; Gomme and Rupert, "Per Capita Income Growth"; Barro and Sala-i-Martin, *Economic Growth*; Niemi, *State and Regional Patterns*; Newman, *Growth*.

7. BEA, "State Annual Personal Income." The comparisons are based on an analysis of data from 1970 to 2005, using real personal income and employment. During the four expansions, the average income gain for North Carolina equaled 34.5 percent, compared to 26 percent for the nation, while North Carolina's average employment gain totaled 22.5 percent, versus 16.8 percent for the nation. During the five recessions, North Carolina's average income loss equaled 2.6 percent, compared to 1.6 percent for the nation. North Carolina lost average employment of 4 percent, while the nation lost an average of 2.1 percent.

8. BEA, "Gross Domestic Product." The relative importance of manufacturing, measured by the value of manufacturing production to total production, fell 47 percent in North Carolina between 1970 and 2006 but 50 percent for the nation.

9. BEA, "State Annual Personal Income." North Carolina's economic expansion, as measured by growth in real income, was 52 percent stronger than the national expansion in the 1980s, 34 percent stronger in the 1990s, but only 13 percent stronger between 2000 and 2005. In contrast, North Carolina's economic recession was 100 percent more severe than the national recession of the 1980s, 56 percent worse in the 1990s, and 88 percent more severe after 2000.

10. BEA, "Gross Domestic Product." The export-oriented industries are often called basic industries because they form the basis for other supporting and service firms in the state. Basic industries are identified by comparing the share of gross state product for each industry in North Carolina to the similar share in the nation. Industries with a larger share in North Carolina than in the nation are basic industries. In 1970, industries fitting this definition were (with the percentage by which their share of the gross state product exceeded the national industry's share in parentheses): agriculture (44 percent), furniture/lumber and wood/paper (110 percent), tobacco products (2,150 percent), and textiles/apparel (594 percent). In 2005, these industries remained classified as basic, although to a diminished degree, but were joined by food processing (293 percent), chemical products (153 percent), and banking (124 percent). Although North Carolina's share in transportation equipment was less than the national share in 2005, this industry was included as basic because its share of North Carolina's gross state product doubled between 1970 and 2005, while the national share was cut in half over the same period. In addition, computer and electronic equipment product manufacturing (technology) was included as basic in 2005 even though North Carolina's share was the same as the national share because of this industry's importance to some regions in the state.

11. In 1970, the Big Three accounted for 25 percent of the total gross state product, while the Big Five accounted for 8 percent. Despite the downsizing, in 2007, the Big Three still provided 178,000 manufacturing jobs, one-third of all manufacturing employment in the state (BEA, "Gross Domestic Product"; U.S. Census Bureau, "Annual Survey of Manufactures," North Carolina, table 1).

12. BEA, "Gross Domestic Product." Even though health care and professional and management services strongly increased their share of the state economy, their shares in 2005 remained less than the comparable national shares. In addition, economists often list tourism as a major component of the North Carolina economy. But published statistics do not identify tourism as a separate industry; instead, tourism involves parts of other industries, such as retail trade, entertainment, food service, and transportation. A 2005 estimate puts the economic value of tourism at $6 billion (Minges, *How Important Is Tourism?*, 8). At that time, the principal components of tourism—arts, entertainment, recreation, accommodations, and food service—collectively accounted for a smaller share of the economy in North Carolina than in the nation.

13. See, for example, Tootell, Kopcke, and Triest, "Investment and Employment"; Davis, Haltiwanger, and Schuh, *Job Creation and Destruction*; Kodrzycki, "Geographic Shifts"; Henry, Barkley, and Li, "Education and Nonmetropolitan Income Growth"; Goetz and Rupasingha, "Returns"; Gould and Ruffin, "What Determines Economic Growth?"; Kusmin, Redman, and Sears, *Factors*; Coughlin and Segev, "Location Determinants."

14. Levy and Murnane, *New Division*, 52.

15. Murnane, Willett, and Levy, "Growing Importance," 256–58.

16. StatAbt 1965, table 148; StatAbt 1955, table 131.

17. StatAbt 2006, table 218.

18. StatAbt 2007, table 218; StatAbt 1973, table 180.

19. N.C. Public Schools, "North Carolina 2005 SAT Report," 28.

20. *National Assessment of Educational Progress*, state profiles.

21. Garrett, "Growth in Manufacturing," 357–59; Wright, *Old South, New South*, 124–55.

22. BEA, "Gross Domestic Product."

23. Crandall, *Manufacturing*, 45.

24. Crone, "Where Have All the Factory Jobs Gone?"; Hekman, "Branch Plant Location"; Coughlin and Segev, "Location Determinants."

25. Tootell, Kopcke, and Triest, "Investment and Employment," 46.

26. Greenwood, "Changing Patterns"; Olsen, "South Will Fall Again"; Bartik, "Business Location Decisions."

27. Moomaw and Williams, "Total Factor Productivity," 29–32.

28. Bauer and Lee, "Labor Productivity Growth Rates," 1–2.

29. Compensation, which includes the value of firm paid benefits in addition to salaries and wages, would have been a better measure than only salaries and wages, but compensation data are available only since the late 1990s. In an independent analysis, Bauer and Lee ("Labor Productivity Growth Rates") found growth in the productivity of North Carolina's workers to be the eighth-fastest among states between 1977 and 2000 and third-fastest between 2000 and 2004.

30. World Trade Organization, "Understanding the WTO"; Asian Development Bank, "WTO Toolkit."

31. Tan, "Liberalization of Trade," 9–12.

32. Mankiw, *Essentials*, 192.

33. Canadian Border Services Agency, "Guide."

34. Asian Development Bank, "WTO Toolkit."

35. Jonquieres, "Garment Industry."

36. Tan, "Liberalization of Trade," 25–33. China's labor costs in general manufacturing were estimated to be 12 percent lower than U.S. costs in 2002 (Dullien, "China's Changing Competitive Position," table 1). WTO members have some ability to impose emergency restrictions on Chinese textile and apparel imports through 2013 (Tan, "Liberalization of Trade," 13).

37. BEA, "Exports and Imports."

38. BEA, "Gross Domestic Product."

39. BLS, "Employment, Hours, and Earnings." North Carolina's textile employment peaked in 1973, apparel employment reached its height in 1984, furniture jobs topped out in 1988, and employment in tobacco has been dropping since the 1940s.

40. Raymond Vernon ("International Investment") originated the theory of the product cycle.

41. Ritter and Sternfels, "When Offshore Manufacturing Doesn't Make Sense."

42. BEA, "Exports and Imports."

43. North Carolina is estimated to be one of the leading states in NAFTA- and WTO-related job losses (Robert E. Scott, "NAFTA's Hidden Costs," 7; Robert E. Scott, *U.S.–China Trade*, 42–45).

44. Chen, Imbs, and Scott (*Competition*, 10) estimate that greater world trade has reduced the inflation rate by 0.14 percentage points annually. Kohn ("Globalization," 5) says that total inflation from the mid-1990s to the mid-2000s has been reduced by between 0.5 and 1.0 percentage points as a result of increased world trade.

45. Author's calculations based on applying Kohn's estimates of the reduced inflation rate to North Carolina's employment base and using Robert E. Scott's estimate of seventy thousand jobs lost in North Carolina from NAFTA and WTO (*U.S.–China Trade*).

46. See Kahn, *Lessons from Deregulation*, a review by the person many observers consider the father of deregulation.

47. Ennis, "On the Size Distribution," 17–20.

48. Broaddus, "Bank Merger Wave," 4.

49. Jayaratne and Strahan, "Benefits," 16–19.

50. Dicken, *Global Shift*, 400.

51. Bartik, "Small Business Start-Ups," 1012–15.

52. Capehart, "U.S. Tobacco Industry."

53. U.S. Department of Agriculture, Foreign Agricultural Service, "NAFTA Agriculture Fact Sheet."

54. Allyn Taylor et al., "Impact," 347.

55. Capehart, "U.S. Tobacco Industry."

56. Tiller, "U.S. Tobacco Economic and Policy Outlook," 4.

57. Alenezi and Walden, "New Look," 102–3.

58. *2004 North Carolina Agricultural Statistics*, 25, 39; Perrin and Sappie, *North Carolina Farm Income and Production*, 53–56.

59. BEA, "Gross Domestic Product."

60. Bhagwati, *In Defense of Globalization*; Martin Wolf, *Why Globalization Works*.

61. In 2005, manufacturing's share of the North Carolina economy was 20 percent, compared to 12 percent for the nation (BEA, "Gross Domestic Product").

62. Energy prices averaged 13 percent higher in North Carolina than in the nation from 1977 to 2004 (U.S. Department of Energy, "State Energy Consumption").

63. Author's calculations based on forecasts from Berman, "Industry Output."

64. Ibid.

65. Ibid.

66. Forecasts from the ESC show annual job growth in North Carolina at 1.6 percent annually through 2014, compared to 1.2 percent annually for the nation (ESC, "Occupational Projections").

67. Berman, "Industry Output," 59–69.

68. Ibid. While the value of production from the information services sector is expected to grow at an above-average rate, employment is forecasted to expand at slightly less than average. In 2005, information services did not yet fit the definition of a basic industry, with its share of the state economy 22 percent below the national share.

69. Atkinson, *Past and Future*, 154.

70. Jensen and Kletzer, *Tradable Services*, 15–17.

71. Engardio, "Future of Outsourcing," 55–56.

72. Bradford, Grieco, and Hufbauer, "Payoff to America," 95.

73. Scheve and Slaughter, *Globalization*, 77–86.

Chapter 3

1. Lacy, *Whither North Carolina Furniture Manufacturing?*, 4–6.

2. U.S. Census Bureau, "Building Permits."

3. Duke University, "North Carolina."

4. U.S. Census Bureau, "U.S. International Trade Statistics."

5. Robb and Xie, "Survey," 484–86.

6. Bryson et al., "Furniture Industry," 11–13.

7. BEA, "Gross Domestic Product."

8. BLS, "Employment, Hours, and Earnings."

9. Nwagbara, Buehlmann, and Schuler, *Impact*, 31–32.

10. Ibid., 30–31.

11. Schuler and Buehlmann, *Identifying Future Competitive Business Strategies*, 6.

12. Berman, "Industry Output," 63.

13. Schuler and Buehlmann, *Identifying Future Competitive Business Strategies*, 8.

14. The U.S. Bureau of Labor Statistics predicts 10 percent fewer furniture manufacturing workers nationwide in 2014 than in 2004 (Berman, "Industry Output," 63).

15. BEA, "Gross Domestic Product"; BLS, "Employment, Hours, and Earnings."

16. U.S. Census Bureau, "U.S. International Trade Statistics."

17. Berman, "Industry Output," 68.

18. BEA, "Gross Domestic Product"; BLS, "Employment, Hours, and Earnings."

19. U.S. Census Bureau, "U.S. International Trade Statistics."

20. Luo, "Two Essays," 2.

21. Mirabelli and Wing, "Proximity"; Spivey, "Study."

22. Berman, "Industry Output," 60.

23. Austin, "N.C. State Researchers"; Simmons, "New Life."

24. Luo, "Two Essays," 2.

25. BLS, "Employment, Hours, and Earnings."

26. Levinsohn and Petropoulos, *Creative Destruction*, 2–8.

27. Hekman, "Product Cycle."

28. Abernathy et al., *Stitch in Time*.

29. "Closing the Circle."

30. U.S. Census Bureau, "U.S. International Trade Statistics."

31. Duke University, "North Carolina."

32. BEA, "Gross Domestic Product"; BLS, "Employment, Hours, and Earnings."

33. U.S. Department of Labor, "Report to Congress," 56–64. Conway's research also supports the idea of productivity improvements in textile manufacturing having an independent effect on reducing industry employment (Conway, *Downsizing, Layoffs*, 28–35).

34. BLS, "Employment, Hours, and Earnings."

35. Berman, "Industry Output," 59.

36. Levinsohn and Petropoulos, *Creative Destruction*, 30; U.S. Census Bureau, "U.S. International Trade Statistics." Comparisons are based on real dollars.

37. "Threads That Think"; Duke University, "North Carolina"; Simmons, "New Uses."

38. Parker, "Spinning Success."

39. Employment in textile mill products, which encompasses the nonapparel component of textiles, increased from 8,800 in 1992 to 12,144 in 2005 (U.S. Census Bureau, "Annual Survey," North Carolina, table 2).

40. BLS, "Consumer Price Index."

41. Walden, *Smart Economics*, 95.

42. BEA, "Gross Domestic Product."

43. BLS, "Employment, Hours, and Earnings."

44. BLS, "Consumer Price Index." Cigarette taxes also increased over the period, but the cigarette tax per pack as a percentage of the price per pack declined between 1977 and 2005 (Campaign for Tobacco-Free Kids, "Federal Cigarette Tax").

45. Paul R. Johnson, *Economics of the Tobacco Industry*, 64; Capehart, *Tobacco Outlook*.

46. Paul R. Johnson, *Economics of the Tobacco Industry*, 64; Capehart, *Tobacco Outlook*; *ERP*, table B-34.

47. BLS, "Consumer Price Index."

48. Hansen, "North Carolina to Raise Cigarette Tax."

49. Capehart, "Trends," 2.

50. Ibid., 4.

51. For a listing of studies on this topic, see Chaloupka, Web site; Robert Wood Johnson Foundation, "Impacteen."

52. For estimates of the impacts of these health concerns and restrictions, see Meier and Licari, "Effect of Cigarette Taxes"; Borland et al., "Effects"; Bardsley and Olekalns, "Cigarette and Tobacco Consumption."

53. FAO Corporate Depository, "Issues."

54. Capehart, "U.S. Tobacco Industry."

55. World Health Organization, *Tobacco Atlas*, 88–89.

56. Durham, "About Durham."

57. Capehart, "U.S. Tobacco Industry." In 2002, the U.S. share of the world tobacco trade was 8 percent, down from 20 percent in 1972 and 27 percent in 1960.

58. Berman, "Industry Output," 59.

59. Woellert, "Tobacco May Be Partying Too Soon."

60. From 1977 to 2005, agriculture's share of the gross domestic product fell from 2.5 percent to 0.9 percent, while its share of national employment declined from 4 percent to 1.4 percent (BEA, "Gross Domestic Product"; *ERP*, tables B-36, B-100).

61. Between 1974 and 2004, the number of farms in North Carolina dropped from ninety-one thousand to fifty-two thousand, while the average farm size rose from 123 acres to 173 acres. Agricultural productivity increased 150 percent between 1977 and 2005 (U.S. Department of Agriculture, "Census of Agriculture," North Carolina, table 1; *2004 North Carolina Agricultural Statistics*, 13; BEA, "Gross Domestic Product").

62. U.S. Census Bureau, "Statistical Abstract: Historical Abstract," no. HS-44.

63. U.S. Department of Agriculture, "Census of Agriculture," North Carolina, table 1.

64. Perrin and Sappie, *North Carolina Farm Income and Production*, 46; *2004 North Carolina Agricultural Statistics*, 60–61.

65. Perrin and Sappie, *North Carolina Farm Income and Production*, 46; *2004 North Carolina Agricultural Statistics*, 60–61.

66. U.S. Department of Agriculture, "Census of Agriculture," North Carolina, table 1; *2004 North Carolina Agricultural Statistics*, 25.

67. Barkema, Drabenstott, and Novack, "New U.S. Meat Industry," 39.

68. Ibid., 40–44.

69. Ibid., 43.

70. "Development of Environmentally Superior Technologies."

71. U.S. Department of Agriculture, "Census of Agriculture," Georgia, table 1.

72. Muth et al., *Profile*, 1–3.

73. Laura L. Martin and Zering, "Relationships," 45–49.

74. Drabenstott, "This Little Piggy," 81–84.

75. Bacon, "Oink"; Duke University, "North Carolina"; Muth et al., *Profile*, chapter 2.

76. The plant in Bladen County can process up to forty thousand hogs daily.

77. U.S. Department of Agriculture, "Census of Agriculture"; U.S. Department of Agriculture, "National Agricultural Statistics Service," North Carolina, table 1.

78. N.C. General Assembly, "Session Law 2007-523."

79. Duke University, "North Carolina."

80. "Development of Environmentally Superior Technologies," appendix D, 12.

81. Rawlins, "Pork Giant"; Steve Ford, "Caution."

82. "Development of Environmentally Superior Technologies," statement of Dr. Richard Whisnant, appendix D, 1–14; "Harnessing of Nature's Bounty."

83. National hog production is expected to increase only 1.5 percent from 2001 to 2011 (Muth et al., *Profile*, 5–14).

84. Federal Emergency Management Administration, U.S. Fire Administration, "Chicken Processing Plant Fires."

85. Collins, "Hog Plant."

86. Congressional Budget Office, "Potential Influenza Pandemic," 10–14.

87. Estimates are based on 2003 poultry values in the state.

88. U.S. Department of Agriculture, Economics Research Service, "Agricultural Baseline Projections," 1–2.

89. U.S. Department of Agriculture, "Census of Agriculture," North Carolina, table 1; *2004 North Carolina Agricultural Statistics*, 52–53.

90. Blake Brown, *Global Cotton Trends*, 3.

91. Any significant reduction in federal government cotton subsidies to producers could reduce cotton income by one quarter or more ("Tangle of Troubles"). The World Trade Organization has ruled that these subsidies are illegal (Hitt, "At the Crossroads").

92. U.S. Department of Agriculture, "Census of Agriculture," North Carolina, table 36; *2004 North Carolina Agricultural Statistics*, 7.

93. N.C. Department of Agriculture and Consumer Services, "Study."

94. "North Carolina's Strategic Plan"; Simmons, "Turning Potatoes, Grass into Ethanol."

95. Mayer, "Fueling Ethanol."

96. von Haefen, "Can Ethanol End Our Oil Addiction?" Rather than helping North Carolina agriculture, the run-up in corn prices as a result of increased demand for ethanol may hurt the state's farmers because corn serves as a feed for the state's dominant livestock sector.

97. North Carolina is a corn-deficit state—that is, it is a net importer of corn from other states.

98. The economic sector identified is "machinery manufacturing." Its contribution to North Carolina's gross state product has ranged between 0.9 percent and 1.2 percent between 1997 and 2005 (BEA, "Gross Domestic Product").

99. This sector is "electrical equipment and appliance manufacturing" and includes electrical appliances, parts, electric motors, generators, transformers, and switch-gear apparatus (BEA, "Gross Domestic Product").

100. BEA, "Personal Consumption Expenditures."

101. Luger and Goldstein, *Technology*, 78.

102. Ibid.; Duke University, "North Carolina."

103. The comparison to 1977 is approximate because industrial machinery and equipment serves as the proxy sector in that year.

104. BEA, "Gross Domestic Product"; BLS, "Employment, Hours, and Earnings."

105. CBC News, "Nortel."

106. BEA, "Gross Domestic Product"; BLS, "Employment, Hours, and Earnings."

107. Prices for computer hardware fell an incredible 76 percent between 1999 and 2005 (BLS, "Consumer Price Index").

108. "Digital Dragon."

109. BEA, "Trade in Goods and Services."

110. McDougall, "IBM Completes Sale."

111. Chandler, Hikino, and von Nordenflycht, *Inventing*, 81; Dalesio, "IBM in N.C."

112. Duke University, "North Carolina."

113. Holahan, "Why Dell, Apple Declined."

114. Kharif, "Dell." In 2007, Dell began selling its products in Wal-Mart stores (Oswald, "Dell, Wal-Mart Sign Retail Pact").

115. Berman, "Industry Output," 62, 65.

116. Carlson, "Software Industry Trends," 77.

117. Riefler, "New Geography," 3–5.

118. ESC, "Occupational Projections."

119. "Future of Technology"; Kirkpatrick, "IBM's Quasar."

120. Ruettgers, "America's Eroding Knowledge Edge."

121. Stuart, "Manufacturing," 194.

122. BEA, "Gross Domestic Product"; BLS, "Employment, Hours, and Earnings."

123. U.S. Census Bureau, *Economic Census, 1977*, North Carolina, Manufacturing, table 1; U.S. Census, "Annual Survey of Manufactures," North Carolina, table 2. Percentages are based on the value added of production.

124. Hitner and Nagle, *Pharmacology*, chapter 1.

125. Chandler, *Shaping*, 52–53.

126. BEA, "Gross Domestic Product."

127. U.S. Census Bureau, "Annual Survey of Manufactures," North Carolina, table 2.

128. Ernst and Young, "Beyond Borders," 4.

129. Duke University, "North Carolina."

130. Luger and Goldstein, *Technology*, 98–99.

131. Chandler, *Shaping*, 260–61. Some writers use the term "biotechnology" to imply the entire pharmaceutical industry.

132. U.S. Department of Commerce, Technology Administration, "Survey," 15; U.S. Census Bureau, *Economic Census 1992*; U.S. Census Bureau, *Economic Census 2002*, North Carolina, table 1 (which defines "biotechnology" as medicinal, botanical, biological, and in-vitro diagnostic substantive manufacturing).

133. Worthington, "North Carolina Research Campus Plans Unveiled"; "$700 Million Biotech Campus."

134. Berman, "Industry Output," 60.

135. The ESC projects a forty-eight-hundred-job gain in the state for chemical product manufacturing between 2002 and 2012 (ESC, "Industry Projections"). Projections specifically for pharmaceutical manufacturing are not provided.

136. BLS, "Consumer Price Index."

137. John A. Vernon, "Drug Research," 24–25.

138. Estimates for bringing a drug to market range as high as $800 million (Tufts Center for the Study of Drug Development, "Backgrounder").

139. Danson, Wang, and Wang, Impact, 18–24.

140. U.S. Department of Commerce, Technology Administration, "Survey," 89–90.

141. Burrill, "State," 30–35.

142. Mathews and Abboud, "For Booming Biotech Firms." Allowing faster marketing of generic drugs would shorten the period during which the company that developed the drug could recover the costs of discovery and development.

143. Duke University. "North Carolina."

144. Ibid.

145. Ernst and Young, "Beyond Borders," 17–25.

146. Armstrong-Hough, "Good Fit."

147. U.S. Census Bureau, "Annual Survey of Manufactures," North Carolina, table 1.

148. BEA, "Gross Domestic Product."

149. BLS, "Employment, Hours, and Earnings."

150. Even with its large meat-processing facilities, North Carolina exported a large percentage of its live animals, especially hogs, outside the state for slaughter. The gradual reduction in this exportation and the consequent increase in the share of live North Carolina hogs sent to North Carolina processing plants was a major factor behind the growth of the state's meat-processing sector after 1997 (Kelly Zering, associate professor of agricultural and resource economics, North Carolina State University, personal communication, 9 February 2007).

151. The U.S. Department of Labor forecasts annual production in food processing to increase 1.7 percent from 2004 to 2014, compared to a rate of 3.6 percent for aggregate production in the economy (Berman, "Industry Output," 59).

152. Meyer, Grimes, and Plain, "From #1 Importer to #1 Exporter."

153. Engardio, "Emerging Giants."

154. The trade deficit for "food and kindred products" increased from $20 billion in 2000 to $27 billion in 2005 in real 2005 dollars (U.S. Census Bureau, "U.S. International Trade Statistics").

155. Cox, "Eastern Counties."

156. Transportation manufacturing fell from 2.8 percent of the national economy in 1977 to 1.3 percent in 2005 (BEA, "Gross Domestic Product").

157. Greenwood, "Changing Patterns," 72–79.

158. "Southeastern Auto Industry."

159. Ibid.

160. U.S. Census Bureau, "Annual Survey of Manufactures," North Carolina, table 1.

161. N.C. Department of Commerce, "North Carolina Automotive," 6–9.

162. Klier, "Does 'Just in Time' Mean 'Right Next Door?,'" 54. On the negative side, industry experts say North Carolina lacks large sites that are ready for construction (Cox, "Lack of Ready Sites").

163. U.S. Census Bureau, "Annual Survey of Manufactures," North Carolina, table 1.

164. Batson, "China's Rise."

165. Berman, "Industry Output," 63.

166. Kenneth D. Jones and Critchfield, "Consolidation," 36–37.

167. Ibid.; Fitzpatrick, "How Charlotte Became a Banking Giant." Based on assets, Charlotte ranks as the world's tenth-biggest banking center (Dicken, *Global Shift*, 400).

168. Duke University, "North Carolina."

169. Berman, "Industry Output," 64.

170. Hanc, "Future," 5.

171. Spieker, "Bank Branch Growth," 1.

172. Hanc, "Future," 3–4.

173. Kenneth D. Jones and Critchfield, "Consolidation," 47.

174. Gratton, "Future of Banking Study," 29.

175. Zellner, "Wal-Mart Moves."

176. Duke University, "North Carolina."

177. Cox and Krishnan, "Fidelity Deal."

178. Airports and seaports in North Carolina are operated by self-financing governmental authorities.

179. BEA, "Gross Domestic Product." The measure used is the quantity index for accommodations.

180. N.C. Department of Commerce, "Fast Facts." The comprehensive contribution for tourism measures visitor expenditures. To be comparable to the economic activity measures for the other sectors, the amount of expenditures was multiplied by the ratio of value-added expenditures to total expenditures in the North Carolina tourist sector ("IMPLAN for North Carolina"). This ratio for North Carolina (0.57) was very close to the same ratio for the national tourism sector, 0.56 (Kuhbach and Herauf, "U.S. Travel and Tourism Satellite Accounts," 18–22). Using value-added tourism expenditures eliminates that spending associated with tourist-related products and services but produced outside of North Carolina. For example, the price of a Topsail Beach hat bought in North Carolina but manufactured in China would be included in total tourism expenditures, but the value-added expenditure would eliminate the component of the price used to pay the Chinese supplier. The employment number comes directly from the N.C. Department of Commerce, "Fast Facts."

181. N.C. Department of Commerce, "Fast Facts."

182. Berman, "Industry Output," 67. The accommodations, amusement, and recreation industries were used as the tourism sector.

183. Shifflet and Associates, "North Carolina Tourism Conference 2006."

184. BEA, "Gross Domestic Product."

185. BLS, "Employment, Hours and Earnings."

186. U.S. Census Bureau, "Building Permits"; LogNC. For the nation between 2000 and 2005, both new housing units and additional households increased by 8 percent (U.S. Census Bureau, "Building Permits"; U.S. Census Bureau, "Housing Units").

187. Knox, "Second Homes 40% of Market." The 1997 change in the homeowner capital gains tax law eliminated the requirement that sellers purchase a new home of comparable or higher value to claim the allowable tax exemption on capital gains from sale of a principal residence.

188. Burns, "Boomers Make Carolinas Their Second Home."

189. The Inner Banks has more than three thousand miles of mainland waterfront (Price, "Coastal Boom").

190. Between 2000 and 2005, commercial fishing harvests in coastal North Carolina, measured in pounds, fell almost 50 percent (Collins and Price, "Development Hurts"). If global warming raises sea levels and submerges coastal property, multi-billion-dollar losses could result (Rawlins, "Climate Change").

191. From July 2005 to July 2006, existing home sales in several coastal counties fell at double-digit rates while rising 2 percent statewide (N.C. Association of Realtors, "Existing Home Sales").

192. StatAbt 1973, no. 949; StatAbt 2004–5, no. 1068.

193. StatAbt 1973, no. 949; StatAbt 2004–5, no. 1068; "North Carolina Ports Tonnage and Trade Statistics."

194. StatAbt 2006, no. 1066.

195. The data are from "IMPLAN for North Carolina" (for 2003) and BEA, "Gross Domestic Product" (for 2002). Some studies find a much higher value of ports—near $800 million annually—by including the value of inputs used in the ports' operations and including spending by port employees (Martin and Associates, "Economic Impact Study," 34).

196. Barrett, "Southport to Be Key Port."

197. BEA, "Gross Domestic Product."

198. Thomas and Foyle, *Economic Impacts*, 8.

199. Two analyses attempting to measure only the economic value created at airports put the annual amount at near $1 billion and 12,500 employees ("IMPLAN for North Carolina"; BEA, "Gross Domestic Product").

200. StatAbt 2006, no. 1054.

201. El Nasser, "New 'Cities.'"

202. Kasarda, "Rise."

203. Green, "Airports and Economic Development." One issue is to what degree airport availability and activity result from or cause economic development. Green employs statistical techniques that separate the two lines of causation and finds that airport activity, as measured by boardings per capita and cargo per capita, exerts an independent positive impact on population and employment growth.

204. StatAbt 2006, no. 1150.

Chapter 4

1. The state's population increased 16 percent during the 1970s, 13 percent in the 1980s, a tremendous 21 percent in the 1990s, and as of 2005 was on track to rise 16 percent during the 2000s (LogNC).

2. StatAbt 1973, nos. 69, 83; StatAbt 2006, nos. 76, 103.

3. Internal growth accounted for 34.3 percent of North Carolina's population increase between 1970 and 2005. This proportion was calculated by applying the difference between the state's average birth and death rates between 1970 and 2003 (latest year available) to the population in 1970 and then compounding the growth through 2005. The resulting population was compared to the actual population in 2005 to derive the proportion that resulted from internal growth.

4. The same procedure as described in n. 3 was applied to all states to arrive at this ranking.

5. U.S. Census Bureau, "Population Born outside State of Residence."

6. LogNC.

7. N.C. State Data Center, "County/State Population Projections."

8. Ibid.

9. Kasarda and Johnson, "Economic Impact," 1. Following the convention of the U.S. Census Bureau, "Hispanic" is defined as persons primarily of a Spanish-speaking origin, including those from Mexico, Cuba, the Dominican Republic, and Central American countries. Hispanic is an ethnic, not racial, designation.

10. Kochhar, Suro, and Tafoya, *New Latino South*, 2.

11. Kasarda and Johnson, "Economic Impact," 10–13; U.S. Census Bureau, "American Community Survey," 2004.

12. Kasarda and Johnson, "Economic Impact," 20.

13. LogNC.

14. Borjas, "For a Few Dollars Less." For similar estimates, see James P. Smith and Edmonston, *Immigration Debate*, chapters 2, 3, 4.

15. Keeton and Newton, "Does Immigration Reduce Imbalances?"; Doug Campbell, "Illegal Immigrant Effect."

16. Kasarda and Johnson, "Economic Impact," 18–21.

17. U.S. Census Bureau, "Public-Use Microdata Samples," North Carolina; U.S. Census Bureau, "American Community Survey," 2005, North Carolina. The analysis compared median real wage rates for full-time workers between the ages of 18 and 60 in North Carolina in 1990 and 2005. Real wage rates increased 3 percent for construction workers, the slowest increase among all industries except for personal services, where real wage rates declined by 1.5 percent.

18. Kasarda and Johnson, "Economic Impact," 26; BEA, "Gross Domestic Product." Kasarda and Johnson's estimate (for 2004) is based on the purchasing power of Hispanic workers in North Carolina and includes the multiplier effects of spending that generates additional rounds of respending throughout the economy.

19. Kremer and Watt, "Globalization."

20. Kasarda and Johnson, "Economic Impact," 33.

21. N.C. State Data Center, "County/State Population Projections."

22. The gap in infant mortality rates narrowed in absolute terms: in 1970, it was 16.8 babies higher for African Americans than for whites, while in 2005 that number dropped to 9.7 babies. On a percentage basis, however, the gap actually widened: the rates were 87 percent higher for African Americans in 1970 and 164 percent higher for African Americans in 2005.

23. Centers for Disease Control, "Behavioral Risk Factor Surveillance System."

24. The nominal spending amount for each category was converted to real spending values by using the consumer price index values specific for that category. The result is a proxy for quantity purchased.

25. Crafts workers are workers in construction and mining trades and workers with skills in repairing and maintaining equipment. Operatives are assembly workers in factories, truckers, and equipment operators.

26. U.S. Census Bureau, 1980 Census of Population and Housing; U.S. Census Bureau, "American Community Survey," 2005, North Carolina.

27. The occupational shift in agriculture between 1980 and 2005 was out of managers and farmers and into clerical and sales workers, crafts workers, and operatives.

28. State of the North Carolina Workforce, 22. In 2007, forecasts show that 24.6 percent of jobs will require a college education, 41.0 percent will require a high school education, and 34.4 percent will require no high school education. Forecasts for 2017 have 26.1 percent requiring college, 38.7 percent requiring high school, and 35.2 percent requiring no high school.

29. ESC, "Occupational Projections." Forecasts are based on the 2004–14 period.

30. The subtraction of net government monetary transfers eliminates the effect of federal government assistance to North Carolina households, which typically increases during recessions and subsides during expansions. These net government transfers do not represent earnings of North Carolina workers.

31. For 1970, the measure is median family income; median household income was not available that year.

32. The wage rate for 1970 is based on the midpoints of work hour intervals given in the data.

33. In 1970, workers received 89 percent of their compensation in wages and salaries and 11 percent in benefits. In 2005, the split was 81 percent for wages and salaries and 19 percent for benefits (BEA, "Personal Income").

34. Statistics for 1970 are not presented because of lack of specific work hours data.

35. Full-time workers are those working 2,080 hours or more annually.

36. The educational attainment of workers of other races in North Carolina went in the opposite direction as for Hispanics. The percentage of "other race" workers with some college or college degrees jumped from 27 percent in 1980 to 57 percent in 2005.

37. The Earned Income Tax Credit is a federal program that provides income supplements to low-income households with a working head and financial dependents. Begun

in 1975, it has become the largest cash assistance program for low-income households, costing $36 billion in 2004 (U.S. House Ways and Means Committee, 2004 *Green Book*, table 13-13).

38. For more discussion of this point, see Blau, Ferber, and Winkler, *Economics of Women, Men, and Work*, 188–235; Waldfogel, "Understanding the 'Family Gap,'" 149.

39. The premiums and discounts in table 4-4 take into account the worker's age, which may be a proxy for experience (see appendix B).

40. Studies supporting the conclusion of limited racial/ethnic discrimination in pay include Ferguson, "Shifting Challenges"; Maxwell, "Effect"; Neal and Johnson, "Role." Neal and Johnson include an analysis of Hispanic workers. Support for the alternative view of lingering discrimination is found in Darity and Mason, "Evidence"; Goldsmith, Hamilton, and Darity, "Does a Foot in the Door Matter?"

41. For evidence of cost-of-living differences within North Carolina, see Walden, "How Much Income Variation 'Really' Exists?" The wage rate premium of roughly 20 percent for urban workers corresponds to the findings in this article.

42. DeNavas-Walt, Proctor, and Lee, "Income, Poverty, and Health Insurance Coverage"; Piketty and Saez, "Income Inequality"; Reynolds, *Income and Wealth*; Fortin and Lemieux, "Institutional Changes"; Topel, "Factor Proportions"; George E. Johnson, "Changes in Earnings Inequality." Some economists also point to an interaction of education premiums with marriage that has contributed to income inequality—specifically, workers with similar education backgrounds are most likely to marry (Burtless, "Effects").

43. This difference between household and family income should not change the qualitative trends in the income distribution. A comparison of the distribution of real household income in 2005 to real household income in 1980 showed the same trends.

44. Author's calculations from data from the U.S. Census Bureau, "Public-Use Microdata Samples." National data show an increase from 43 percent in 1970 to 50 percent in 2005 in the income share of the top 20 percent of income-earning households (DeNavas-Walt, Proctor, and Lee, "Income, Poverty, and Health Insurance Coverage," table A-3).

45. Gottschalk, "Inequality," 36–38. Analysts debate whether income variability and hence household mobility between income levels has increased or decreased during the Connected Age. For different conclusions, see Dynan, Elmendorf, and Sichel, "Evolution"; Congressional Budget Office, "Trends."

46. W. Keith Bryant and Wang ("American Consumption Patterns," 302–3) argue that the development of time-saving household equipment and technologies was prompted, in part, by the increasing value of women's time in the paid workplace. The pull factors thus motivated part of the push factor, as working women were more interested in purchasing time-saving household equipment, thereby prompting firms to develop and produce the equipment.

47. U.S. Census Bureau, "Public-Use Microdata Samples," North Carolina.

48. Desai, Chase-Lonsdale, and Michael, "Mothers or Markets?"; Desai, Michael, and Chase-Lonsdale, "Home Environment"; Hewlett, *When the Bough Breaks*.

49. Between 1970 and 2005, food prices rose 377 percent and clothing prices rose 102 percent, while the price index for all consumer goods and services grew 403 percent (BLS, "Consumer Price Index"). One adverse consequence of the falling real price of food may be the rising obesity rate among both children and adults.

50. LogNC.

51. Ibid.

52. "Economic Impact of the Child Care Industry," 2.

53. BLS, "Consumer Expenditure Survey." The data are for the nation. No comparable data exist for North Carolina.

54. The growth rate for the number of firms of all types was 6 percent, with an increase in sales of 230 percent (LogNC).

55. The comparisons are for married households with household heads aged between 25 and 60 working full time (U.S. Census Bureau, "Public-Use Microdata Samples"). One reason for the greater gains made by households with two working spouses may be that a higher proportion of such households have at least one college graduate, and income gains have been greater for college graduates during the Connected Age (Winkler, "Earnings of Husbands and Wives," 44–46).

56. U.S. Census Bureau, "Public-Use Microdata Samples."

57. ESC, "Announced Business Closings."

58. Estes, Schweke, and Lawrence, *Dislocated Workers*, 4.

59. Schweke, "Economic Dislocation," 4.

60. *Facing the Facts*, 1.

61. Schweke, "Economic Dislocation," 13–15; Estes, Schweke, and Lawrence, *Dislocated Workers*, 6. Schweke's period of unemployment is a national average, while Estes, Schweke, and Lawrence's rate is for North Carolina workers.

62. *Facing the Facts*, 2.

63. Schweke, "Economic Dislocation," 16; Estes, Schweke, and Lawrence, *Dislocated Workers*, 7.

64. Schweke, "Economic Dislocation," 16.

Chapter 5

1. The saying is attributed to former speaker of the U.S. House of Representatives Tip O'Neill (O'Neill and Hymel, *All Politics Is Local*, chapter 1).

2. N.C. State Data Center, "State Demographics."

3. Killian and Tolbert, "Commuting-Based Definition."

4. Commuting zones can cross state lines, and three North Carolina counties are part of zones in other states. However, given this book's focus on North Carolina's economy, the counties are included in the nearest in-state zone (Alleghany in Greater Wilkes, Rutherford in Greater Gaston, and Macon in the Far West).

5. Walden, "How Much Income Variation 'Really' Exists?," 245.

6. Renkow, "Income Non-Convergence," 1017–18, found increasing income dispari-

ties among North Carolina counties in the 1980s (the extent of his time period), results that are consistent with the findings here.

7. The change in the number of firms, rather than the change in employment, is used to gauge changes in traditional and new economy industries at the local level because employment data are suppressed (for disclosure reasons) if a limited number of firms comprise the industry in a locality, such as a county. The number of firms, however, is not suppressed (U.S. Census Bureau, *County Business Patterns, 1970*; U.S. Census Bureau, *County Business Patterns, 2004*).

8. These regions also could be termed "micropolitan," but I do not use this term because all of the regions do not meet the U.S. Census criteria for such classification (U.S. Census Bureau, "Current Lists"). I sought to indicate a settlement pattern that fell between those of the large urbanized regions and those of the rural regions.

9. Rappaport, *Local Growth Empirics*, 34–39.

10. Wheeler, *Employment Growth*, 6–14.

11. Henry, Barkley, and Li, "Education and Nonmetropolitan Income Growth," 232–37.

12. Goetz and Rupasingha, "Returns," 252–55.

13. Kusmin, Redman, and Sears, *Factors*, 31–37.

14. Renkow, "Income Non-Convergence," 1022–25.

15. Denaux, "Taxes, Government Spending, and Endogenous Growth," 107.

16. I used counties rather than commuting zones in the analysis to have more variation in the measures and thus improved estimation.

17. "Look at America."

18. No government estimates of gross local product exist for individual counties. However, estimates are available from MIG's IMPLAN (impact planning and analysis) data services. The IMPLAN data are widely used for substate analysis, and the earliest available series for North Carolina dates from 1990.

19. For example, Forbes.com named Raleigh-Cary the "best city for jobs" in 2006 (Alan M. Wolf, "Raleigh Works Way").

20. Collectively, Duke, North Carolina State University, and the University of North Carolina at Chapel Hill have seventy thousand students and graduate seventeen thousand each year (data are for 2006). The Raleigh-Durham metropolitan area, the largest within the Triangle commuting zone, ranks fourth nationally in the number of doctoral degrees per capita but ranks first among metropolitan areas with populations of five hundred thousand or more (U.S. Census Bureau, "American Community Survey," 2004, North Carolina). The Carnegie Foundation developed the Research 1 university designation to indicate the institutions of higher education that receive the greatest amounts of federal science research funding (Carnegie Foundation, "Carnegie Classification").

21. Research Triangle Park, "Quick Facts."

22. ESC, "Employment and Wages." The measure is employment in computer and electronic product manufacturing.

23. Research Triangle Region Partnership, "State," 2.

24. Nilsen and John, "Credit Suisse"; Cox, "Giving Away More"; "RBC Centura Mov-

ing Headquarters." Since 9/11, the Triangle has also been viewed favorably as a location for backup operations for major financial firms (Mattson-Teig, "Wanted").

25. Blue Ribbon Committee, *Inaugural Report*, 3.

26. The committee also recommended the more frequent revaluation of real property. Wake and many other North Carolina counties revalue real property only every eight years. In rapidly growing counties, the property tax base quickly becomes outdated and undervalued relative to actual market values and therefore is inadequate to fund current infrastructure needs. More frequent revaluations would remedy this problem. Chapter 6 includes a more extensive discussion of this issue.

27. ESC, "Employment and Wages."

28. In 2006, the American Chamber of Commerce Researchers Association's *Cost of Living Index* gave Raleigh and Durham index values of 99.1 and 90.4 respectively, below the national average of 100 and lower than values for New York (215), Washington, D.C. (139), and San Jose (151).

29. In 2004, the Rocky Mount–Wilson region led all regions in the share of GLP devoted to wholesale trade (8.5 percent), with Greater Charlotte second at 7.8 percent. However, on a dollar-value basis, Greater Charlotte's wholesale trade led the state and was almost ten times larger than Rocky Mount–Wilson's value.

30. Hopkins, "Philip Morris Plant Closing."

31. ESC, "Employment and Wages." The measure is employment in computer and electronic product manufacturing.

32. Connaughton et al., "Economic Impacts," 29.

33. Boyum, "Experts Analyze."

34. Charlotte Regional Partnership, "Industry Clusters."

35. University of North Carolina at Charlotte, Long Range Enrollment Planning Task Force, "Enrollment Projections."

36. LogNC.

37. "Scrapping Special Charlotte Tax."

38. For example, Mecklenburg County (Charlotte) voters defeated a multi-hundred-million-dollar school construction bond in 2004.

39. For example, in 2006, Charlotte's cost-of-living index was 92.7, compared to 98.8 for Atlanta (*Cost of Living Index*).

40. N.C. Department of Commerce, "Tourism."

41. LogNC.

42. These three industries accounted for 43 percent of Greater Wilmington's 2004 employment, compared to 39 percent for the state (ESC, "Employment and Wages").

43. United Press International, "Strike at Biggest Pork Processing Plant."

44. LogNC.

45. From January 2006 to January 2007, sales of existing homes in Greater Wilmington fell 21 percent, while such sales rose by 6 percent in both the Triangle and Triad and dropped by just 2 percent in Greater Charlotte (N.C. Association of Realtors, "Existing Home Sales").

46. Aon, "Recent Atlantic Basin Hurricane Frequency Shift."

47. Sack, "North Carolina Picks Up."

48. Schreiner, "Brunswick Port Price Tag?"

49. "GPS Tour of Asheville."

50. ESC, "Employment and Wages." For the state as a whole, personal services industries accounted for 26 percent of total employment in 1990.

51. LogNC. The state in-migration rate in 2000 was 1.2 percent, compared to a rate of 1.6 percent for the Greater Asheville region. The rate estimates the annual increase in population resulting from people moving to the region from outside the area.

52. ESC, "Employment and Wages." For the state as a whole in 2004, finance and professional services accounted for 8 percent of jobs, while the number for the Triangle region was 10 percent.

53. Leslie A. Scott and Linton, "Vision Plan," 18.

54. University of North Carolina at Asheville, "About UNC Asheville"; Asheville-Buncombe Technical Community College, "Academic Programs."

55. Charles Taylor, "Congressman Taylor and ERC."

56. For examples of these issues, see Wake-Up Wake County, "Growth Issues"; Western North Carolina Tomorrow, "Mission and Goals."

57. Collectively, the three regions only account for 2 percent of gross state product and 3 percent of state employment, compared to 52 percent of gross state product and 48 percent of employment for the racehorse regions.

58. Appalachian State University, "Enrollment History."

59. BEA, "Local Area Personal Income."

60. The federal military and nonmilitary spending is affiliated primarily with the U.S. Coast Guard Air Station, an associated repair and supply center, and a training and support center.

61. Enrollment grew from eighteen hundred in 1990 to twenty-six hundred in 2004 (University of North Carolina, *Statistical Abstract*, table 2).

62. LogNC.

63. Center for Competitive Economics, *Regional Partnership Vision Plan*, 18.

64. The Northeast region ranked seventh among the state's twenty-one regions in its cost-of-living indicator (see table 5-2). However, this relatively high ranking resulted entirely from the resort county of Currituck, where the cost-of-living indicator came in fourth among the state's one hundred counties. The remaining five counties in the region had cost-of-living indicators among the state's lowest.

65. LogNC.

66. Others observers fear that the U.S. military will threaten the regional environment. The U.S. Navy has proposed building a landing strip in rural Washington County to allow aircraft to practice nighttime landings. Local groups have objected, saying that the landings would create unwanted noise and jeopardize the tens of thousands of migratory birds that winter in the region. In early 2007, political pressure mounted to cancel the plan (Barrett, "Bill Could Kill Navy's Airfield Plan").

67. LogNC. In 2000, the number was 47 percent.

68. Powell and Mazzocchi, *Encyclopedia*, 967.

69. "Harrah's Cherokee Great Smoky Mountains Resort."

70. The MIG IMPLAN model for the Highlands region shows one job created outside the casino industry for every three jobs directly in the casino industry and thirty-four cents of spending outside the casino industry generated for every dollar of spending in the casino industry. One research study estimated that the opening of a large casino was associated with a 0.6 percentage point drop in the host county's unemployment rate (Baxandall and Sacerdote, *Betting*, 4).

71. Western Carolina University, "Enrollment History."

72. For the Highlands region in 2004, this rate is 15 percent, more than three times the rate for the Triangle region (LogNC).

73. Fontana Lake, in the western part of the Highlands region, was created by the Tennessee Valley Authority when Fontana Dam was constructed in 1944 ("Visitor's Guide").

74. The combined average salary in the regions in 2004 was second-lowest among all North Carolina regions.

75. American Gaming Association, "Casino Employment."

76. Western Carolina University, "State of the University Address."

77. Wagner, "'Smart Growth' Fever."

78. Atlanta 575 Real Estate.

79. The region is still the headquarters of Branch Banking and Trust Corporation, the third-leading bank in employment in the state (Duke University, "North Carolina").

80. Vollmer, "Rivals May Steal RTP's Thunder."

81. N.C. Office of the Governor, "Easley Announces."

82. ESC, "Unemployment Rates."

83. Sadovi, "New Arrivals." A cost-of-living index for the fourth quarter of 2006 puts Winston-Salem's value at 9 percent below the national average (*Cost of Living Index*).

84. Perry, "High Point Paper."

85. Krishnan, "Honda Jets"; Cox, "Honda, N.C. Take a Chance."

86. Direct hub employment is estimated at fifteen hundred, with the remaining jobs created from supplier firms and from the induced economic activity of consumer spending. Multiyear economic impact estimates range from $2.4 billion to $7.5 billion (Vera Brown, "FedEx, PTIA Propose Nighttime Cargo Hub").

87. Global Security.org, "Military: Ft. Bragg."

88. Consumer spending and direct military spending together account for as much as 32 percent of GLP (author's calculations using data from "IMPLAN for North Carolina").

89. Because of disclosure limitations, the 1970 employment estimate is based on limited available data.

90. "IMPLAN for North Carolina."

91. North Carolina's Southeast, "Regional Data Book."

92. In 2004, Fayetteville State University had fifty-four hundred students (Fayetteville State University, "Fact Book").

93. U.S. Census Bureau, *County Business Patterns, 1970*, North Carolina, table 2; ESC, "Employment and Wages."

94. Leffler and Newsome, *North Carolina*, 632.

95. The loss of textile and apparel output reached $906 million in Greater Greensboro (table D11) but topped $1 billion in Greater Gaston (table D13).

96. U.S. Census Bureau, *County Business Patterns, 1970*; U.S. Census Bureau, *County Business Patterns, 2004*, North Carolina, table 2.

97. In 2000, the region ranked fifteenth out of twenty-one regions in the percentage of the population with a college degree. Belmont Abbey College and Gaston College are small higher-education institutions in the region focusing on the liberal arts.

98. Luger and Lane, "Opportunities," 5–7.

99. N.C. Office of the Governor, "Governor Easley Announces 856 Jobs."

100. Powell and Mazzocchi, *Encyclopedia*, 752.

101. U.S. Census Bureau, *County Business Patterns, 1970*, North Carolina, table 2; BEA, "Local Area Personal Income."

102. "IMPLAN for North Carolina."

103. ESC, "Employment and Wages."

104. "IMPLAN for North Carolina"; ESC, "Unemployment Rates."

105. ESC, "Unemployment Rates." In January 2007, the Foothills had a regional unemployment rate of 6.4 percent, compared to the state rate of 5 percent. Between 2003 and 2004, the region added approximately one hundred technology jobs ("IMPLAN for North Carolina").

106. Cox, "Lenoir Gets Google."

107. "New Bern History"; U.S. Marine Corps, "Camp Lejeune History"; Hutson, "Place in History."

108. The BRAC recommendation calls for a net reduction of 192 personnel at Camp Lejeune through 2013 (U.S. Department of Defense, "Base Realignment and Closure").

109. Bender, "Analysts Question."

110. The Marine Corps Air Station at Cherry Point (Havelock) did not fare as well as Camp Lejeune in the BRAC recommendations. Through 2015, the base is expected to lose 628 mostly civilian personnel (U.S. Department of Defense, "Base Realignment and Closure"). However, most of the losses will result from the privatization of functions (Global Security.org, "Cherry Point").

111. The state's other medical schools are at the University of North Carolina at Chapel Hill and Duke University in the Triangle region and Wake Forest University in the greater Winston-Salem region.

112. For example, the region's Pitt County was long the largest flue-cured tobacco producing county in the United States. But from 1999 to 2006, tobacco production in the county declined 49 percent (Mitch Smith, "General Tobacco Facts").

113. Fisher, "ECU Dental School OK'd."

114. U.S. Census Bureau, *County Business Patterns, 1970*, North Carolina, table 2. Not all employment is revealed due to disclosure restrictions.

115. U.S. Census Bureau, *County Business Patterns, 1970*; U.S. Census Bureau, *County Business Patterns, 2004*, North Carolina, table 2.

116. The region's 2000 cost-of-living index is tenth-lowest among the state's twenty-one regions (table 5-2).

117. "Cheesecake Factory."

118. On this score, local leaders proposed converting the private North Carolina Wesleyan College to a public University of North Carolina campus. Such a change, they hoped, would bring added gravitas to the institution, along with the possibility of additional funding and programs, particularly in the sciences. What the ECU medical school had done for the Greenville-Jacksonville region, these leaders hoped a University of North Carolina campus could do for the Rocky Mount–Wilson area (Stancill, "UNC-Rocky Mount?"). However, a University of North Carolina System study commission recommended against the proposal (Stancill, "Bowles Tries to Smooth Feathers").

119. U.S. Census Bureau, *County Business Patterns, 1970*, North Carolina, table 2. Again, disclosure restrictions prevent a total count of county-level employment in textiles, apparel, and furniture.

120. Baxter, "History."

121. Employee compensation in 2004 was fifty-two thousand dollars per worker, compared to twenty-eight thousand dollars for all workers in the region ("IMPLAN for North Carolina").

122. *2004 North Carolina Agricultural Statistics*, 33; LogNC.

123. James R. Jones, *History*, 3.

124. In 2004, these sectors accounted for less than 1 percent of gross state product (BEA, "Gross Domestic Product").

125. "Seymour Johnson Air Force Base History."

126. U.S. Census Bureau, *County Business Patterns, 1970*; U.S. Census Bureau, *County Business Patterns, 2004*, North Carolina, table 2.

127. Carey, "Officials: BRAC Decisions a Victory."

128. Educational attainment in the region, as measured by the percentage of college graduates, ranked seventeenth among the state's twenty-one regions in 2000. The rate was just over half that for the nation (table 5-2).

129. Powell and Mazzocchi, *Encyclopedia*, 469.

130. Ibid., 1139.

131. "Lowes Foods Corporate History"; North Wilkesboro, "Brief History."

132. Powell and Mazzocchi, *Encyclopedia*, 760, 77.

133. "Miss America 1984 Delegates."

134. Only the Lakes and Greater Gaston regions lost jobs between 1990 and 2004. The percentage loss in the Lakes region (–6.3 percent) exceeded that in the Greater Gaston region (–4.3 percent).

135. "Welcome to Kerrlakenc.com."

136. "Lake Gaston."

137. The Lakes county with the most shoreline, Vance, added 5 percent to its real estate value from 2000 to 2005 (LogNC).

138. Stewart and Luger, "Implementation Plan."

139. Powell and Mazzocchi, *Encyclopedia*, 979–80.

140. Corbin, "Rural Work Ethic."

141. Average annual employment in Hertford County was 9,013 in 2000, 8,999 in 2001, 9,192 in 2002, 8,982 in 2003, 8,989 in 2004, and 9,161 in 2005 (ESC, "Unemployment Rates").

142. Roanoke Valley Chamber of Commerce, "Entertainment District."

Chapter 6

1. *ERP*, tables 28, 31. Total government spending as a percentage of total economic income (gross domestic product) was 28 percent in 1970 and 31 percent in 2005.

2. An alternative way of looking at revenue and spending amounts is as real amounts per capita. The difference between the two methods is subtle but important. Real amounts per capita control for inflation and for population size, so higher spending as a result of inflation or of more people living in North Carolina are not counted as increases. Revenues and spending expressed as a percentage of GSP also take out the effect of inflation, which is imbedded in both the numerator (tax or spending amount) and denominator (GSP) and is therefore canceled. This measure also accounts for population size, which is an implicit part of GSP (that is, more population increases GSP). The element that the GSP-based measure adds that is not included in tax or spending amounts per capita is income gains beyond inflation. That is, GSP accounts for increases in North Carolinians' standard of living. When a revenue or spending amount is presented as a percentage of GSP, that number answers the question of what part of North Carolina's standard of living, as represented by GSP, is devoted to a particular revenue or a particular spending category.

3. Indeed, North Carolina's state government has a more prominent role in both public revenues and spending than is the case in other states. In North Carolina in 2005, 59 percent of public revenues were raised at the state level, while 41 percent were raised by localities; comparable numbers were 55 percent and 45 percent, respectively, for the average state. On the public spending side, North Carolina's state-local division was 47 percent versus 53 percent, compared to 45 percent/55 percent for the average state (U.S. Census Bureau, "State and Local Government Finances," North Carolina).

4. Spending includes operating and capital expenditures. Revenues and expenditures from public enterprises or publicly regulated private monopolies—specifically, utilities providing electricity, gas, and water; state-regulated liquor stores; and the state-run unemployment insurance trust fund—are not included.

5. The category of public revenues termed "charges and fees" can present issues of comparability, both over time and between North Carolina and the United States. One

such issue is charges for public hospitals. North Carolina and other states that have a relatively high share of public hospitals will consequently have a higher component of public hospital charges. However, these public charges largely substitute for private hospital charges in states with low shares of public hospitals. Indeed, in 2005, public hospital charges in North Carolina totaled 1 percent of GSP, two-thirds larger than the 0.6 percent figure for the nation. In addition, between 1972 and 2005, North Carolina's public hospital charges as a percentage of GSP more than tripled from 0.3 percent to 1 percent. The increase in North Carolina public hospital charges accounted for almost 40 percent of the increase in total state charges and fees (from 2.2 percent to 4 percent) between 1972 and 2005.

6. The "other" category includes public programs in the environment and housing, government administration, other education spending such as libraries, and debt interest.

7. In 2007, North Carolina's ranking had risen to nineteenth (Dubay, "State and Local Tax Burdens," 4). In this analysis, taxes are taken as a percentage of total personal income rather than GSP. However, total personal income accounts for more than three-quarters of the GSP.

8. Walden, *North Carolina's Relative Tax Burden*, 4.

9. Public charges and fees, the largest of which involve public university and college tuitions and costs at public hospitals, are discussed in the subsequent section on spending.

10. Z. Smith Reynolds Foundation and Institute for Emerging Issues, Preparatory Materials, section 5, table 1.

11. Mullen and Williams, "Marginal Tax Rates," 695–701.

12. *Recommendations* (Income Tax Modernization Subcommittee), 1.

13. North Carolina's corporate income tax rate is first among southeastern states for the lowest applicable rate and second for the highest applicable rate (Z. Smith Reynolds Foundation and Institute for Emerging Issues, Preparatory Materials, section 5, table 2).

14. John Locke Foundation, "State Tax Reform."

15. N.C. Governor's Commission, "Final Report"; Economic Future Study Commission, *Fiscal Realities*, 3. A subcommittee of the 2007 N.C. State and Local Fiscal Modernization Study Commission also recommended lowering the corporate income tax rate (*Recommendations* [Income Tax Modernization Subcommittee], 1).

16. *Recommendations* (Income Tax Modernization Subcommittee), 1.

17. Russo, "State Tax Reform," 3.

18. N.C. Governor's Commission, "Final Report"; Economic Future Study Commission, *Fiscal Realities*, 3; *Recommendations* (Sales Tax Modernization Subcommittee), 1.

19. *Recommendations* (Sales Tax Modernization Subcommittee), 1.

20. Research shows that states with broader-based sales taxes have greater revenue gains as the economy expands (Mullen and Williams, "Marginal Tax Rates," 695–700).

21. Bruce and Fox, "State and Local Sales Tax Revenue Losses," 7–11.

22. U.S. Census Bureau, "State and Local Government Finances." Property taxes ac-

counted for 39 percent of North Carolina's locally raised public revenue from taxes, fees, and charges in 2005.

23. N.C. Department of Revenue, "Property Tax Rates."

24. North Carolina law effectively encourages the rollback of rates by requiring county commissioners to report the revenue-neutral property tax rate (the property tax rate that would keep the average property tax payment unchanged) after each revaluation.

25. *Recommendations* (Local Taxation Modernization Subcommittee), 1.

26. A system of annually reassessing property values and using market values as the basis for taxation would have yielded an average 10 percent increase in property tax revenues for North Carolina counties over the 1980–1995 period (Walden and Denaux, "Lags," 210–11).

27. In fiscal year 2004, the two taxes accounted for 80 percent of the state revenues collected for highways (N.C. Office of Management and Budget, "North Carolina Tax Guide," 41, 66).

28. In real 2005 dollars, the North Carolina motor fuels tax rate was 60 cents per gallon in 1970 and 29.9 cents per gallon in 2006, based on calculations from the N.C. Department of Revenue, "Motor Fuels Tax Rate," and the BEA, "Consumer Price Index."

29. If the motor fuels tax rate is calculated on a per-mile-driven basis, the drop is 60 percent between 1970 and 2005.

30. From 1970 to 2006, average new vehicle prices rose 160 percent, compared to an average price increase for all goods and services of 420 percent (BEA, "Consumer Price Index").

31. North Carolina's motor fuels tax rate ranked fourth in the nation and first in the Southeast (Virginia, North Carolina, South Carolina, Tennessee, Georgia, Florida) in 2006 (Dubay, "Facts and Figures," table 20).

32. In 2005, local governments accounted for only 14 percent of North Carolina's highway spending (U.S. Census Bureau, "State and Local Government Finances"). However, the financing for the local spending comes from state-raised highway funds that are transferred to local governments (N.C. General Assembly, "Transportation Funding," 6).

33. Prior to 2006, part of the North Carolina motor fuels tax was indexed. The tax was composed of a nonindexed flat rate component plus a component indexed to the wholesale price of gasoline. In 2005, this formula resulted in 59 percent of the rate not being indexed and 41 percent being indexed. In 2006, responding to public dissatisfaction regarding gas prices, the N.C. General Assembly capped the indexed component at its current rate.

34. Stern, "Innovative Transportation Funding," 2. North Carolina is participating in a nationwide study of the mileage fee (Siceloff, "Drivers Might Pay"). One downside of a mileage tax is that it would remove the incentive for drivers to purchase more fuel-efficient vehicles that is created when a per-gallon tax is used.

35. For the economic benefits of moving to consumption-type taxation, see Edwards, "Simplifying Federal Taxes."

36. Cameron, "Following the Money," 6–7.

37. The North Carolina sales tax has two parts, a state component and a local (county) component. Groceries (foods consumed at home) are exempt from the state component but not the local component.

38. For Friedman's ideas for a negative income tax, see his *Capitalism and Freedom*, chapter 12.

39. Gray, "Strategies." A broader question is whether a state EITC would be used simply to refund part of paid income taxes or whether it could pay more to households than they owed in income tax payments. The second proposition is, of course, more expensive to the state budget. The form of the EITC approved in North Carolina in 2007 followed the second approach and piggybacked on federal rules by setting the state EITC at 3.5 percent of the federal EITC.

40. This growth rate does not exclude inflation. Doing so gives a negative growth rate.

41. Colorado and Missouri have adopted this restriction (Stallman, "Impacts"). In North Carolina, the John Locke Foundation has proposed such a restriction ("State Budget").

42. The Economic Future Study Commission recommended this budget limitation (*Fiscal Realities*, 3).

43. David Crotts, chief economist, Fiscal Research Division, N.C. General Assembly, personal communication, 14 May 2007.

44. Zahradnik, "Rainy Day Funds," 3.

45. N.C. Office of Management and Budget, "Post-Legislative Budget Summary."

46. The relative size of debt is often expressed as real debt per person (per capita) in the state, suggesting the amount of public debt each person owes. Although intuitively appealing, this measure fails to include the economic measure that supports debt—income. Hence, a single measure such as debt as a percentage of GSP or as a percentage of total personal income is preferred.

47. Atkins, *Analysis*, 8.

48. Siceloff, "N.C. Public Works."

49. David Jones, "Amendment One."

50. Adams, "Carolina Beat."

51. StatAbt 2007, table 218; StatAbt 1973, no. 180.

52. N.C. Public Schools, "North Carolina 2006 SAT Report."

53. StatAbt 2007, tables 121, 122, 123, 124.

54. StatAbt 2007, table 245; StatAbt 1973, nos. 160, 163. Spending is only for current, or operational, functions; capital spending is not included. Also, as table 6-2 shows, the spending increases have only kept up with the growing North Carolina economy.

55. StatAbt 2007, table 245; StatAbt 1973, nos. 160, 163. The spending gap does not account for any differences in the cost of living between North Carolina and the nation.

56. StatAbt 2007, table 240; StatAbt 1971, table 190. The pupil/teacher ratio is total pupils divided by all instructional personnel. The latter includes classroom teachers as

well as school specialists such as fine arts teachers, special resource teachers, and guidance counselors. Hence, the pupil/teacher ratio is not the same as average classroom size.

57. Considerable debate takes place regarding the comparison of teacher salaries among states. A straight comparison of salaries does not include differences in the purchasing power of dollars in different states, in numbers of hours and days worked per year, in experience and ability, and in pension systems. More elaborate comparisons yield differing results, with some studies reporting that North Carolina's salaries are at the national average (Stoops, "Learning") and others finding that North Carolina's salaries remain below the national average (Walden and Newmark, "Interstate Variation"; Greene and Winters, *How Much Are Public School Teachers Paid?*).

58. Average real salaries for all North Carolina workers rose 38 percent from 1972 to 2004 (BEA, "State Annual Personal Income").

59. Tucker, "Challenge from Asia."

60. James H. Johnson Jr., "Shaping the Business Leaders of Tomorrow."

61. For dropout rate rankings, see U.S. Department of Education, National Center for Education Statistics, "Dropout Rates." For trends in the dropout rate, see N.C. Public Schools, *Report*. The dropout rate rose from 4.78 percent in 2002–3 to 5.04 percent in 2005–6.

62. Hui, "Only 68% Graduate on Time."

63. Warren, "State-Level High School Completion Rates," table 2.

64. N.C. Public Schools, "North Carolina 2005 SAT Report," 13.

65. James H. Johnson Jr., "Shaping the Business Leaders of Tomorrow," 1.

66. James H. Johnson Jr., "Changing Face," 30.

67. Silberman, "Study"; Stephens and Riggsbee, "Talented Students on Hold."

68. Nationally, the percentage of all teachers who are female increased from 66 percent in 1970 to 79 percent in 2001 (DES 2005, table 68).

69. Rockoff, "Impact," 248–49.

70. Reform K–12, "Future Teachers."

71. The comparison was to business occupations, science jobs, architects and engineers, and social service workers. The exception was social service workers. The ESC defines experienced wage rates as the rate in the upper two-thirds of the wage distribution. The comparisons are imperfect because they do not adjust for the occupations' nonsalary characteristics.

72. Greene and Winters, *How Much Are Public School Teachers Paid?*, table 1b.

73. New Commission on the Skills of the American Workforce, *Tough Choices or Tough Times?*, 127–35. In the first decade of the twenty-first century, North Carolina focused on increasing beginning teacher salaries by having raises include a flat dollar amount, which results in a greater percentage increase for lower-paid starting teachers (Dan Kane, "House Budget Ups Teacher Pay").

74. Clodfelter et al., *Would Higher Salaries Keep Teachers?*

75. Figlio and Kenny, *Teacher Incentives.* The authors note, however, that their results

cannot distinguish whether teacher merit pay plans lead to improved student performance or whether schools that already have more accomplished students choose to implement merit pay plans.

76. Whoriskey, "Florida to Link Teacher Pay."

77. Stegall, "State to Measure."

78. Figlio and Kenny, *Teacher Incentives.*

79. "Into the Hornet's Nest."

80. Darling-Hammond, *Teacher Quality*, 18–23.

81. Boyd et al., *How Changes in Entry Requirements Alter the Teacher Workforce*; Thomas
Kane, Rockoff, and Staiger, *What Does Certification Tell Us?* Using North Carolina data,
Clodfelter, Ladd, and Vigdor, *How and Why Do Teacher Credentials Matter?*, also suggest
that teachers with advanced degrees have little positive impact on student achievement
and instead found teaching experience to be much more important.

82. DES 2005, tables 161, 165; DES 1992, table 407.

83. Szulik, "Why Schools Need Open-Source Software."

84. "Effectiveness of Reading and Mathematics Software Products."

85. Walden and Sisak, "School Inputs," 607.

86. N.C. Office of the Governor, "Governor Easley Announces "Learn and Earn"; N.C.
Office of the Governor, "Governor Mike Easley's 2007–2009 Budget Highlights."

87. *State of the North Carolina Workforce*, appendix 2.

88. Neumark and Rothstein, *Do School-to-Work Programs Help?*, 12–18.

89. Kakadelis, "School to Work Reconsidered."

90. For a reasoned discussion of school choice, see Peterson, "Choice."

91. Bifulco and Ladd, *Impacts*, table 1.

92. Ibid.; Hoxby, "Achievement."

93. Newmark, "Another Look."

94. For the United States as a whole in 2003–4, the state share was 47 percent, the
local share was 43 percent, and the federal share was 10 percent (U.S. Department of
Education, National Center for Education Statistics, "Common Core").

95. Expenditures per pupil are only for current, or operating, expenditures. Local
governments are responsible for capital expenditures. Current expenditures per pupil,
in 2005 dollars, for the twenty highest-wealth counties rose from $3,665 in 1980 to
$7,363 in 2005. Similar spending in the twenty lowest-wealth counties rose from $3,639
to $7,943 (wealth definitions are from the *2006 Local School Finance Study*, 10; data are
from LogNC).

96. New Commission on the Skills of the American Workforce, *Tough Choices or Tough
Times?*, 130–31.

97. Walden and Sisak, "School Inputs," 607.

98. Card and Rothstein, *Racial Segregation*, 24–34; Tough, "What It Takes."

99. University of North Carolina at Chapel Hill, "Carolina."

100. Fahy, *Workforce Development*, 2.

101. "Constitution of North Carolina."

102. DES 2005, table 189; LogNC.

103. LogNC. The comparable national change in college enrollment as a percentage of college-aged persons was from 36 percent in 1972 to 59 percent in 2005 (StatAbt 1974, no. 34; DES 2006, table 173; U.S. Census Bureau, "Public-Use Microdata Samples").

104. Ibid. The comparable national increase was from 10.7 percent in 1970 to 27.6 percent in 2005.

105. DES 2005, table 313.

106. Nordstrom et al., "Education Budget Overview," 32, 49.

107. Financial aid to athletics is not included in the net tuition measures. The measures are formed by taking total tuition paid by students, subtracting the designated type of financial aid, and then dividing the result by the number of students. Aid includes awards from all sources. The N.C. State Education Assistance Authority has performed similar calculations for the late 1990s through early twenty-first century (Knapp, "Benchmarks").

108. DES 2005, table 327.

109. Ibid.

110. Dynarski, "Does Aid Matter?," 282–84.

111. Vedder, Going Broke, 67.

112. Knapp, "Benchmarks," table 18.

113. Annual enrollments for both the University of North Carolina System and the North Carolina Community College System are expected to rise more than 3 percent annually between about 2005 and 2015 (Mabe, "Long-Term Planning Process," 25; Pappas Consulting Group, Staying a Step Ahead, 87). By comparison, North Carolina's population is forecast to increase 1.6 percent annually over the same period (N.C. State Data Center, "County/State Population Projections").

114. University of North Carolina Board of Governors, "Retention, Graduation, and Persistence Rates." This rate has edged up slightly since 1990, when it stood at 52 percent.

115. Şahin, Incentive Effects, 24–27.

116. Data regarding average class sizes are not available for either the University of North Carolina System or the North Carolina Community College System. However, the ratio of students to full-time faculty in the University of North Carolina System increased from 14 to 1 in 1971 to 18 to 1 in 2003 (University of North Carolina, Statistical Abstract, table 40; DES 2005, tables 191, 225).

117. Research has found that student interaction is reduced in larger classes and that the room setting and lighting become more important with greater numbers of students (DeLeone et al., "Class Size Effects"). For a review of the research on learning and class size in university settings, see Minnesota State University–Mankato, "Class Size."

118. University of North Carolina Board of Governors, "Report."

119. Ibid.

120. Walden, Smart Economics, chapter 48.

121. James H. Johnson Jr., "North Carolina's Higher Education," 14.

122. DES 2005, table 237; University of North Carolina, *Statistical Abstract*, table 48; Nordstrom et al., "Education Budget Overview," 37. Peer comparisons at a point in time are also relevant. Here, University of North Carolina System faculty compensation compares well to average compensation with peer institutions (Sanders, "Faculty Compensation"), but salaries of community college faculty members fall behind those of both their southeastern and national colleagues (Nordstrom et al., "Education Budget Overview," 37).

123. Vedder, *Going Broke*, 141. Alaska, Hawaii, and the District of Columbia were excluded from the analysis.

124. See, for example, Frances A. Campbell and Ramey, "Effects."

125. U.S. House Ways and Means Committee, *2004 Green Book*, table 15-33; N.C. Department of Health and Human Services, "North Carolina Child Care Snapshot."

126. Currie and Thomas, "Does Head Start Make a Difference?"; Currie and Thomas, "School Quality and the Longer-Term Effects"; Oden, Schweinhart, and Weikart, *Into Adulthood*.

127. N.C. Partnership for Children, "Smart Start."

128. Acord et al., "Effective Practices," 2.

129. Donna Bryant et al., *Smart Start*, 9–13.

130. Peisner-Feinberg and Schaaf, *Evaluation*, 22–34.

131. Jacobson, LaLonde, and Sullivan, *Should We Teach Old Dogs New Tricks?*, 2.

132. Schweke, "Promising Practices," 23. Programs developed specifically to assist workers displaced by trade agreements have been especially limited. From 1995 to 2002, only $188 million annually was spent nationwide, with the assistance received by a mere thirty-two thousand workers (U.S. House Ways and Means Committee, *2004 Green Book*, table 6-3).

133. A clear break in clothing prices occurred in 1994, with prices rising prior to that year and falling thereafter. Calculations are by the author, with savings obtained by applying to purchases of apparel products in 2003 the additional clothing price consumers would have paid if pre-1994 price trends had continued. The notion that displaced workers require more assistance than they currently receive is echoed in Aldonas, Lawrence, and Slaughter, *Succeeding*. However, these authors propose that the augmented assistance come from general tax revenues, rather than revenues raised from targeted taxes.

134. A related controversy arose in the early twenty-first century regarding the degree to which state highway funds were being diverted to nonhighway spending. In 1989, one of the state's two highway funds (the Highway Trust Fund, which taxed vehicle sales) was created to replace a general sales tax on vehicle sales, the proceeds of which went to the state's General Fund for purposes other than highway construction and maintenance. Legislators enacted an annual transfer from the Highway Trust Fund to the General Fund to replace the vehicle taxes previously allocated to the General Fund. From fiscal year 2002 to fiscal year 2006, the legislature authorized additional transfers averaging $103 million annually above the replacement amounts. These "excess" transfers totaled 3.5

percent of all highway spending in the state over the period ("History of Transfers"). In 2007, the General Assembly voted to end these transfers by 2013 (N.C. General Assembly, "Transportation Funding," 20). Some public highway monies are used for functions other than road construction and maintenance, most notably the State Highway Patrol.

135. Hartgen, "Looming Highway Condition Crisis," 24–30.

136. Ibid.

137. Hartgen, "Traffic Congestion," figure II.A.2.

138. Siceloff, "N.C. Public Works."

139. Capital Area Metropolitan Planning Organization, "NCDOT Spending."

140. Capital Area Metropolitan Planning Organization, "Transportation Revenue Return Map and Table." The percentages for the period were Mecklenburg, 70 percent; Wake, 71 percent; Forsyth, 51 percent; and Guilford, 92 percent.

141. Roth, *Liberating the Roads*, 16–17.

142. Baysden, "New Law."

143. Siceloff, "In Charlotte."

144. Hartgen, "Policy and Performance," 22–25.

145. Roth, *Street Smart*, part 3.

146. BEA, "Local Area Personal Income."

147. Ibid.; *2006 Local School Finance Study*, 10.

148. N.C. Department of Health and Human Services, "History," 48; LogNC.

149. N.C. Department of Health and Human Services, "History," 48; BEA, "Gross Domestic Product"; estimates by the author based on the state's share of total Medicaid spending.

150. N.C. General Assembly, Fiscal Research Division, "Medicaid Program Overview," 46–47.

151. For a history of the expansion in coverage of the Medicaid program, see N.C. Department of Health and Human Services, "History."

152. N.C. General Assembly, Fiscal Research Division, "Medicaid Program Overview," 20.

153. Monetary values are estimates by the author using a procedure suggested by the N.C. Association of County Commissioners (personal communication, 25 May 2007).

154. N.C. Association of County Commissioners, "Medicaid Burden."

155. N.C. Association of County Commissioners, "Current Issues." A half cent of the local sales tax was transferred to the statewide sales tax. Counties had the option of replacing this revenue with a .25 cent local sales tax or a 0.4 percent land transfer tax, with both subject to voter approval.

156. Congressional Budget Office, "Budget Projections," table 1-4.

157. The measures are Medicaid payments per person served and Medicaid spending per state resident (John Locke Foundation, "Medicaid and Health Choice"). The state has implemented several cost-containment strategies since the end of the twentieth century (N.C. General Assembly, Fiscal Research Division, "Medicaid Program Overview," 35–43).

158. Kent, "Sooner State Reforms Medicaid." Voucher supporters see the current supply-side Medicaid program as encouraging spending because the participant bears little or none of the financial costs of treatment. Under this structure, participants have an incentive to use care until the marginal benefit to them is zero. Where participants face some costs for treatment, as they likely would with a private-market insurance policy, participants are likely to be more frugal in using care, doing so only when the benefits they reap exceed their costs.

159. After three years, the recipient can reapply for assistance (N.C. Department of Health and Human Services, "North Carolina's Temporary Assistance for Needy Families State Plan," 21).

160. LogNC.

161. Grogger and Karoly, *Welfare Reform*, 239–42.

162. Cobb, *Selling*, 73.

163. Rork, "Getting What You Pay For," 37.

164. Ibid.

165. Cameron, "Following the Money," 40.

166. Cox and Bonner, "Tire Makers." To be eligible for the incentives, existing firms must be located in one of the state's most distressed counties, employ at least two thousand full-time workers, pay wages at least 40 percent above the county average, and invest at least $200 million in infrastructure upgrades.

167. Cox, "Incentives Get a Tweak." As a result, the program has been changed to increase the number of low-income counties eligible for the largest grants.

168. Luger and Bae, "Effectiveness," 331–38. The authors offer several caveats regarding their methodology and findings, including paucity of data, inadequate time to measure the full effects of the programs, and failure to consider multiplier effects.

169. Cameron, "Following the Money," 38–39.

170. Cox, "Google Breaks." The biggest such incentives packages were for Dell in 2004 ($280 million), Google in 2006 ($100 million), Fidelity in 2006 ($69 million), Novartis in 2006 ($41.5 million), and Merck in 2004 ($39.4 million). Localities can also add incentives packages (*Incentives Game*).

171. ABCMoney.co.uk, "Dell Case."

172. Stanek, "N.C. Judge Dismisses Dell Incentives Suit."

173. Mejia, Nordstrom, and Schweke, "Getting Our Money's Worth," 12–18. The study specifically analyzed the Dell incentives package and argued that the outcomes of the benefit/cost calculation were less positive (and sometimes negative) when more modest production values from the factory were assumed. N.C. Department of Commerce officials, who manage and operate the model, countered that the incentives packages are performance based, meaning that lower-than-expected production levels would result in lowered tax benefits (Cox, "Incentive Model").

174. This is the same logic used in the area of college tuitions and student financial aid. To the best of my knowledge, the application to business recruitment financial incentives is original. Wilson makes a similar but more narrow argument that business recruitment

financial incentives provide compensation for subsequent higher taxes paid by the firm when moving becomes more expensive (Wilson, "Tax Treatment").

175. For an example of the survey method, see Rondinelli and Burpitt, "Do Government Incentives Attract and Retain International Investment?" For examples of the statistical approach, see Tim C. Ford, Rork, and Elmslie, "Foreign Direct Investment"; Goodman, "Are Economic Development Incentives Worth It?"; Gabe and Kraybill, "Effect." For a statistical analysis that found a positive impact of business incentives but only for low-unemployment counties, see Goss and Phillips, "Do Business Tax Incentives Contribute." Calcagno and Hefner, "State Targeting," found that business incentive programs led to increases in state corporate tax revenue.

176. Calzonetti and Walker, "Factors," 235–36.

177. Greenstone and Moretti, *Bidding*, 20–26.

178. Mather, "Air Cargo Complex," 29–30.

179. Speizer, "Aerotropolis." The most notable prospective tenant is an aircraft components manufacturer, who in 2008 promised to eventually bring approximately 1,000 jobs to the site (Cox, "Firm Pledges Jobs for Transpark").

180. Walden, "Global Transpark"; Burtman, "Jet Lag." Indeed, in some eyes, the FedEx facility at the Piedmont Triad International Airport fills the Transpark's intended role (Speizer, "Aerotropolis").

181. In 2004 the state attempted to revive its investment in the Global Transpark by offering more than $500 million in financial incentives to Boeing to turn the site into an assembly plant for the 787 Dreamliner Aircraft. However, Boeing ultimately selected Everett, Washington, for the factory location (Wagner, "Post-Boeing, Incentives Debate Rages").

182. Bruce, Fox, and Tuttle, "Tax Base Elasticities," 336–37.

183. Shields and Snyder, "Building a 21st Century Rural Workforce," 40–41.

184. The incentives provided by the Job Development Investment Grant program require that job targets be met at regular intervals (Cox, "Employers Meet Goals").

185. Joining the majority of other states, North Carolina implemented a lottery in 2006, with the proceeds allocated primarily to K–12 education. On average, however, since net lottery revenues account for less than 2 percent of state-raised public revenues, the lottery is not a solution to long-run public funding issues (Hansen, "Gambling," 17).

186. Greater efficiencies would result if, by using more of their own money, college students took less time to graduate, drivers consolidated trips, and health care users engaged in personal behavior that reduced use of the health care system.

Chapter 7

1. *State of the North Carolina Workforce*, 22.

2. BEA, "Gross Domestic Product."

3. Meredith, *Elephant and the Dragon*, chapters 8, 9.

4. From 2000 to 2006, the percentage increase in U.S. exports to China and India exceeded the percentage increase in imports from those countries to the United States. However, the United States still ran a trade deficit with those countries because the volume of imports was much larger than the volume of exports (BEA, "Trade in Goods and Services").

5. BLS, "Consumer Price Index."

Primer on Economic Concepts

1. National Bureau of Economic Research, "Business Cycle Expansions and Contractions."

2. One of the classic studies of business cycles in the United States is Milton Friedman and Schwartz, *Monetary History*. The current chair of the Federal Reserve Board, Ben Bernanke, has contributed to this field with his book, *Essays on the Great Depression*.

Appendix A

1. In the reported regression results, all variables are contemporaneous in time. Other forms of the regression equations were run, including using measures of the explanatory variables from one year earlier and using economy-wide output and jobs as the national variables. None of these alternatives provided superior results. Parameter values for the intercept are not shown in the tables.

2. Miernyk, "Rising Energy Prices," 5–6.

3. Poot, "Synthesis," 531–37.

Appendix C

1. The years used for each measure are the earliest and latest years for which data are available within the 1970–2004 period. Where only one year of data was available (as in the case of OPENSPACE), it was used.

2. The definition of urban is that used by the N.C. Rural Economic Development Center, "Water 2030: Glossary of Terms."

3. Kusmin, Redman, and Sears, *Factors*, 12–13, 38–39.

4. Dinlersoz, "Cities," 85–100.

5. In place of HIGHWAYS, the impact of road infrastructure was measured as a categorical variable indicating whether an interstate highway went through the county. However, this alternative measure as not statistically significant in either economic growth equation. Also, following Kusmin, Redman, and Sears, a categorical variable was developed that indicated counties within fifty miles of a commercial airport. When used in Version 2, this variable too was not statistically significant in either equation.

Bibliography

ABCMoney.co.uk. "Dell Case at N.C. Appeals Court." 26 April 2007. <http://www
.abcmoney.co.uk/news/26200762681.htm>. Accessed 20 July 2007.

Abernathy, Frederick H., John T. Dunlop, Janice H. Hammond, and David Weil. *A
Stitch in Time: Lean Retailing and the Transformation of Manufacturing — Lessons from
the Apparel and Textile Industries.* Oxford: Oxford University Press, 1999.

Acord, Phil, Flora Gee, Rhonda Laird, Mary Ann Rasberry, and Cynthia Wheeler.
"Effective Practices between Public Schools and Private Pre-Kindergarten Programs
in Three States." Paper presented at the Smart Start Conference, Greensboro, North
Carolina, May 10, 2007.

Adams, Chad. "Carolina Beat, No. 767: Amendment One Is Still a Bad Idea." *Carolina
Journal Online*, 14 July 2004. <http://www.carolinajournal.com/opinions/display_
story.html?id=1668>. Accessed 17 December 2007.

Aldonas, Grant D., Robert Z. Lawrence, and Matthew J. Slaughter. *Succeeding in the
Global Economy: A New Policy Agenda for the American Worker.* Washington, D.C.:
Financial Services Forum, 2007.

Alenezi, Mohammad, and Michael L. Walden. "A New Look at Husbands' and Wives'
Time Allocation." *Journal of Consumer Affairs* 38 (June 2004): 81–106.

American Gaming Association. "Casino Employment." 2003. <http://www
.americangaming.org/industry/factsheets/general_info_detail.cfv?id=28>. Accessed
16 July 2007.

Aon. "Recent Atlantic Basin Hurricane Frequency Shift." 2006. <http://www.aon.com/
about/publications/issues/rp_06_Atlantic_Basin_Hurricane_Frequency_Shift.jsp>.
Accessed 4 April 2007.

Appalachian State University. "Enrollment History." N.d. <http://www.appstate.edu/
www_docs/depart/irp/factbook/factbook0405/S9HeadcountEnrollmentHistory
.pdf>. Accessed 1 July 2007.

Armstrong-Hough, Mari. "A Good Fit: North Carolina's Place in the Biotechnology
Value Chain." January 2006. <http://www.soc.duke.edu/NC_GlobalEconomy/pdfs/
paper/armstrong_hough_1.pdf>. Accessed 17 December 2007.

Asheville-Buncombe Technical Community College. "Academic Programs." N.d.
<http://www.abtech.edu/programs.asp>. Accessed 9 July 2007.

Asian Development Bank. "The WTO Toolkit." 30 June 2005. <http://www.adb.org/Documents/Others/OGC-Toolkits/WTO/default.asp>. Accessed 21 June 2007.

Atkins, Cathy. *Analysis of Innovative State Legislation to Encourage Infrastructure Finance Options.* Washington, D.C.: National Association of Homebuilders, 2006.

Atkinson, Robert D. *The Past and Future of America's Economy.* Northampton, Mass.: Elgar, 2004.

Atlanta 575 Real Estate. <http://www.atlanta575realestate.com>. Accessed 16 July 2007.

Austin, Chad. "N.C. State Researchers Look to Improve Pulp Paper Process with $2.8 Million Grant." 3 March 2005. <http://www.ncsu.edu/news/press_releases/05_03/054.htm>. Accessed 17 December 2007.

Bacon, J. A. "Oink: Not North Carolina." *Virginia Business,* June 1993, 55–56.

Baily, Martin N., and Diana Farrell. "Exploding the Myths of Offshoring." *McKinsey Quarterly,* July 2004. <http://www.mckinseyquarterly.com>. Accessed 16 July 2007.

Bardsley, Peter, and Nilss Olekalns. "Cigarette and Tobacco Consumption: Have Anti-Smoking Policies Made a Difference?" *Economic Record* 75 (September 1999): 225–40.

Barkema, Alan, Mark Drabenstott, and Nancy Novack. "The New U.S. Meat Industry." *Economic Review* (Federal Reserve Bank of Kansas City), 2nd Quarter 2001, 33–56.

Barrett, Barbara. "Bill Could Kill Navy's Airfield Plan." *Raleigh News and Observer,* 10 May 2007. <http://www.newsobserver.com/159/story/572592.html>. Accessed 26 June 2007.

———. "Southport to Be Key Port." *Raleigh News and Observer,* 31 December 2005. <http://www.newsobserver.com/print/saturday/front/story/383713.html>. Accessed 17 December 2007.

Barro, Robert J., and Xavier Sala-i-Martin. *Economic Growth.* 2nd ed. Cambridge: MIT Press, 2004.

Bartik, Timothy J. "Business Location Decisions in the U.S.: Estimates of the Effects of Unionization, Taxes, and Other Characteristics of States." *Journal of Business and Economic Statistics* 3 (January 1985): 14–22.

———. "Small Business Start-Ups in the United States: Estimates of the Effects of Characteristics of States." *Southern Economic Journal* 55 (April 1989): 1004–18.

Batson, Andrew. "China's Rise as Auto Parts Power Reflects New Manufacturing Edge." *Wall Street Journal,* 1 August 2006, A1, A6.

Bauer, Paul, and Yoonsoo Lee. "Labor Productivity Growth across States." *Economic Commentary* (Federal Reserve Bank of Cleveland), June 2005, 1–4.

Baxandall, Phineas, and Bruce Sacerdote. *Betting on the Future: The Economic Impact of Legalized Gambling.* PB-2005-1. Cambridge: Rappaport Institute for Greater Boston, Kennedy School of Government, Harvard University, 2005.

Baxter. "History." N.d. <http://www.baxter.com/about_baxter/company_profile/sub/history.html>. Accessed 8 July 2007.

Baysden, Chris. "New Law Allows Counties to Build Roads Using Local Tax Dollars." *Triangle Business Journal,* 21 December 2007. <http://triangle.bizjournals.com/triangle/stories/2007/12/24/story9.html>. Accessed 23 January 2008.

Bender, Bryan. "Analysts Question Need for Boost in Combat Troops." *Boston Globe*, 5 March 2007. <http://www.boston.com/news/nation/washington/articles/2007/03/05/analysts_question_need_for_boost_in_combat_troops>. Accessed 7 April 2007.

Berman, Jay M. "Industry Output and Employment Projections to 2014." *Monthly Labor Review*, November 2005, 45–69.

Bernanke, Ben S. *Essays on the Great Depression*. Princeton: Princeton University Press, 2000.

Bhagwati, Jagdish N. *In Defense of Globalization*. New York: Oxford University Press, 2004.

Bhide, Amar. "Venturesome Consumption, Innovation, and Globalization." Paper presented at a joint conference of CESIFO and the Center on Capitalism and Society, Venice, Italy, 21–22 July 2006.

Bifulco, Robert, and Helen F. Ladd. *The Impacts of Charter Schools on Student Achievement: Evidence from North Carolina*. Working Paper SAN04-01. Durham, N.C.: Terry Sanford Institute of Public Policy, Duke University, 2004.

Blau, Francine D., Marianne A. Ferber, and Anne E. Winkler. *The Economics of Women, Men, and Work*. 3rd ed. Upper Saddle River, N.J.: Prentice Hall, 1998.

Blinder, Alan S. "Offshoring: The Next Industrial Revolution?" *Foreign Affairs* 85 (March–April 2006): 113–28.

Blue Ribbon Committee on the Future of Wake County. *Inaugural Report of the Blue Ribbon Committee on the Future of Wake County*. Raleigh, N.C.: Greater Raleigh Chamber of Commerce, 2006.

Borjas, George J. "For a Few Dollars Less." *Wall Street Journal*, 18 April 2006, A18.

———. *Heaven's Door: Immigration Policy and the American Economy*. Princeton: Princeton University Press, 1999.

———. "The Labor Demand Curve Is Downward Sloping: Reexamining the Impact of Immigration on the Labor Market." *Quarterly Journal of Economics* 118 (November 2003): 1335–74.

Borland, R., S. Chapman, N. Owen, and D. Hill. "Effects of Workplace Smoking Bans on Cigarette Consumption." *American Journal of Public Health* 80 (February 1990): 178–80.

Boyd, Donald, Pamela Grossman, Hamilton Lankford, Susanna Loeb, and James Wyckoff. *How Changes in Entry Requirements Alter the Teacher Workforce and Affect Student Achievement*. Working Paper 11844. Boston: National Bureau of Economic Research, 2005.

Boyum, Tim. "Experts Analyze Textile Industry's Future." News14 Carolina, 9 December 2004. <http://news14.com/Default.aspx?ArID=556214>. Accessed 17 December 2007.

Bradford, Scott C., Paul L. E. Grieco, and Gary Clyde Hufbauer. "The Payoff to America from Global Integration." In *The United States and the World Economy: Foreign Economic Policy for the Next Decade*, edited by C. Fred Bergsten, 65–109. Washington, D.C.: Institute for International Economics, 2005.

Broaddus, J. Alfred. "The Bank Merger Wave: Causes and Consequences." *Economic Quarterly* (Federal Reserve Bank of Richmond) 84 (Summer 1998): 1–11.

Brown, Blake. *Global Cotton Trends*. Raleigh: Department of Agricultural and Resource Economics, North Carolina State University, 2004.

Brown, Clair, John Haltiwanger, and Julia Lane. *Economic Turbulence*. Chicago: University of Chicago Press, 2006.

Brown, Vera. "FedEx, PTIA Propose Nighttime Cargo Hub." *Guilfordian*, 16 February 2001. <http://www.guilfordian.com>. Accessed 3 May 2007.

Bruce, Donald, and William F. Fox. "State and Local Sales Tax Revenue Losses from E-Commerce: Updated Estimates." September 2001. <http://cber.bus.utk.edu/ecomm/ecom0901.pdf>. Accessed 17 December 2007.

Bruce, Donald, William F. Fox, and M. H. Tuttle. "Tax Base Elasticities: A Multi-State Analysis of Long-Run and Short-Run Dynamics." *Southern Economic Journal* 73 (October 2006): 315–41.

Bryant, Donna, Kelly Maxwell, Karen Taylor, Michelle Poe, Ellen Peisner-Feinberg, and Kathleen Bernier. *Smart Start and Preschool Child Care Quality in North Carolina: Change over Time and Relation to Children's Readiness*. Chapel Hill: Frank Porter Graham Child Development Institute, 2003.

Bryant, W. Keith, and Yan Wang. "American Consumption Patterns and the Price of Time: A Time-Series Analysis." *Journal of Consumer Affairs* 24 (Winter 1990): 280–306.

Bryson, Virginia, Gianni Lanzillotti, Josh Myerberg, Elizabeth Miller, and Fred Tian. "The Furniture Industry (Case Goods): Future of the Industry, United States versus China." 7 March 2003. <www.kenan-flagler.unc.edu/assets/documents/furn_paper.pdf>. Accessed 17 December 2007.

Burns, Jenny. "Boomers Make Carolinas Their Second Home." *Myrtle Beach Sun News*, 16 August 2006. <http://www.myrtlebeachonline.com>. Accessed 26 June 2007.

Burrill, G. Steven. "State of the Biotechnology Industry: An Outlook for 2005." 13 January 2005. <http://www.burrillandco.com/pdfs/duke_011305.pdf>. Accessed 17 December 2007.

Burtless, Gary. "Effects of Growing Wage Disparities and Changing Family Composition on the U.S. Income Distribution." *European Economic Review* 43 (April 1999): 853–65.

Burtman, Bob. "Jet Lag: How Long before the Global Transpark Takes Off—and at What Cost?" *Independent Weekly*, 3 August 1994, 10–13.

Calcagno, Peter T., and Frank Hefner. "State Targeting of Business Investment: Does Targeting Increase Corporate Tax Revenue?" *Journal of Regional Analysis and Policy* 37, no. 2 (2007): 90–102.

Calzonetti, F. J., and Robert T. Walker. "Factors Affecting Industrial Location Decisions: A Survey Approach." In *Industry Location and Public Policy*, edited by Henry W. Herzog Jr. and Alan M. Schlottman, 221–40. Knoxville: University of Tennessee Press, 1991.

Camarota, Steven A. "A Jobless Recovery?: Immigrant Gains and Native Losses."

October 2004. <http://www.cis.org/articles/2004/back1104.html>. Accessed 17 December 2007.

Cameron, Amna. "Following the Money: A Guide to North Carolina's Tax System and a Blueprint for Reform and Modernization." 2004. <http://www.ncjustice.org/assets/library/38_taxprimer04.pdf>. Accessed 17 December 2007.

Campaign for Tobacco-Free Kids. "The Federal Cigarette Tax Is Much Lower than Historical Levels." 26 July 2007. <http://tobaccofreekids.org/research/factsheets/pdf/0092.pdf>. Accessed 17 December 2007.

Campbell, Doug. "The Illegal Immigrant Effect." *Region Focus* (Federal Reserve Bank of Richmond) 10 (Summer 2006): 19–23.

Campbell, Frances A., and Craig T. Ramey. "Effects of Early Intervention on Intellectual and Academic Achievement: A Follow-Up Study of Children from Low-Income Families." *Child Development* 65 (April 1994): 684–98.

Canadian Border Services Agency. "Guide to the Treatment of Textiles, Textile Articles, and Apparel under NAFTA." RC4236. 2001. <http://www.cbsa-asfc.gc.ca/E/pub/cp/rc4236/rc4236-e.pdf>. Accessed 21 June 2007.

Capehart, Thomas C., Jr. "Trends in the Cigarette Industry after the Master Settlement Agreement." TBS-250-01. November 2001. <http://www.ers.usda.gov/Publications/TBS/Oct01/TBS250-01/>. Accessed 17 December 2007.

———. *Tobacco Outlook.* TBS-260. Washington, D.C.: U.S. Department of Agriculture Economic Research Service, April 2006. <http://usda.mannlib.cornell.edu/usda/ers/TBS//2000s/2006/TBS-04-28-2006.pdf>. Accessed 17 December 2007.

———. "U.S. Tobacco Industry Responding to New Competitors, New Challenges." *Amber Waves*, September 2003. <http://www.ers.usda.gov/AmberWaves/September03/Features/USTobaccoIndustry.htm>. Accessed 16 February 2007.

Capital Area Metropolitan Planning Organization. "NCDOT Spending per 1000 VMT Map and Table." N.d. <http://www.campo-nc.us/Statistics/CAMPO_Trans_Stats.htm>. Accessed 20 July 2006.

———. "Transportation Revenue Return Rate Map and Table." N.d. <http://www.campo-nc.us/Statistics/CAMPO_Trans_Stats.htm>. Accessed 20 July 2006.

Card, David, and John E. DiNardo. "Technology and U.S. Wage Inequality: A Brief Look." *Economic Review* (Federal Reserve Bank of Atlanta) 87 (3rd Quarter 2002): 45–62.

Card, David, and Jesse Rothstein. *Racial Segregation and the Black-White Test Score Gap.* Working Paper 12078. Boston: National Bureau of Economic Research, 2006.

Carey, Renee. "Officials: BRAC Decisions a Victory." *Goldsboro News-Argus*, 28 August 2005. <http://www.newsargus.com/news/archives/2005/08/28/officials_brac_decisions_a_victory/index.shtml>. Accessed 26 June 2007.

Carlino, Gerald A., and Leonard O. Mills. "Are U.S. Regional Incomes Converging?" *Journal of Monetary Economics* 32 (November 1993): 335–46.

Carlson, Pete. "Software Industry Trends." In *An Analysis of Market and Skill Changes: The Impact of Globalization on American Jobs in Selected Industries,* edited by Mark Troppe and Pete Carlson, 69–79. National Center on Education and the Economy,

New Commission on the Skills of the American Workforce, 2006. <http://www.skillscommission.org/pdf/Staff%20Papers/Industry_Papers.pdf>. Accessed 17 December 2007.

Carnegie Foundation for the Advancement of Teaching. "The Carnegie Classification of Institutions of Higher Education." 2007. <http://www.carnegiefoundation.org/classifications/index.asp>. Accessed 12 July 2007.

CBC News. "Nortel: Canada's Closely-Watched Tech Giant." 12 March 2007. <http://www.cbc.ca/news/background/nortel/>. Accessed 10 July 2007.

Center for Competitive Economics. *Regional Partnership Vision Plan — North Carolina's Northeast Partnership*. Chapel Hill: Kenan-Flagler School of Business, University of North Carolina, 2005.

Centers for Disease Control. "Behavioral Risk Factor Surveillance System." 2006. <http://apps.nccd.cdc.gov/brfss/>. Accessed 9 July 2007.

Chandler, Alfred D., Jr. *Shaping the Industrial Century: The Remarkable Story of the Modern Chemical and Pharmaceutical Industries*. Cambridge: Harvard University Press, 2005.

Chandler, Alfred D., Jr., with Takashi Hikino and Andrew von Nordenflycht. *Inventing the Electronic Century: The Epic Story of the Consumer Electronics and Computer Industries*. New York: Free Press, 2001.

Chaloupka, Frank J. Web site. N.d. <http://tigger.uic.edu/~fjc>. Accessed 23 July 2007.

Charlotte Regional Partnership. "Industry Clusters." N.d. <http://www.charlotteusa.com/Regional/regional_industry.asp>. Accessed 3 July 2007.

"Cheesecake Factory to Build Eastern U.S. Bakery in Nash County." *Triangle Business Journal*, 27 July 2005. <http://triangle.bizjournals.com/triangle/stories/2005/07/25/daily25.html>. Accessed 7 March 2007.

Chen, Natalie A., Jean M. Imbs, and Andrew Scott. *Competition, Globalization, and the Decline of Inflation*. Discussion Paper 4695. London: Center for Economic Policy Research, 2004.

Choi, Chi-Young. "A Reexamination of Output Convergence in the U.S. States: Toward Which Level(s) Are They Converging?" *Journal of Regional Science* 44 (November 2004): 713–41.

Clodfelter, Charles, Elizabeth Glennie, Helen Ladd, and Jacob Vigdor. *Would Higher Salaries Keep Teachers in High-Poverty Schools?: Evidence from a Policy Intervention in North Carolina*. Working Paper 12285. Boston: National Bureau of Economic Research, 2006.

Clodfelter, Charles, Helen Ladd, and Jacob Vigdor. *How and Why Do Teacher Credentials Matter for Student Achievement?* Working Paper 12828. Boston: National Bureau of Economic Research, 2007.

"Closing the Circle: Automated Tailoring Comes Closer." *The Economist*, 13 July 2006, 79.

Cobb, James C. *The Selling of the South: The Southern Crusade for Industrial Development, 1936–1990*. 2nd ed. Urbana: University of Illinois Press, 1993.

Collins, Kristin. "Hog Plant Wants Union Vote." *Raleigh News and Observer*, 2 July 2006. <http://www.newsobserver.com/news/story/456899.html>. Accessed 17 December 2007.

Collins, Kristin, and Jay Price. "Development Hurts Ailing Fishing Industry." *Raleigh News and Observer*, 16 July 2006. <http://www.newsobserver.com/front/story/461206.html>. Accessed 17 December 2007.

Congressional Budget Office. "Budget Projections." 2007. <http://www.cbo.gov/budget/budproj.shtml>. Accessed 17 December 2007.

―――. "A Potential Influenza Pandemic: Possible Macroeconomic Effects and Policy Issues." 8 December 2005. <http://www.cbo.gov/ftpdocs/69xx/doc6946/12-08-BirdFlu.pdf>. Accessed 17 December 2007.

―――. "Trends in Earnings Variability over the Past 20 Years." April 2007. <http://www.cbo.gov/ftpdocs/80xx/doc8007/04-17-EarningsVariability.pdf>. Accessed 17 December 2007.

―――. "What Accounts for the Decline in Manufacturing Employment?" 18 February 2004. <http://www.cbo.gov/ftpdoc.cfm?index=5078&type=0>. Accessed 17 December 2007.

Connaughton, John E., Ronald A. Madsen, John M. Gandar, Joseph D. Arthur, and Alain A. Krapl. "The Economic Impacts of the Motorsports Industry on the North Carolina Economy." October 2004. <http://www.nccommerce.com/NR/rdonlyres/D1E0B2EB-A3AC-4261-A434-4F51918D0D28/0/EconomicImpactsoftheMotorsportsIndustryontheNorthCarolinaEco.pdf>. Accessed 17 December 2007.

"The Constitution of North Carolina." N.d. <http://statelibrary.dcr.state.nc.us/nc/stgovt/preconst.htm>. Accessed 20 July 2007.

Conway, Patrick. *Downsizing, Layoffs, and Plant Closures: The Impacts of Import Price Pressure and Technological Growth on U.S. Textile Producers*. Working Paper 06-10. Washington, D.C.: U.S. Census Bureau, Center for Economic Studies, 2006.

Corbin, Laura Hendrix. "Rural Work Ethic Means Big Business." *Southern Business and Development* (Summer 2003). <http://www.sb-d.com/issues/summer2003/ruralamericansouth/NorthCarolina.asp>. Accessed 21 June 2007.

Cost of Living Index (4th Quarter). Arlington, Va.: American Chamber of Commerce Researchers Association, 2006.

Coughlin, Cletus C., and Eran Segev. "Location Determinants of New Foreign-Owned Manufacturing Plants." *Journal of Regional Science* 40 (May 2000): 323–51.

Council of Economic Advisers. *Economic Report of the President, 2007*. Washington, D.C.: U.S. Government Printing Office, 2007.

Cox, Jonathan B. "Eastern Counties Support Food Industry." *Raleigh News and Observer*, 12 July 2006. <http://www.newsobserver.com/business/story/459724.html>. Accessed 17 December 2007.

―――. "Employers Meet Goals." *Raleigh News and Observer*, 18 May 2007. <http://www.newsobserver.com/business/nc/story/575383.html>. Accessed 17 December 2007.

———. "Firm Pledges Jobs for Transpark." *Raleigh News and Observer*, 15 May 2008. <http://www.newsobserver.com/business/nc/story/1073203.html>. Accessed 23 May 2008.

———. "Giving Away More to Lure Jobs to North Carolina." *Raleigh News and Observer*, 23 January 2007. <http://www.newsobserver.com/business/story/535184.html>. Accessed 17 December 2007.

———. "Google Breaks May Top $100M." *Raleigh News and Observer*, 16 January 2007. <http://www.newsobserver.com/104/story/532914.html>. Accessed 20 July 2007.

———. "Honda, N.C. Take a Chance." *Raleigh News and Observer*, 18 July 2007. <http://www.newsobserver.com/business/story/640790.html>. Accessed 17 December 2007.

———. "Incentive Model Called Too Rosy." *Raleigh News and Observer*, 22 March 2007. <http://www.newsobserver.com/business/nc/story/556067.html>. Accessed 20 July 2007.

———. "Incentives Get a Tweak Next Year." *Raleigh News and Observer*, 14 December 2006. <http://www.newsobserver.com/front/story/521260.html>. Accessed 17 December 2007.

———. "Lack of Ready Sites Hurts N.C." *Raleigh News and Observer*, 4 April 2007. <http://www.newsobserver.com/front/story/560675.html>. Accessed 17 December 2007.

———. "Lenoir Gets Google, at a Cost." *Raleigh News and Observer*, 20 January 2007. <http://www.newsobserver.com/102/story/534390.html>. Accessed 17 December 2007.

———. "Offshoring Blamed on Talent Gap." *Raleigh News and Observer*, 1 November 2006. <http://www.newsobserver.com/business/story/504972.html>. Accessed 17 December 2007.

Cox, Jonathan B., and Lynn Bonner. "Tire Makers Win State Incentives." *Raleigh News and Observer*, 12 September 2007. <http://www.newsobserver.com/politics/story/701029.html>. Accessed 28 December 2007.

Cox, Jonathan B., and Anne Krishnan. "Fidelity Deal May Launch Triangle into New Orbit." *Raleigh News and Observer*, 3 August 2006. <http://www.newsobserver.com/business/nc/story/467102.html>. Accessed December 17, 2007.

Crandall, Robert W. *Manufacturing on the Move.* Washington, D.C.: Brookings Institution, 1993.

Crone, Theodore M. "Where Have All the Factory Jobs Gone—and Why?" *Business Review* (Federal Reserve Bank of Philadelphia), May–June 1997, 1–16.

Cunningham, Thomas. "Structural Booms: Why the South Grows." *Economic Review* (Federal Reserve Bank of Atlanta) 80 (May–June 1995): 1–10.

Currie, Janet, and Duncan Thomas. "Does Head Start Make a Difference?" *American Economic Review* 85 (June 1995): 341–64.

———. "School Quality and the Longer-Term Effects of Head Start." *Journal of Human Resources* 35 (Autumn 2000): 755–74.

Dalesio, Emery P. "IBM in N.C. Hums at Center of Outsourcing Debate." *USA*

Today, 17 March 2004. <http://www.usatoday.com/tech/news/2004-03-17-ibm-outsource_x.htm>. Accessed 8 July 2007.

Danson, Patricia M., Y. Richard Wang, and Liang Wang. *The Impact of Price Regulation on the Launch Delay of New Drugs—Evidence from Twenty-five Major Markets in the 1990s.* Working Paper 9874. Boston: National Bureau of Economic Research, 2003.

Darity, William A., Jr., and Patrick L. Mason. "Evidence on Discrimination in Employment: Codes of Color, Codes of Gender." *Journal of Economic Perspectives* 12 (Spring 1998): 63–90.

Darling-Hammond, Linda. *Teacher Quality and Student Achievement: A Review of State Policy Evidence.* Seattle: Center for the Study of Teaching and Policy, University of Washington, 1999.

Davis, Steven J., John C. Haltiwanger, and Scott Schuh. *Job Creation and Destruction.* Cambridge: MIT Press, 1996.

DeLeone, Charles J., Wendell H. Potter, Catherine M. Ishikawa, Jacob A. Blickenstaff, and Patrick L. Hession. "Class Size Effects in Active Learning Physics Courses." 2001. <http://piggy.cis.rit.edu/franklin/perc2001/DeLeone.doc>. Accessed 15 December 2007.

Denaux, Zulal. "Taxes, Government Spending, and Endogenous Growth: A Theoretical Analysis with an Empirical Application to North Carolina." Ph.D. diss., North Carolina State University, 2001.

DeNavas-Walt, Carmen, Bernadette D. Proctor, and Cheryl Hill Lee. "Income, Poverty, and Health Insurance Coverage in the United States: 2005." P60-231. August 2006. <http://www.census.gov/prod/2006pubs/p60-231.pdf>. Accessed 17 December 2007.

"Deregulation Was Supposed to Cut Prices, Expand Choice, Enhance Service—Improve Your Life. So Why Aren't You Smiling?" *Consumer Reports*, July 2002. <http://www.consumersunion.org/pdf/cudereg.pdf>. Accessed 17 December 2007.

Desai, Sonalde, P. Lindsay Chase-Lonsdale, and Robert T. Michael. "Mothers or Markets?: Effects of Maternal Employment on the Intellectual Ability of 4-Year-Old Children." *Demography* 26 (November 1989): 545–61.

Desai, Sonalde, Robert T. Michael, and P. Lindsay Chase-Lonsdale. "The Home Environment: A Mechanism through Which Maternal Employment Affects Child Development." Paper presented at the conference of the Population Association of America, Toronto, May 1990.

"Development of Environmentally Superior Technologies, Phase 3 Report." 8 March 2006. <http://www.cals.ncsu.edu/waste_mgt/smithfield_projects/phase3report06/phase3report.htm>. Accessed 18 December 2007.

Dicken, Peter. *Global Shift: Mapping the Changing Contours of the World Economy.* 5th ed. New York: Guilford, 2007.

Dietz, Richard, and James Orr. "A Leaner, More Skilled U.S. Manufacturing Workforce." *Current Issues in Economics and Finance* (Federal Reserve Bank of New York) 12 (February–March 2006): 1–7.

"Digital Dragon." *The Economist*, 14 December 2005, 58.

Dinlersoz, Emin M. "Cities and the Organization of Manufacturing." *Regional Science and Urban Economics* 34 (January 2004): 71–100.

Drabenstott, Mark. "This Little Piggy Went to Market: Will the New Pork Industry Call the Heartland Home?" *Economic Review* (Federal Reserve Bank of Kansas City), 3rd Quarter 1998, 79–97.

Dubay, Curtis S., ed. "Facts and Figures: How Does Your State Compare?" 1 March 2007. <"http://www.taxfoundation.org/publications/show/2181.html>. Accessed 18 December 2007.

———. "State and Local Tax Burdens Hit 25-Year High." 4 April 2007. <http://www.taxfoundation.org/publications/show/22320.html?>. Accessed 17 December 2007.

Duke University. "North Carolina in the Global Economy." N.d. <http://www.soc.duke.edu/NC_GlobalEconomy/>. Accessed 24 July 2007.

Dullien, Sebastian. "China's Changing Competitive Position: Lessons from a Unit-Labor-Cost-Based REER." *EconWPA* (February 2005). <http://129.3.20.41/eps/it/papers/0502/0502016.pdf>. Accessed 22 June 2007.

Durham, City of. "About Durham: A History of Transformation—A City on the Move." 2006. <http://www.durhamnc.gov/about/>. Accessed 24 January 2008.

Dynan, Karen E., Douglas W. Elmendorf, and Daniel E. Sichel. "The Evolution of Household Income Volatility." October 2007. <http://www.federalreserve.gov/pubs/feds/2007/200761/200761pap.pdf>. Accessed 17 December 2007.

Dynarski, Susan M. "Does Aid Matter?: Measuring the Effect of Student Aid on College Attendance and Completion." *American Economic Review* 93 (March 2003): 279–88.

Eckstein, Zvi, and Eva Nagypal. "The Evolution of U.S. Earnings Inequality: 1961–2002." *Quarterly Review* (Federal Reserve Bank of Minneapolis) 28 (December 2004): 10–29.

Economic Future Study Commission. *Fiscal Realities for the 90s.* Raleigh: State of North Carolina, 1991.

"The Economic Impact of the Child Care Industry in North Carolina: Executive Summary." June 2004. <http://www.nedlc.org/NCEIRExecSum.pdf>. Accessed 17 December 2007.

Edwards, Chris. "Simplifying Federal Taxes: The Advantages of Consumption-Based Taxation." Policy Analysis 416. 17 October 2001. <http://www.cato.org/pubs/pas/pa416.pdf>. Accessed 17 December 2007.

"Effectiveness of Reading and Mathematics Software Products: Findings for the First Student Cohort." March 2007. <http://ies.ed.gov/ncee/pdf/20074005.pdf>. Accessed 18 December 2007.

El Nasser, Haya. "New 'Cities' Springing Up around U.S. Cities." *USA Today,* 25 September 2003. <http://www.usatoday.com/travel/news/2003/09/25-airport-cities.htm>. Accessed 3 July 2007.

Employment Security Commission of North Carolina. "Announced Business Closings and Permanent Layoffs." N.d. <http://eslmi23.esc.state.nc.us/masslayoff/>. Accessed 9 July 2007.

————. "Employment and Wages by Industry, 1990 to Most Recent." N.d. <http://www.ncesc.com/lmi/industry/industryMain.asp#industry/wages>. Accessed 12 July 2007.

————. "Industry Projections, North Carolina, 2002–2012." <http://eslmi23.esc.state.nc.us/projections/>. Accessed 27 October 2006.

————. "Occupational Projections, North Carolina, 2004–2014." <http://www.ncesc.com/lmi/occupational/occupational_Projections_NC_2004_2014.pdf>. Accessed 22 June 2007.

————. "Unemployment Rates." <http://www.ncesc.com/lmi/laborStats/laborStatMain.asp>. Accessed 16 July 2007.

Engardio, Pete. "Emerging Giants." *Business Week*, 31 July 2006. <http://www.businessweek.com/magazine/content/06_31/b3995001.htm>. Accessed 17 December 2007.

————. "The Future of Outsourcing." *Business Week*, 30 January 2006. <http://www.businessweek.com/magazine/content/06_05/b3969401.htm?chan=search>. Accessed 17 December 2007.

Engemann, Kristie M., and Michael T. Owyang. "Working Hard or Hardly Working?: The Evolution of Leisure in the United States." *Regional Economist*, January 2007. <http://stlouisfed.org/publications/re/2007/a/pages/leisure.html>. Accessed 17 December 2007.

Ennis, Humberto. "On the Size Distribution of Banks." *Economic Review* (Federal Reserve Bank of Richmond) 87 (Fall 2001): 1–25.

Ernst and Young. "Beyond Borders: Technology Report 2005." <http://www.ey.com/global/content.nsf/International/Biotechnology_Library_Beyond_Borders_2005>. Accessed 17 December 2007.

Estes, Chris, William Schweke, and Sara Lawrence. *Dislocated Workers in North Carolina: Aiding Their Transition to Good Jobs*. Raleigh: N.C. Justice and Community Development Center, 2002. <http://www.ncjustice.org/assets/library/180_dislwkrsum.pdf>. Accessed 17 December 2007.

Facing the Facts: Dislocated Workers. Raleigh: N.C. Rural Economic Development Center, 2004. <http://www.ncruralcenter.org/rdwi/NCREconomyWinter.pdf>. Accessed 17 December 2007.

Fahy, Pat. *Workforce Development in the State of North Carolina: An Overview*. Washington, D.C.: National Center on Education and the Economy, 2006. <http://www.skillscommission.org/pdf/Staff%20Papers/North_Carolina_Workforce.pdf>. Accessed 17 December 2007.

FAO Corporate Depository. "Issues in the Global Tobacco Economy: Selected Case Studies." 2003. <http://www.fao.org/docrep/006/y4997e/y4997e00.htm>. Accessed 17 December 2007.

Fayetteville State University. "Fact Book." Fall 2004. <http://www.uncfsu.edu/ir/Fact%20Book%20Fall%202004.pdf>. Accessed 3 June 2007.

Federal Emergency Management Administration, U.S. Fire Administration. "Chicken

Processing Plant Fires, Hamlet, North Carolina and North Little Rock, Arkansas."
Technical Report Series 057. 1992. <http://www.interfire.com/res_file/pdf/Tr-057
.pdf>. Accessed 19 December 2007.

The Federal Register. N.d. <http://www.gpoaccess.gov/fr/index.html>. Accessed 31 July
2007.

Federal Reserve Bank of St. Louis. "Economic Data—FRED." N.d. <http://research
.stlouisfed.org/fred2/categories/2>. Accessed 23 July 2007.

Federal Reserve Board. "Bank Structure Data." N.d. <http://www.federalreserve.gov/
releases/>. Accessed 23 July 2007.

———. "Flow of Funds Accounts of the United States." <http://www.federalreserve
.gov/releases/z1>. Accessed 23 July 2007.

———. "Selected Interest Rates." <http://www.federalreserve.gov/releases/h15>.
Accessed 23 July 2007.

Ferguson, Ronald F. "Shifting Challenges: Fifty Years of Economic Change toward
Black-White Earnings Equality." *Daedalus* 124 (Winter 1995): 37–76.

Fields, Gary S., and Efe A. Ok. "Measuring Movements of Incomes." *Economica* 66
(November 1999): 455–71.

Figlio, David, and Lawrence Kenny. *Teacher Incentives and Student Performance.*
Working Paper 12627. Boston: National Bureau of Economic Research, 2006.

Fisher, Jean P. "ECU Dental School OK'd." *Raleigh News and Observer,* 11 November
2006. <http://www.newsobserver.com/102/story/509261.html>. Accessed 17 June
2007.

Fitzpatrick, Dan. "How Charlotte Became a Banking Giant, Outpacing Pittsburgh's
Banks." *Pittsburgh Post-Gazette,* 25 June 2006. <http://www.post-gazette.com/
06176/701039-28.stm>. Accessed 7 August 2006.

Florida, Richard. *The Flight of the Creative Class: The New Global Competition for Talent.*
New York: Harper Collins, 2005.

———. *The Rise of the Creative Class and How It's Transforming Work, Leisure,
Community and Everyday Life.* New York: Perseus, 2002.

Ford, Steve. "Caution: More Hogs in the Pipeline." *Raleigh News and Observer,* 29 July
2007. <http://www.newsobserver.com/opinion/columns/story/653007.html>.
Accessed 17 December 2007.

Ford, Tim C., Jonathan C. Rork, and Bruce. T. Elmslie. "Foreign Direct Investment,
Economic Growth, and the Human Capital Threshold: Evidence from the U.S.
States." Unpublished paper, 2005.

Fortin, Nicole, and Thomas Lemieux. "Institutional Changes and Rising Wage
Inequality: Is There a Linkage?" *Journal of Economic Perspectives* 11 (Spring 1997):
75–96.

Friedman, Milton. *Capitalism and Freedom.* Chicago: University of Chicago Press,
1962.

Friedman, Milton, and Anna Jacobson Schwartz. *A Monetary History of the United
States, 1867–1960.* Princeton: Princeton University Press, 1963.

Friedman, Thomas L. *The World Is Flat: A Brief History of the Twenty-first Century*. New York: Farrar, Straus, and Giroux, 2005.

"The Future of Technology." *Business Week*, 20 June 2005. <http://www.businessweek .com/magazine/toc/05_25/B3938o5it100.htm>. Accessed 3 July 2007.

Gabe, Todd M., and David S. Kraybill. "The Effect of State Economic Development Incentives on Employment Growth of Establishments." *Journal of Regional Science* 42 (November 2002): 703–30.

Garrett, Martin A., Jr. "Growth in Manufacturing in the South, 1947–58: A Study in Regional Industrial Development." *Southern Economic Journal* 34 (January 1968): 352–64.

Gittleman, Maury, and Mary Joyce. "Have Family Income Mobility Patterns Changed?" *Demography* 36 (August 1999): 299–314.

Global Security.org. "Cherry Point Marine Corps Air Station." N.d. <http://www .globalsecurity.org/military/facility/cherry-point.htm>. Accessed 7 March 2007.

———. "Military: Ft. Bragg." N.d. <http://www.globalsecurity.org/military/facility/fort-bragg.htm>. Accessed 7 March 2007.

Goetz, Stephan J., and Anil Rupasingha. "The Returns to Education in Rural Areas." *Review of Regional Studies* 34 (Winter 2004): 245–59.

Goldsmith, Arthur, Darrick Hamilton, and William Darity Jr. "Does a Foot in the Door Matter?: White-Nonwhite Differences in the Wage Return to Tenure and Prior Workplace Experience." *Southern Economic Journal* 73 (October 2006): 267–306.

Goodman, D. Jay. "Are Economic Development Incentives Worth It?: A Computable General Equilibrium Analysis of Pueblo, Colorado's Efforts to Attract Business." *Journal of Regional Analysis and Policy* 33, no. 1 (2003): 43–55.

Gomme, Paul, and Peter Rupert. "Per Capita Income Growth and Disparity in the United States, 1929–2003." *Economic Commentary* (Federal Reserve Bank of Cleveland), August 2004, 1–4.

Gordon, Edward E. *The 2010 Meltdown: Solving the Impending Jobs Crisis*. Westport, Conn.: Praeger, 2005.

Goss, Ernest P., and Joseph M. Phillips. "Do Business Tax Incentives Contribute to a Divergence in Economic Growth?" *Economic Development Quarterly* 13 (August 1999): 217–28.

Gottschalk, Peter. "Inequality, Income Growth, and Mobility: The Basic Facts." *Journal of Economic Perspectives* 11 (Spring 1997): 21–40.

Gould, David M., and Roy J. Ruffin. "What Determines Economic Growth?" *Economic Review* (Federal Reserve Bank of Dallas), 2nd Quarter 1993, 25–40.

"GPS Tour of Asheville." 31 July 2007. <http://www.travelbygps.com/premium/ asheville/asheville.php>. Accessed 17 December 2007.

Gratton, Heather. "Future of Banking Study: Regional and Other Midsize Banks: Recent Trends and Short-Term Prospects." Draft FOB-2004-06.1, FDIC, June 2004. <http://www.fdic.gov/bank/analytical/future/fob_06.pdf>. Accessed 15 December 2007.

Gray, Meg. "Strategies for Helping Low-Income Taxpayers: Comparing a No-Tax Floor to a State EITC." *BTC Reports* 13 (March 2007). <http://www.ncjustice.org/assets/library/898_btcrptmar607.pdf>. Accessed 17 December 2007.

Green, Richard K. "Airports and Economic Development." *Real Estate Economics* 35 (Spring 2007): 91–112.

Greene, Jay P., and Marcus A. Winters. *How Much Are Public School Teachers Paid?* Civic Report 50. New York: Center of Civic Innovation, Manhattan Institute, 2007. <http://www.manhattan-institute.org/html/cr_50.htm>. Accessed 17 December 2007.

Greenspan, Alan. "Economic Outlook: Testimony before the Joint Economic Committee, U.S. Congress." 3 November 2005. <http://www.federalreserve.gov/BOARDDOCS/Testimony/2005/20051103/default.htm>. Accessed 21 January 2008.

Greenstone, Michael, and Enrico Moretti. *Bidding for Industrial Plants: Does Winning a "Million Dollar Plant" Increase Welfare?* Working Paper 9844. Boston: National Bureau of Economic Research, 2003.

Greenwood, Michael. "Changing Patterns of Migration and Regional Growth in the U.S.: A Demographic Perspective." *Growth and Change* 19 (Fall 1988): 68–87.

Grogger, Jeffrey, and Lynn A. Karoly. *Welfare Reform: Effects of a Decade of Change.* Cambridge: Harvard University Press, 2005.

Grossman, Gene M., and Esteban Rossi-Hansberg. "Trading Tasks: A Simple Theory of Offshoring." October 2006. <http://www.princeton.edu/~erossi/TT.pdf>. Accessed 17 December 2007.

Hacker, Jacob S. *The Great Risk Shift: The Assault on American Jobs, Families, Health Care, and Retirement and How You Can Fight Back.* New York: Oxford University Press, 2006.

Hanc, George. "The Future of Banking in America: Summary and Conclusions." *FDIC Banking Review* 16, no. 1 (2004): 1–28.

Hanna, Frank A. "Income in the South since 1929." In *Essays in Southern Economic Development*, edited by Melvin L. Greenhut and W. Tate Whitman, 239–92. Chapel Hill: University of North Carolina Press, 1964.

Hansen, Alicia. "Gambling with Tax Policy: States' Growing Reliance on Lottery Tax Revenue." Background Paper 54. 3 July 2007. <http://www.taxfoundation.org/publications/show/22457.html>. Accessed 18 December 2007.

———. "North Carolina to Raise Cigarette Tax." *Tax Policy Blog*, 8 August 2005. <http://www.taxfoundation.org/blog/show/1001.html>. Accessed 18 December 2007.

"The Harnessing of Nature's Bounty." *The Economist*, 5 November 2005, 73–75.

"Harrah's Cherokee Great Smoky Mountains Resort." <http://www.emporis.com/en/wm/cx/?id=harrahscherokeegreatsmokymountainsresort-cherokee>. Accessed 2 February 2008.

Hartgen, David. "The Looming Highway Condition Crisis: Performance of State Highway Systems, 1984–2002." 10 February 2004. <http://www.johnlocke.org/

acrobat/policyReports/state_highway_report_2004.pdf>. Accessed 18 December 2007.

———. "Policy and Performance: Directions for North Carolina's Largest Transit Systems." 4 May 2006. <http://www.johnlocke.org/policy_reports/2006050471 .html>. Accessed 18 December 2007.

———. "Traffic Congestion in North Carolina: Status, Prospects, and Solutions." 21 March 2007. <http://www.lockefan.org/research/display_article.html?id=51>. Accessed 18 December 2007.

Heckler, Daniel E. "Occupational Employment Projections to 2014." *Monthly Labor Review*, November 2005. <http://www.bls.gov/opub/mlr/2005/11/art5full.pdf>. Accessed 18 December 2007.

Hekman, John S. "Branch Plant Location and the Product Cycle in Computer Manufacturing." *Journal of Economics and Business* 37 (May 1985): 89–102.

———. "The Product Cycle and New England Textiles." *Quarterly Journal of Economics* 94 (June 1980): 697–717.

Henry, Mark, David Barkley, and Haizhen Li. "Education and Nonmetropolitan Income Growth in the South." *Review of Regional Studies* 34 (Winter 2004): 223–44.

Hewlett, Sylvia Ann. *When the Bough Breaks—The Cost of Neglecting Our Children.* New York: Basic Books, 1991.

"History of Transfers from the Highway Trust Fund to the General Fund." Unpublished paper. N.C. General Assembly, Fiscal Research Division, 2007.

Hitner, Henry, and Barbara Nagle. *Pharmacology: An Introduction.* Boston: McGraw-Hill, 2005.

Hitt, Greg. "At a Crossroads: Failed Trade Talks Cloud WTO's Future." *Wall Street Journal*, 31 July 2006, A2.

Holahan, Catherine. "Why Dell, Apple Declined." *Business Week*, 13 July 2006. <http://www.businessweek.com/bwdaily/dnflash/content/jul2006/db20060712_955118 .htm?chan=tc&chan=technology_technology+index+page_today's+top+stories>. Accessed 3 July 2007.

Hopkins, Stella M. "Philip Morris Plant Closing." *Raleigh News and Observer*, 27 June 2007. <http://www.newsobserver.com/business/story/618312.html>. Accessed 12 July 2007.

Hotchkiss, Julie L. *What's Up with the Decline in Female Labor Force Participation?* Working Paper 2005–18. Atlanta: Federal Reserve Bank of Atlanta, 2005.

Hoxby, Caroline M. "Achievement in Charter Schools and Regular Public Schools in the U.S.: Understanding the Differences." Harvard University Program on Education Policy and Governance Working Paper, December 2004.

Huber, Peter W., and Mark P. Mills. *The Bottomless Well: The Twilight of Fuel, the Virtue of Waste, and Why We Will Never Run Out of Energy.* New York: Basic Books, 2005.

Hufbauer, Gary Clyde, and Jeffrey J. Schott. *NAFTA Revisited: Achievements and Challenges.* Washington, D.C.: Institute for International Economics, 2005.

Hui, T. Keung. "Only 68% Graduate on Time." *Raleigh News and Observer*, 1 March

2007. <http://www.newsobserver.com/146/story/548421.html>. Accessed 17 December 2007.

Hutson, Jeannine Manning. "A Place in History: Nearing Its 20th Birthday, the ECU School of Medicine." *ECU Report* 27 (April 1996). <http://www.ecu.news.edu/april96tab/hist67.html>. Accessed 18 December 2007.

"IMPLAN for North Carolina." Stillwater, Minn.: MIG, 1990, 2003, 2004.

The Incentives Game: North Carolina Local Economic Development Incentives. Raleigh: N.C. Institute for Constitutional Law, 2007. <http://www.ncicl.org/Incentives/NCICLincetiveRpt.pdf>. Accessed 18 December 2007.

International Trade Data System. "The NAFTA." <http://www.itds.treas.gov/nafta.html>. Accessed 21 June 2007.

"Into the Hornet's Nest: Merit Pay for Teachers." *The Economist*, 12 May 2007, 30–31.

Jacobson, Louis, Robert LaLonde, and Daniel G. Sullivan. *Should We Teach Old Dogs New Tricks?: The Impact of Community College Retraining on Older Displaced Workers.* Working Paper 25. Chicago: Federal Reserve Bank of Chicago, 2003.

Jayaratne, Jith, and Philip E. Strahan. "The Benefits of Branching Deregulation." *Economic Policy Review* (Federal Reserve Bank of New York) 3 (December 1997): 13–29.

Jensen, J. Bradford, and Lori G. Kletzer. *Tradable Services: Understanding the Scope and Impact of Services Outsourcing.* Working Paper 05-9. Washington, D.C.: Institute for International Economics, 2005. <http://www.iie.com/publications/wp/wp05-9.pdf>. Accessed 18 December 2007.

John Locke Foundation. "Medicaid and Health Choice." 2006. <http://www.johnlocke.org/agenda2006/medicaid.html>. Accessed 20 July 2007.

———. "The State Budget, 2006." <http://www.johnlocke.org/agenda2006/statebudget.html>. Accessed 19 July 2007.

———. "State Tax Reform, 2006." <http://www.johnlocke.org/agenda2006/taxreform.html>. Accessed 18 July 2006.

Johnson, George E. "Changes in Earnings Inequality: The Role of Demand Shifts." *Journal of Economic Perspectives* 11 (Spring 1997): 41–54.

Johnson, James H., Jr. "The Changing Face of North Carolina." Unpublished paper. Kenan Institute of Private Enterprise, 2006.

———. "North Carolina's Higher Education Demographic Challenges." Unpublished paper. Kenan-Flagler School of Business, University of North Carolina, 2007.

———. "Shaping the Business Leaders of Tomorrow: America's K–12 Education Crisis Is a Higher Education Problem." *Sustainable Enterprise Quarterly* 3 (March 2007). <www.kenan-flagler.unc.edu/assets/documents/cseSpring2007.pdf>. Accessed 18 December 2007.

Johnson, Paul R. *The Economics of the Tobacco Industry.* New York: Praeger, 1984.

Jones, David. "Amendment One: Zero Deals." *Charlotte Business Journal*, 4 November 2005. <http://charlotte.bizjournals.com/charlotte/stories/2005/11/07/editorial1.html>. Accessed 21 January 2008.

Jones, James R. *History of North Carolina Swine Extension and the Industry, 1918–1994*. Raleigh: Department of Animal Science, North Carolina State University, 1995.

Jones, Kenneth D., and Tim Critchfield. "Consolidation in the U.S. Banking Industry: Is the 'Long, Strange Trip' about to End?" *FDIC Banking Review* 17, no. 4 (2005): 31–61.

Jones, Larry E., Rodolfo E. Manuelli, and Ellen R. McGrattan. *Why Are Married Women Working So Much?* Research Department Staff Report 317. Minneapolis: Federal Reserve Bank of Minneapolis, 2003.

Jonquieres, Guy de. "Garment Industry Faces a Global Shake-Up. *Financial Times*, 19 July 2004. Reprinted in *Yale Global On-line*, <http://www.yaleglobal.yale.edu/display.article?id=4269>. Accessed 23 January 2007.

Jorgensen, Dale W., Mun S. Ho, and Kevin J. Stiroh. "Projecting Productivity Growth: Lessons from the U.S. Growth Resurgence." *Economic Review* (Federal Reserve Bank of Atlanta) 87 (3rd Quarter, 2002): 1–14.

Jorgensen, Dale W., and Kevin J. Stiroh. "Raising the Speed Limit: Economic Growth in the Information Age." *Brookings Papers on Economic Activity* 1, no. 1 (2000): 125–235.

Kahn, Alfred E. *Lessons from Deregulation: Telecommunications and Airlines after the Crunch*. Washington, D.C.: AEI Brookings Joint Center for Regulatory Studies, 2003.

Kakadelis, Lindalyn. "School to Work Reconsidered." *Carolina Journal* 16 (May 2007): 9.

Kane, Dan. "House Budget Ups Teacher Pay." *Raleigh News and Observer*, 4 May 2007. <http://www.newsobserver.com/politics/story/570538.html>. Accessed 25 September 2007.

Kane, Thomas, Jonah E. Rockoff, and Douglas O. Staiger. *What Does Certification Tell Us about Teacher Effectiveness?: Evidence from New York City*. Working Paper 12155. Boston: National Bureau of Economic Research, 2006.

Kasarda, John D. "The Rise of the Aerotropolis." *Next American City* 10 (May 2006). <http://www.americancity.org/article.php?id_article=148>. Accessed 3 July 2007.

Kasarda, John D., and James H. Johnson Jr. "The Economic Impact of the Hispanic Population on the State of North Carolina." January 2006. <https://www.kenan-flagler.unc.edu/assets/documents/2006_KenanInstitute_HispanicStudy_ExecutiveSummary.pdf>. Accessed 15 December 2007.

Keeton, William R., and Geoffrey B. Newton. "Does Immigration Reduce Imbalances among Labor Markets or Increase Them?: Evidence from Recent Migration Flows." *Economic Review* (Federal Reserve Bank of Kansas City), 4th Quarter 2005, 47–80.

Kent, Christina. "The Sooner State Reforms Medicaid: Vouchers for the Commercial Market." *State News*, 10 July 2006. <http://www.ncsl.org/programs/health/shn/2006/sn471.htm>. Accessed 20 July 2007.

Kharif, Olga. "Dell: Time for a New Model?" *Business Week*, 6 April 2005. <http://www.businessweek.com/technology/content/apr2005/tc2005046_6483_tc119.htm?chan=search>. Accessed 3 July 2007.

Killian, Molly, and Charles Tolbert. "A Commuting-Based Definition of Metropolitan Local Labor Markets in the United States." In *Inequalities in Labor Market Areas*, edited by Joachim Singelmann and Forrest Desaran, 69–79. Boulder, Colo.: Westview, 1993.

Kirkpatrick, David. "IBM's Quasar: Is It the Future of the Company?" *CNN Money*, 3 March 2006. <http://money.cnn.com/2006/03/02/technology/fastforward_fortune/index.htm>. Accessed 18 December 2007.

Kletzer, Lori. *Job Loss from Imports: Measuring the Costs.* Washington, D.C.: Institute for International Economics, 2001.

Klier, Thomas H. "Does 'Just in Time' Mean 'Right Next Door?': Evidence from the Auto Industry on the Spatial Concentration of Supplier Networks." *Journal of Regional Analysis and Policy* 30, no. 1 (2000): 41–57.

Knapp, Laura Greene. "Benchmarks: Measures of College Affordability and Student Aid in North Carolina." December 2004. <http://www.ncseaa.edu/pdf/Benchmarks_1_31_05_Final.pdf>. Accessed 18 December 2007.

Knox, Noelle. "Second Homes 40% of Market." *USA Today*, 5 April 2006. <http://www.usatoday.com>. Accessed 11 May 2007.

Kochhar, Rakesh, Roberto Suro, and Sonya Tafoya. *The New Latino South: The Context and Consequences of Rapid Population Growth.* Washington, D.C.: Pew Hispanic Center, 2005. <http://pewhispanic.org/reports/report.php?ReportID=50>. Accessed 18 December 2007.

Kodrzycki, Yolanda K. "Geographic Shifts in Higher Education." *New England Economic Review* (Federal Reserve Bank of Boston), July–August 1999, 27–47.

Kohn, Donald L. "Globalization, Inflation, and Monetary Policy." Remarks at the College of Wooster, Wooster, Ohio, October 2005. <http://www.federalreserve.gov/boarddocs/speeches/2005/20051011/default.htm>. Accessed 18 December 2007.

Kotlikoff, Laurence, and Scott Burns. *The Coming Generational Storm: What You Need to Know about America's Economic Future.* Cambridge: MIT Press, 2004.

Kremer, Michael, and Stanley Watt. "The Globalization of Household Production." 5 October 2005. <http://www.brookings.edu/papers/2005/1005globaleconomics_kremer.aspx>. Accessed 18 December 2007.

Krishnan, Anne. "Honda Jets to Be Built in Triad." *Raleigh News and Observer*, 10 February 2007. <http://www.newsobserver.com/print/saturday/business/story/541743.html>. Accessed 17 December 2007.

Kuhbach, Peter, and Bradlee A. Herauf. "U.S. Travel and Tourism Satellite Accounts for 2001–2004." *Survey of Current Business* 85 (June 2005): 17–29.

Kusmin, Lorin D., John M. Redman, and David W. Sears. *Factors Associated with Rural Economic Growth: Lessons from the 1980s.* Economic Research Service, U.S. Department of Agriculture, Technical Bulletin 1850. Washington, D.C.: U.S. Government Printing Office, 1996.

Lacy, Robert L. *Whither North Carolina Furniture Manufacturing?* Working Paper 04-07. Richmond, Va.: Federal Reserve Bank of Richmond, 2004.

"Lake Gaston." N.d. <http://www.tourbrunswick.org/lake_gaston.htm>. Accessed 9 July 2007.

Landes, David S. *The Wealth and Poverty of Nations: Why Some Are So Rich and Some So Poor.* New York: Norton, 1999.

Leamer, Edward E. "A Flat World, a Level Playing Field, a Small World After All, or None of the Above?: A Review of Thomas L. Friedman's *The World Is Flat." Journal of Economic Literature* 45 (March 2007): 83–126.

Leffler, Hugh Talmage, and Albert Ray Newsome. *North Carolina: The History of a Southern State.* 3rd ed. Chapel Hill: University of North Carolina Press, 1973.

Levinsohn, Jim, and Wendy Petropoulos. *Creative Destruction or Just Plain Destruction?: The U.S. Textile and Apparel Industries since 1972.* Working Paper 8348. Boston: National Bureau of Economic Research, 2001.

Levinson, Marc. *The Box: How the Shipping Container Made the World Smaller and the World Economy Bigger.* Princeton: Princeton University Press, 2006.

Levy, Frank, and Richard J. Murnane. *The New Division of Labor: How Computers Are Creating the Next Job Market.* New York: Sage, 2004.

"A Look at America, Up Close and Personal." *Wall Street Journal,* 26 October 2006, D2.

"Lowes Foods Corporate History." 2006. <http://www.lowesfoods.com/CorporateHistory.cfm>. Accessed 5 July 2007.

Luger, Michael I., and Suho Bae. "The Effectiveness of State Business Tax Incentive Programs: The Case of North Carolina." *Economic Development Quarterly* 19 (November 2005): 327–45.

Luger, Michael I., and Harvey A. Goldstein. *Technology in the Garden: Research Parks and Regional Economic Development.* Chapel Hill: University of North Carolina Press, 1991.

Luger, Michael I., and Edward Lane. "Opportunities for Job Creation and Economic Growth in Cleveland County, North Carolina." July 2004. <http://www.kenan-flagler.unc.edu/assets/documents/cceOpportunitiesCleveland.pdf>. Accessed 15 December 2007.

Luo, Jifeng. "Two Essays on the Demand for and Supply of Paper and Paperboard Products." Master's thesis, Georgia Institute of Technology, 2003.

Mabe, Alan. "Long-Term Planning Process." Unpublished paper. University of North Carolina General Administration, 2007.

Mankiw, N. Gregory. *Essentials of Economics.* 4th ed. Mason, Ohio: Thomson-Southwestern, 2007.

Martin and Associates. "Economic Impact Study of the North Carolina State Ports Authority." June 2006.

Martin, Joyce A., Brady E. Hamilton, Paul D. Sutton, Stephanie J. Ventura, Fay Menacher, and Martha L. Munson. "Births: Final Data for 2003." *National Vital Statistics Report* 54 (September 2005). <http://www.cdc.gov/nchs/data/nvsr/nvsr54/nvsr54_02.pdf>. Accessed 15 December 2007.

Martin, Laura L., and Kelly D. Zering. "Relationships between Industrialized

Agriculture and Environmental Consequences—The Case of Vertical Coordination in Broilers and Hogs." *Journal of Agricultural and Applied Economics* 29 (July 1997): 45–56.

Mather, Tom. "Air Cargo Complex: Flight or Fancy?" *North Carolina Insight* 14 (September 1992): 26–39.

Mathews, Anna Wilde, and Leila Abboud. "For Booming Biotech Firms, a Threat: Generics." *Wall Street Journal*, 14 March 2007, A1, A13.

Mattson-Teig, Beth. "Wanted: Secure Locations." 2006. <http://www.fastfacility.com/FastInfo/info10.asp>. Accessed 21 September 2007.

Maxwell, Nan L. "The Effect on Black-White Wage Differences of Differences in the Quantity and Quality of Education." *Industrial and Labor Relations Review* 47 (January 1994): 249–64.

Mayer, Steve. "Fueling Ethanol: Implications for Livestock Producers." Paper presented at the National Institute for Animal Agriculture, Paragon Economics, 2007. <www.zimmcomm.biz/niaa/NIAA-07-Steve-Meyer.ppt>. Accessed 18 December 2007.

McDougall, Paul. "IBM Completes Sale of PC Business to Lenovo." *Information Week*, 2 May 2005. <http://www.informationweek.com>. Accessed 3 July 2007.

Meier, K. J., and M. J. Licari. "The Effect of Cigarette Taxes on Cigarette Consumption, 1955 through 1994." *American Journal of Public Health* 87 (July 1997): 1126–30.

Mejia, Elaine, Kristopher Nordstrom, and William Schweke. "Getting Our Money's Worth: An Evaluation of the Economic Model Used for Awarding State Business Subsidies." March 2007. <http://www.cfed.org/imageManager/_documents/getting_our_moneys_worth.pdf>. Accessed 18 December 2007.

Meredith, Robyn. *The Elephant and the Dragon: The Rise of India and China and What It Means for All of Us.* New York: Norton, 2007.

Meyer, Steve, Glenn Grimes, and Ron Plain. "From #1 Importer to #1 Exporter." *Pork Checkoff Report and the University of Missouri.* N.d. <http://www.pork.org/newsandinformation/news/porkcheckoff16.aspx>. Accessed 5 August 2006.

Miernyk, William. "Rising Energy Prices and Regional Economic Development." *Growth and Change* 8 (July 1977): 2–7.

Minges, Lynn. *How Important Is Tourism in North Carolina?* Report prepared for the N.C. Economic Development Board. Boston: Global Insight, 2005.

Minnesota State University–Mankato. "Class Size." N.d. <http://www.mnsu.edu/cetl/teachingresources/articles/classsize.html>. Accessed 20 July 2007.

Mirabelli, Maria C., and Steve Wing. "Proximity to Pulp and Paper Mills and Wheezing Symptoms among Adolescents in North America." *Environmental Research* 102 (September 2006): 96–100.

"Miss America 1984 Delegates." N.d. <http://www.geocities.com/missusamagicf/MA1984Delegates.html>. Accessed 29 June 2007.

Moomaw, Ronald L., and Martin Williams. "Total Factor Productivity in Manufacturing: Further Evidence from the States." *Journal of Regional Science* 31 (February 1991): 17–34.

Mullen, John K., and Martin Williams. "Marginal Tax Rates and State Economic Growth." *Regional Science and Urban Economics* 24 (December 1994): 687–705.

Murnane, Richard J., John B. Willett, and Frank Levy. "The Growing Importance of Cognitive Skills in Wage Determination." *Review of Economics and Statistics* 77 (May 1995): 251–66.

Murphy, Kevin M., and Finis Welch. "Empirical Age-Earnings Profiles." *Journal of Labor Economics* 8 (April 1990): 202–29.

Muth, Mary, Robert Blackard, Brian Murray, Kelly Zering, and Michael Wohlgenant. *A Profile of the N.C. Hog Industry in Relation to the U.S. and International Markets.* Raleigh: RTI International, 2003.

National Assessment of Educational Progress (NAEP): The Nation's Report Card. N.d. <http://nces.ed.gov/nationsreportcard/>. Accessed 12 June 2007.

National Bureau of Economic Research. "Business Cycle Expansions and Contractions." N.d. <http://www.nber.org/cycles/cyclesmain.html>. Accessed 11 June 2007.

National Center for Public Policy and Higher Education. "Income of U.S. Workforce Projected to Decline *If* Education Doesn't Improve." *Policy Alert*, November 2005. <http://www.highereducation.org/reports/pa_decline/index.shtml>. Accessed 15 December 2007.

N.C. Association of County Commissioners. "Current Issues." 2007. <http://www.ncacc.org/currentissues.htm>. Accessed 20 July 2007.

———. "Medicaid Burden by the Numbers." 2007. <http://www.ncacc.org/documents/medicaidestimates_2007-08.pdf>. Accessed 20 July 2007.

N.C. Association of Educators. "A History of Statewide Monthly Salaries for North Carolina Classroom Teachers with Bachelor's Degrees." Unpublished paper. N.C. Association of Educators, 2007.

———. "Teacher Salary Percentage Increases, 2006–07." 2006. <http://www.ncae.org/salaries/0607salary.pdf>. Accessed 19 December 2007.

N.C. Association of Realtors. "Existing Home Sales." <http://www.ncrealtors.com/market_statistics.cfm>. Accessed 3 July 2007.

N.C. Department of Agriculture and Consumer Services. "Study: N.C. Green Industry Has $8.6 Billion Economic Impact." March 2007. <http://www.ncagr.com/paffairs/release/2007/3-07greenindustryimpact.htm>. Accessed 23 January 2008.

N.C. Department of Commerce. "Fast Facts: 2005 Economic Impact of Tourism." 2006. <http://www.nccommerce.com/NR/rdonlyres/558DE042-E448-4C99-AB92-1C4FF6064759/0/FastFactsEI_05.pdf>. Accessed 27 June 2007.

———. "North Carolina Automotive." 2008. < http://www.nccommerce.com/NR/rdonlyres/B5AA7235-B969-42A0-AD48-489175BB1C24/0/Automotive_815x11.pdf>. Accessed 23 January 2008.

———. "Tourism: 2005 County Statistics." <http://www.nccommerce.com/tourism/econ/countystats.asp>. Accessed 12 July 2007.

N.C. Department of Health and Human Services. "History of North Carolina Medicaid

Program: State Fiscal Years 1970 to 2006." N.d. <http://www.dhhs.state.nc.us/dma/historyofmedicaid.pdf>. Accessed 20 July 2007.

———. "North Carolina Child Care Snapshot." N.d. <http://ncchildcare.dhhs.state.nc.us/general/mb_snapshot.asp#Head%20Start>. Accessed 20 July 2007.

———. "North Carolina's Temporary Assistance for Needy Families State Plan: The Work First Program." N.d. <http://www.dhhs.state.nc.us/dss/publications/docs/TANF_StatePlan_0405.pdf>. Accessed 19 December 2007.

N.C. Department of Revenue. "Motor Fuels Tax Rates." 15 June 2007. <http://www.dor.state.nc.us/taxes/motor/rates.html>. Accessed 19 July 2007.

———. "Property Tax Rates and Latest Year of Revaluation for North Carolina Counties and Municipalities." 2007. <http://www.dornc.com/publications/propertyrates.html>. Accessed 19 July 2007.

N.C. General Assembly. "Session Law 2007-523." 31 August 2007. <http://www.ncleg.net/EnactedLegislation/SessionLaws/HTML/2007-2008/SL2007-523.html>. Accessed 2 February 2008.

N.C. General Assembly, Fiscal Research Division. "Medicaid Program Overview." 31 January 2007. <http://www.ncleg.net/fiscalresearch/topics_of_interest/topics_pdfs/medicaid_program_overview_jan_2007.pdf>. Accessed 20 July 2007.

———. "Transportation Funding in North Carolina." December 2007.

N.C. Governor's Commission to Modernize State Finances. "Final Report." December 2002. <http://www.osbm.state.nc.us/files/pdf_files/final_rpt_gov_comm.pdf>. Accessed 18 December 2007.

N.C. Office of Management and Budget. "Certified Budget 2005–07." N.d. <http://sdc.state.nc.us/budget_narratives/certified_budget.html>. Accessed 20 July 2007.

———. "North Carolina Tax Guide 2004." <http://www.osbm.state.nc.us/files/pdf_files/2004_Tax_Guide.pdf>. Accessed 19 December 2007.

———. "Post-Legislative Budget Summary, 2006–2007." November 2006. <http://www.osbm.state.nc.us/files/pdf_files/pls2006_07.pdf>. Accessed 19 December 2007.

N.C. Office of the Governor. "Easley Announces Dell to Locate in Piedmont Triad." News release, 9 November 2004. <http://www.governor.state.nc.us/News_FullStory.asp>. Accessed 23 May 2007.

———. "Gov. Easley Announces 856 Jobs for Gaston County." News release, 2 August 2005. <http://www.governor.state.nc.us/News_FullStory.asp?id=2287>. Accessed 6 June 2007.

———. "Gov. Easley Announces 'Learn and Earn' High School Program." News release, 8 September 2004. <http://www.governor.state.nc.us/reform/_pdf/20040908.pdf>. Accessed 23 May 2007.

———. "Governor Mike Easley's 2007–2009 Budget Highlights: High School Reform Expansion and EARN Scholarship Program." News release, 31 July 2007. <http://www.governor.state.nc.us/Reform/_pdf/Easleys%20High%20School%20Reform%20and%20EARN%20Scholarships.pdf>. Accessed 18 December 2007.

N.C. Partnership for Children. "Smart Start." 2007. <http://www.ncsmartstart.org/about/whatissmartstart.htm>. Accessed 21 January 2008.

N.C. Public Schools. "The North Carolina 2005 SAT Report." August–September 2005. <http://www.ncpublicschools.org/accountability/reporting/sat/2005>. Accessed 18 December 2007.

———. "The North Carolina 2006 SAT Report." August–September 2006. <http://www.ncpublicschools.org/accountability/reporting/sat/2006>. Accessed 18 December 2007.

———. *Report to the Joint Legislative Education Oversight Committee.* Raleigh: N.C. Department of Public Instruction and N.C. School Board, 2007. <http://www.ncpublicschools.org/docs/research/dropout/reports/2005-06dropout.pdf>. Accessed 25 July 2007.

N.C. Rural Economic Development Center. "Water 2030: Glossary of Terms." N.d. <http://www.ncruralcenter.org/water2030/glossary.htm>. Accessed 23 July 2007.

N.C. State Data Center. "County/State Population Projections." N.d. <http://demog.state.nc.us>. Accessed 15 July 2007.

———. "Log into North Carolina." N.d. <http://linc.state.nc.us/>. Accessed 9 June 2007.

———. "State Demographics." N.d. <http://demog.state.nc.us/>. Accessed 12 July 2007.

Neal, Derek A., and William R. Johnson. "The Role of Premarket Factors in Black-White Wage Differences." *Journal of Political Economy* 104 (October 1996): 869–95.

Neumark, David, and Donna Rothstein. *Do School-to-Work Programs Help the "Forgotten Half"?* Working Paper 11636. Boston: National Bureau of Economic Research, 2005.

"New Bern History." N.d. <http://www.newbern.com/history/>. Accessed 15 June 2007.

New Commission on the Skills of the American Workforce. *Tough Choices or Tough Times?* Washington, D.C.: National Center on Education and the Economy, 2007.

Newman, Robert J. *Growth in the American South: Changing Regional Employment and Wage Patterns in the 1960s and 1970s.* New York: New York University Press, 1984.

Newmark, Craig M. "Another Look at the Effect of Charter Schools on Student Test Scores in North Carolina." April 2005. <http://www.johnlocke.org/acrobat/policyReports/charterschoolreport.pdf>. Accessed 19 December 2007.

Niemi, Albert W., Jr. *State and Regional Patterns in American Manufacturing, 1860–1900.* Westport, Conn.: Greenwood, 1974.

Nilsen, Kim, and Leo John. "Credit Suisse a Different Kind of Win for RTP." *Triangle Business Journal,* 22 October 2004. <http://www.bizjournals.com/triangle/stories/2004/10/18/daily30.html>. Accessed 23 January 2008.

Nordstrom, Kristopher, Adam Levinson, Jennifer Haygood, and Richard Bostic. "Education Budget Overview." 13 February 2007. <http://www.ncga.state.nc.us/fiscalresearch/topics_of_interest/topics_pdfs/total_ed_overview_presentation_feb_13_2007.pdf>. Accessed 19 December 2007.

"North Carolina Ports Tonnage and Trade Statistics." N.d. <http://www.ncports
.com/web/ncports.nsf/a5e75a4ee8d2dc808525666a005c2487/
3fddf4439cb5c9ac85256f150071b475?OpenDocument>. Accessed 19 June 2007.

North Carolina's Southeast. "Regional Data Book." Vol. 8 (2006). <http://www.ncse
.org/2006-databook/military/pope.htm>. Accessed 11 April 2007.

"North Carolina's Strategic Plan for Biofuels Leadership." 1 April 2007. <http://www
.ncbiotech.org/biotechnology_in_nc/strategic_plan/documents/biofuels_plan
.pdf>. Accessed 19 December 2007.

North Wilkesboro, Town of. "A Brief History of North Wilkesboro." N.d. <http://www
.north-wilkesboro.com/history/>. Accessed 5 July 2007.

Nwagbara, Ucheoma, Urs Buehlmann, and Al Schuler. *The Impact of Globalization
on North Carolina's Furniture Industries.* Raleigh: N.C. Department of Commerce,
2002.

Oden, Sherri, Lawrence J. Schweinhart, and David P. Weikart. *Into Adulthood: A Study
of the Effects of Head Start.* Ypsilanti, Mich.: High/Scope, 2000.

Oliner, Stephen D., and Daniel E. Sichel. "The Resurgence of Growth in the Late
1990s: Is Information Technology the Story?" *Journal of Economic Perspectives* 14
(Fall 2000): 3–22.

Olsen, Mancur. "The South Will Fall Again: The South as Leader and Laggard in
Economic Growth." *Southern Economic Journal* 49 (April 1983): 917–32.

O'Neill, Tip, and Gary Hymel. *All Politics Is Local, and Other Rules of the Game.* Avon,
Mass.: Adams Media, 1995.

Oswald, Ed. "Dell, Wal-Mart Sign Retail Pact." *BetaNews*, 24 May 2007. <http://www
.betanews.com/article/Dell_WalMart_Sign_Retail_Pact/1180026053>. Accessed
3 July 2007.

Ottaviano, Gianmarco I. P., and Giovanni Peri. *Rethinking the Gains from Immigration:
Theory and Evidence from the U.S.* Working Paper 11672. Boston: National Bureau of
Economic Research, 2005.

Pappas Consulting Group. "Staying a Step Ahead: Higher Education Transforming
North Carolina's Economy." May 2005. <http://intranet.northcarolina.edu/docs/
econ_transform/Pappas_Core.pdf>. Accessed 6 February 2008.

Parker, Vickie Lee. "Spinning Success as Rivals Fall Away." *Raleigh News and Observer*,
22 March 2006. <http://www.newsobserver.com/print/wednesday/business/
story/420662.html>. Accessed 17 December 2007.

Peisner-Feinberg, Ellen S., and Jennifer M. Schaaf. "*Evaluation of the North Carolina
More at Four Pre-Kindergarten Program: Year 5 Report (July 1, 2005–June 30, 2006).*"
February 2007. <http://www.fpg.unc.edu/~mafeval/pdfs/year_5_final_report.pdf>.
Accessed 19 December 2007.

Perrin, R. K., and G. P. Sappie. *North Carolina Farm Income and Production.* Economic
Information Report 83. Raleigh: Department of Agricultural and Resource
Economics, North Carolina State University, 1990.

Perry, David. "High Point Paper Downplays Vegas Threat." *Furniture Today*, 7 February

2007. <http://www.furnituretoday.com/article/CA6414725.html>. Accessed 16 July 2007.

Peterson, Paul E. "Choice in American Education." In *A Primer on America's Schools*, edited by Terry M. Moe, 249–83. Stanford, Calif.: Hoover Institution Press, Stanford University, 2001. <http://media.hoover.org/documents/0817999426_10.pdf>. Accessed 19 December 2007.

Piketty, Thomas, and Emmanuel Saez. "Income Inequality in the United States, 1913–1998." *Quarterly Journal of Economics* 118 (February 2003). <http://elsa.berkeley.edu/~saez/pikettyqje.pdf>. Accessed 19 December 2007.

Poot, Jacques. "A Synthesis of Empirical Research on the Impact of Government on Long-Run Growth." *Growth and Change* 31 (Fall 2000): 516–46.

Powell, William S., and Jay Mazzocchi, eds. *Encyclopedia of North Carolina*. Chapel Hill: University of North Carolina Press, 2006.

Price, Jay. "Coastal Boom Moves Inland." *Raleigh News and Observer*, 4 June 2006. <http://www.newsobserver.com/news/growth/story/446961.html>. Accessed 17 December 2007.

Rappaport, Jordan. *Local Growth Empirics*. CID Working Paper 23. Cambridge: Center for International Development, Harvard University, 1999.

Rawlins, Wade. "Climate Change Could Hit Homes, Beaches, Business." *Raleigh News and Observer*, 21 June 2007. <http://www.newsobserver.com/2660/story/611485.html>. Accessed 17 December 2007.

———. "Pork Giant Agrees to New Waste Curbs." *Raleigh News and Observer*, 21 January 2006. <http://www.newsobserver.com/print/saturday/city_state/story/390998.html>. Accessed 17 December 2007.

"RBC Centura Moving Headquarters to Raleigh." 30 August 2005. <http://www.rbccentura.com/about/news/083005_hqmove.html>. Accessed 12 July 2007.

Recommendations. Raleigh: N.C. State and Local Fiscal Modernization Study Commission, Income Tax Modernization Subcommittee, 2007.

Recommendations. Raleigh: N.C. State and Local Fiscal Modernization Study Commission, Local Taxation Modernization Subcommittee, 2007.

Recommendations. Raleigh: N.C. State and Local Fiscal Modernization Study Commission, Sales Tax Modernization Subcommittee, 2007.

Reform K–12. "Future Teachers and SAT Scores." 6 February 2004. <http://www.reformK12.com/archives/000094.nclk>. Accessed 13 July 2007.

Renkow, Mitch. "Income Non-Convergence and Rural-Urban Earnings Differentials: Evidence from North Carolina." *Southern Economic Journal* 62 (April 1996): 1017–28.

Research Triangle Park. "Quick Facts: RTP Companies." <http://www.rtp.org/main/index.php?pid=166&sec=1>. Accessed 12 July 2007.

Research Triangle Region Partnership. "State of the Research Triangle Region." 2006. <http://www.researchtriangle.org/staying%20on%20top/state%20of%20the%20region/documents/StateoftheRegion2006.pdf>. Accessed 15 December 2007.

Reynolds, Alan. "For the Record." *Wall Street Journal*, 18 May 2005. <http://www
    .opinionjournal.com/editorial/feature.html?id=110006704>. Accessed 19
    December 2007.

————. *Income and Wealth*. Westport, Conn.: Greenwood, 2006.

————. "Unreal Wages." 22 September 2005. <http://www.cato.org/pub_display
    .php?pub_id=5044>. Accessed 28 December 2007.

Riches, Erin. "Top 10 Best Selling Vehicles in 2000." 8 January 2001. <http://www
    .edmunds.com/reviews/list/top10/45758/article.html>. Accessed 12 June 2007.

Riefler, Roger. "A New Geography for Information Technology Activity?" *Journal of
    Regional Analysis and Policy* 35, no. 2 (2005): 1–10.

Ritter, Ronald, and Robert Sternfels. "When Offshore Manufacturing Doesn't Make
    Sense." *McKinsey Quarterly*, November 2004. <http://www.mckinseyquarterly.com/
    home.aspx>. Accessed 13 January 2007.

Roanoke Valley Chamber of Commerce. "Entertainment District—Major Travel
    Destination Announced for Roanoke Rapids." Press release, 30 June 2005. <http://
    www.rvchamber.com/edistrict.php>. Accessed 20 June 2007.

Robb, David, and Bin Xie. "A Survey of Manufacturing Strategy and Technology in the
    Chinese Furniture Industry." *European Management Journal* 21 (August 2003): 484–96.

Robert Wood Johnson Foundation. "Impacteen." N.d. <http://www.impacteen.org/>.
    Accessed 23 July 2007.

Rockoff, Jonah E. "The Impact of Individual Teachers on Student Performance:
    Evidence from Panel Data." *American Economic Review* 94 (May 2004): 247–52.

Rondinelli, Dennis A., and William J. Burpitt. "Do Government Incentives Attract
    and Retain International Investment?: A Study of Foreign-Owned Firms in North
    Carolina." *Policy Sciences* 33 (June 2000): 181–205.

Rork, Jonathan. "Getting What You Pay For: The Case of Southern Economic
    Development." *Journal of Regional Analysis and Policy* 35, no. 2 (2005): 37–53.

Roth, Gabriel. *Liberating the Roads: Reforming U.S. Highway Policy*. Policy Analysis 538.
    Washington, D.C.: Cato Institute, 2005. <http://www.cato.org/pubs/pas/pa538
    .pdf>. Accessed 19 December 2007.

————, ed. *Street Smart: Competition, Entrepreneurship, and the Future of Roads*. New
    Brunswick, N.J.: Transaction, 2006.

Ruettgers, Mike. "America's Eroding Knowledge Edge." *Business Week*, 11 May 2005.
    <http://www.businessweek.com/technology/content/may2005/tc20050511_2924
    .htm>. Accessed 3 July 2007.

Russo, Benjamin. "State Tax Reform: Evidence, Logic, and Lessons from the Trenches."
    State Tax Notes 39 (13 February 2006): 467–77.

Sack, Kevin. "North Carolina Picks Up after the Hurricane." *New York Times*, 22
    September 1996. <http://www.nytimes.com>. Accessed 7 July 2007.

Sadovi, Maura Webber. "New Arrivals Could Revive Piedmont Triad." *Wall Street
    Journal*, 31 January 2007. <http://triadcommercial.com/news/01_07wsj.pdf>.
    Accessed 19 December 2007.

Şahin, Ayşegül. *The Incentive Effects of Higher Education Subsidies on Student Effort.* Staff Report 192. New York: Federal Reserve Bank of New York, 2004. <http://www.newyorkfed.org/research/staff_reports/sr192.pdf>. Accessed 19 December 2007.

Sanders, Jon. "Faculty Compensation in the University of North Carolina System: How UNC Schools Compare with National Peers." May 2007. <http://www.johnlocke.org/acrobat/pope_articles/pope_facultycomp.pdf>. Accessed 19 December 2007.

Scheve, Kenneth F., and Matthew J. Slaughter. *Globalization and the Perceptions of American Workers.* Washington, D.C.: Institute for International Economics, 2001.

Schreiner, Mark. "Brunswick Port Price Tag: $1 Billion." *Wilmington Star News,* 31 December 2005. < http://www.starnewsonline.com/article/20051231/NEWS/51231001>. Accessed 2 February 2008.

Schuler, Al, and Urs Buehlmann. *Identifying Future Competitive Business Strategies for the U.S. Wood Furniture Market: Benchmarking and Paradigm Shifts.* Washington, D.C.: U.S. Forest Service, U.S. Department of Agriculture, 2003. <http://www.fs.fed.us/ne/newtown_square/publications/technical_reports/pdfs/2003/gtrne304.pdf>. Accessed 19 December 2007.

Schweke, William. "Economic Dislocation: Issues, Facts, and Alternatives: A Literature Review." September 2004. <http://www.ncruralcenter.org/rdwi/LiteratureReview.pdf>. Accessed 19 December 2007.

———. "Promising Practices to Assist Dislocated Workers." September 2004. <http://www.ncruralcenter.org/rdwi/PromisingPractices.pdf>. Accessed 19 December 2007.

Scott, Leslie A., and Brenda L. Linton. "Vision Plan for the Economy of the Advantage West Region." April 2004. <http://www.advantagewest.com/uploads/File/AdvWest_plan_and_report.pdf>. Accessed 19 December 2007.

Scott, Robert E. "NAFTA's Hidden Costs." April 2001. <http://www.epinet.org/content.cfm/briefingpapers_nafta01_us>. Accessed 19 December 2007.

———. *U.S.-China Trade, 1989–2003: Impact on Jobs and Industries, Nationally and by State.* Working Paper 270. Washington, D.C.: Economic Policy Institute, 2005. <http://www.epinet.org/workingpapers/epi_wp270.pdf>. Accessed 19 December 2007.

"Scrapping Special Charlotte Tax Would Boost Efficiency." 15 March 2007. <http://www.johnlocke.org/press_releases/display_story.html?id=240>. Accessed 19 December 2007.

"$700 Million Biotech Campus Envisioned for Kannapolis." *BT Catalyst,* September–October 2005. <http://www.highbeam.com/doc/1G1-138048567.html>. Accessed 24 July 2007.

"Seymour Johnson Air Force Base History." N.d. <http://www.seymourJohnson.af.mil/library/factsheets/factsheet.asp?id=4331>. Accessed 1 July 2007.

Sherwood-Call, Carolyn. "The 1980s Divergence in State per Capita Incomes: What Does It Tell Us?" *Economic Review* (Federal Reserve Bank of San Francisco), no. 1 (1996): 14–25.

Shields, Martin, and Anastasia Snyder. "Building a 21st Century Rural Workforce." *Journal of Regional Analysis and Policy* 37, no. 1 (2007): 40–43.

Shifflet and Associates. "North Carolina Tourism Conference 2006." 2006. <http://www.dksa.com/North%20Carolina%20Leisure%20Outlook%20Speech06B.pdf>. Accessed 13 October 2006.

Siceloff, Bruce. "Drivers Might Pay Road Taxes by Mile." *Raleigh News and Observer*, 17 June 2007. <http://www.newsobserver.com/news/story/607113.html>. Accessed 17 December 2007.

———. "In Charlotte, Light Rail Is on Track." *Raleigh News and Observer*, 27 August 2006. <http://www.newsobserver.com/front/story/479639.html>. Accessed 20 July 2007.

———. "N.C. Public Works Earn Mediocre Grade." *Raleigh News and Observer*, 19 September 2006. <http://www.newsobserver.com/news/story/488107.html>. Accessed 17 December 2007.

Silberman, Todd. "Study: Broaden Education." *Raleigh News and Observer*, 17 January 2007. <http://www.newsobserver.com/news/story/533115.html>. Accessed 17 December 2007.

Simmons, Tim. "New Life for Paper Mills: Ethanol Plants." *Raleigh News and Observer*, 27 September 2007. <http://www.newsobserver.com/business/story/717702.html>. Accessed 17 December 2007.

———. "New Uses Widen Textiles' Realm." *Raleigh News and Observer*, 4 December 2005. <http://www.newsobserver.com/front/story/374296.html>. Accessed 17 December 2007.

———. "Turning Potatoes, Grass into Ethanol." *Raleigh News and Observer*, 8 March 2007. <http://www.newsobserver.com/business/nc/story/550952.html>. Accessed 17 December 2007.

Smith, James P., and Barry Edmonston, eds. *The Immigration Debate: Studies on the Economic, Demographic, and Fiscal Effects of Immigration.* Washington, D.C.: National Academy Press, 1998.

Smith, Mitch. "General Tobacco Facts, Pitt County." 2006. <http://www.ces.ncsu.edu/pitt/ag/tobacco/tobfacts.html>. Accessed 3 July 2007.

"The Southeastern Auto Industry: Moving into the Fast Lane." *EconSouth* (Federal Reserve Bank of Atlanta), 2nd Quarter 2001, 2–7.

Speizer, Irwin. "Aerotropolis." *Business North Carolina*, 1 July 2007. <http://www.redorbit.com/news/business/1024072/aerotropolis/index.html>. Accessed 19 December 2007.

Spieker, Ronald. *Bank Branch Growth Has Been Steady—Will It Continue?* Future of Banking Study. Washington, D.C.: FDIC, 2004. <http://www.fdic.gov/bank/analytical/future/fob_08.pdf>. Accessed 19 December 2007.

Spivey, Angela K. "Study Shows Increased Suicide Rate with Possible Link to Nearby Industry Chemicals in Second N.C. Community." No. 560. University of North Carolina at Chapel Hill News Services, 7 November 2005. <http://www.unc.edu/news/archives/nov05/haywood110705.html>. Accessed 15 December 2007.

Stallman, Judith. "Impacts of Tax and Expenditure Limitations on Small Local Governments: Lessons from Colorado and Missouri." *Journal of Regional Analysis and Policy* 37, no. 1 (2007): 62–65.

Stancill, Jane. "Bowles Tries to Smooth Feathers in Rocky Mount." *Raleigh News and Observer*, 4 April 2007. <http://www.newsobserver.com/news/higher_education/story/560700.html>. Accessed 17 December 2007.

———. "UNC–Rocky Mount?: System to Study Idea." *Raleigh News and Observer*, 16 August 2006. <http://www.newsobserver.com/102/story/471409.html>. Accessed 7 April 2007.

Stanek, Steve. "NC Judge Dismisses Dell Incentives Suit; Appeal Promised." *Budget and Tax News*, 1 July 2006. <http://heartland.org/Article.cfm?artId=19294>. Accessed 20 July 2007.

State of the North Carolina Workforce: An Assessment of the State's Labor Force Demand and Supply, 2007–2017. Raleigh: N.C. Commission on Workforce Development, 2007. <http://www.nccommerce.com/NR/rdonlyres/CE53BE9D-DDF7-4AA9-9430-B9ACF559B197/0/StateoftheNorthCarolinaWorkforceFinal.pdf>. Accessed 15 December 2007.

Stegall, Jim. "State to Measure 'Value-Added' in Schools." *Carolina Journal* 16 (February 2007): 10.

Stephens, Kristen, and Jan Riggsbee. "Talented Students, on Hold." *Raleigh News and Observer*, 30 January 2007. <http://www.newsobserver.com/print/tuesday/opinion/story/537523.html>. Accessed 17 December 2007.

Stern, Jay. "Innovative Transportation Funding." Unpublished paper. N.C. Aggregates Association, 2007.

Stewart, Leslie S., and Michael I. Luger. "Implementation Plan for a Mini-Hub in the Kerr-Tar Region." February 2004. <www.kenan-flagler.unc.edu/assets/documents/ed_Kerr_Tar_Hub_Report.pdf>. Accessed 19 December 2007.

Stoops, Terry. "Learning about Teacher Pay: N.C. Teachers Are Favorably Compensated; What They Need Is Merit Pay." *John Locke Foundation Spotlight*, 14 February 2007. <http://www.johnlocke.org/acrobat/spotlights/spotlight_307-teacherpay.pdf>. Accessed 15 December 2007.

Stuart, Alfred W. "Manufacturing." In *The North Carolina Atlas: Portrait for a New Century*, edited by Douglas M. Orr Jr. and Alfred W. Stuart, 177–98. Chapel Hill: University of North Carolina Press, 2000.

Su, Betty W. "The U.S. Economy to 2014." *Monthly Labor Review*, November 2005, 10–24. <http://www.bls.gov/opub/mlr/2005/11/art2full.pdf>. Accessed 19 December 2007.

Summers, Peter M. "What Caused the Great Moderation?: Some Cross-Country Evidence." *Economic Review* (Federal Reserve Bank of Kansas City), 3rd Quarter 2005, 5–27.

Suranovic, Steven M. "U.S Tariff Policy: Historical Notes." 2006. In *International Trade Theory and Policy*. <http://internationalecon.com/Trade/Tch20/T20-3.php>. Accessed 24 July 2007.

Szulik, Matthew. "Why Schools Need Open-Source Software." *E School News On-Line*, 1 November 2001. <http://www.eschoolnews.com/search/?id=33925;_hbguid= 3e031783-ebce-449f-9e31-7a4c93fb830b>. Accessed 19 July 2007.

Tan, Junyuan. "The Liberalization of Trade in Textiles and Clothing: China's Impact on the ASEAN Countries." Ph.D. diss., Stanford University, 2005.

"A Tangle of Troubles." *The Economist*, 20 July 2006, 35.

Taylor, Allyn, Frank J. Chaloupka, Emmanuel Guindon, and Michaelyn Corbett. "The Impact of Trade Liberalization on Tobacco Consumption." In *Tobacco Control in Developing Countries*, edited by Prabhat Jha and Frank Chaloupka, 343–64. New York: Oxford University Press, 2000. <http://www1.worldbank.org/tobacco/tcdc/ 343TO364.PDF>. Accessed 19 December 2007.

Taylor, Charles, Office of. "Congressman Taylor and ERC Bring Cost Efficient High-Speed Internet Access Connection to Region." N.d. <http://www.ercwc.org/press/ 2004/2003_telecom_congressmanTaylorERCBringCostEfficient.doc>. Accessed 7 July 2007.

Thomas, David H., and Robert S. Foyle. *Economic Impacts of N.C. Airports*. Raleigh: N.C. Department of Transportation, 2006. <http://www.ncdot.org/transit/aviation/ download/economics/Airport_Briefing_Oct_2006.pdf>. Accessed 3 August 2007.

"Threads That Think." *The Economist*, 10 December 2005, 32–34.

Tiller, Kelly J. "U.S. Tobacco Economic and Policy Outlook." 23 September 2003. <US%20Tobacco%20Economic%20and%20Policy%20Outlook%20Sept03.pdf>. Accessed 19 December 2007.

Toossi, Mitra. "A New Look at Long-Term Labor Force Projections to 2050." *Monthly Labor Review*, November 2006. <http://www.bls.gov/opub/mlr/2006/11/art3full .pdf>. Accessed 28 December 2007.

Tootell, Geoffrey, Richard W. Kopcke, and Robert K. Triest. "Investment and Employment by Manufacturing Plants." *New England Economic Review* (Federal Reserve Bank of Boston), no. 2, 2001, 41–58.

Topel, Robert H. "Factor Proportions and Relative Wages: The Supply-Side Determinants of Wage Inequality." *Journal of Economic Perspectives* 11 (Spring 1997): 55–74.

Tough, Paul. "What It Takes to Make a Student." *New York Times Magazine*, 26 November 2006. <http://www.nytimes.com/2006/11/26/magazine/26tough.html>. Accessed 20 July 2007.

Tucker, Marc. "The Challenge from Asia." Paper prepared for the New Commission on the Skills of the American Workplace. April 2006. <http://skillscommission.org/ pdf/Staff%20Papers/The%20Challenge%20From%20Asia.pdf>. Accessed 19 December 2007.

Tufts Center for the Study of Drug Development. "Backgrounder: A Methodology for Counting Costs for Pharmaceutical R&D." 1 November 2001. <http://www.csdd .tufts.edu/NewsEvents/RecentNews.asp?newsid=5>. Accessed 30 June 2007.

2004 North Carolina Agricultural Statistics. No. 204. Raleigh: N.C. Department of Agriculture and Consumer Services, October 2005.

2006 Local School Finance Study. Raleigh: Public School Forum of North Carolina, 2006.

"Underemployment Affects 18 Percent of Entry Level Job Seekers." *CollegeGrad.com,* 18 September 2004. <http://www.collegegrad.com/press/underemployed.shtml>. Accessed 12 June 2007.

University of North Carolina. *Statistical Abstract of Higher Education in North Carolina.* Chapel Hill: General Administration Program Assessment and Public Service Division, University of North Carolina, 1971/72–2006/7.

University of North Carolina at Asheville. "About UNC Asheville." N.d. <http://www.unca.edu>. Accessed 10 July 2007.

University of North Carolina at Chapel Hill. "Carolina: A Brief History." N.d. <http://www.unc.edu/about/history.html>. Accessed 20 July 2007.

University of North Carolina at Charlotte, Long Range Enrollment Planning Task Force. "Enrollment Projections for UNC Charlotte: 2020." 31 January 2007. <http://www.provost.uncc.edu/SpecialProjEvents/LongRangeEnrollmentPlanningReport.pdf>. Accessed 17 June 2007.

University of North Carolina Board of Governors. "Report on Expanding Access to Higher Education through State-Funded Distance Education Programs." May 2004. <http://intranet.northcarolina.edu/docs/aa/planning/reports/DERpt2004.pdf>. Accessed 20 July 2007.

——. "Retention, Graduation, and Persistence Rates of First-Time Full-Time Freshmen at All UNC Institutions." 2007. <http://www.northcarolina.edu/content.php/assessment/reports/student_info/retention.htm>. Accessed 19 December 2007.

United Press International. "Strike at Biggest Pork Processing Plant." 17 November 2006. <http://www.upi.com/NewsTrack/Business/2006/11/17/strike_at_biggest_pork_processing_plant/>. Accessed 12 July 2007.

U.S. Census Bureau. *1970 Census of Population and Housing.* Vol. 1, *Characteristics of the Population.* Washington, D.C.: U.S. Government Printing Office, 1972.

——. *1980 Census of Population and Housing.* Vol. 1, *Characteristics of the Population.* Washington, D.C.: U.S. Government Printing Office, 1982.

——. "American Community Survey." 2004, 2005. <http://factfinder.census.gov/servlet/DatasetMainPageServlet?_program=ACS&_submenuId=&_lang=en&_ts=>. Accessed 15 December 2007.

——. "Annual Survey of Manufactures." 1994, 2005. <http://www.census.gov/mcd/asm-as3.html>. Accessed 15 July 2007.

——. "Building Permits." N.d. <http://www.census.gov/const/www/permitsindex.html>. Accessed 22 June 2007.

——. *County Business Patterns, 1970.* Washington, D.C.: U.S. Government Printing Office, 1973.

——. *County Business Patterns, 2004.* Washington, D.C.: U.S. Government Printing Office, 2007.

———. "Current Lists of Metropolitan and Micropolitan Statistical Areas and Definitions." <http://www.census.gov/population/www/estimates/metrodef.html>. Accessed 24 July 2007.

———. *Economic Census, 1977.* Washington, D.C.: U.S. Government Printing Office, 1978.

———. *Economic Census, 1992.* Washington, D.C.: U.S. Government Printing Office, 1993.

———. *Economic Census, 2002.* Washington, D.C.: U.S. Government Printing Office, 2003.

———. "Families and Living Arrangements." N.d. <http://www.census.gov/population/www/socdemo/hh-fam.html>. Accessed 24 July 2007.

———. "Historical Income Tables—Households." N.d. <http://www.census.gov/hhes/www/income/histinc/h05.html>. Accessed 24 July 2007.

———. "Housing Units." N.d. <http://www.census.gov/popest/housing/>. Accessed 19 December 2007.

———. "Population Born outside State of Residence." January 2005. <http://www.census.gov/population/cen2000/phc-t38/phc-t38.pdf>. Accessed 8 October 2006.

———. "Public-Use Microdata Samples." 11 October 2005. <http://www.census.gov/main/www/pums.html>. Accessed 9 July 2007.

———. "State and Local Government Finances." N.d. <http://www.census.gov/govs/www/estimate.html>. Accessed 18 July 2007.

———. "Statistical Abstract: Historical Abstract." N.d. <http://www.census.gov/compendia/statab/hist_stats.html>. Accessed 2 July 2007.

———. "Statistical Abstract of the United States." N.d. <http://www.census.gov/prod/www/statistical-abstract-1995_2000.html>. Accessed 19 December 2007.

———. "U.S. International Trade Statistics." N.d. <http://censtats.census.gov/naic3_6/naics3_6.shtml>. Accessed 2 July 2007.

U.S. Department of Agriculture. "The Census of Agriculture, 2002." <http://www.agcensus.usda.gov/Publications/2002/index.asp>. Accessed 19 December 2007.

U.S. Department of Agriculture, Economics Research Service. "Agricultural Baseline Projections: U.S. Livestock, 2007–2017." 14 February 2007. <http://www.ers.usda.gov/Briefing/Baseline/livestock.htm>. Accessed 15 December 2007.

U.S. Department of Agriculture, Foreign Agricultural Service. "NAFTA Agriculture Fact Sheet: Tobacco." 18 November 2005. <http://www.fas.usda.gov/itp/policy/nafta/tobacco.html>. Accessed 25 July 2007.

U.S. Department of Agriculture, National Agricultural Statistics Service. N.d. <http://www.nass.usda.gov>. Accessed 24 July 2007.

U.S. Department of Commerce, Bureau of Economic Analysis. N.d. <http://www.bea.gov>. Accessed 24 July 2007.

———. "Exports and Imports of Goods and Services by Type of Product." N.d. <http://www.bea.gov/national/nipaweb/TableView.asp?SelectedTable=116&FirstYear=2005&LastYear=2007&Freq=Qtr>. Accessed 24 July 2007.

———. "Gross Domestic Product by State." N.d. <http://www.bea.gov/regional/gsp/>. Accessed 7 July 2007.

———. "Local Area Personal Income." N.d. <http://www.bea.gov/regional/reis>. Accessed 12 July 2007.

———. "Personal Consumption Expenditures by Type of Expenditure." <http://www.bea.gov/national/nipaweb/TableView.asp?SelectedTable=73&FirstYear=2005&LastYear=2006&Freq=Year>. Accessed 24 July 2005.

———. "Personal Income and Its Disposition." N.d. <http://www.bea.gov/national/nipaweb/TableView.asp?SelectedTable=58&FirstYear=2005&LastYear=2007&Freq=Qtr>. Accessed 7 July 2007.

———. "Real Gross Domestic Product, Chained Dollars." N.d. <http://www.bea.gov/national/nipaweb/TableView.asp?SelectedTable=6&FirstYear=2006&LastYear=2007&Freq=Qtr>. Accessed 24 July 2007.

———. "State Annual Personal Income." N.d. <http://www.bea.gov/regional/spi/>. Accessed 29 June 2007.

———. "Trade in Goods and Services." <http://www.bea.gov/international/index.htm#trade>. Accessed 8 July 2007.

U.S. Department of Commerce, Technology Administration. "A Survey of the Use of Biotechnology in U.S. Industry." October 2003. <http://www.technology.gov/reports/Biotechnology/CD120a_0310.pdf>. Accessed 19 December 2007.

U.S. Department of Defense. "Base Realignment and Closure, 2005." <http://www.dod.mil/brac/>. Accessed 11 July 2007.

U.S. Department of Education. "Digest of Education Statistics." 1992, 2005. <http://nces.ed.gov/programs/digest/>. Accessed 19 July 2007.

U.S. Department of Education, National Center for Education Statistics. "Common Core of Data." N.d. <http://nces.ed.gov/ccd/>. Accessed 19 December 2007.

———. "Dropout Rates in the United States, 2004." NCES 2007-024. November 2006. <http://nces.ed.gov/pubs2007/dropout/>. Accessed 15 December 2007.

U.S. Department of Energy. "Energy Consumption by Sector, Selected Years 1949–2006." 2006. <http://www.eia.doe.gov/emeu/aer/pdf/pages/sec2_4.pdf>. Accessed 19 July 2007.

———. "State Energy Consumption, Price and Expenditure Estimates." N.d. <http://www.eia.doe.gov/emeu/states/_seds.html>. Accessed 19 July 2007.

U.S. Department of Housing and Urban Development. "Fair Market Rents." <http://www.huduser.org/datasets/fmr.html>. Accessed 26 July 2007.

U.S. Department of Labor. "Report to Congress: The Past, Present, and Future of Employment in the Textile and Apparel Industries: An Overview." May 2004. <http://www.doleta.gov/whatsnew/new_releases/textile_apparel_report.pdf>. Accessed 15 December 2007.

U.S. Department of Labor, Bureau of Labor Statistics. <http://www.bls.gov>. Accessed 24 July 2007.

———. "Alternative Measures of Labor Underutilization." 6 February 2004. <http://www.bls.gov/webapps/legacy/cpsatab12.htm>. Accessed 24 July 2007.

———. "Consumer Expenditure Survey." <http://www.bls.gov/cex/home.htm>. Accessed 7 July 2007.

———. "Consumer Price Index." N.d. <http://www.bls.gov/cpi/>. Accessed 7 July 2007.

———. "Employment, Hours, and Earnings from the Current Employment Statistics Survey." N.d. <http://www.bls.gov/ces/>. Accessed 7 July 2007.

U.S. House Ways and Means Committee. *2004 Green Book: Background Material and Data on Programs within the Jurisdiction of the Committee on Ways and Means.* Washington, D.C.: U.S. Government Printing Office, 2004.

U.S. Marine Corps. "Camp Lejeune History." N.d. <http://www.lejeune.usmc.mil/mcb/history.asp>. Accessed 6 July 2007.

Vedder, Richard. *Going Broke by Degree: Why College Costs Too Much.* Washington, D.C.: AEI Press, 2004.

Vernon, John A. "Drug Research and Price Controls." *Regulation* 25 (Winter 2002–3). <http://www.cato.org/pubs/regulation/regv25n4/v25n4-7.pdf>. Accessed 19 December 2007.

Vernon, Raymond. "International Investment and International Trade in the Product Cycle." *Quarterly Journal of Economics* 80 (May 1966): 190–207.

"Visitor's Guide to Bryson City, Swain County, and the Great Smoky Mountains: Fontana Lake." N.d. <http://www.greatsmokies.com/fontana.asp>. Accessed 16 July 2007.

Vollmer, Sabine. "Rivals May Steal RTP's Thunder." *Raleigh News and Observer*, 18 January 2007. <http://www.newsobserver.com/business/story/533531.html>. Accessed 17 December 2007.

von Haefen, Roger H. "Can Ethanol End Our Oil Addiction?" *N.C. State Economist*, March–April 2007. <http://www.ag-econ.ncsu.edu/VIRTUAL_LIBRARY/ECONOMIST/marapr07.pdf>. Accessed 19 December 2007.

Wagner, Richard. "Post-Boeing, Incentives Debate Rages." *Carolina Journal*, 22 March 2004. <http://www.carolinajournal.com/exclusives/display_exclusive.html?id=1433>. Accessed 15 December 2007.

———. "'Smart Growth' Fever Hits Jackson County." *Carolina Journal*, 4 June 2007. <http://www.carolinajournal.com/articles/display_story.html?id=4109>. Accessed 19 December 2007.

Wake-Up Wake County. "Growth Issues." 2006. <http://www.wakeupwakecounty.com/issues.htm>. Accessed 19 December 2007.

Walden, Michael L. "Global Transpark Is a Risky Investment for the State." *North Carolina Insight* 14 (September 1992): 49–57.

———. "How Much Income Variation 'Really' Exists within a State?" *Review of Regional Studies* 27 (Winter 1997): 237–50.

———. *North Carolina's Relative Tax Burden.* Raleigh: Department of Agricultural and Resource Economics, North Carolina State University, 2003. <http://www.ag-econ.ncsu.edu/faculty/walden/nctaxburdenranking.PDF>. Accessed 18 July 2007.

———. *Smart Economics: Commonsense Answers to 50 Questions about Government, Taxes, Business, and Households.* Westport, Conn.: Praeger, 2005.

Walden, Michael L., and Zulal Denaux. "Lags in Real Property Revaluations and Estimates of Shortfalls in Property Tax Collections in North Carolina." *Journal of Agricultural and Applied Economics* 34 (April 2002): 205–13.

Walden, Michael L., and Craig M. Newmark. "Interstate Variation in Teacher Salaries." *Economics of Education Review* 14 (December 1995): 395–402.

Walden, Michael L., and Mark R. Sisak. "School Inputs and Educational Outcomes in North Carolina: Comparison of Static and Dynamic Analyses." *Journal of Agricultural and Applied Economics* 31 (December 1999): 593–609.

Waldfogel, Jane. "Understanding the 'Family Gap' in Pay for Women with Children." *Journal of Economic Perspectives* 12 (Winter 1998): 137–56.

Warnock, Francis E., and Veronica C. Warnock. "International Capital Flows and U.S. Interest Rates." Discussion Paper 840. September 2005. <http://www.federalreserve.gov/pubs/ifdp/2005/840/ifdp840.pdf>. Accessed 19 December 2007.

Warren, John Robert. "State-Level High School Completion Rates: Concepts, Measures, and Trends." Paper presented at the annual meeting of the American Sociological Association, Atlanta, August 2003.

"Welcome to Kerrlakenc.com." N.d. <http://www.kerrlakenc.com>. Accessed 9 July 2007.

Western Carolina University. "Enrollment History." N.d. <http://www.wcu.edu/inst_studies/Detailed/fb12.html>. Accessed 16 July 2007.

———. "State of the University Address." 29 January 2004. <http://www.wcu.edu/chancellor/speeches/stateoftheuniversity.html>. Accessed 16 July 2007.

Western North Carolina Tomorrow. "Mission and Goals." N.d. <http://www.wnct.org/wnct2.html>. Accessed 5 July 2007.

Wheeler, Christopher H. *Employment Growth in America: Exploring Where Good Jobs Grow.* St Louis: Federal Reserve Bank of St. Louis, 2005.

———. "Evidence on Wage Inequality, Worker Education, and Technology." *Review* (Federal Reserve Bank of St. Louis) 87 (May–June 2005): 375–93.

Whoriskey, Peter. "Florida to Link Teacher Pay to Student Scores." *Washington Post,* 22 March 2006. <www.washingtonpost.com/wp-dyn/content/article/2006/03/21/AR2006032101545.htm>. Accessed 19 December 2007.

Willis, Robert J. "Economic Theory of Fertility Behavior." In *Economics of the Family: Marriage, Children, and Human Capital,* edited by Theodore W. Schultz, 25–80. Chicago: University of Chicago Press, 1974.

Wilson, John Douglas. "The Tax Treatment of Imperfectly Mobile Firms: Rent-Seeking, Rent-Protection, and Rent-Destruction." In *The Political Economy of Trade Policy: Papers in Honor of Jagdish Bhagwati,* edited by Robert C. Feenstra, Gene M. Grossman, and Douglas A. Irwin, 225–44. Cambridge: MIT Press, 1996.

Winkler, Anne E. "Earnings of Husbands and Wives in Dual-Earner Families." *Monthly*

Labor Review, April 1998. <http://www.bls.gov/opub/mlr/1998/04/art4exc.htm>. Accessed 19 December 2007.

Winston, Clifford. "U.S. Industry Adjustment to Economic Deregulation." *Journal of Economic Perspectives* 12 (Summer 1998): 89–110.

Woellert, Lorraine. "Tobacco May Be Partying Too Soon." *Business Week*, 24 July 2006. <http://www.businessweek.com/magazine/content/06_30/b3994040.htm?chan=search>. Accessed 18 December 2007.

Wolf, Alan M. "Raleigh Works Way atop Forbes Job List." *Raleigh News and Observer*, 17 February 2007. <http://www.newsobserver.com/print/saturday/business/story/544185.html>. Accessed 17 December 2007.

Wolf, Martin. *Why Globalization Works*. New Haven: Yale University Press, 2004.

World Health Organization. "The Tobacco Atlas." <http://www.who.int/tobacco/statistics/tobacco_atlas/en/>. Accessed 24 June 2006.

World Trade Organization. "Understanding the WTO." N.d. <http://www.wto.org/english/thewto_e/whatis_e/tif_e/tif_e.htm>. Accessed 21 June 2007.

Worthington, Joni. "North Carolina Research Campus Plans Unveiled." 12 September 2005. <http://www.ci.kannapolis.nc.us/news_0.asp?newID=736>. Accessed 27 June 2007.

Wright, Gavin. *Old South, New South: Revolutions in the Southern Economy since the Civil War*. New York: Basic Books, 1986.

Z. Smith Reynolds Foundation and Institute for Emerging Issues. Preparatory Materials for Leadership Retreat. Asheville, N.C., 11–12 June 2006.

Zahradnik, Robert. "Rainy Day Funds: Opportunities for Reform." 9 March 2005. <http://www.cbpp.org/3-9-05sfp.htm>. Accessed 19 December 2007.

Zellner, Wendy. "Wal-Mart Moves into Banking and Financial Services." *Business Week*, 27 January 2005. <http://www.reclaimdemocracy.org/walmart/banking_financial.php>. Accessed 10 October 2006.

Index

African Americans, 85, 88, 96, 97, 100, 174, 262 (n. 22)

Aging population, 13–14, 16, 66, 68, 71, 82, 106

Agriculture: history of, xiii; shifts in, xv, 203; production in, 3, 54–55, 81, 255 (n. 61); employment in, 6, 25–26, 55, 90, 107, 127, 133, 134, 206, 223, 262 (n. 27); and women's labor force participation, 56; and niche products, 59–60; and alternative fuels, 60, 133–34, 256 (n. 96); and median wage rate, 97, 98; and Roanoke region, 156; as basic industry, 250 (n. 10). *See also* Livestock industry; Tobacco industry

Air cargo industry, 140–41, 144, 197–98, 268 (n. 86), 281 (n. 180)

Air-conditioning, 14, 24

Airports, 77, 80–82, 118, 123, 211, 259 (n. 178), 260 (nn. 199, 203)

Alternative fuels, 60, 133–34, 256 (n. 96)

Appalachian State University, 132

Apparel industry: development of, xiii; competitiveness of, 26, 51; and world trade, 31, 32, 33, 48, 51; and women's labor force participation, 37; production in, 38, 39, 48, 49, 51, 81; employment in, 48, 49, 50, 206; investment in, 50–51; and median wage rate, 98; and Greater Charlotte region, 123, 124, 125, 130; and Greater Wilmington region, 126; and Greater Asheville region, 129; and Greater Boone region,

132; and Midcoast region, 134; and Far West region, 137; and Highlands region, 137; and Greater Greensboro region, 138, 140, 269 (n. 95); and Sandhills region, 138, 141, 142; and Greater Winston-Salem region, 139; and Greater Gaston region, 143, 269 (n. 95); and Foothills region, 145; and Greenville-Jacksonville region, 147; and Rocky Mount–Wilson region, 148; and Greater Mountain region, 150; and Down East region, 152; and Greater Wilkes region, 153; and Lakes region, 154; and Roanoke region, 156; as basic industry, 250 (n. 10)

Auto racing, 124, 153

Avian flu, 58–59

Baby boom generation, 13, 14, 19, 75, 210

Banking industry: development of, xv, 21, 61; and Greater Charlotte region, xv, 34, 74–75, 123, 124, 125, 139; competitiveness of, 26, 203; deregulation of, 33–34, 36, 124; and technological developments, 74; employment in, 75; production in, 75, 82; and mergers, 75–76, 77; and Greater Wilmington region, 126; and Greater Asheville region, 129; and Greater Boone region, 132; and Greater Winston-Salem region, 138, 139, 268 (n. 79); and Greater Wilkes region, 154; as basic industry, 250 (n. 10)